THOMAS S. BURACK AND KEVIN R. MURRAY, EDITORS

DISASTER AND HAZARDOUS MATERIALS INCIDENT RESPONSE

A Lawyer's Guide

AMERICAN BAR ASSOCIATION
Environment, Energy, and Resources Section

Cover design by Elizabeth Kulak/ABA Design

Printed in the United States of America.

29 28 27 26 25 5 4 3 2 1

ISBN 978-1-63905-569-2

Contents

Preface

Mary Ellen Ternes

The idea for this book sprang from the April 18–19, 2019, National Summit on Homeland Security Law and ACOEL Regional Conference, organized by the American College of Environmental Lawyers (ACOEL) and the Murrah Center for Homeland Security Law and Policy. This well-attended two-day conference was held at the Oklahoma City University School of Law on the 24th anniversary of the Oklahoma City Bombing. One day of the conference covered the general topic of disaster preparedness, response, and recovery, and another the related topics of environmental and emergency management issues within that broader context. The conference brought together professionals from many fields, including private practitioners; environmental consultants; insurance experts; and local, state, and federal environmental and disaster managers, including EPA and FEMA managers, who deal with natural and man-made disasters of all kinds. Panelists included some whose focus is largely on incidents involving discrete releases of hazardous or toxic substances or materials and others who manage natural disasters impacting municipalities and larger regions. It was apparent that there was much that the participants were learning from each other, and much more the attendees wanted to learn. It was also apparent that the kind of information presented at the conference could and should be shared more broadly across a nation and in a world facing seemingly more frequent disasters through industrialization exacerbated by the increasing effects of climate change that are posing ever-greater threats to public health and safety, environmental quality, and the livelihoods of many millions of people.

As a Vanderbilt University degreed chemical engineer, former on-scene coordinator for EPA emergency response and removal actions at abandoned hazardous waste sites and sites of hazardous substance releases, hazardous waste management industry compliance manager, and environmental attorney, I've long had an interest in ensuring that attorneys, environmental professionals, and all entities using, producing, and managing hazardous materials, wastes, and substances are properly prepared for potential emergencies and broader disaster response, including mitigation of damages following such events, pursuant to environmental law, emergency management, and homeland security requirements. This body of law includes requirements to prevent release incidents through emergency preparedness and to mitigate impacts from incidents involving these materials. It also includes provisions on responding to and recovering from these events to achieve protective and restorative outcomes as expeditiously as possible. At the same time, as the frequency and severity of natural disasters have been increasing due to a rapidly changing climate, high-risk facilities pose much greater potential for catastrophic releases from the increasing intensity and frequency of tropical storms, hurricanes, tornadoes, changing precipitation patterns, new flooding impacts, wildfires, and droughts, thus increasing the overall risks, dangers, and potential damages and compelling more focus on climate change adaptation to mitigate these risks.

This book constitutes a modest and early effort to provide the legal community, environmental and disaster response professionals, as well as community and business leaders some basic background and guidance materials for measures to prepare for and prevent environmental releases before they occur, respond to disasters of all kinds through coordination under national and state response plans and structures, including a particular focus on events involving hazardous substances and materials, and actions to mitigate and recover from damages following such events. Designed to provide general background information on incident management, specific regulatory requirements mandating emergency preparedness, immediate guidance in the first minutes and hours of a disaster, as well as more detailed background materials for consideration in the following days, it is hoped that this book will serve as a handy desktop reference and help to better equip all of us to be better prepared for, to respond and coordinate more effectively to, and to recover more quickly from, disasters of all kinds, including those involving releases of hazardous and toxic substances and materials.

Finally, note that as this book moves toward publication, efforts appear to be underway to shift federal government policy away from climate change recognition, mitigation, and adaptation. Regardless of federal policy, risks from environmental disasters addressed herein remain, as well as liability and the risk of litigation resulting therefrom.[1] Thus, the intent and scope of the authority addressed herein remain relevant and instructive for preparing for, mitigating, and responding to these increasing risks.

1. *See* Mary Ellen Ternes, ***Legal Liability, Good Engineering Judgment and Adaptation***, Wiley, Process Safety Progress: Volume 38, Issue 3, Special Section: Process Safety and Climate Change, September 2019, https://doi.org/10.1002/prs.12083 (adapted from the Ternes presentation at the American Institute of Chemical Engineers 2019 Spring Meeting, 15th Global Congress on Process Safety, New Orleans, Louisiana, March 31–April 3, 2019).

Reporting and Response Timeline for Incidents Involving Hazardous Materials, Hazardous Substances, Pollutants or Contaminants, Radionuclides, or Biological Agents

Thomas S. Burack

This timeline identifies some of the key steps that typically must be taken by the responsible party within the first 24 hours of the response to most incidents involving a release of hazardous materials, hazardous substances, pollutants, contaminants, radionuclides, or biological agents. This timeline can serve as an initial "to do list" in the first minutes and hours of responding to an emergency involving these types of releases, and is not intended as a substitute for identifying, reviewing, and following the specific statutory and regulatory requirements that may apply to each particular incident or release. This timeline only covers a limited number of federal reporting provisions. There may also be state, territorial, local, or tribal government reporting obligations. The references to chapters in some of the parentheticals are to specific chapters in this book.

Within the First Hour (0–60 Minutes)

- Identify nature of incident and gather information to characterize the release, including:
  - Location, date/time, duration, and possible source(s) of release
  - Substance name, estimated quantity, and possible source(s) of hazardous substance(s)/material(s) released
  - Media (air, water, land, etc.) and approximate number of people (if any) affected, and known or anticipated acute or chronic health risks
  - Name and phone number of contact person
- Make initial report to local emergency response agencies (call 911).
- Activate facility/organization emergency response team and applicable provisions of emergency operations plan/emergency response plan/emergency action plan.
- Report incident to all federal, tribal, state, and local regulatory authorities that must be notified "immediately":
  - National Response Center: (800) 424-8802 – For Certain Federal Reporting
    - Clean Water Act (CWA): Release of harmful quantity of oil, within 15 minutes of "knowledge" of release (40 C.F.R. Part 110; Chapters 3, 5, and 6)
    - Facility with Spill Prevention Control Countermeasures (SPCC) Plan (CWA): Release of oil to navigable waters of the U.S. (40 C.F.R. Part 112; Chapters 3 and 5)
    - EPCRA: release of extremely hazardous substance equal to or greater than the reportable quantity (RQ), within 15 minutes of actual or constructive knowledge of release; also report to SERC/LEPC (40 C.F.R. §§ 355.30–355.43; Chapters 3 and 5)
    - CERCLA: release of hazardous substance equal to or greater than the reportable quantity (RQ), within 15 minutes of actual or constructive knowledge of release; includes certain radionuclides (40 C.F.R. § 302.6; Chapters 3, 5, and 6)

  - RCRA: release, fire, or explosion at a treatment, storage, or disposal facility (TSDF) that could threaten human health, or the environment, outside the facility; and must also notify local authorities if an evacuation of local areas may be advisable (40 C.F.R. § 264.56; Chapter 3)
  - TSCA: fire in an electrical transformer containing PCBs (40 C.F.R. § 761.30; Chapter 3)
  - PHMSA/Pipelines: operators of gas, hazardous liquids, or carbon dioxide pipeline must report accidents and incidents at the earliest practicable moment following discovery, but no later than one hour after confirmed discovery (49 C.F.R. §§ 191.1, 195.1) (Chapter 6)
- Atomic Energy Act/Radionuclides. Report to Nuclear Regulatory Commission Operations via Emergency Notification System Center (301-816-5100): any event involving byproduct, source, or special nuclear material that may have caused an individual to receive a dose of radiation specified in the rule (10 C.F.R. § 20.2202; Chapter 3)
- Public Health Security and Bioterrorism or Agricultural Bioterrorism/Select Agents and Toxins. Each registered individual or entity must report to Centers for Disease Control and Prevention (CDC) (800-432-2636 or other published number) and/or the Animal and Plant Health Inspection Service (APHIS) of the U.S. Department of Agriculture (USDA) (844-820-2234 or other published number) a discovery of the theft or loss, or the release of a select agent or toxin causing occupational exposure or outside of the primary barrier of the biocontainment area (9 C.F.R. § 121.19 and 7 C.F.R. § 331.19; Chapter 3)

• Ensure that all facility personnel are safe (e.g., sheltering in place or evacuated from the facility), they have all been accounted for, and their locations and status are known.
• Take all other actions necessary to protect human health, human life, and the environment.

Within the Second Hour (60 to 120 Minutes)

- Follow all directives given by the incident commander.
- Ensure that responsible party has notified its emergency response contractor and requested site mobilization if warranted.
- Preserve evidence and documents that may help determine the cause(s) of the incident (Note: only once access is deemed safe by the incident commander).
- Identify potentially applicable reporting obligations other than those requiring "immediate" notification.

Within Four Hours

- National Response Center (800-424-8802)
  - Clean Air Act. An accidental release of a regulated substance or extremely hazardous substance to ambient air from a stationary source of air pollution that causes a death or inpatient hospitalization, or property damage outside the stationary source exceeding $1 million; obtain the NRC identification number *and* within 30 minutes thereafter report same to the Chemical Safety and Hazard Investigation Board (CSB) at (202) 261-7600 or report@csb.gov (40 C.F.R. § 1604.3(b)), or make report to CSB within eight hours (see below) (Chapter 3)

Within Eight Hours

- Make all additional incident reports to regulatory authorities required within eight hours of the release or other event, such as:
  - Chemical Safety Board (CSB): (202) 261-7600
    - Clean Air Act: An accidental release of a regulated substance or extremely hazardous substance to ambient air from a stationary source of air pollution that causes a death or inpatient hospitalization, or property damage outside the

stationary source exceeding $1 million; or make report to NRC within four hours (see above) (40 C.F.R. § 1604.3(c); Chapters 3 and 9)

- Occupational Safety and Health Administration (OSHA): (800) 321-6742 or www.osha.gov
  - Workplace fatality: After the death of any employee as a result of a workplace incident (33 C.F.R. § 1904.39(a)(1); Chapter 9)

Within 12 Hours

- National Response Center (800-424-8802) – HMTA, reporting of incidents arising during the course of transportation in commerce (including loading, unloading, and temporary storage), as soon as practicable but no later than 12 hours after the occurrence of any incident involving:
  - Hazardous materials: Eash person in physical possession of hazardous materials must report if, as a direct result of a hazardous material: a person is killed or hospitalized; the general public is evacuated for one hour or more; a major transportation artery or facility is closed or shut down for one hour or more; or, the operational flight pattern or routine of an aircraft is altered. (49 C.F.R. § 171.15(a), (b)(1); Chapters 3 and 6)
  - Radioactive materials: Eash person in physical possession of radioactive materials must report: (1) any fire, breakage, spillage, or suspected radioactive contamination involving radioactive material, and (2) if, as a direct result of the radioactive material: a person is killed or hospitalized; the general public is evacuated for one hour or more; a major transportation artery or facility is closed or shut down for one hour or more; or, the operational flight pattern or routine of an aircraft is altered. (49 C.F.R. §§ 171.15(a), (b)(1) and (2); see also C.F.R. § 176.48; Chapter 3)

- Infectious substances (other than regulated medical wastes): Each person in physical possession of infectious substances must report (1) any fire, breakage, spillage, or suspected contamination involving infectious substances, and (2) if, as a direct result of the infectious substance: a person is killed or hospitalized; the general public is evacuated for one hour or more; a major transportation artery or facility is closed or shut down for one hour or more; or, the operational flight pattern or routine of an aircraft is altered. (49 C.F.R. §§ 171.15(a), (b)(1), and (3); Chapter 3)

Within 24 Hours

- RCRA: Owner or operator of treatment, storage, or disposal facility (TSDF) must report leak from a hazardous waste tank system or secondary containment to the EPA regional administrator (40 C.F.R. §§ 264.196(d)(1), 265.196(d)(1); Chapter 3)
- RCRA: Underground storage tank (UST) for petroleum or hazardous substance: Report release to the implementing agency (typically a state environmental agency) (40 C.F.R. 280.61; Chapter 3)
- TSCA: Spill of more than one pound of material containing more than 50 ppm PCBs, as soon as possible and within 24 hours, to NRC and EPA Regional Office branch of Office of Pesticides and Toxic Substances (40 C.F.R. § 761.125; Chapter 3)
- Make all additional incident reports to regulatory authorities required within 24 hours of the release, such as:
  - Occupational Safety and Health Administration (OSHA): (800) 321-6742
    - Workplace injury: After the in-patient hospitalization of one or more employees or an employee's amputation of a limb or loss of an eye, as a result of a work-related incident (33 C.F.R. § 1904.39(a)(2); Chapter 9)

- Review and activate all applicable provisions of business continuity plan / continuity of operations plan.
- Determine post-incident investigation plan.
- Initiate on-site post-incident internal investigation (only once safety considerations permit).
- Put insurance carrier(s) on notice of potential claim(s).

IMPORTANT: Practically every federal or state statute or regulation that requires an initial report of a release also requires the submittal of one or more follow-up written reports within a few days or weeks after the initial report. It is beyond the scope of this timeline to enumerate examples of such additional reporting requirements.

About the Editors

Thomas S. Burack, a shareholder and consultant with Sheehan Phinney, focuses on environmental, energy, real estate, and nonprofit organization matters. Tom is a practical problem solver whose clients benefit from his experiences serving in all three branches of government and in board leadership roles for numerous nonprofit organizations. As commissioner of the NH Department of Environmental Services for over ten years, Tom guided development and deployment of the agency's emergency preparedness, response, and recovery capabilities, including in collaboration with local, state, and federal partners. Trained in incident management, Tom has helped lead responses to hurricanes, snow and ice storms, floods, droughts, tornadoes, anthrax exposures, dam emergencies, river avulsions, oil and hazardous materials spills, and the most widespread environmental incident in the state's history—atmospheric deposition of PFAS that contaminated soil, groundwater, and drinking water supplies across thousands of properties spanning more than 64 square miles across at least five communities.

Tom counsels businesses, municipalities, nonprofits, and individuals on release and other emergency responses, brownfields redevelopment, dam repairs and removals, water supply issues, compliance, and litigation under the full suite of state and federal environmental laws; he also facilitates development of strategic and scenario plans that contemplate hazards and disasters. Tom is a Fellow of the American College of Environmental Lawyers, a Harry S. Truman Scholar, and served as president of the Environmental Council of the States. A professional raconteur, Tom is known for calling moose, performing as Daniel Webster, and regaling audiences with tales of the North Country.

Olivia Cronquist is an associate attorney at Holland & Hart's Salt Lake City office. Her practice focuses on helping clients navigate labor and employment disputes and supporting them through litigation when matters go unresolved. She strives to achieve sensible outcomes for her clients through recommended changes to workplace policies or employment procedures and can audit companies for compliance with state and local rules and regulations. Olivia's experience also extends into general commercial litigation, including breach of contract disputes, real estate and construction matters, and noncompete agreement disputes. Olivia earned her MA in English from Brigham Young University, where she gained editing experience and taught undergraduate students both first-year writing and persuasive writing. She graduated cum laude with her JD from BYU's J. Reuben Clark Law School, where she assisted with scholarly research and writing.

Kevin R. Murray is known for his innovative and unique resolutions to complex contamination issues, especially involving multi-jurisdictional and multi-agency matters (particularly EPA and NRC) in the mining, real estate, energy, petroleum, nuclear, and manufacturing industries. His practice focuses on managing environmental liabilities, repurposing real estate assets, and creating value through property remediation and planning. Kevin is respected for his strategic approach to crafting cutting-edge legal solutions that deliver maximum value for his clients, ranging from the largest international corporations to individual landowners. He has been the lead attorney for billions of dollars of acquisitions and development of environmentally challenged assets worldwide, including many Superfund sites. Kevin has significant experience with CERCLA, RCRA, state hazardous waste laws, and related programs, and substantial experience with uranium mine and mill remediation and decommissioning. His work in the disaster arena comes in advising on planning for private development sustainability and resilience. Kevin is a former president of the American College of Environmental Lawyers and the editor of the fifth edition of *Environmental Aspects of Real Estate and Commercial Transactions: Acquisition, Development, and Liability Management*, published by the ABA. He is a member of the editorial board of the ABA SEER Natural Resources & Environment Journal, a member of the American Law Institute, and a member of the Environmental Law Institute where he serves on the Leadership Steering Committee of the Leadership Council.

About the Authors

Robert Ayers represents clients in environmental and workplace safety matters, including government investigations, emergency response, compliance counseling, internal investigations, and litigation. He has counseled clients through several of the largest workplace incidents and regulatory enforcement actions in the United States.

Robert routinely advises clients following major industrial incidents, including process safety events and workplace fatalities. He represents clients in connection with investigations by various government agencies, including the Occupational Safety and Health Administration (OSHA), the Chemical Safety Board (CSB), the Environmental Protection Agency (EPA), the Mine Safety and Health Administration (MSHA), the Pipeline and Hazardous Materials Safety Administration (PHMSA), and various state and local agencies. Robert also counsels clients on regulatory compliance, workplace safety culture, and process safety management.

Robert also defends clients in regulatory enforcement actions, including matters before the Occupational Safety and Health Review Commission, Federal Mine Safety and Health Review Commission, the Interior Board of Land Appeals, and various state-level environmental and occupational safety appeals boards. He also represents clients in civil litigation following industrial incidents. Robert has litigated disputes relating to oil and gas development, personal injury, groundwater contamination, and breach of contract in state and federal courts across the United States.

Susan Parker Bodine is an environmental attorney with over 36 years of public and private experience with environmental public policy issues including water pollution control, wetlands, regulation of wastes, remediation of contaminated properties, and water resources development.

Ms. Bodine's experience includes serving as the assistant administrator of EPA's Office of Enforcement and Compliance Assurance, which secures cleanup commitments from private parties using the liability provisions of the Superfund law, and as the assistant administrator of EPA's

Office of Solid Waste and Emergency Response (now the Office of Land and Emergency Management), which oversees Superfund cleanups and carries out EPA's emergency management responsibilities. Ms. Bodine also conducted oversight and worked on legislation related to the Superfund program while serving as the chief counsel for the Senate Committee on Environment and Public Works, and as the staff director and senior counsel for the Subcommittee on Water Resources and Environment of the House Transportation and Infrastructure Committee.

Before and after her government service, Ms. Bodine practiced environmental law at Covington & Burling and at Barnes & Thornburg. She currently is a partner with Earth & Water Law. Ms. Bodine is a graduate of Princeton University and the University of Pennsylvania School of Law.

Thomas S. Burack, a shareholder and consultant with Sheehan Phinney, focuses on environmental, energy, real estate, and nonprofit organization matters. Tom is a practical problem solver whose clients benefit from his experiences serving in all three branches of government. As commissioner of the NH Department of Environmental Services for over ten years, Tom guided development and deployment of the agency's emergency preparedness, response, and recovery capabilities, including in collaboration with local, state, and federal partners. Trained in incident management, Tom has helped lead responses to hurricanes, snow and ice storms, floods, droughts, tornadoes, anthrax exposures, dam emergencies, river avulsions, oil and hazardous materials spills, and the most widespread environmental incident in the state's history—atmospheric deposition of PFAS that contaminated soil, groundwater, and drinking water supplies across thousands of properties spanning more than 64 square miles across at least five communities.

Tom counsels businesses, municipalities, nonprofits, and individuals on release and other emergency responses, brownfields redevelopment, dam repairs and removals, water supply issues, compliance, and litigation under the full suite of state and federal environmental laws; he also facilitates development of strategic and scenario plans that contemplate hazards and disasters. Tom is a Fellow of the American College of Environmental Lawyers.

Greg Dillard chairs the Catastrophic Accident Response and OSHA Safety practices at BakerHostetler, and has been responding to high-stakes incidents, commonly involving hazardous materials, across the United States for more than 20 years. A nationally recognized leader in crisis response, Greg's work spans numerous industries, including transportation and logistics. Greg provides both strategic guidance to companies' legal and executive teams and on-site tactical support for the affected facility and its personnel. Greg ensures that clients' contamination and hazardous materials incidents are handled expeditiously with the priority on protecting people, the environment, and a company's business reputation. Greg has first-chair trial experience defending corporations, post-incident, against enforcement actions by state and federal agencies, such as NTSB, ATF, EPA, and OSHA. Greg is a frequent author and speaker on environmental crisis response and has participated in rulemaking advocacy for revisions to the EPA Clean Air Act Risk Management Plan and process safety management regulations in multiple states.

Scott Elliott has over 15 years of experience advising clients on a wide range of environmental, health, and safety matters. He is a leading crisis response lawyer, representing clients nationwide in the wake of explosions, fires, fatalities, and other major incidents. Scott's experience includes working on some of the most significant industrial accidents of the last decade across a range of industries, including refining and chemical manufacturing, warehousing, manufacturing, and food products. Scott has represented clients in connection with administrative, civil and criminal investigations, litigation and enforcement, and has extensive experience working on investigations by the Chemical Safety Board, DOJ, EPA, OSHA, and multiple other state-level agencies across the country. Scott also frequently assists clients in performing internal investigations relating to safety issues.

Scott leverages his incident response and enforcement experience to advise companies on a broad range of environmental, health, and safety matters, with a particular focus on requirements under federal and state process safety regulations. He also works with clients to develop and review EHS compliance programs and to analyze emerging EHS regulations.

Marshall Gilinsky is a shareholder in Anderson Kill's Boston office and practices in the firm's Insurance Recovery and Commercial Litigation groups. Marshall is co-chair of the firm's Sexual Harassment and Abuse Insurance Recovery Group and Sports, Media and Entertainment Group, and a member of the firm's Banking and Lending Group and Restaurant, Retail & Hospitality Group.

During his 30-year career representing policyholders, Marshall has recovered hundreds of millions of dollars for his clients, successfully litigating disputed claims under a variety of insurance products, including property and business interruption insurance, commercial general liability (CGL) insurance, errors and omissions (E&O) insurance, directors and officers (D&O) insurance, and life insurance. Marshall has represented clients on numerous high-stakes, complex insurance claims arising out of prominent losses such as 9/11, Hurricane Katrina, Superstorm Sandy, and the "Big Dig" in Boston.

Marshall frequently writes and lectures on a variety of topics of interest to professionals and practitioners in the insurance arena, and is frequently quoted in the press, including appearances in *The New York Times*, *The Wall Street Journal*, *National Law Review*, *CNN*, and *Business Insurance*, among others.

Gregory Goldberg, a fierce advocate, defends companies and individuals—including directors and other executives—in government investigations and related civil and criminal litigation. Drawing on his experience as a former prosecutor with the U.S. Department of Justice, Greg has credibility with DOJ and federal agencies around the country to help clients navigate potential parallel civil, regulatory, and criminal proceedings. Understanding that timing is critical in any government investigation, Greg leverages in-depth knowledge of key inflection points in the case to drive solutions.

Greg's demeanor and responsiveness put clients at ease in disputes with the government where corporate reputation and governance, personal liberty, and serious financial risk are on the line. He advises corporate boards, officers, and individuals in achieving results aligned with each client's interests and objectives.

Greg handles complex civil and criminal cases, including under various state and federal environmental statutes, and in every phase of False Claims Act (FCA) proceedings, including government investigation and declination, litigation with relators and DOJ, the Granston Memo, suspension and debarment, and appeal. Greg also counsels museums and collectors in responding to investigations by foreign nations and state and federal governments regarding the provenance, repatriation, and forfeiture of pieces of artwork.

Pamela Hans is the managing shareholder of Anderson Kill's Philadelphia office. Her practice concentrates in the area of insurance coverage on behalf of policyholders. A civil engineer and lawyer, she combines the two disciplines to bring practical solutions to complex problems in the energy, mining, oil and gas, and manufacturing sectors. With a practice that spans numerous U.S. jurisdictions, Canada, and overseas, Pam has represented companies in bet-the-company matters including those involving coverage for environmental liabilities, catastrophic personal injuries and property losses, and cyber incidents. Pam has been recognized for appellate victories and important decisions on matters including trigger of coverage and attorney-client privilege; she is most recognized by her clients for putting their interests and goals at the center of every representation to drive favorable results, whether through litigation or negotiations.

Pam is a Fellow of the American College of Coverage Counsel, recognized by Chambers USA, The Legal 500, and Best Lawyers®. Law360 identified her as a Legal Lion for a $58 million Appeals Court Win for TransCanada Energy and as a 2014 Female Powerbroker.

Pam is a board member (corporator/director) of the American School for the Deaf.

Seán McCabe is an attorney in Anderson Kill's New York office and a member of the firm's White Collar Defense and Insurance Recovery groups. Seán has had a key role in trial preparation and legal research on federal criminal cases arising out of the Southern District of New York, including major white collar criminal cases, conspiracy, and RICO cases. He also represents policyholders in insurance coverage disputes.

Before entering private practice, Seán worked at the Philadelphia District Attorney's Office as part of an LLM Program at Temple University. He also interned with the Hon. Charles J. Cunningham III in Philadelphia. In Ireland, Seán worked with a large, multidisciplinary firm, where he served as a summer associate for a partner, focusing on commercial, criminal, and malpractice litigation. He is admitted to practice in New York State Court and Federal District Courts for the Southern and Eastern Districts of New York.

A native of Ireland, Seán graduated from the University College of Cork School of Law in Ireland with a bachelor's of law, magna cum laude, concentrating on international criminal law. During his studies, he spent a year at Temple University's Beasley School of Law in its LLM program.

Emily Mott is an experienced crisis response attorney with the law firm of BakerHostetler in Houston, Texas. As a member of the firm's Catastrophic Accident Response team, Emily has deployed to manage a variety of environmental crisis incidents across the transportation, oil and gas, energy, chemical, and manufacturing industries. Emily provides immediate support and counsel in response to major incidents, including performing on-site investigations, managing regulatory and legal obligations, and defending against resulting enforcement and litigation. She is well versed in performing complex internal investigations and simultaneously managing federal and state agency investigations in the wake of incidents, including investigations by the U.S. Environmental Protection Agency, U.S. Chemical Safety Board, Occupational Safety and Health Administration, and National Transportation Safety Board. Emily uses her background in investigations, including root cause analyses and whistleblower complaints, to help companies foresee and prevent future liability and strengthen emergency preparedness.

Kevin R. Murray is known for his innovative and unique resolutions to complex contamination issues, especially involving multi-jurisdictional and multi-agency matters (particularly EPA and NRC) in the mining, real estate, energy, petroleum, nuclear, and manufacturing industries. His practice focuses on managing environmental liabilities, repurposing real estate assets, and creating value through property remediation and planning. Kevin is respected for his strategic approach to crafting cutting-edge legal solutions that deliver maximum value for his clients, ranging from the largest international corporations to individual landowners. He has been the lead attorney for billions of dollars of acquisitions and development of environmentally challenged assets worldwide, including many Superfund sites. Kevin has significant experience with CERCLA, RCRA, state hazardous waste laws, and related programs, and substantial experience with uranium mine and mill remediation and decommissioning. His work in the disaster arena comes in advising on planning for private development sustainability and resilience. Kevin is a former president of the American College of Environmental Lawyers and the editor of the fifth edition of *Environmental Aspects of Real Estate and Commercial Transactions: Acquisition, Development, and Liability Management*, published by the ABA.

Rhonda D. Orin is the managing shareholder of Anderson Kill's Washington, D.C., office and co-chair of the firm's Climate Change and Disaster Recovery group. As a senior partner at AK, Rhonda has decades of experience representing policyholders. She has been lead counsel in multiple coverage trials and has substantial appellate experience. Two of her cases have been decided by the U.S. Supreme Court.

Rhonda is distinguished by her substantive knowledge. In addition to expertise with first-party property damage and business interruption claims, third-party tort and environmental liability claims, directors & officers, and errors & omissions claims, she is knowledgeable about cyber liability, disability policies, and health insurance.

Rhonda is a Fellow of the American Bar Foundation, an honor reserved for less than 1 percent of attorneys, a Fellow of the Litigation Counsel of America, and ranked in *Chambers USA*. She has been honored by *The Legal 500*, awarded "Star of the Bar" by the Women's Bar Association of D.C., and included in Best Lawyers in America and Super Lawyers continuously since 2011. She also is a prolific and influential author, including of *Making Them Pay: How to Get the Most from Health Insurance and Managed Care* (St. Martin's Press 2000), honored by *The Wall Street Journal*.

Regan Samson is an attorney in Anderson Kill's New York office. She focuses her practice on insurance recovery, exclusively on behalf of policyholders.

While attending Benjamin N. Cardozo School of Law, Regan worked as a summer law clerk at Anderson Kill. Also, while at Cardozo, she served as a pro bono scholar at Lawyers for Children, where she represented children in cases involving custody, visitation, voluntary foster care placement, abuse, neglect, and termination of parental rights. She also worked as a summer ADR Department legal intern with the U.S. District Court for the Southern District of New York, designing dispute resolution programs responsive to the needs of local communities, and as a mediator at the Cardozo Mediation Clinic, where she mediated cases in Manhattan Small Claims Court between landlords and tenants, business partners, vendors and consumers, family members, and employees and employers.

At Cardozo, Regan was the recipient of the 2021 Jacob Burns Medal, the 2021 Inspire! Award for Pro Bono Services, and the Dean's Merit Scholarship. She was also co-editor in chief for the Cardozo Moot Court Honor Society.

Mary Ellen Ternes is a 1984 Vanderbilt degreed chemical engineer, former EPA CERCLA Emergency Response On-Scene Coordinator, EPA RCRA hazardous waste incinerator permit writer, and a commercial hazardous waste incineration industry permitting and compliance officer, who then became an environmental attorney. Since 1995, Mary Ellen has represented a broad range of clients with complex technical issues arising under environmental law, particularly as they arise with chemical process and waste facility crisis preparedness, response, and remediation, exacerbated by the effects of climate change, as well as permitting, compliance, enforcement, transactions, and litigation.

Mary Ellen's engagement in environmental issues extends beyond client counseling to leadership, education, and publication regarding science-based policy development, both nationally and internationally, particularly regarding the issues of chemical plant safety, anthropogenic climate change mitigation and adaptation, and plastic pollution and solutions. Mary Ellen is a Fellow and former president of the American

College of Environmental Lawyers, Fellow of the American Institute of Chemical Engineers, Senior Fellow for Law and Policy of the Global Council for Science and the Environment, for which she has served as Delegate to the United Nations Intergovernmental Negotiating Committee on Plastic Pollution, and Senior Fellow of The Judge Alfred P. Murrah Center for Homeland Security Law & Policy. Mary Ellen is also a former chair of the Air Quality, Climate Change, and Ethics Committees of the ABA Section of Environment, Energy and Resources, and lead editor of the ABA SEER's NR&E spring 2024 issue, "Plastic." Vanderbilt University Center for Sustainability, Energy and Climate has created an endowed lectureship emphasizing the importance of interdisciplinary education in Mary Ellen's honor.

Mary Ellen is currently a partner with Earth & Water Law, LLC.

Jordan Wimpy is a partner at Mitchell, Williams, Selig, Gates & Woodyard, P.L.L.C. in Little Rock, Arkansas, where his practice covers issues across the spectrum of environmental, agricultural, energy, and natural resources. Jordan represents trade associations, utilities, and business clients in administrative rulemaking matters and in all aspects of the environmental permitting, compliance, and enforcement processes. He advises landowners and local governments regarding land use, environmental mitigation/reclamation standards, and complex regulatory matters. He also counsels agricultural producers and landowners regarding agricultural conservation programs, conservation easements, and land stewardship activities.

Jordan is a frequent speaker on environmental law. He is a regular presenter at the National Clean Water Law and Enforcement seminar hosted by the National Association of Clean Water Agencies; the Arkansas Environmental Federation's Water, Air, and Land Seminars; and the Arkansas Bar Association's Environmental Law Conference.

Jordan is a member of the American Bar Association's Environment, Energy and Resources Section where he has served in numerous leadership roles for the Agricultural Management Committee. Before joining active practice, Jordan earned his JD and master of environmental law and policy, both magna cum laude, from Vermont Law School.

Chapter 1

The National Emergency Response System as the Backdrop for Disaster Preparedness, Response, and Recovery

Thomas S. Burack

Introduction: Destruction and Hope[1]

DISASTER! The very word instantly instills fear and portends tragedy, catastrophe, destruction, and death. Disasters have stalked, afflicted, and brought despair to humankind throughout recorded history. In 79 AD, a violent volcanic eruption of Mt. Vesuvius rapidly covered the nearby towns of Herculaneum and Pompeii in hot ash, pumice, debris, and burning clouds, killing some 16,000 people in what is today Italy.[2] On August 27, 1900, a hurricane packing estimated wind speeds in excess of 130 miles per hour and a storm surge of nearly 16 feet caught the seaside town of Galveston, Texas, largely by surprise, leveling much of

1. This chapter is based in part upon a compilation initially prepared by Mary Ellen Ternes, Earth & Water Law, LLC, with contributions from Thomas S. Burack, Sheehan Phinney Bass & Green, PA, and Kevin R. Murray, Holland & Hart, for educational purposes at The Judge Alfred P. Murrah Center for Homeland Security Law & Policy 2019 National Summit, which was held at Oklahoma City University in 2019.

2. *See generally Eruption of Mount Vesuvius of 79 AD*, https://bomv.commons.gc.cuny.edu/eruption-of-mount-vesuvius-of-79-ad/ (last visited Mar. 29, 2025).

the town and killing an estimated 6,000 to 8,000 people.[3] And over the course of about three and a half weeks in January 2025, a series of uncontrolled wildfires in the Los Angeles region of California—fanned by Santa Ana winds of near hurricane force—killed at least 29 people, razed at least 16,000 homes and businesses, and caused billions of dollars of economic loss.[4]

One of the most tragic human-caused disasters occurred on December 3, 1984, when 40 tons of methyl isocyanate—a poisonous gas—were emitted into the air from a pesticide plant in Bhopal, India, killing as many as 3,800 people immediately, an estimated 10,000 within days, and another 15,000 to 20,000 due to premature deaths during the next two decades, and leaving a lingering legacy of health issues.[5] The largest offshore oil spill in U.S. history was the result of an April 20, 2010, explosion on the Deepwater Horizon oil platform that killed 11 workers on the platform; released 134 million gallons of oil into ocean waters over the course of 87 days; fouled 1,300 miles of shoreline across five states along the U.S. Gulf Coast; and caused billions of dollars in damages to natural resources, fisheries, and lost livelihoods.[6]

While the attention-grabbing disasters tend to be large in scale and impact, the vast majority of disasters are of a much smaller scale and come and go quickly in the daily news cycle; nevertheless, they can have catastrophic impacts. Today, every hurricane gets a name, and in recent

---

3. *See generally* NOAA, *The Great Galveston Hurricane of 1900*, https://celebrating200years.noaa.gov/magazine/galv_hurricane/welcome.html#pred (last visited Mar. 29, 2025).

4. *See generally* NCEI, *Destructive California Wildfires Fueled by Strong Santa Ana Winds in January; an Arctic Blast Brought a Blanket of Snowfall to the Gulf Coast States* (Feb. 10, 2025), https://www.ncei.noaa.gov/news/national-climate-202501; *see also* Rebecca Lindsey, *The Weather and Climate Influences on the January 2025 Fires Around Los Angeles*, NOAA Climate.gov (Feb. 19, 2025), https://www.climate.gov/news-features/event-tracker/weather-and-climate-influences-january-2025-fires-around-los-angeles#:~:text=On%20January%207%2C%202025%2C%20a,quality%20for%20millions%20of%20people.

5. Edward Broughton, *The Bhopal Disaster and Its Aftermath: A Review*, 4(6) Env't Health (May 10, 2005), https://pmc.ncbi.nlm.nih.gov/articles/PMC1142333/.

6. *See* NOAA, *Deepwater Horizon Oil Spill: Longterm Effects on Marine Mammals, Sea Turtles* (Apr. 20, 2017), https://oceanservice.noaa.gov/news/apr17/dwh-protected-species.html#:~:text=As%20the%20largest%20offshore%20oil,of%20shoreline%20along%20five%20states. *See also* EPA, *Deepwater Horizon—BP Gulf of America Spill*, https://www.epa.gov/enforcement/deepwater-horizon-bp-gulf-america-oil-spill#:~:text=On%20April%2020%2C%202010%2C%20the,of%20marine%20oil%20drilling%20operations (last updated Feb. 6, 2025).

decades we've experienced many—Sandy, Katrina, Milton, and Helene, to mention just a few. Major wildfires also get names, typically associated with the geographic name of the affected community, such as Oakland Hills, Paradise, Marshall, or Maui. But tornadoes, which occur sometimes on an almost daily basis and may not affect as large a land area, can still do just as much destruction to an individual community as any hurricane or wildfire. Perhaps because we don't give tornadoes names, they tend to be forgotten, except by those who managed to live through them.

It is certainly helpful that in this modern era some disasters are foreseeable or even predicted days in advance (often thanks to highly sophisticated, super-computer-enhanced weather or seismic forecasting), but the stark reality is that most disasters occur with little or no warning. Moreover, as some of the preceding examples illustrate, many disasters are the result of natural forces over which humankind has little or no immediate control, and others may be the result of human error or poor judgment; process operation flaws; or flawed engineering, design, construction, or technology. There are even disasters within disasters, such as when flooding results in the release of hazardous or toxic chemicals into the environment.

Regardless of its type or cause, a disaster's combined effects of economic losses, environmental damages, societal disruption, loss of life, and physical and mental health impacts can be devastating on an affected community or region. The Federal Emergency Management Agency estimates that "[a]bout 25 percent of businesses do not reopen after disasters."[7] Direct economic losses to a community from a disaster may "include the destruction of residences, businesses, productive capital, infrastructure, crops, livestock, and (monetized) physical and mental health impacts."[8] For example, an early estimate of the economic impact of the January 2025 Los Angeles wildfires projects total property and capital losses ranging from $76 to $131 billion (of which only $45 billion is insured), a 0.48 percent decline in county gross domestic product

7. FEMA, *Stay in Business After a Disaster by Planning Ahead* (Oct. 30, 2018), https://www.fema.gov/press-release/20250121/stay-business-after-disaster-planning-ahead#:~:text=About%2025%20percent%20of%20businesses%20do%20not%20reopen%20after%20disasters.

8. W.J. Wouter Botzen, Olivier Deschenes & Mark Sanders, *The Economic Impacts of Natural Disasters: A Review of Models and Empirical Studies*, 13(2) Rev. Env't Econ. & Pol'y 167–88 (2019).

in 2025, and 2025 wage losses of $297 million for local businesses and employees.[9] Numerous studies document that those who live through natural disasters are likely to experience an increased risk of mental health consequences, including but not limited to anxiety, depression, and post-traumatic stress disorder.[10]

If there is a hopeful message amid all this carnage, damage, and despair, it is that regardless of the cause of a disaster, its impact can be mitigated with appropriate planning, preparedness, and resiliency measures; that a speedy and well-equipped response (such as with modern firefighting equipment) can lessen the overall damages; and that recovery can proceed more quickly with a pre-established and well-structured system of financial and technical support. A recent analysis found that insurance recoveries and government aid are important factors in a community's ability to bounce back, and may eventually bolster the economies of communities affected by natural disasters.[11] Case studies also show that when communities "build back better" following a disaster, they will be more resilient in the face of future disasters, be more economically competitive, and offer their residents a better quality of life.[12]

Here in the United States, the current system for addressing disasters and incidents of all kinds (an "all hazards" approach) is tiered based on the premise that most responses will be handled initially at the local level by municipal, county, and tribal governments, as well as by cooperating businesses and nonprofit organizations. The system also assumes that help and support will be provided as necessary by the affected state or

9. Zhiyun Li & William Yu, *Economic Impact of the Los Angeles Wildfires*, UCLA Anderson Sch. of Mgmt., https://www.anderson.ucla.edu/about/centers/ucla-anderson-forecast/economic-impact-los-angeles-wildfires (last updated Mar. 3, 2025); *see also* LAEDC, Impact of 2025 Los Angeles Wildfires and Comparative Study (Feb. 2025), https://laedc.org/wpcms/wp-content/uploads/2025/02/LAEDC-2025-LA-Wildfires-Study.pdf.

10. Eamin Z. Heanoy & Norman R. Brown, *Impact of Natural Disasters on Mental Health: Evidence and Implication*, 12(18) Healthcare 1812 (2024), https://www.mdpi.com/2227-9032/12/18/1812.

11. *See* Brigitte Roth Tran & Daniel J. Wilson, *The Local Economic Impact of Natural Disasters* (Aug. 2024), Fed. Rsrv. Bank of S.F. Working Paper Series 2020-34 (Aug. 2024), https://www.frbsf.org/wp-content/uploads/wp2020-34.pdf.

12. *See* NADO, *Lessons from the Storm: Case Studies on Economic Recovery and Resilience*, https://www.nado.org/lessons-from-the-storm-case-studies-on-economic-recovery-and-resilience/ (last visited Mar. 29, 2025).

states and, in turn, by the federal government, although typically only as requested by a state and deemed warranted by federal officials. While there are some types of incidents, such as releases of hazardous substances or petroleum products into offshore federal waters, in which the federal government will likely be the "first responder," the federal government usually serves as the backstop for state, tribal, and local government responses to incidents of all kinds, including natural, technological, and human-caused disasters and emergencies. One complication of an all-hazards approach is that it brings together literally hundreds, if not many thousands, of different laws and regulations, all of which have their own defined terms that may not be consistent with similar terms used in other laws or regulations that may also apply to a given situation. Accordingly, this book often uses the terms "disaster" and "incident" interchangeably to refer collectively to all forms and types of disasters, incidents, accidents, and emergencies, and under some circumstances uses "incident" to describe situations limited to unpermitted releases of pollutants, chemicals, or biological or nuclear hazards into the environment.

Of note, on March 18, 2025, President Trump issued Executive Order 14239, "Achieving Efficiency Through State and Local Preparedness,[13] whose stated purpose is to "empower [] State, local, and individual preparedness and inject[] common sense into infrastructure prioritization and strategic investments through risk-informed decisions that make our infrastructure, communities, and economy resilient to global and dynamic threats and hazards."[14] Section 2 of Executive Order 14239 asserts, "It is the policy of the United States that State and local governments and individuals play a more active and significant role in national resilience and preparedness, thereby saving American lives, securing American livelihoods, reducing taxpayer burdens through efficiency, and unleashing our collective prosperity."[15] A further policy of the United States states "that my Administration streamline its preparedness operations; update relevant government policies to reduce complexity and better protect and serve

13. Exec. Order No. 14239, 90 Fed. Reg. 13267, Achieving Efficiency Through State and Local Preparedness (Mar. 18, 2025).

14. *Id.* § 1.

15. *Id.* § 2.

Americans; and enable State and local governments to better understand, plan for, and ultimately address the needs of their citizens."[16] Under the heading, "Updating Federal Policy to Save Lives and End the Subsidization of Mismanagement," Section 3 of the executive order calls for publication within 90 days of a National Resilience Strategy, and for review within 180 days of "all critical infrastructure policies" accompanied by recommended "revisions, recissions, and replacements necessary to achieve a more resilient posture[,] shift from an all-hazards approach to a risk-informed approach[,] move beyond information sharing to action[, and] implement the National Resilience Strategy[.]"[17]

It is too early to know just what this executive order will bring in the future, but taking it at face value, among other things, it may result in greater reliance on state and local resources to prepare for disasters, and fewer federal resources—both financial and expert personnel—to support states, localities, and individuals in disaster response and recovery. This executive order also signals a doctrinal shift from an "all-hazards" approach to a "risk-informed" approach (a term that has not yet been fleshed-out but sounds similar to the "risk-based" approach mandated for FEMA by the Post-Katrina Emergency Management Reform Act of 2006, discussed later in this chapter). The concept of resilience (the ability to withstand and recover quickly from harms), on which this new, overall approach is based, has deep roots in the field of disaster and incident management, so this may be more about semantics and incremental change rather than a radical shift. And this is because, in very practical terms, regardless of the hazards or risks being addressed, all communities, businesses, and individuals affected by a disaster will typically need the same basic goods and services in order to help them get back on their feet and ultimately recover—namely, drinking water, food, emergency shelter, clothing, medicines and medical services, debris removal, and infrastructure and utility repair and replacement—all as the foundation for building new homes and other structures better suited to surviving future disasters. In short, terminology and approach may change, but human needs and hope for the future will not.

16. *Id.*
17. *Id.* § 3.

The remainder of this chapter is structured to provide an overview of the purpose, players, history, legal authority, structure, and operations of incident management in the United States. It explains how the different layers and branches of government currently collaborate under established frameworks and plans to help communities prepare for, respond to, and recover from incidents of all types.

The Goals, Challenges, and Key Players in Disaster and Emergency Management

The federal government's approach to disaster and emergency prevention, protection, mitigation, response, and recovery envisions a community-wide scope, dynamic adaptation, and continually building on past experiences. The National Preparedness Goal of the Federal Emergency Management Agency (FEMA) reads: "A secure and resilient nation with the capabilities required across the whole community to prevent, protect against, mitigate, respond to, and recover from the threats and hazards that pose the greatest risk."[18]

Invariably, disasters and emergencies are disruptive, expensive, and time-consuming to address. They can result in loss of human life, including mass casualties, extensive if not permanent property damage, and substantial economic losses. Happily, many kinds of disasters are preventable, or their impacts can at least be mitigated with preparedness and resiliency measures. Long experience has taught that the scale and extent of some disasters is far greater than individual communities and states can handle on their own, even with the benefit of mutual aid agreements, and that a disaster affecting one state or region can have ripple effects on other states or regions, such as when a large number of people are displaced by a flood and need to be relocated (either temporarily or permanently). In short, the exigencies of disaster response can easily exceed the financial and personnel resources of individual communities and states and demonstrate the necessity of the federal government's central role in the disaster management framework.

---

18. FEMA, *National Preparedness Goal*, https://www.fema.gov/emergency-managers/national-preparedness/goal (last updated Mar. 14, 2025).

Fortunately, the federal government is uniquely positioned and currently equipped to track and anticipate changing threats, such as the ever-evolving tactics of foreign and domestic terrorists, extreme weather events exacerbated by climate change, and the possibility of future pandemics. Societal shifts and evolving technologies also pose potential challenges, including the influence of smart phones and other technologies which may, depending on the circumstances, either impede or enhance local community engagement, possibly impacting communities' resilience in a disaster. There are also ever-present tensions between federal and state government jurisdiction. Federal jurisdiction is both authorized and limited by constitutional powers and enabled by federal statute and thus, at least in the first instance, limited in scope to the enabling authority. State government jurisdiction confers generally broader authority—particularly with respect to police powers—than the federal government to address issues at the community level, but states nevertheless find themselves asking the federal government for emergency supplies, as well as for financial, managerial, logistical, and technical assistance to help them prepare for, respond to, and recover from the full array of incident types. And then there are the constant challenges presented by periodic changes in leadership at all levels of government, agency reorganizations, budget limitations, and ever-changing priorities.

The ever-current question is: Are we ready for the next event? The nation's disaster professionals are certainly working hard to make sure our governmental agencies and communities are prepared. Federal, tribal, state, and local agencies and communities prepare hazard mitigation plans and emergency operations plans pursuant to federal and state laws and consistent with national frameworks, while volunteer entities such as the American Red Cross continually coordinate resources.

Private entities, including businesses and regulated entities, may not be directly involved in the regulatory aspects of disaster planning, but are often governed by environmental programs, homeland security, or other regulatory programs imposing preparedness and response requirements. Many private and nonprofit organizations are increasingly involved in this work because they play a vital role in ensuring both that supply chains of vital goods like food and medicines are not interrupted by disasters, and that vital services and needs are met at the community level. And while basic coverage such as flood insurance is likely a recognized priority, more comprehensive hazard assessment and mitigation is often overlooked, as is simple business continuity planning. Expanded notions of foreseeability and recent litigation appear to compel renewed focus on business risk management in this area. It is critical that businesses, nonprofit organizations, and other regulated entities have reasonable expectations of government resources through the various scenarios that can arise during a disaster. But it is even more critical that all of these entities properly evaluate and mitigate hazards, evaluate and obtain appropriate insurance, and develop continuity of operations plans (COOPs) or business continuity plans (BCPs). COOPs and BCPs help public and private entities to remain viable during and following a disaster and also ensure that their operations don't become a source of further harm in this context.

Key Elements of Disaster and Emergency Management

The Department of Homeland Security (DHS) describes "national preparedness" as encompassing five separate "mission areas," namely, prevention, protection, mitigation, response, and recovery.[19] Importantly, the "prevention" and "protection" mission areas in this context are focused heavily on reducing the risks and potential consequences of terrorist activities and attacks—a topic outside the scope of this book. While acknowledging the broad scope and cross-cutting themes of the DHS definition of "national preparedness," this book primarily uses the term "preparedness" to encompass prevention, protection, and mitigation as a combined set of activities that precedes an incident and treats response and recovery as separate stages that follow an incident.

It is also instructive to note that the National Preparedness Goal's five mission areas are supported by 32 "core capabilities."[20] For example, the core capabilities of planning, public information and warning, and operational coordination support all five mission areas. The core capabilities

19. FEMA, *Mission Areas and Core Capabilities*, https://www.fema.gov/emergency-managers/national-preparedness/mission-core-capabilities (last updated July 20, 2020).
20. *Id.*

of physical protective measures and cybersecurity only support the protection mission area. Others, such as environmental response/health and safety as well as fire management and suppression only support the response mission, while health and social services, economic recovery, and housing focus on the recovery mission.

The following concepts and terms are referred to periodically in this book. Prevention measures are intended to prevent or reduce the occurrence of future disasters, and could include, for example, building dams or levees to prevent future flooding. Hazard mitigation is a planning and action step that aims to reduce loss of life and damage to property by minimizing the potential impact of future disasters. For example, restricting development in low-lying areas, elevating buildings, and increasing the capacity of drainage systems are common ways to mitigate against the impacts, damages, and consequences of future flooding. Preparedness, particularly in the context of a number of environmental laws, focuses on ensuring that human systems are ready to respond effectively to future incidents through such measures as planning, training, and practicing incident response techniques. This can include everything from conducting emergency drills such as tabletop or field exercises to ensuring that all response personnel and agencies have interconnected communication systems. Response usually consists of three phases: (1) the immediate response by local emergency responders (fire, police, emergency medical) to put out fires, undertake evacuations, and take other actions to reduce the risk of injuries or deaths; (2) deployment of additional personnel for site investigation and emergency removals of dangerous structures or hazardous materials; and (3) ongoing remedial actions, such as collection and disposal of debris. Recovery involves longer-term cleanup, rebuilding, occasionally permanent relocation of structures or inhabitants, and getting life back to normal. Recovery measures might include replacing culverts and bridges with structures equipped to handle larger volumes of precipitation and providing supplemental mental health support services.

Regardless of the incident type, protection in the form of threat monitoring is almost always being conducted in the background—whether it's tracking potential terrorist activity, monitoring seismic activity, or forecasting hurricanes. Sometimes there's advance notice of an incident (such as when a bad actor posts a shooting threat on social media). But there are also no-notice incidents (such as train derailments leading to releases of hazardous materials). Regardless of the threat type, once the incident occurs, it's typically followed by four phases of emergency management: immediate response (1–24 hours), community stabilization (24–72 hours), sustained operations (72 hours–30 days), and recovery (30+ days). This timeline is depicted in Figure 1.1.[21]

FIGURE 1.1 Emergency management operational phases

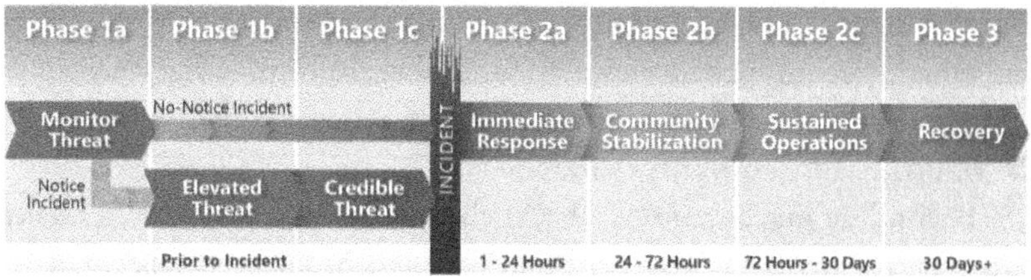

Federal and State Authority

The federal government draws on constitutional authority for its jurisdiction in responding to disasters. This includes congressional authority to raise armies,[22] the President's authority as commander in chief,[23] the federal government's duty to protect the states,[24] and Congress's authority to muster the military to enforce federal law.[25]

Of course, while the powers of the federal government are specifically enumerated, the Tenth Amendment provides that "[t]he powers not delegated to the United States by the Constitution, nor prohibited by it to the States, are reserved to the States respectively, or to the people."[26] Thus, the states implement general powers including police powers to protect citizens' general health, safety, and welfare, including disaster response as limited by the Constitution or otherwise preempted by Congress.

21. FEMA, OIL AND CHEMICAL INCIDENT ANNEX (Feb. 2021), https://www.fema.gov/sites/default/files/documents/fema_incident-annex-oil-chemical.pdf.
22. U.S. CONST. art. I, § 8, cl. 12.
23. *Id.* art. II, § 2.
24. *Id.* art. IV, § 4.
25. *Id.* art. I, § 8, cl. 15.
26. *Id.* amend. X.

Congress may preempt state action by enacting legislation. For example, Congress utilizes its Commerce Clause authority[27] when the "regulated activity 'substantially affects' interstate commerce,"[28] but in a disaster, Congress and the President can rely broadly on Congress's Spending Clause authority,[29] which requires the support of no other enumerated power to spend federal funds for the general welfare.[30] The Spending Clause allows Congress to condition the receipt of federal funds on compliance with certain requirements. Accordingly, congressional disaster relief funding is often tied to state adoption of disaster preparedness plans and other prerequisite conditions.[31] Additional authorities that may come into play in the context of disasters include the Taxing Clause authority,[32] the Militia Clause authority,[33] and the Fourteenth Amendment.[34]

Beyond serving as commander in chief of the military, the President has executive power to "take Care that the Laws be faithfully executed."[35] The scope of executive power is sometimes controversial and uncertain, considering recent examples of possible "disasters" and proposed uses

---

27. *Id.* art. I, § 8, cl. 3 (providing Congress with the power to "regulate Commerce with foreign Nations, and among the several States, and with the Indian Tribes").

28. United States v. Lopez, 514 U.S. 549, 559 (1995).

29. U.S. Const. art. I, § 8, cl. 1 (providing Congress with the power to "lay and collect taxes, duties, imposts and excises, to pay the debts and provide for the common defense and general welfare of the United Sates").

30. United States v. Butler, 297 U.S. 1 (1936).

31. Daniel A. Farber, Robert R.M. Verchick, James Ming Chen & Lisa Grow Sun, Disaster Law and Policy 93 (3d ed. 2015) (citing Pet Evacuation and Transportation Standards Act of 2006, 42 U.S.C. § 5196 (conditioning emergency shelter funding on state adoption of disaster plans for households with domestic pets) and Disaster Mitigation Act of 2000, 42 U.S.C. § 5165 (conditioning hazard mitigation funds on state adoption of approved natural disaster mitigation plans)).

32. U.S. Const. art. I, § 8, cl. 1 (providing Congress with the power to "lay and collect taxes, duties, imposts and excises, to pay the debts and provide for the common defense and general welfare of the United States").

33. *Id.* art. I, § 8, cl. 15–16 (providing Congress with the power to "provide for calling forth the militia to execute the Laws of the Union, suppress insurrections and repel invasions" and "for organizing, arming, and disciplining the militia, and for governing such part of them as may be employed in the service of the United States, reserving to the States respectively, the appointment of officers, and the authority of training the militia according to the discipline prescribed by Congress").

34. *Id.* amend. XIV, § 5 (providing the power to "enforce, by appropriate legislation" compliance by the states with the guarantees of equal protection and due process of law established by § 1 of the Fourteenth Amendment).

35. *Id.* art. II, § 3.

of executive power along our southern border.[36] But, as discussed later in this chapter, the Stafford Act expressly delegates broad power to the President to immediately respond to disasters. This power is so broad for a federal government with limited enumerated powers that it can cause, and has caused, confusion and delay when working with states' more general police powers.[37]

Federal Government Involvement Before the Creation of FEMA

The federal government has long played a role in disaster response, and in more recent decades that role has expanded to include disaster preparedness and prevention. Between 1803 and 1950, the federal government assisted states in responding to over 100 emergencies, including earthquakes, fires, floods, and tornadoes.[38]

During this period, disaster assistance was available through various federal entities that were not internally coordinated. For example, in the 1930s, the Reconstruction Finance Corporation had authority to grant loans to fund public entity recovery efforts following natural and other disasters.[39] In 1934, funding for recovery efforts for transportation infrastructure was provided by the Bureau of Public Roads.[40] In 1965, the Flood Control Act provided the Army Corps of Engineers with authority to implement flood control projects.[41] In 1968, the National Flood

---

36. *See generally* Farber et al., *supra* note 31, at 98 (referencing for further reading, David J. Barron & Martin S. Lederman, *The Commander in Chief at the Lowest Ebb—A Constitutional History*, 121 Harv. L. Rev. 941 (2008); Candidus Dougherty, *"Necessity Hath No Law": Executive Power and the Posse Comitatus Act*, 31 Campbell L. Rev. 1 (Sept. 2008)).

37. *See* Farber et al., *supra* note 31, at 100; Erin Ryan, *Federalism and the Tug of War Within: Seeking Checks and Balance in the Interjurisdictional Gray Area*, 66 Md. L. Rev. 503, 522–36 (2007).

38. *See* Farber et al., *supra* note 31, at 106 (citing The White House & Executive Office of the President, *The White House, The Federal Response to Hurricane Katrina: Lessons Learned*, 11–12, 158–59 n.11 (2006)).

39. *See generally* James Butkiewicz, *Reconstruction Finance Corporation*, Econ. Hist. Ass'n (July 19, 2002), https://eh.net/encyclopedia/reconstruction-finance-corporation/.

40. *See generally* Richard Weingroff, *A Moment in Time: FDR and the Federal-Aid Highway Program Part 1: Roosevelt Applies the Brakes*, FHWA, https://highways.dot.gov/highway-history/general-highway-history/moment-time-fdr-and-federal-aid-highway-program-part-1#:~:text=The%20Hayden%2DCartwright%20Act%20seeks,tapering%20off%20of%20emergency%20highway (last updated Mar. 25, 2024).

41. *See, e.g.*, The Flood Protection Authority, Comprehensive Regional Flood Defense, https://www.floodauthority.org/wp-content/uploads/2018/04/Info-Sheet-Flood-Defense-System.pdf (last visited Mar. 31, 2025).

Insurance Act created the Federal Insurance Administration and made flood insurance available to homeowners for the first time.[42] Known as the National Flood Insurance Program (NFIP), its primary goals are to "reduc[e] future flood damage and protect[] property owners."[43] The NFIP accomplishes these goals by working with private insurers and insurance agents to make flood insurance available for purchase by eligible residential and commercial property owners in communities that adopt and enforce floodplain management standards, which numbered some 22,600 as of 2023.[44] The Flood Disaster Protection Act of 1973 made the purchase of flood insurance mandatory to protect property located in Special Flood Hazard Areas,[45] as shown on flood maps developed by FEMA and used by participating communities to identify flood prone areas.[46]

In 1974, President Nixon signed the Disaster Relief Act of 1974 (1974 Act), which for the first time established a process whereby the President could issue disaster declarations.[47] The 1974 Act also broadened the authorities of the federal government to assist states and communities by providing federal assistance for disaster recovery while also creating incentives for disaster preparedness and hazard mitigation. This law provided the programmatic framework upon which the Federal Emergency Management Agency (FEMA) was subsequently established four years later.

---

42. 42 U.S.C. §§ 4001, *et seq.*

43. *See* NFIP, *A Brief History of the NFIP* (Oct. 2023), https://agents.floodsmart.gov/articles/brief-history-nfip.

44. *See* NFIP, *Flood Insurance 101: Getting Started Selling Flood Insurance*, https://agents.floodsmart.gov/agents-guide/background (last visited Mar. 28, 2025). For detailed history on the NFIP, *see* Scott G. Knowles & Howard C. Kunreuther, *Troubled Waters: The National Flood Insurance Program in Historical Perspective*, 26(3) J. Pol'y Hist. 327–53 (July 2014), and Cong. Rsch. Serv., Introduction to the National Flood Insurance Program (Apr. 2025), https://www.congress.gov/crs-product/R44593; *see also* American Institutes for Research, A Chronology of Major Events Affecting the National Flood Insurance Program (Oct. 2002), https://www.dhs.gov/xlibrary/assets/privacy/privacy_pia_mip_apnd_h.pdf.

45. *Id.*

46. *See generally* FEMA, *Flood Maps*, https://www.fema.gov/flood-maps (last updated Jan. 22, 2024).

47. 42 U.S.C. §§ 5121, *et seq.*

The Creation and Early History of FEMA and the Stafford Act

In June 1978, in response to state requests for greater federal disaster coordination, President Carter created FEMA pursuant to Reorganization Plan No. 3.[48] On March 31, 1979, President Carter's Executive Order 12127 transferred three sets of functions to FEMA, including the National Fire Prevention and Control Administration from the Department of Commerce, the Federal Insurance Administration (which administers the National Flood Insurance Program) from the Department of Housing and Urban Development, and the President's authority over the Emergency Broadcasting system.[49] In July 1979, via Executive Order 12148, President Carter then delegated to FEMA broad disaster relief authority as well as civil defense responsibilities and brought additional existing government programs and authorities under FEMA's umbrella, including the Defense Civil Preparedness Agency from the Department of Defense, the Federal Disaster Assistance Administration from the Department of Housing and Urban Development, the Federal Preparedness Agency from the General Services Administration, and the National Weather Service Community Preparedness Program from the Department of Commerce.[50]

As discussed later, FEMA's authorities and responsibilities were codified in 1988 by the Robert T. Stafford Disaster Relief and Emergency Assistance Act (Stafford Act), which was signed into law on November 23, 1988, and amended the 1974 Act.[51] Today, the Stafford Act is the statutory authority for most federal disaster response activities, especially as they pertain to FEMA and its programs. The 1988 Stafford Act provides the authority for awarding federal disaster aid, including in response to requests by a state government, and for the President to issue a disaster declaration.

---

48. Reorganization Plan No. 3 of 1978, 43 FR 41943 (1978).

49. Exec. Order No 12127, 44 FR 19367 (1979).

50. Exec. Order 12148, 44 FR 43239.

51. Robert T. Stafford Disaster Relief and Emergency Assistance Act, 42 U.S.C.S. §§ 5141, *et seq.* (1988) (amending the Disaster Relief Act of 1974, Pub. L. No. 93-288. This act constitutes the statutory authority for most federal disaster response activities, especially as they pertain to FEMA and FEMA programs.).

In 1993, President Clinton appointed James Lee Witt, an experienced emergency manager, as FEMA director.[52] Director Witt reformed FEMA, which at the time was charged with coordinating 26 different federal agencies through the Federal Response Plan for disasters.[53] FEMA was elevated to cabinet-level status in 1996.[54]

In 2001, however, as a result of the terrorist attack known as 9/11, the nation's attention was diverted to counterterrorism. Following 9/11, Congress passed the Homeland Security Act of 2002, signed into law by President Bush, which created the Department of Homeland Security and moved FEMA to DHS as a sub-department.[55] Within DHS, FEMA suffered significant budget cuts. In July 2004, a year before Hurricane Katrina, the initial phase of a disaster planning exercise, "Hurricane Pam," identified the potential for some 60,000 deaths and large-scale evacuations as the consequences of a scenario in which a major hurricane hit New Orleans.[56] FEMA delays and budget cuts were subsequently blamed for the lack of additional planning efforts to prepare New Orleans for an incident of this magnitude.[57]

After Hurricane Katrina devastated the Gulf Coast in 2005, President Bush signed the Post-Katrina Emergency Management Reform Act into law on October 4, 2006.[58] This significantly modified Title V of the Homeland Security Act of 2002 to reorganize FEMA and ensure sufficient enabling legislation to support FEMA's mission: " to reduce the loss of life and property and protect the Nation from all hazards, including natural disasters, acts of terrorism, and other man-made disasters, by leading and supporting the Nation in a risk-based, comprehensive emergency management system of preparedness, protection, response,

52. R. Steven Daniels & Carolyn L. Clark-Daniels, Transforming Government: The Renewal and Revitalization of the Federal Emergency Management Agency, The PricewaterhouseCoopers Endowment for The Business of Government 13 (Apr. 2000).

53. *Id.* at 12.

54. *Id.* at 13.

55. 6 U.S.C. § 238 (2002).

56. Preparing for a Catastrophe: The Hurricane Pam Exercise: Hearing Before the Comm. on Homeland Security and Gov. Affairs United States Senate, 109th Cong. (2006).

57. *Id.* at 2.

58. The Post-Katrina Emergency Management Reform Act was enacted as part of P.L. 109-295, an act making appropriations for the Department of Homeland Security for the fiscal year ending September 30, 2007.

recovery, and mitigation."[59] This mission explicitly included The Directorate of Preparedness and preserved FEMA's identity as a "distinct entity" within DHS.[60]

Under this mission, FEMA directs and supervises terrorism preparedness grant programs for emergency response providers and incorporates the strategy priorities into planning guidance on an agency level for overall national preparedness efforts.[61] For example, the 2022–2026 FEMA Strategic Plan, entitled "Building the FEMA Our Nation Needs and Deserves," emphasizes three goals: Instill Equity as a Foundation of Emergency Management; Lead Whole of Community in Climate Resilience; and, Promote and Sustain a Ready FEMA and Prepared Nation.[62] It can reasonably be anticipated that this Strategic Plan will be revised based on Executive Order 14239 discussed earlier in this chapter.

FEMA's Authority Under the Stafford Act

Overview

The Stafford Act provides authority for federal and state disaster preparedness programs, disaster warnings, pre-disaster hazard mitigation and an interagency task force.[63] It authorizes the President to establish a program of disaster preparedness that uses the services of all appropriate agencies. This includes, for example, preparation of disaster preparedness plans for mitigation, warning, emergency operations, rehabilitation, and recovery. It also includes training and exercises, annual program review, coordination of federal, state, and local preparedness programs, application of science and technology, and research.[64]

The law also grants FEMA authority to administer major disaster and emergency assistance. This includes a diverse scope of provisions, including appointment of federal coordinating officers and formation of

59. 6 U.S.C. § 313.

60. *Id.* § 316.

61. 42 U.S.C.S. §§ 5131–5134.

62. FEMA, *FEMA Releases New Strategic Plan*, https://www.fema.gov/sites/default/files/documents/fema_2022-2026-strategic-plan.pdf (last updated Jan. 21, 2025).

63. 42 U.S.C. §§ 5121 *et seq.* This act constitutes the statutory authority for most federal disaster response activities, especially as they pertain to FEMA and FEMA programs.

64. *Id.* §§ 5170–5189h.

emergency support and response teams; authority to reimburse federal agencies; a broad assertion of sovereign immunity for federal government actions taken under the Stafford Act; use of local resources; prohibitions against discrimination in the administration of disaster relief; use and coordination of relief organizations; requirements that recipients of certain relief obtain insurance against similar future losses; protection of the environment (effectively exempting restoration of a facility to its pre-disaster condition from NEPA review); and mitigation planning.[65]

Major Disaster Assistance Programs

The Stafford Act's Major Disaster Assistance Programs[66] establish authority for the procedures governing the disaster declaration process, federal assistance, hazard mitigation, response, and debris removal. It also authorizes ancillary activities providing care for the public, which are necessitated by the disaster. This can include food, relocation, legal services, crisis counseling, loans, communications, transportation, as well as case management.

Subchapter IV-A of the act provides authority for the procedures governing the emergency declaration process, federal assistance, and the amount of that assistance.[67] There are two types of disaster declarations provided for in the Stafford Act: emergency declarations and major disaster declarations. Both declaration types authorize the President to provide supplemental federal disaster assistance. The type of declaration establishes the scope and amount of assistance the federal government will provide.

"Emergency" is defined as "any occasion or instance for which, in the determination of the President, Federal assistance is needed to *supplement State and local efforts and capabilities to save lives and to protect property and public health and safety, or to lessen or avert the threat of a catastrophe in any part of the United States*."[68] "Major disaster" is defined as "any natural catastrophe (including any hurricane, tornado, storm, high water, wind

65. *Id.* §§ 5131–5136a (Disaster Preparedness and Mitigation Assistance).
66. *Id.* §§ 5170–5189h (Major Disaster Assistance Programs).
67. *Id.* §§ 5191–5193.
68. *Id.* § 5122(1) (emphasis added).

driven water, tidal wave, tsunami, earthquake, volcanic eruption, landslide, mudslide, snowstorm, or drought), or, regardless of cause, any fire, flood, or explosion, in any part of the United States, which in the determination of the President causes damage of sufficient severity and magnitude to warrant major disaster assistance under this Act *to supplement the efforts and available resources of States, local governments, and disaster relief organizations in alleviating the damage, loss, hardship, or suffering caused thereby*."[69]

Emergency and major disaster declarations are within the sole discretion of the President and will only be issued upon request by the governor of the affected state or territory[70] or the leadership of a federally recognized Indian tribal government.[71] Such a request is typically preceded by a Preliminary Damage Assessment (PDA), which is conducted by a team of local, state, tribal, and federal employees led by the regional FEMA office and whose findings can support and justify the request.[72] The PDA team will conduct a thorough assessment of the impacted area to determine the extent of the disaster, its impact on individuals and public facilities, and the types of federal assistance that may be needed. This information is included in the governor or tribal chief executive's request to show that the disaster is of such severity and magnitude that effective response is beyond the capabilities of the state and the affected local governments or Indian tribal government, and that supplemental federal assistance is necessary. Generally, the PDA is completed before the governor or tribal chief executive requests a major disaster declaration. However, when an obviously severe or catastrophic event occurs, the governor or tribal chief executive's request may be submitted before the PDA is complete.

---

69. *Id.* § 5122(2) (emphasis added).

70. *Id.* § 5191.

71. *Id.* § 5191(c); *see also* FEMA, *Tribal Declarations Pilot Guidance* (Jan. 2017), https://www.fema.gov/disaster/tribal-declarations.

72. *See generally* FEMA, *Preliminary Damage Assessments*, https://www.fema.gov/disaster/how-declared/preliminary-damage-assessments (last updated Feb. 10, 2025).

FEMA Grant Programs

FEMA administers a number of grant programs, all of which are targeted to specific needs. Emergency and major disaster declarations can trigger certain types of public assistance grant awards by FEMA, including Category A (debris removal) and Category B (emergency protective measures). They may also trigger various categories of funding for permanent work (e.g., roads and bridges, and public utilities), under which the federal government pays 75 percent of eligible costs and the state and local communities pay 25 percent.[73] For high-impact events where the level of damage to residences is empirically overwhelming, the declaration may also include individual assistance.[74] Additional forms of assistance may be added later, pending the completion of PDAs. FEMA also administers hazard mitigation assistance grants to assist communities in planning for and implementing measures that can reduce the impact of future disasters.[75]

Emergency Preparedness

Subchapter IV-B of the act provides authority for the procedures governing emergency preparedness as a joint effort of the federal government and the states and their political subdivisions, recognizes that this organizational structure can provide relief and assistance to those affected by a hazard, provides definitions and vests authority in FEMA to oversee these efforts, and also includes a 2001 amendment that focuses on the protection of "critical infrastructure"—physical or virtual—"so vital to the United States that the incapacity or destruction of such systems and assets would have a debilitating impact on security, national economic security, national public health or safety, or any combination of those matters."[76] In 2006, based on lessons learned from Hurricane Katrina, the Post-Katrina Emergency Management Reform Act

---

73. *See generally* FEMA, *FEMA Public Assistance*, https://www.fema.gov/fact-sheet/fema-public-assistance (last updated Jan. 21, 2025).

74. *See generally* FEMA, *Individual Assistance*, https://www.fema.gov/assistance/individual (last updated Feb. 7, 2025).

75. *Id.* § 5170c; *see generally* FEMA, *Hazard Mitigation Assistance Grants*, https://www.fema.gov/grants/mitigation (last updated Mar. 25, 2025).

76. 42 U.S.C. §§ 5195–5195c.

(PKEMRA) significantly reorganized FEMA and provided substantial new authority to remedy gaps in response and include a more robust preparedness mission for FEMA.[77] Among other things, the PKEMRA provided a definitive description of FEMA's primary mission and detailed specific responsibilities for FEMA with respect to preparedness, protection, response, and recovery, including developing and coordinating "the implementation of a risk-based, all-hazards strategy for preparedness[.]"[78] Following Hurricane Sandy in 2012, FEMA's authority provided by the Stafford Act was amended further by the Sandy Recovery Improvement Act of 2013 with an eye toward simplifying and streamlining numerous FEMA processes, including for public assistance and community disaster loans, and authorizing federally recognized Indian tribal governments to either request a presidential emergency or major disaster declaration on their own or under a state's request.[79] The Stafford Act was amended again in 2018 by the Disaster Recovery Reform Act of 2018, enacting a set of 56 reforms that "acknowledge the shared responsibility for disaster response and recovery, aim to reduce the complexity of FEMA, and build the nation's capacity for the next catastrophic event."[80]

---

77. Post-Katrina Emergency Management Reform Act, 109 P.L. 295 (2006) (amending the Homeland Security Act of 2002 to make extensive revisions to emergency response provisions while keeping FEMA within DHS); *see also* The PETS Act of 2006, 109 P.L. 308 (2006) (amending the Robert T. Stafford Disaster Relief and Emergency Assistance Act to require the FEMA Administrator to ensure that state and local emergency preparedness operational plans address the needs of individuals with household pets and service animals prior to, during, and following a major disaster or emergency and authorizes federal agencies to provide, as assistance essential to meeting threats to life and property resulting from a major disaster, rescue, care, shelter, and essential needs to individuals with household pets and service animals and to such pets and animals).

78. Post-Katrina Emergency Management Reform Act, 109 P.L. 295 (2006), enacting 6 U.S.C. § 313.

79. The Sandy Recovery Improvement Act, 113 P.L. 2 (2013). The act became law on January 29, 2013, amending the Robert T. Stafford Disaster Relief and Emergency Assistance Act; authorizing provisions modifying FEMA's delivery of federal disaster assistance with the goals of (1) reducing the costs to the federal government of providing such assistance; (2) increasing flexibility in the administration of assistance; (3) expediting the provision of assistance to a state, tribal, or local government, or owner or operator of a private nonprofit facility; and (4) providing financial incentives and disincentives for the timely and cost-effective completion of projects). *See also* summary at https://www.fema.gov/disaster/sandy-recovery-improvement-act-2013 (last visited Mar. 28, 2025).

80. *See generally* FEMA, *Disaster Recovery Reform Act of 2018*, https://www.fema.gov/disaster/disaster-recovery-reform-act-2018 (last updated July 6, 2021).

FEMA's National Preparedness Structure

Consistent with its preparedness duties under the Stafford Act, and on the premise that preparedness is a shared responsibility, FEMA seeks to engage the "Whole Community"—including individuals, families, businesses, faith-based and community organizations, nonprofits, schools and academia, media outlets, and all governments (local, regional/metropolitan, state, tribal, territorial, insular area, and federal)—in accomplishing the nation's National Preparedness Goal.[81]

National Preparedness Goal: Five Mission Areas[82]

As part of its National Preparedness Goal, FEMA has adopted five mission areas with 32 core capabilities. The five mission areas are:

1. **Prevention.** Prevent, avoid, or stop an imminent, threatened, or actual act of terrorism.
2. **Protection.** Protect our citizens, residents, visitors, and assets against the greatest threats and hazards in a manner that allows our interests, aspirations, and way of life to thrive.
3. **Mitigation.** Reduce the loss of life and property by lessening the impact of future disasters.
4. **Response.** Respond quickly to save lives, protect property and the environment, and meet basic human needs in the aftermath of a catastrophic incident.
5. **Recovery.** Recover through a focus on the timely restoration, strengthening, and revitalization of infrastructure; housing and a sustainable economy; as well as the health, social, cultural, historic, and environmental fabric of communities affected by a catastrophic incident.

81. *See* FEMA, *Whole Community*, https://www.fema.gov/glossary/whole-community (last updated Oct. 6, 2020); *see also* FEMA, National Preparedness Goal, Second Edition, Department of Homeland Security iii (Sept. 2015), https://www.fema.gov/emergency-managers/national-preparedness/goal.

82. FEMA, *National Incident Management System*, https://www.fema.gov/emergency-managers/nims (last updated Feb. 14, 2025) (The five mission areas are presented in five National Framework documents.).

The concept of preparedness incorporates the first three mission areas (prevention, protection, and mitigation), mandates for which exist variously in other federal legislation and regulatory programs. For example, high-risk chemical and other hazardous materials activities are regulated by the DHS as well as the USEPA. As discussed further in Chapter 5, the USEPA administers several programs that mandate emergency response and preparedness measures under the National Contingency Plan. These response and preparedness measures provide important foundational elements for the system that is now deployed nationwide for managing the response to incidents of all kinds.

The National Incident Management System and National Response Framework

Issued in 2003, Homeland Security Presidential Directive (HSPD) 5[83] established the National Incident Management System (NIMS), which has since shown its value as a consistent doctrinal framework for incident management at all jurisdictional levels.[84] By establishing a "unified command" approach, NIMS is intended to serve as a single, comprehensive management system for all "domestic incidents," including terrorist attacks, major disasters, and other emergencies. This enables "Federal, State, and local governments to work effectively and efficiently together to prepare for, respond to, and recover from domestic incidents, regardless of cause, size, or complexity."[85] HSPD 5 also directed the development of the National Response Plan (NRP) to align federal coordination structures, capabilities, and resources into a unified, all-discipline, and all-hazards approach to domestic incident management.[86] In 2008, DHS replaced the NRP with the National Response Framework (NRF), which established "a comprehensive, national, all-hazards approach to domestic incident

83. U.S. Dep't of Homeland Security, Homeland Security Presidential Directive 5, ¶ 15, https://www.dhs.gov/publication/homeland-security-presidential-directive-5 (last updated Sept. 7, 2022).

84. FEMA, National Incident Management System, 3d ed. (2017), https://www.fema.gov/sites/default/files/2020-07/fema_nims_doctrine-2017.pdf.

85. Homeland Security, *supra* note 83, at ¶ 15.

86. *Id.* ¶ 16.

response."[87] Most states have formally adopted the NIMS principles and policies for all of their departments and agencies because adoption is mandatory for states that wish to apply for federal preparedness grants.[88]

The NRF provides the structure for the nation's emergency response capabilities and contemplates both Stafford Act responses (following an Emergency Declaration or Major Disaster Declaration) as well as non-Stafford Act responses. The NRF is always in effect and elements can be implemented at any time. The NRF also explains the relationship between the NRF and NIMS—the template for how all the different levels of government and other parties can work together to best achieve success across the five mission areas of prevention, protection, mitigation, response, and recovery.[89] NIMS is applied almost universally to incidents of all types, sizes, and complexities. It provides consistency, predictability, efficiency, and harmonious collaboration among responding agencies and organizations across all phases of an incident.

NIMS includes an Incident Command Structure (ICS), which follows a consistent structure whether it is led by a single incident commander or a unified command and includes three command staff posts (public information officer, safety officer, and liaison officer), and four general staff posts (operations section chief, planning section chief, logistics section chief, and finance/administration section chief). Depending on the scale, complexity, and duration of an incident response, and the number of organizations involved, each of these posts may have multiple supporting staff members from a variety of services and entities assigned to them, including, for example, staff from law enforcement, fire, public health, public works, environmental protection, and humanitarian agencies such as the Red Cross. Figure 1.2 illustrates this structure.[90]

---

87. U.S. Dep't of Homeland Security, Introducing . . . National Response Framework (2008), https://www.fema.gov/pdf/emergency/nrf/about_nrf.pdf.

88. *See generally* FEMA, *NIMS Implementation and Training*, https://www.fema.gov/emergency-managers/nims/implementation-training (last updated Feb. 14, 2025).

89. FEMA, *supra* note 84.

90. FEMA, *supra* note 84, at 26, Fig. 4.

Figure 1.2 Example of an ICS organization with unified command

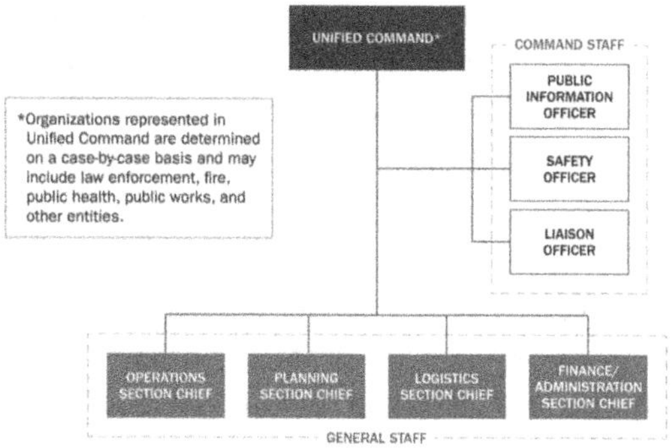

The NRF includes a set of 15 Emergency Support Functions (ESFs) that describe functional areas where resources and capabilities are most frequently needed to support a national response, whether undertaken pursuant to the Stafford Act or as a non-Stafford Act response:[91]

ESF #1—Transportation
ESF #2—Communications
ESF #3—Public Works and Engineering
ESF #4—Firefighting
ESF #5—Information and Planning
ESF #6—Mass Care, Emergency Assistance, Housing, and Human Services
ESF #7—Logistics
ESF #8—Public Health and Medical Services
ESF #9—Search and Rescue
ESF #10—Oil and Hazardous Materials Response
ESF #11—Agriculture and Natural Resources
ESF #12—Energy
ESF #13—Public Safety and Security
ESF #14—Cross-Sector Business and Infrastructure
ESF #15—External Affairs

91. *See* FEMA, *National Response Framework*, https://www.fema.gov/emergency-managers/national-preparedness/frameworks/response#esf (last updated Mar. 10, 2025) (descriptions of each of the ESFs).

There are also support annexes to the National Response Framework that describe how support is organized among private sector, NGO, and federal partners in the arenas of financial management, international coordination, public affairs, tribal relations, volunteer and donations management, and worker health and safety.[92]

A large-scale natural disaster or terrorist incident can require the activation of all ESFs. A localized flood or tornado might only require activating a few ESFs. Each ESF has one or two coordinating federal agencies that are in charge of orchestrating federal support and managing staff and resources for that functional area, and additional agencies that have supporting roles.

In the case of environmental incidents, ESF #10 (Oil and Hazardous Materials Response) is the most frequently activated. EPA serves as the coordinator and one of the primary agencies, along with the Department of Homeland Security/U.S. Coast Guard.[93] ESF #10 provides a coordinated federal response to actual or potential oil and hazardous materials incidents. Response under ESF #10 occurs when there has been a Presidential Disaster Declaration under the Stafford Act or there is a need to support a response under the National Oil and Hazardous Substances Contingency Plan (NCP)[94] with additional resources. As more thoroughly discussed in Chapter 5, pursuant to the NCP, in a matter on which EPA is the lead federal agency, EPA will appoint an on-scene coordinator (OSC) to serve as the incident commander and oversee and direct the response phase under the NRF. EPA's participation is scalable based on the OSC's assessment of the incident and a determination by the OSC or other official, or, in the case of significant incident, by the President by means of a Major Disaster or Emergency Declaration.

---

92. *Id.* The Support Annexes, the contents of which may be superseded by changes and updates to legislation, are available at https://www.fema.gov/emergency-managers/national-preparedness/frameworks/response#support.

93. FEMA, Emergency Support Function #10—Oil and Hazardous Materials Response Annex (2016), https://www.fema.gov/sites/default/files/2020-07/fema_ESF_10_Oil-Hazardous-Materials.pdf. In addition to its coordinating role under ESF #10, EPA is also a supporting agency for ESF #3, Public Works and Engineering; ESF #4, Firefighting; ESF #5, Emergency Management; ESF #8, Public Health and Medical Services; ESF #11, Agriculture and Natural Resources; ESF #13, Public Safety and Security; and ESF #15, External Affairs.

94. 40 C.F.R. § 300.

Recovery

The National Disaster Recovery Framework provides resources for economic recovery, community planning and capacity building, housing recovery, health and social services, infrastructure and natural and cultural resources.[95] Notably, the goal is more than the community's return to pre-disaster circumstances, especially when the community determines that these circumstances are no longer sustainable, competitive, or functional as shown by the post-disaster condition. This reflects an opportunity to merge pre-disaster planning with post-disaster resilience-building by making necessary or appropriate modifications to avoid future issues.

The recovery process is best described as a sequence of interdependent and often concurrent activities that advance a community toward its planned recovery outcomes. Decisions made and priorities set by a community pre-disaster and early in the recovery process have a cascading effect on the nature, speed, and inclusiveness of recovery. Figure 1.3 depicts the recovery phase as a cyclical process.[96]

Figure 1.3 Disaster recovery life cycle

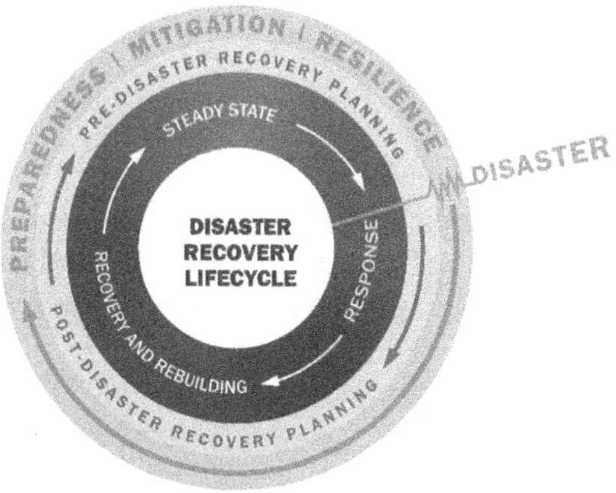

95. *See* FEMA, National Disaster Recovery Framework, 3d Ed. (2024), https://www.fema.gov/sites/default/files/documents/fema_national-disaster-recovery-framework-third-edition_2024.pdf. Additional resources available at https://www.fema.gov/emergency-managers/national-preparedness/frameworks/recovery.

96. *See id.* at 4.

The recovery phase is usually a long-term process that can extend from months to years, as depicted in Figure 1.4.[97]

FIGURE 1.4 Recovery continuum

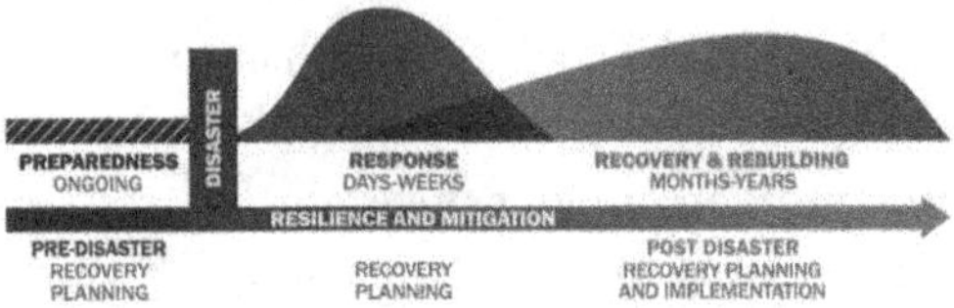

The recovery phase often involves a whole community approach, and its long-term success will also often be a function of the ability and willingness of a range of nongovernmental and governmental entities to collaborate through planning and implementation activities to put a community back on its feet and better equipped for, and more resilient in the face of, future incidents.

Regulations promulgating and implementing authority for both the Department of Homeland Security and the Federal Emergency Management Agency are codified in Title 44 of the Code of Federal Relations. Among other topics, these regulations cover insurance and hazard mitigation, fire prevention and control, disaster assistance, and preparedness.[98]

Additional Resources

National Voluntary Organizations Active in Disaster (VOAD)[99]

National VOAD is a nonprofit "association of organizations that mitigate and alleviate the impact of disasters."[100] National VOAD's mission is to "provide[] a forum promoting cooperation, communication, coordination

97. *Id.* at 3.

98. Title 44 of the Code of Federal Regulations is entitled "Emergency Management and Assistance," and includes six subchapters: Subchapter A, 44 C.F.R. 0-49, General (standard FEMA authorities); Subchapter B, 44 C.F.R. 50-149, Insurance and Hazard Mitigation; Subchapter C, 44 C.F.R. 150-199, Fire Prevention and Control; Subchapter D, 44 C.F.R. 200-294, Disaster Assistance; Subchapter E, 44 C.F.R. 295-299, Fire Assistance; and, Subchapter F, 44 C.F.R. 300-399, Preparedness.

99. *See* NATIONAL VOLUNTARY ORGANIZATIONS ACTIVE IN DISASTER, https://www.nvoad.org/ (last visited Jan. 10, 2025.

100. *See* NVOAD, *Our Mission, Vision, Guiding Principles and Core Values*, https://www.nvoad.org/our-mission/ (last visited Mar. 31, 2025).

and collaboration; and foster[] more effective delivery of services to communities affected by disasters."[101] The NVOAD coalition includes well more than 100 member organizations, which represent national members, state VOADs, local/regional VOADs, and hundreds of other member organizations throughout the country.

VOAD members include faith-based, community-based, and other nonprofit, nongovernmental organizations. VOAD also works with government agencies, for-profit corporations, foundations, and educational and research institutions.

Flood Preparedness and Response: The Silver Jackets Program

In recent decades, the nation has experienced increasingly frequent and severe flooding in many states due to a variety of natural causes including hurricanes and severe local storms. The cost and complexity of these events has caused federal, state, and local governments to face greater demands than ever before for close coordination in preparing for and responding to these disasters. One broadly adopted approach for achieving greater coordination in addressing flooding is known as "Silver Jackets."[102] This program is supported by the U.S. Army Corps of Engineers through its Flood Risk Management Program.[103]

The Silver Jackets approach is to bring together federal, state, local, and tribal government personnel to learn from each other and share their knowledge and understanding of flood preparedness, prevention, restoration, and recovery techniques. This can help reduce the risk of flooding and other natural disasters and can also speed the response and recovery efforts when floods occur. By getting to know each other's personnel, programs, resources, and capabilities in advance of flood events, the participating agencies can more effectively, efficiently, and responsively leverage their collective financial, technical, and regulatory authorities to assist in the response and recovery phases of floods and other natural disasters.

---

101. *Id.*

102. *See* Silver Jackets, https://www.iwr.usace.army.mil/Silver-Jackets/ (last visited Mar. 31, 2025).

103. *See* U.S. Army Corps of Engineers, *IWR Mission: Flood Risk Management*, https://www.iwr.usace.army.mil/Missions/Flood-Risk-Management/Flood-Risk-Management-%20Program/ (last visited Mar. 31, 2025).

Practically every state now has a state-led team, which typically includes, at a minimum, an array of state and federal agencies. Typical state agency members include departments of emergency response, environmental protection, public safety, public health, transportation, commerce, natural and cultural resources, fish and game, energy, and governors' offices. Typical federal members include FEMA, the Army Corps of Engineers, the Natural Resources Conservation Service (USDA), the U.S. Geological Survey, NOAA (National Weather Service, and the U.S. Fish and Wildlife Service), and, depending on the federal land holdings within a state, may also include the U.S. Forest Service, the National Park Service, or the Bureau of Land Management, among others. Silver Jackets groups may have formal charters or memoranda of understanding and typically are focused on pre- and post-incident response and recovery.

One of the greatest challenges communities face after a major flood is quickly determining what may be the most appropriate technical and engineering solutions to help recover from the event while also helping to prevent similar damages from occurring due to a similar future flood. And then there's the question of funding: What sources of funding are available to help communities address these needs, which are often extremely expensive? By bringing together all the technical and financial capabilities of the federal and state governments into a single Silver Jackets team, the program helps to streamline the recovery process and ensure that the most appropriate and applicable resources are identified, prioritized, and deployed. While the existence of a Silver Jackets program does not ensure that there will always be adequate financial resources for every flood-related disaster, it does greatly increase the prospects for promptly identifying the most suitable funding sources and providing coordinated and collaborative guidance and support to affected communities and property owners.

State Authority

While the Stafford Act enables federal agencies to implement programs and provide resources for disaster preparedness, response, and recovery, the states and local agencies are always most engaged, given the localized impact of disasters. During such incident responses, state and local officials typically rely primarily upon the police powers conferred on them by state laws because the Stafford Act and other applicable federal statutes do not as a general matter grant them any additional authorities other than, in the case of a state, the authority to request emergency assistance from the federal government. All states have emergency management agencies whose emergency operations centers (EOCs) serve as communication, management, and leadership hubs for coordinating disaster and emergency responses.[104] These agencies also typically provide support for hazard mitigation planning at the local and county levels as well as assist with coordination or administration of associated federal or state grants.

Conclusion and Overview of Book Contents

The system of incident response in the United States is, arguably, the envy of the world, as it has evolved to provide a comprehensive set of tools, resources, tactics, and management structures and strategies for addressing all forms of incidents, ranging from natural to man-made disasters, from terrorist attacks to chemical explosions, and from cybersecurity threats to major fires or pandemics. This system is structured to first take full advantage of local emergency response personnel and equipment, to supplement these with state-level resources, and to provide backup and expertise with federal resources when and as necessary. For example, in the case of incidents involving environmental disasters, including unpermitted releases of hazardous materials or substances, pollutants, or contaminants, local fire and rescue personnel are typically the first on scene to assess and control the hazards; as warranted, they will then call in private contractors, as well as county- or state-level personnel and resources to assist with containment, removal, and investigation activities. Depending on the scale, nature, or extent of the incident, there may be authority for direct federal involvement, but otherwise federal agencies such as the EPA would typically engage only upon the request of the state's governor.

---

104. For a link to find each state's agency, *see* https://www.usa.gov/state-emergency-management.

The eight chapters that follow cover a wide range of issues, challenges, and opportunities that may arise in the sequence of disaster or incident preparedness, response, and recovery. Chapter 2, Preparedness, Including Prevention, Protection, and Mitigation, provides practical guidance on how organizations of all kinds, including governments, businesses, and nonprofits can make themselves more resilient, so they are better equipped to handle the next disaster or incident—whether it be due to natural, technological, or human-caused hazards. The second portion of Chapter 2 identifies additional preparedness requirements for workplaces that handle hazardous materials in their operations. Chapter 3, Release Reporting, focuses on the vital importance of, and legal requirements pertaining to, reporting to governmental authorities as one of the very first and ongoing components of a responsible party's response to incidents involving a release of hazardous substances, materials, pollutants, contaminants, oil, or biological or nuclear materials into the environment (air, water, or land) or inside a workplace. A Reporting and Response Timeline, which identifies some key actions to be taken within the first 24 hours of such types of releases, appears at the front of the book. Chapter 4, FEMA Response and Recovery, kicks off an exploration of the response and recovery phases of disaster management by detailing the federal disaster declaration process and a number of FEMA's most significant programs for assisting communities and individuals in recovering from a disaster.

Chapter 5, The National Contingency Plan, continues the exploration of the response phase by focusing on the regulations that guide federal (and often state) responses to incidents involving releases of oil, hazardous substances, pollutants, or contaminants into the environment. This chapter provides an example of how one Emergency Support Function (Oil and Hazardous Materials Response, ESF #10) of disaster management fits and interacts within the larger, government-wide, National Response Framework and is implemented using the National Incident Management System. Chapter 6, Responses to Transportation-Related Hazardous Materials Incidents: Trains, Pipelines, Ships, and Trucks, rounds out the book's coverage of the response phase with a focus on the laws, regulations, and good practices associated with releases of hazardous materials from incidents that may occur during their movement by train, pipeline, ship, or truck from one location to another.

Chapter 7, Liability and Defenses for Hazardous Substance Incidents, kicks off the exploration of the recovery phase with an in-depth analysis of liability and defenses arising in the contexts of spills or releases of hazardous substances. This chapter focuses on the Comprehensive Environmental Response, Compensation, and Liability Act (CERCLA) and common law, as examples of statutory principles and legal theories that may be useful in analyzing liability or defenses for other types or releases or even other technological or human-caused incidents or disasters. Chapter 8, The Multifaceted Role of Insurance in Environmental Disasters and Climate Change, examines the potential role of insurance in helping a business or other entity recover from a weather-related or other type of environmental disaster. This chapter analyzes four key types of insurance coverage, explains how they may protect an insured against losses and damages incurred due to a disaster or incident, and provides practical guidance for insureds in making insurance claims in order to secure funds to help with their disaster recovery. Finally, Chapter 9, Handling Civil and Criminal Investigations, provides an overview of standard or recommended procedures for organizations in responding to governmental investigations triggered by incidents or disasters. While the focus is on investigations involving potential violations of environmental, health, and safety laws and regulations, the general lessons are broadly applicable to all types of investigations that may arise during the recovery phase of an incident or disaster.

The book's Foreword identifies the genesis of this book as a 2019 conference on Disaster Preparedness, Response, and Recovery. From that gathering came a recognition that a seeming increase in the frequency of disasters posing ever-greater and costlier threats to our environment and society called for an effort to share background information and insights with the legal community, environmental and disaster response professionals, as well as community and business leaders in an effort to spread the word and build deeper bench strength, including among attorneys, to help the nation's communities, businesses, and organizations build resiliency to future disasters of all kinds.

This book is an early entrant into the exploration of legal issues in a rapidly evolving field of work and study that seeks ever-more sophisticated, streamlined, and effective approaches to meeting community and human needs during times of crisis. The applicable laws, regulations, ordinances, and programs at the local, state, tribal, and federal levels will continue to evolve based on lessons learned and ever-new challenges. Accordingly, this book's readers will find it essential to stay current with updates to the materials covered (and not covered) in this book and to follow the latest developments in disaster management programs at all levels of government as well as in the private and nonprofit sectors.

Chapter 2

Preparedness, Including Prevention, Protection, and Mitigation[1]

Thomas S. Burack and Scott Elliott

The best kind of incident is one that never happens. Unfortunately, however, "bad stuff" does happen. Fortunately, though, whether the incident was preventable or not, the most serious consequences to communities, including their families, workforces, businesses, organizations, facilities, and neighbors, can often be reduced if not eliminated through advance efforts focused on preparedness, prevention, protection, and mitigation. When organizations plan and equip themselves for events they hope to never encounter, they can often limit the scope of an incident, save lives, protect property and the environment, enhance safety, and reduce suffering and economic hardship. In many instances, preparedness, particularly in the form of planning for a disaster or emergency, is also required by law. This chapter summarizes some broadly applicable key principles and elements of preparedness and highlights various statutory and regulatory requirements for preparedness efforts by governments, businesses, and other entities, including those that manufacture, use, or transport hazardous substances or materials.

1. The authors wish to express their gratitude to Mary Ellen Ternes, Esq., who shared initial research materials and presentations she had given on the topic of preparedness in the context of releases of hazardous substances and materials. Her materials assisted the authors in organizing their thoughts and covering a wide range of regulatory programs.

Planning for Incidents: What Is Preparedness?

The concept of preparedness has more than one formulation. From a process standpoint, the Department of Homeland Security has focused on continual improvement, explaining that preparedness is "a continuous cycle of planning, organizing, training, equipping, exercising, evaluating, and taking corrective action in an effort to ensure effective coordination during incident response."[2] Expressed more broadly, "national preparedness" is defined in Presidential Policy Directive / PPD-8: National Preparedness as "the actions taken to plan, organize, equip, train, and exercise to build and sustain the capabilities necessary to prevent, protect against, mitigate the effects of, respond to, and recover from those threats that pose the greatest risk to the security of the Nation."[3] In other words, national preparedness includes all the steps necessary to try to reduce the likelihood or potential consequences of an incident, but also to be ready to respond to and recover from any incident that does occur. Thus, the overall goal of national preparedness is to make communities more resilient—that is, to ensure that communities have the capacity to withstand and recover from an incident, ideally in as self-reliant a manner as possible, and for there to be an effective and responsive federal backstop when communities and states are simply overwhelmed by the scale or complexity of an incident.

Preparedness can also be thought of more narrowly as a set of activities that can be taken before an incident—both as an activity itself and as an overall concept that encompasses prevention, protection, and mitigation, including compliance with all applicable federal, state, or local requirements for preparedness. The following working definitions of prevention, protection, mitigation, and preparedness are helpful in this context:[4]

---

2. DHS, *Plan and Prepare for Disasters*, https://www.dhs.gov/archive/plan-and-prepare-disasters (last updated Sept. 17, 2024).

3. Barack Obama, Presidential Policy Directive: National Preparedness (Mar. 30, 2011), https://www.dhs.gov/presidential-policy-directive-8-national-preparedness.

4. Some of the examples included in these working definitions are drawn from FEMA's description of Mission Areas and Core Capabilities in support of the National Preparedness Goal. *See* FEMA, *Mission Areas and Core Capabilities*, https://www.fema.gov/emergency-managers/national-preparedness/mission-core-capabilities (last updated July 20, 2020).

- "Prevention" is a focus on preventing natural, technological, or human-caused hazards from occurring. And although not all hazards are preventable, measures such as evacuation plans and the consideration of prevention in environmental, architectural, and engineering designs can help reduce the risks of loss of life or injury that may result from hazards.
- "Protection" includes both process and physical measures. Processes that provide protection include, among others, hazard information collection and dissemination, cybersecurity, access control and identity verification, and strengthening the supply chain. Physical measures that provide protection include everything from flood walls and levees to tornado shelters.
- "Mitigation" entails reducing loss of life and property damage by reducing the impacts of hazards.[5] For example, in a coastal setting, mitigation measures may include land use ordinances or building codes that require new or modified structures to be set back a certain distance from the high tide line or elevated (e.g., on pilings or stilts) above anticipated flooding levels.
- "Preparedness," as an overarching concept, is all about planning and preparing for hazards before they occur. It's an ongoing and continuous process of organizing resources, training personnel, obtaining and maintaining equipment, conducting practice exercises, evaluating successes and failures, and constantly improving systems to ensure the capabilities exist to respond to hazards quickly, efficiently, and effectively with the goal of minimizing the potential resulting loss of life, property damage, and economic and societal disruption.

This chapter's analysis of preparedness best practices and key requirements considers these concepts first in the "all hazards" context of disasters and emergencies as they affect communities generally, and then in the specific context of incidents involving releases of hazardous and other potentially harmful materials.

5. The Mitigation Planning regulations adopted to implement the provisions of section 322 of the Stafford Act, 42 U.S.C. § 5165 and § 1366 of the National Flood Insurance Act of 1968, 42 U.S.C. § 4104c define "hazard mitigation" as "any sustained action taken to reduce or eliminate the long-term risk to human life and property from hazards." 44 C.F.R. § 201.2.

General Incident Preparedness (What to Do So Incidents Don't Become Crises)

Basic emergency planning for any forward-looking organization (e.g., government, school, business, nonprofit) typically includes the following steps:[6]

- Conduct a risk assessment: Identify the most significant potential hazards and analyze their potential impacts and consequences, using the following or a similar list as a starting point:[7]
  - Common potential hazards: There are several principal categories of hazards, including:
    - Human-caused incidents (e.g., civil unrest, cyber incident, terrorism, violence; common incidents that may be human-caused, including structural fire, medical emergency);
    - Natural hazards (e.g., biological incident (such as anthrax exposure), pandemic, weather-related incidents (drought, extreme temperatures, winter storm, flood, hurricane, tornado, tsunami, wildfire), geologic incidents (earthquake, seismic eruptions/volcanic ash)); and,
    - Technological hazards (e.g., electric power outage, internet outage, equipment failure, dam or levee breach, release of lethal chemicals or munitions, radiological release, hazardous materials spill).[8]

---

6. *See generally* FEMA, Developing and Maintaining Emergency Operations Plans, Comprehensive Preparedness Guide 101 (Version 3.0, Sept. 2021), https://www.pge.com/assets/pge/docs/outages-and-safety/outage-preparedness-and-support/fema-cpg-101-developing-and-maintaining-eops-v3.pdf (identifying many of the hazards listed in the risk assessment bullets that follow, as well as some of the general tasks falling within) [hereinafter Comprehensive Preparedness Guide]. *See also* FEMA, Developing and Maintaining Emergency Operations Plans, Comprehensive Preparedness Guide (CPG) 101: Compilation of checklists (Sept. 2021), https://www.fema.gov/sites/default/files/documents/fema_cpg-101-v3-developing-maintaining-eops-chechlist.pdf, and FEMA, Developing and Maintaining Emergency Operations Plans (Version 2.0, Nov. 2010), https://www.fema.gov/sites/default/files/2020-05/CPG_101_V2_30NOV2010_FINAL_508.pdf.

7. Helpful risk assessment tools may be found at https://www.ready.gov/business/planning/risk-assessment. FEMA also provides extensive online materials to assist individuals and families to plan and prepare for emergencies and disasters, at https://www.ready.gov/.

8. *See, e.g.*, Comprehensive Preparedness Guide, *supra* note 6 (identifying many of the hazards listed in these three bullets).

   - Facility-specific technological hazards associated with operations: both OSHA's Process Safety Management standard and EPA's Risk Management Program regulations require facilities that exceed certain threshold amounts of hazardous chemicals to perform process hazard analyses.[9] These periodic reviews are required to follow specific methodologies and must "identify, evaluate, and control the hazards involved in the process."[10]

- Even when not required by law, facilities can benefit from engaging in a structured process to identify hazards associated with their operations. Creatively imagining the types of incidents that can arise and evaluating their severity and likelihood can provide critical information when making plans and deploying the organization's resources to most effectively limit the impact of these incidents. Moreover, these plans will be most helpful if they imagine a wide range of potential, possibly even somewhat unlikely external or internal events, and how they could affect the safety and security of personnel, facilities, records, and raw or finished products.
   - Tragic or life-threatening incidents involving hazardous materials often co-occur with or as a result of natural or man-made disasters. For example, in the middle of Hurricane Harvey in 2017, a chemical facility near Houston, Texas, suffered major damage, caused substantial pollution, and led to the evacuation of over 200 residents living within a one and a half mile radius of the facility.[11] The U.S. Chemical Safety and Hazard Investigation Board (CSB) determined that the facility's OSHA-mandated process hazard analysis (PHA) failed to analyze its susceptibility to extreme weather events such as floods, and to ensure

9. *See* 29 C.F.R. § 1910.119(e); 40 C.F.R. pt. 68.

10. *See* 29 C.F.R. § 1910.119(e); 40 C.F.R. pt. 68.

11. *See* CSB, Investigation Report: Organic Peroxide Decomposition, Release, and Fire at Arkema Crosby Following Hurricane Harvey Flooding (May 2018), https://www.csb.gov/arkema-inc-chemical-plant-fire-/ (noting that 350,000 pounds of organize peroxide combusted during fires). *See also* CSB, Executive Summary, https://www.csb.gov/assets/1/20/csb_arkema_exec_summary_08.pdf?16265 (last visited Feb. 20, 2025).

adequate and independent levels of process safeguards. Most significantly, the facility was not sited or constructed to be able to withstand an extreme flooding event, so that when both the electrical supply and the backup power generators had to be shut off due to four-foot deep flood waters, there was no means of keeping organic peroxides (which must be refrigerated to preserve their stability) from combusting.[12]

- Establish reporting protocols: These protocols ensure that all personnel are trained in how to recognize and immediately report incidents to emergency response personnel within a facility and to local emergency responders, and how necessary information is quickly gathered and assessed to determine if additional reports must be timely made, such as to the National Response Center in the event of a spill of oil or hazardous materials or substances (see Chapters 3 and 5).
- Develop response strategies: These are actions that can be implemented immediately to save lives, reduce suffering, prevent the spread of contamination (in air, water, land, or person-to-person or animal-to-person), or reduce economic damages.
- Assign roles and responsibilities: This ensures that all personnel within an organization know what's expected of them before, during, and after an incident to help implement the appropriate response actions and strategies.
- Establish communication protocols: Ensure that all personnel know how to collect and share vital information and directives within the organization and with third parties, including through use of existing communication channels (e.g., cell phones, email, social media sites, broadcast radio), and through backup or other specialized emergency response channels (e.g., police/fire/EMS radio systems, satellite phones, door-to-door visits, public address systems).
- Create evacuation or sheltering plans: Establish a system, including alarms, for (1) notifying residents, employees, students, or other groups of the need to shelter in place or evacuate from a

12. *Id.*

facility or general area; (2) ensuring transportation and other logistics systems to support such evacuations; (3) identifying, marking, and managing evacuation routes; and (4) developing and operating locations for temporary or permanent relocation or sheltering.

- Gather, inventory, and maintain emergency supplies: Collect, store, and keep up-to-date essential supplies such as bottled water, ready-to-eat foods, first aid supplies, backup generators and fuel supplies, bedding and blankets,
- Establish standing agreements with specialized response contractors, such as those with oil and hazardous materials spill response capabilities, so they're "on call" when needed.
- Develop an emergency response plan: Compile all the preceding measures into a written emergency response plan (ERP) that complies with all applicable laws and regulations, and then regularly review and revise the plan based on updated hazard assessments, changes in laws or regulations, and lessons learned from practice exercises and responses to actual incidents.
    - For example, OSHA requires that certain employers develop written emergency action plans that address multiple considerations in an emergency, such as how to report an emergency and how to evacuate in the event of an emergency.[13] EPA also requires that certain facilities subject to its RMP regulations develop an emergency response plan that includes procedures for informing the public and government authorities about accidental releases as well as procedures and measures for an emergency response.[14]
    - Even where the regulations do not require a facility to have a written emergency plan, having these types of plans may still be advisable. A continuity of operations plan (COOP) or business continuity plan (BCP) can make all the difference in terms of an organization's ability to continue operating after a significant incident or disaster. These plans consider a wide range of

13. *See* 29 C.F.R. § 1910.38.
14. *See* 40 C.F.R. § 68.95.

logistical and other factors, including such topics as temporary relocation; remote work; ensuring backup off-site storage of essential customer, business, or other records; and means of communicating between and among organization personnel when the standard modes are not available.

- Foster regular communications, collaboration, and information exchanges with local emergency response agencies, including by providing site or facility tours.
- Keep essential records, including the ERP, additional facility or site plans, emergency contact lists, and other vital documents in protected locations, including in off-site electronic storage.
- Conduct drills, exercises, and training: Practice responding to different scenarios involving one or more of the identified hazards and involve all the different personnel and organizations (including local emergency response agencies) who have assigned response roles and responsibilities, so they can experience what's expected of them in the event of an actual incident. For example, it's vital that security personnel and receptionists receive focused training on communications protocols for emergency situations.
  - Developing plans and procedures for responding to an incident could have limited effectiveness if the persons tasked with implementation are not familiar with their content. Training and drills are critical to establishing familiarity with the plans, and to maintaining readiness for an incident. As the federal website ready.gov[15] explains, "[e]veryone needs training to become familiar with protective actions for life safety (e.g., evacuation, shelter, shelter-in-place and lockdown). Employees should receive training to become familiar with safety, building security, information security and other loss prevention programs."[16] Benefits associated with training include

15. According to the website, ready.gov was "[l]aunched in February 2003" as a "public service campaign designed to educate and empower the American people to prepare for, respond to and mitigate emergencies and disasters. The goal of the campaign is to promote preparedness through public involvement." *See About Us*, Ready.gov, http://ready.gov/about-us (last updated Sept. 20, 2023).

16. *Training and Testing*, Ready.gov, https://www.ready.gov/business/training (last updated Sept. 7, 2023).

clarifying roles and responsibilities and developing experience and knowledge with procedures and equipment, among others. Ready.gov also promotes conducting exercises, explaining that these "enhance knowledge of plans, allow individuals to improve their own performance and identify opportunities to improve capabilities to respond to real events."[17]

There are many resources available that provide guidance on good practices for any facility or organization to take when preparing for emergencies. For example, OSHA's Emergency Preparedness webpage and the federal government's ready.gov provide extensive guidance on preparing for emergencies.[18]

In summary, effective preparedness is based on knowing the hazards, knowing the requirements, making plans for emergencies, and practicing those emergency plans.

Examples of Emergency Response Plans

The following discussion describes various types of emergency response plans for a range of entities, including governments, businesses, nonprofit organizations, and infrastructure systems.

Governmental Plans

In the case of governments (states, territories, tribes, counties, municipalities), emergency response plans are typically referred to as emergency operations plans (EOPs). FEMA provides support for the preparation of EOPs, including incorporation of the National Incident Management System (NIMS), through published guides.[19] In addition, in order to be eligible for many types of FEMA grants, including nonemergency assistance and mitigation projects, state, local, tribal, and territorial

---

17. *Id.*

18. *See* OSHA, *Emergency Preparedness and Response: Getting Started*, https://www.osha.gov/emergency-preparedness/getting-started#v-nav-home (last visited Feb. 20, 2025) [hereinafter OSHA Emergency Preparedness]; *Make a Plan*, Ready.gov, https://www.ready.gov/plan (last updated Apr. 19, 2024).

19. *See generally supra*, note 6; *see also* https://www.fema.gov/emergency-managers/nims/implementation-training.

governments must develop and update a Hazard Mitigation Plan (HMP) not less frequently than every five years.[20] Each state or territory's HMP is structured to include: (1) a risk assessment that characterizes and analyzes state- or territory-wide natural hazards and risks, and the associated vulnerabilities and hazard areas, including potential losses to vulnerable state- or territory-owned or operated buildings, infrastructure, and critical infrastructure; (2) a mitigation strategy for reducing the potential losses identified in the risk assessment; (3) a plan for coordinating with local governments' mitigation planning efforts, including with funding and technical assistance; and (4) a process and schedule for monitoring, evaluating, and updating the plan.[21] A local and tribal government's HMP is coordinated with its state or territory's HMP and is intended to help guide and prioritize natural hazard risk reduction investments within their particular locality or reservation.[22]

It should also be noted that many states require each school or school district (including private, nonpublic, or charter schools) to have EOPs that provide detailed plans for protection of students, faculty, and staff from a wide range of incidents, and to coordinate the development and exercise of those plans with local emergency response agencies.[23] In addition, states typically require publicly and privately owned or operated public water supplies to have some form of emergency plan to ensure their protection and security.[24]

In many instances, the states themselves as well as municipalities have established COOPs for their agencies or departments in order to

---

20. *See* 44 C.F.R. pt. 201, Mitigation Planning, implementing § 322 of the Stafford Act, 42 U.S.C. § 5165, as well as § 1366 of the National Flood Insurance Act of 1968, 42 U.S.C. § 4104c.

21. 44 C.F.R. § 201.4.

22. *See* FEMA, Local Mitigation Planning Policy Guide (Apr. 19, 2022), https://www.fema.gov/sites/default/files/documents/fema_local-mitigation-planning-policy-guide_042022.pdf; FEMA, Tribal Mitigation Plan Review Guide (released Dec. 5, 2017, effective Dec. 5, 2018), a similar document for tribal governments, https://www.fema.gov/sites/default/files/documents/fema-tribal-mitigation-plan-review-guide_12-05-2017.pdf; in addition, FEMA, Tribal Mitigation Planning Handbook (May 2019), https://www.fema.gov/sites/default/files/2020-06/fema-tribal-planning-handbook_05-2019.pdf (last viewed Jan. 2025), may be undergoing modifications by FEMA concurrently with a four-year update of the Tribal Mitigation Planning Policy. *See* https://www.fema.gov/sites/default/files/documents/fema_mit-tribal-mitigation-planning-policy-update-fact-sheet.pdf.

23. *See, e.g.*, N.H. R.S.A. 189:64.

24. *See, e.g.*, N.H. Code of Admin. Rules Env-Dw 503.24.

ensure that they are able to maintain vital public services regardless of the impact that an incident may have on the operations of a given agency or department's operations. For example, such COOPs may identify temporary quarters for an agency's leadership team and staff in the event their primary offices are damaged or destroyed, authorize remote work, put all essential records into the cloud or other electronic storage that is accessible from any location, ensure that agency personnel have computers or other equipment that can be used from remote locations, and provide emergency notification and backup communication systems or plans to ensure command and control capabilities.

Business and Nonprofit Plans

Businesses and nonprofit organizations will often refer to their version of an EOP as a BCP and, depending on the size and complexity of their operations and facilities, may have "nesting" BCPs or separate BCP components for the organization as a whole and for its individual facilities. FEMA provides extensive tools to assist organizations in establishing BCPs.[25] Issues considered at the overall organizational level may include such potential factors as: financial vulnerabilities due to lost or delayed sales or income, increased expenses, regulatory fines, contractual penalties, or loss of customers or new business opportunities; the adequacy of existing insurance coverage, including for property damage or business interruption; supply chain vulnerabilities or interruptions; maintaining communications with customers, clients, suppliers, distributors, and key service providers in the event of technology failures; and, ensuring the protection and accessibility of business and financial records and accounts, payroll systems, operating systems, applications, and other data.[26]

At a facility level, BCPs may focus on such topics as: protection of staff, including with full contact information and emergency notification systems; risks of restricted access to the site or facility due to an event; risks due to nonstructural elements outside or inside the facility

25. *See Ready Business*, Ready.gov, https://www.ready.gov/business (last updated Feb. 5, 2024).

26. *See, e.g., Business Impact Analysis*, Ready.gov, https://www.ready.gov/business/planning/impact-analysis (last updated Dec. 26, 2023).

that could pose a threat to the facility during an event (e.g., trees during a hurricane, or un-anchored furniture during an earthquake); the vulnerabilities of the electrical, water, sewer, HVAC, and internet that support a building's operations; potential damage to manufacturing equipment, machinery, or systems; the vulnerabilities of a building's architectural or structural elements; and, opportunities to engage and serve the surrounding community following an incident.[27]

As discussed further in the second section of this chapter, many businesses and industries regulated by the Occupational Safety and Health Administration (OSHA) are required to have an emergency action plan.[28] In addition, individual types of businesses, operations, facilities, or infrastructure may be legally required to have a customized form of emergency response plan, while others may find it helpful to have such a plan even if one is not required. The following examples of specialized emergency plans are illustrative only, and not an exhaustive list by any means.

Dams and Dam Safety

Emergency action plans (EAPs) are required by the Federal Energy Regulatory Commission (FERC) for electric power generating dams nationwide,[29] and many states require similar types of plans for dams that don't generate electric power, particularly those that pose high or significant hazards.[30] FERC describes an EAP as "a formal document that identifies potential emergency conditions at a dam and specifies

27. *See* Ready Business, How-To Guide, https://www.ready.gov/sites/default/files/2020-04/ready_business_how-to-guide.pdf (last visited Feb. 20, 2025).

28. 29 C.F.R. § 1910.38 (At a minimum, an EAP must be in writing and include procedures pertaining to: reporting a fire or other emergency; emergency evacuation; employees who remain to operate critical plant operations before they evacuate; accounting for all evacuated employees; rescue or medical duties; name or job title of employees who have information or provide training about the plan. The employer must also have and maintain an employee alarm system, train employees to assist in a safe and orderly evacuation of other employees, and review the EAP with each covered employee when the plan is developed, the employee is initially assigned to a job, the employee's responsibilities change, or the EAP is changed.).

29. FERC, *Emergency Action Plan (EAP) Program*, https://www.ferc.gov/emergency-action-plan-eap-program (last updated June 28, 2022); *see also* FERC, Chapter VI: Emergency Action Plans (July 2015), https://www.ferc.gov/sites/default/files/2020-04/chap6.pdf [hereinafter FERC EAP Guidelines].

30. *See, e.g.*, N.H. Code of Admin. Rules CHAPTER Env-Wr 500.

preplanned actions to be followed to minimize property damage and loss of life."[31] FERC defines a dam safety incident as "a malfunction/deviation of a project feature or some other unusual occurrence that could, if left unchecked, lead to an uncontrolled release or excessive controlled release of water from an impounding structure."[32] The principal risks presented by an uncontrolled release from or a breach of a dam are loss of life and property damage in the area downstream that could be flooded by the excessive volume of water resulting from the release (the "inundation zone"). FERC's EAP Guidelines specify standard elements of EAPs for all FERC-licensed dams, are often incorporated by reference in states' dam safety rules, and include requirements for analysis of dam breach and inundation risks; identification of at-risk infrastructure and populations; required protective measures; emergency warning and notification procedures; evacuation plans; preventive actions to address malfunctions or emergencies; and coordination with local, state, and federal emergency responders and regulatory agencies.[33]

Healthcare Providers, Including Hospitals and Long-Term Care Facilities

In 2017, the Centers for Medicare & Medicaid Services (CMS), an agency within the U.S. Department of Health and Human Services (DHHS), promulgated an emergency preparedness rule, which requires most healthcare facilities and providers in the United States to have an emergency preparedness plan. Revised in 2019, the rule, originally entitled the "Emergency Preparedness Requirements for Medicare and Medicaid Participating Providers and Suppliers Final Rules,"[34] serves the purpose of "establish[ing] national emergency preparedness requirements to ensure adequate planning for both natural and man-made disasters, and coordination with federal, state, tribal, regional and local emergency

31. *See* FERC EAP Guidelines, *supra* note 29, at 7.

32. *Id.*

33. *Id.* and *e.g.*, N.H. Code of Admin. Rules CHAPTER Env-Wr 500. Further reference materials are available at the website of the Association of State Dam Safety Officials, https://www.damsafety.org/.

34. 42 C.F.R. §§ 403, 416, 418, 441, 460, 482, 483, 484, 485, 486, 491, 494e.

preparedness systems."[35] This rules applies to all 17 provider and supplier types (under Medicare and Medicaid), requires each provider and supplier to have its own set of emergency preparedness regulations as a condition or requirement of its certification, and to comply with those regulations to participate in the Medicare or Medicaid program.[36]

As a general matter, emergency preparedness in the healthcare arena under this rule has four core elements: (1) risk assessment and emergency planning (i.e., identifying likely hazards such as hurricanes, emerging infectious diseases, care-related emergencies, equipment and power failures, communications interruptions, cyberattacks, loss of all or a portion of a facility or supplies); (2) a communications plan (for contacting staff, physicians), including coordination within the facility and with its healthcare providers and local public health departments and emergency management services; (3) policies and procedures compliant with federal and state laws; and (4) training and at least bi-annual plan updates.[37]

Retail Food Services and Restaurants

Long regulated due to public health concerns, including the risk of foodborne illnesses, restaurants and other food service establishments, including retail grocers, are also recognized as providing essential public services. Accordingly, emergency preparedness by these kinds of facilities—even if not legally required—can protect not only the businesses themselves but also their customers. For example, the Conference for Food Protection[38] developed and published an "Emergency Action Plan for Retail Food Establishments" intended to help restaurants, grocery stores, and other

35. CMS, *Emergency Preparedness Rule*, https://www.cms.gov/medicare/health-safety-standards/quality-safety-oversight-emergency-preparedness/emergency-preparedness-rule (last updated Dec. 20, 2023).

36. *Id.*

37. CMS, *Core EP Rule Elements*, https://www.cms.gov/medicare/health-safety-standards/quality-safety-oversight-emergency-preparedness/core-ep-rule-elements (last updated Dec. 30, 2024).

38. The Conference for Food Protection's website is available at https://www.foodprotect.org/. The Conference for Food Protection is a nonprofit organization "created to provide a formal process whereby members of industry, regulatory, academia, consumer, and professional organizations are afforded equal input in the development and/or modification of food safety guidance [which] is incorporated into food safety laws and regulations at all levels of government throughout the United States."

food service establishments ensure that imminent health hazards such as electrical or water outages, contaminated water supply, sewage back-ups, fires, or floods affecting their operations are handled appropriately.[39] Designed as a template for planning efforts, some state and local public health departments have published their own versions of the document incorporating state or local requirements or concerns.[40] The U.S. Food and Drug Administration also provides guidance on a range of related topics, including food safety during emergencies[41] and the reopening of restaurants and grocery stores following hurricanes or floods.[42]

Transportation, Including Pipelines

Preparedness requirements for railroads, pipelines, ships, and roadway vehicles that carry hazardous substances or materials are discussed in Chapter 6.

Preparedness Requirements Relating to Safety, Health, and the Environment, Including Handling of Hazardous Materials and Substances

Occupational Safety and Health Administration

OSHA has several standards that address emergency planning in the workplace. As OSHA explains on its Emergency Preparedness and Response: Getting Started website,[43] "[e]mployers and workers may be

39. Conference for Food Protection, Emergency Action Plan for Retail Food Establishments (Jan. 22, 2014), https://www.foodprotect.org/media/guide/Emergency%20Action%20Plan%20for%20Retail%20food%20Est.pdf.

40. *See, e.g.*, New Hampshire DHHS, Emergency Action Plan for Retail Food Establishments (2007), https://www.dhhs.nh.gov/sites/g/files/ehbemt476/files/documents/2021-11/fp-emergency.pdf.

41. FDA, *Food Safety During Emergencies*, https://www.fda.gov/food/recalls-outbreaks-emergencies/food-safety-during-emergencies (last updated May 11, 2023).

42. FDA, *Restaurants and Grocers Reopening After Hurricanes and Flooding*, https://www.fda.gov/food/food-safety-during-emergencies/restaurants-and-grocers-reopening-after-hurricanes-and-flooding (last updated Mar. 7, 2022).

43. OSHA Emergency Preparedness, *supra* note 18. OSHA provides additional resources and reference materials at its Emergency Preparedness and Response landing page, https://www.osha.gov/emergency-preparedness.

required to deal with an emergency when it is least expected and proper planning *before* an emergency is necessary to respond effectively."[44] OSHA's standards address a wide range of considerations when preparing for an emergency, including personal protective equipment, fire detection and suppression systems, and alarm systems. Following is a summary of key emergency planning and response requirements relating to facilities that may deal with hazardous chemical incidents.[45]

Emergency Action Plans

Who Must Comply?

OSHA's emergency action plan standard applies to employers with ten or more employees whenever another OSHA standard requires it.[46] Standards requiring emergency action plans include those regulating process safety management (PSM), ethylene oxide (EtO), methylenedianiline (MDA), and 1,3-Butadiene (BD).[47]

What Does It Require?

OSHA explains that "[a]n emergency action plan (EAP) is intended to facilitate and organize employer and worker actions during workplace emergencies and is recommended for all employers. Well-developed emergency plans and proper worker training (i.e., so that workers understand their roles and responsibilities within the plan) will result in fewer and less severe worker injuries and less damage to the facility during emergencies."[48]

Where applicable, this standard requires employers to develop a written plan that includes, among other requirements:

- Instructions on how to report a fire or other emergency;
- Emergency evacuation procedures;

---

44. *Id.*

45. OSHA, Principal Emergency Response and Preparedness: Requirements and Guidance (2004), https://www.osha.gov/sites/default/files/publications/osha3122.pdf (providing a comprehensive overview of OSHA standards addressing preparedness).

46. https://www.osha.gov/laws-regs/regulations/standardnumber/1910/1910.38.

47. 29 C.F.R. §§ 1910.119 (PSM), 1910.1047 (EtO), 1910.1050 and 1926.60 (MDA), and 1910.1051 (BD).

48. OSHA Emergency Preparedness, *supra* note 18.

- Accountability procedures following an evacuation;
- Procedures for essential employees who remain at a facility during an emergency; and
- Contact information for persons who can provide additional information about the emergency action plan.[49]

The Emergency Action Plan standard also requires employers to maintain an employee alarm system, train employees who may assist with an evacuation, and review the emergency action plan when it is developed and also when employee responsibilities change or the emergency procedures change.[50]

Process Safety Management of Highly Hazardous Chemicals

Who Must Comply?

Issued in 1992, the requirements of OSHA's Process Safety Management (PSM) standard are intended to prevent or minimize the consequences of catastrophic releases of toxic, reactive, flammable, or explosive chemicals.[51] The standard applies when a facility has highly hazardous chemicals in excess of threshold quantities set forth in the standard.[52] Certain facilities are exempted from coverage, including retail facilities, oil or gas well drilling and servicing operations, and normally unoccupied remote facilities.[53]

What Does It Require?

The standard contains requirements for the management of hazards associated with processes using highly hazardous chemicals. These requirements are spread out across 14 elements that touch on a variety of issues, such as mechanical integrity, operating procedures, management of change, process hazard analysis, and compliance audits.[54] The PSM

49. 29 C.F.R. § 1910.38(c).
50. *Id.* § 1910.38(e), (f).
51. *Id.* § 1910.119.
52. *Id.* § 1910.119(a).
53. *Id.* § 1910.119(a)(2).
54. *Id.* § 1910.119(e) (process hazard analysis), (f) (operating procedures), (j) (mechanical integrity), and (l) (management of change).

standard mandates implementation of an emergency action plan.[55] This plan must also include procedures for handling small releases.[56]

Other elements address principles of preparedness, mitigation, and prevention. For example, the PSM standard requires that at least every five years after the completion of an initial process hazard analysis, employers assemble a qualified team to update and revalidate the original analysis and confirm that it's consistent with the current process.[57] These analyses must be performed using specified methodologies, and are intended to identify, evaluate, and control the hazards involved in the process.[58] Specific considerations to be addressed with relevance to preparedness include:

- The identification of any previous incident which had a likely potential for catastrophic consequences in the workplace;
- Engineering and administrative controls applicable to the hazards and their interrelationships, such as appropriate application of detection methodologies to provide early warning of releases; and
- Facility siting.[59]

Hazardous Waste Operations and Emergency Response, 29 C.F.R. 1910.120

Who Must Comply?

OSHA issued the Hazardous Waste Operations and Emergency Response (HAZWOPER) rule in 1989.[60] Mandated by the Superfund Amendments Reauthorization Act (SARA) of 1986, the rule addresses five categories of work, including "[e]mergency response operations for releases of, or substantial threats of releases of, hazardous substances without regard to the location of the hazard."[61] The standard defines emergency response or responding to emergencies as:

55. *Id.* §§ 1910.119(n), 1910.38.
56. *Id.* § 1910.119(n).
57. *Id.* § 1910.119(e)(6).
58. *See id.* § 1910.119(e)(2).
59. 29 C.F.R. § 1910.119(e)(3).
60. *Id.* § 1910.120.
61. *Id.* § 1910.120(a)(1)(v). This chapter does not address the other categories of work covered by the HAZWOPER rule.

> a response effort by employees from outside the immediate release area or by other designated responders (i.e., mutual-aid groups, local fire departments, etc.) to an occurrence which results, or is likely to result, in an uncontrolled release of a hazardous substance.[62]

Incidental releases that are controlled by maintenance personnel or employees in the immediate area, or releases of substances that do not pose a safety or health hazard, are not covered by this portion of the standard.[63]

What Does It Require?

One of the key elements of the HAZWOPER standard is the requirement to develop an emergency response plan.[64] The emergency response plan must address:

- Pre-emergency planning and coordination with off-site responders;
- Personnel roles, lines of authority, and communication procedures;
- Possible emergencies and how to prevent them;
- Safe distances and places of refuge;
- Site control and security;
- Evacuation routes and procedures;
- Emergency decontamination procedures;
- Emergency medical treatment and first aid;
- Emergency communication procedures;
- Necessary emergency equipment, including PPE; and
- ERP evaluation criteria.[65]

---

62. *Id.* § 1910.120(a)(3).

63. *Id.*

64. 29 C.F.R. § 1910.120(q)(1). Per the regulation, "Employers who will evacuate their employees from the danger area when an emergency occurs, and who do not permit any of their employees to assist in handling the emergency, are exempt from the requirements of this paragraph if they provide an emergency action plan in accordance with 29 C.F.R. § 1910.38."

65. Bulleted list copied from OSHA's HAZWOPER landing page, https://www.osha.gov/emergency-preparedness/hazardous-waste-operations/preparedness.

In addition to a written ERP, the HAZWOPER rule includes detailed training requirements based on the responder's role.[66] The HAZWOPER rule also provides requirements for medical surveillance, chemical protective clothing, and post-emergency response operations.[67]

Environmental Protection Agency

Like OSHA, the Environmental Protection Agency (EPA) administers several programs that directly address emergency preparedness.

CAA 112(r) Risk Management Program

Who Must Comply?

The Clean Air Act Amendments of 1990 required EPA to issue regulations to prevent catastrophic releases at chemical facilities.[68] One of the unique aspects of the Risk Management Program (RMP) is that portions of the RMP regulations[69] overlap extensively with OSHA's PSM standard. EPA has explained that while the "OSHA PSM standard and EPA RMP regulations are closely aligned in content, policy interpretations, and enforcement," "[t]he focus of OSHA's regulations in the PSM standard is on workplace safety, while EPA's focus in the RMP regulations has been primarily on minimizing the public impacts of accidental releases through prevention and response."[70]

Similar to OSHA's PSM standard, stationary sources are subject to RMP regulations if they exceed threshold quantities of specified extremely hazardous substances.[71] While OSHA and EPA utilize similar lists of chemicals and substances to determine applicability, these lists do not completely overlap, and careful scrutiny is warranted.

Unlike OSHA's PSM standard, facilities subject to RMP then must determine which of three "prevention program levels" are applicable.[72]

66. 29 C.F.R. § 1910.120(q)(4)–(q)(7).
67. *Id.* § 1910.120(q)(9)–(q)(11).
68. 42 U.S.C. § 7412(r)(7)(B).
69. *See* 40 C.F.R. pt. 68, subpt. D (Program 3 Prevention Program).
70. 89 Fed. Reg. 17622, at 17632.
71. 40 C.F.R. § 68.10.
72. *Id.* § 68.10(j)–(l).

The requirements of each program level become more rigorous and specific as the program levels increase, with program 1 having relatively minimal requirements and program 3 being a close match to OSHA's PSM standard. The increasing rigor of the program levels reflects the agency's judgment on potential for public harm associated with processes at each program level.

What Does It Require?

This chapter focuses on the requirements applicable to program 2 and program 3 facilities.[73] One of the key requirements of RMP regulations is for facilities to prepare and submit a written risk management plan to EPA. This plan must be fully updated and resubmitted every five years. Other changes require updates prior to the five-year deadline. The written risk management plan must be certified and include several elements, such as:

- An analysis of off-site consequences. This analysis must include information about worst-case release scenarios for toxic and flammable releases;
- A five-year accident history. This must identify all accidental releases from covered processes that resulted in deaths, injuries, or significant property damage on-site or known off-site deaths, injuries, evacuations, sheltering in place, property damage, or environmental damage;
- Details about implementation of the prevention program; and
- Details about the emergence response program and exercises.[74]

With regard to the prevention program requirements, both programs 2 and 3 require that facilities conduct hazard assessments for off-site consequences.[75] Both programs also require implementation of a prevention

---

73. 40 C.F.R. pt. 68 subpts C (Program 2 Prevention Program) and D (Program 3 Prevention Program) (Program 1 has minimal requirements and applies to facilities with no public receptors and no accidents in the last five years with off-site consequences.).

74. *Id.* § 68.150.

75. *Id.* § 68.50 (hazard review); *id.* § 68.67 (process hazard analysis)

program.[76] Common elements of prevention programs include requirements to:

- Compile safety information;
- Perform hazard reviews (or, in program 3, process hazard analyses);
- Develop and implement written operating procedures;
- Conduct training with operators;
- Implement a mechanical integrity program;
- Perform compliance audits;
- Investigate incidents; and
- Develop a written plan for employee participation.[77]

Similar to the preceding discussion of PSM, many of these prevention program elements address emergency preparedness considerations.

In addition, the RMP regulations require program 2 and 3 facilities to develop and implement an emergency response program.[78] This program is required to contain certain elements, such as:

- Procedures for notifying the public and local emergency response agencies about accidental releases (including partnering with local agencies to ensure a community notification system is in place);
- Documentation of proper emergency medical treatment to treat exposures;
- Procedure for emergency response after an accidental release of a regulated substance;
- Procedures for use and maintenance of emergency response equipment;
- Training for employees; and
- Procedures to review and update the emergency response plan.[79]

The RMP regulations also emphasize coordination with local response authorities. For example, the regulations require that facilities

76. *Id.* § 68.12(c), (d).

77. *See* 40 C.F.R. pt. 68 subpts C (Program 2 Prevention Program) *and* D (Program 3 Prevention Program).

78. *See id.* pt. 68, subpt. E (Emergency Response).

79. *Id.* § 68.95.

develop an exercise program that includes tabletop and field exercises.[80] Local emergency response officials must be invited to participate in these exercises.[81] Facilities are also required to coordinate response needs with local emergency response organizations.[82]

Emergency Preparedness and Community Right to Know, 40 C.F.R. Parts 370, 372

The Emergency Planning and Community Right-to-Know Act (EPCRA) was authorized in 1986 by Title III of the Superfund Amendments and Reauthorization Act (SARA Title III).[83] Following the 1984 chemical disaster in Bhopal, India, this law was intended to reduce the chance of a similar incident happening in the United States.

EPCRA's requirements emphasize notifications relating to the presence of certain extremely hazardous substances and planning.

Who Must Comply?

In general, EPCRA applies to facilities that have specified extremely hazardous substances present in excess of the rule's threshold planning quantities.[84] Facilities may also become subject to the rule's requirements if they are designated for emergency planning purposes by the state emergency response commission, the governor, or the chief executive of the tribe under whose jurisdiction the facility falls.[85]

What Does It Require?

EPCRA provides several notification requirements for covered facilities. These include requirements to:

- Notify local authorities if you are subject to emergency planning requirements,
- Designate a facility emergency coordinator,

---

80. 40 C.F.R. § 68.96.
81. *Id.* § 68.96(b).
82. *Id.* § 68.93.
83. 42 U.S.C. §§ 11001 *et seq.*
84. 40 C.F.R. § 355.10(a).
85. *Id.* § 355.10(b).

- Notify local authorities of any changes relevant to emergency planning, and
- Provide emergency planning information to the local authorities upon request.[86]

The information provided assists local and tribal emergency planning committees (i.e., fire and police departments, and emergency medical services) to prepare emergency response plans tailored to a particular facility's potential issues and needs. In addition, EPCRA facilities are required to provide other notifications and submittals. These include immediate notification of releases of EHSs that exceed a reportable quantity.[87] Facilities are also required to submit Safety Data Sheets (SDSs) of hazardous chemicals present on-site at or above the reporting threshold to their SERC, LEPC, and local fire department, as well as an annual inventory report to these organizations.[88]

Finally, some facilities subject to EPCRA are also required to submit annual Toxic Release Inventory (TRI) reports to EPA documenting the use and release of toxic chemicals at the facility.[89] Facilities subject to this requirement:

- Have ten or more full-time employees on-site;
- Are included in the TRI-covered NAICS codes; and
- Manufacture, process, or otherwise use any EPCRA 313 chemical over applicable thresholds during a calendar year.[90]

Clean Water Act—Spill Prevention, Control, and Countermeasure Plans

Few incidents impact the public's consciousness more than oil spills—the Valdez oil spill, Deepwater Horizon, and others have had significant impacts on communities and the environment. The key federal regulation intended to prevent such spills are the Oil Pollution Prevention

86. 40 C.F.R. § 355.20.
87. *Id.* § 355.30.
88. https://www.govinfo.gov/content/pkg/USCODE-2021-title42/pdf/USCODE-2021-title42-chap116.pdf. Note that the inventory reporting may be either a Tier I report or a Tier II report.
89. 40 C.F.R. § 372.30.
90. *Id.* § 372.22.

regulations.[91] First promulgated in 1973 and updated or streamlined several times since then, these regulations are intended to "prevent oil from reaching navigable waters and adjoining shorelines, and to contain discharges of oil."[92] The regulations seek to achieve this goal in three ways: (1) prevention, (2) preparedness, and (3) response. The regulations aim to accomplish these goals by requiring all regulated facilities to establish and maintain Spill Prevention, Control, and Countermeasure Plans (SPCC Plans).[93]

Who Must Comply?

In general, non-transportation-related facilities engaged in drilling, producing, gathering, storing, processing, refining, transferring, distributing, using, or consuming oil and oil products that exceed certain oil storage thresholds (1,320 gallons aboveground or 42,000 gallons buried[94]) may be covered if there is a reasonable expectation of an oil discharge into or upon navigable waters.[95]

Determining applicability is complex, and the criteria just cited contain several terms that are supported by detailed definitions and/or guidance. These include:

- Oil: The regulation defines this term broadly, as "oil of any kind or in any form, including, but not limited to: fats, oils, or greases of animal, fish, or marine mammal origin; vegetable oils, including oils from seeds, nuts, fruits, or kernels; and, other oils and greases, including petroleum, fuel oil, sludge, synthetic oils, mineral oils, oil refuse, or oil mixed with wastes other than dredged spoil."[96]

---

91. *Id.* pt. 112.

92. EPA, *Overview of the Spill Prevention, Control, and Countermeasure (SPCC) Regulation*, https://epa.gov/oil-spills-prevention-and-preparedness-regulations/overview-spill-prevention-control-and (last updated Feb. 18, 2025).

93. 40 C.F.R. § 112.3.

94. Note that there are exemptions to the general applicability requirements. For example, certain completely buried storage tanks are exempt from this rule if they are subject to the underground storage tank technical requirements in 40 C.F.R. pt. 280 or a state program approved under 40 C.F.R. pt. 281.

95. 40 C.F.R. § 112.1(b).

96. *Id.* § 112.2.

- Transportation-related: The SPCC regulations include appendices with detailed discussion addressing whether a facility is transportation related or non-transportation related (and, therefore, subject to either Department of Transportation (DOT) jurisdiction or EPA jurisdiction, respectively).[97] Facilities can also be "complexes" that have components of both and may be subject to the jurisdiction of more than one agency (typically EPA and either DOT or United States Coast Guard (USCG)).[98]
- Reasonable Expectation of Discharge: "Reasonable expectation" of a discharge is not a defined term, and, therefore, facility owners must consider the unique aspects of their facility.[99] EPA guidance suggests factors to consider include past discharges, facility location, unique geological or geographic features, and precipitation runoff, among others.[100]

These examples are illustrative. Other applicability criteria, such as what constitutes a "discharge" and what is a "navigable water" have equally complex interpretations.[101] Due to these complexities, facility owners will usually consult with experienced technical consultants and legal counsel when determining SPCC applicability.

What Does the SPCC Rule Require?

SPCC regulations are intended to prevent or contain discharges of oil into navigable waters. Logic suggests that the best way to protect navigable waters from oil discharges is to prevent oil spills from occurring in the first place. Hence, the regulations require that oil be stored in suitable containers and that sufficient secondary containment is in place (e.g., in the form of steel, concrete, or clay-lined "bathtubs" around the

97. *See id.*, pt. 112, app. A.
98. *Id.* § 112.2.
99. EPA, *Chapter 2, SPCC Rule Applicability*, *in* SPCC Guidance for Regional Inspectors § 2.6.2 (Dec. 16, 2013), https://www.epa.gov/sites/default/files/2014-04/documents/2_applicability_2014.pdf [hereinafter SPCC Rule Applicability].
100. *Id.*
101. *See* 40 C.F.R. § 112.2 (defining discharge and navigable waters); *see also* "SPCC Rule Applicability, *supra* note 98 § 2.6.1 (addressing discharge), 2.6.4 (addressing navigable waters)."

containers, or other active or passive prevention systems such as sumps and collections systems or spill diversion ponds)[102] so that if the container springs a leak, the spilled oil is entirely contained and "any discharge [of oil] from a primary containment system, such as a tank, will not escape the containment system before cleanup occurs."[103] As a practical matter, this typically means that a secondary containment system should be sized to contain (or divert) the capacity of the largest single tank or container within the containment system with sufficient freeboard for precipitation.

One key aspect of the regulations is to require preparation of an SPCC Plan.[104] The regulation and EPA guidance[105] identify several important elements of an SPCC plan:

- Facility diagram and description of the facility;
- Oil discharge predictions;
- Appropriate secondary containment or diversionary structures;
- Facility drainage;
- Site security;
- Facility inspections;
- Requirements for bulk storage containers including inspections, overfill, and integrity testing requirements;
- Transfer procedures and equipment (including piping);
- Requirements for qualified oil-filled operational equipment;
- Loading/unloading rack requirements and procedures for tank cars and tank trucks; and
- Brittle fracture evaluations for aboveground field-constructed containers.

This is a performance-based regulation that is intended to provide flexibility to owners and operators. As a result, development of an SPCC involves a facility-specific evaluation. For example, with regard to

102. 40 C.F.R. § 112.7(c)(1)(E).

103. *Id.* § 112.7(c).

104. *Id.* § 112.3.

105. EPA, Spill Prevention, Control, and Countermeasure (SPCC) Regulation (June 2010), https://www.epa.gov/sites/default/files/documents/spccbluebroch.pdf.

secondary containment, the regulation explains that "[i]n determining the method, design, and capacity for secondary containment, you need only to address the typical failure mode, and the most likely quantity of oil that would be discharged."[106] The SPCC regulations also allow for deviations from certain rule requirements when the owner or operator develops a plan that provides equivalent environmental protection.[107]

When preparing an SPCC plan, the regulation requires that the plan follow good engineering practices and also receive management approval.[108] These plans must also be certified by a professional engineer (except where the facility is authorized to self-certify).[109] Once developed, facilities must also train oil-handling personnel who operate equipment designed to prevent discharges, designate a person who is accountable for the discharge prevention, and conduct oil-discharge briefings at least annually.[110] These plans must also be reviewed every five years.[111]

The SPCC regulations identify a subset of facilities that must also prepare a Facility Response Plan (FRP). This requirement applies to facilities that "could reasonably be expected to cause substantial harm to the environment."[112] There are several criteria that may trigger this requirement, including:

- Facilities that transfer oil over water and have storage capacity greater than or equal to 42,000 gallons;
- Facilities with oil storage capacity greater than or equal to one million gallons and one of the following:
  - Secondary containment that is not sufficient to contain the capacity of the largest aboveground storage tank plus sufficient freeboard;
  - Located at a distance where a discharge could impact fish, wildlife, or sensitive environments;

106. 40 C.F.R. § 112.7(c).
107. *Id.* § 112.7(a)(2).
108. *Id.* § 112.7.
109. *Id.* § 112.3(d).
110. *Id.* § 112.7(f).
111. *Id.* § 112.5(b).
112. *Id.* § 112.20(a).

- Located at a distance where a discharge could shut down a public water intake; or
- Prior oil discharge in the last five years of 10,000 or more gallons of oil.[113]

Facilities mandated to have a FRP must meet a heightened set of prevention and planning requirements. For example, they must plan for additional scenarios, including a worst-case discharge, which the rule defines as "the largest foreseeable discharge in adverse weather conditions as determined using the worksheets" provided in the regulation.[114]

These facilities are also required to develop and implement a facility response training program and a drill/exercise program that satisfy the requirements of this section.[115] The regulations specifically recommend following the USCG's Training Elements for Oil Spill Response training program as the basis for a facility training program,[116] and note that a drill and exercise program that follows the National Preparedness for Response Exercise Program is also deemed satisfactory.[117]

RCRA Preparedness and Prevention, 40 C.F.R. Part 262 (Generators of Hazardous Waste)

EPA's Hazardous Water Generator Regulations, issued under the Resource Conservation and Recovery Act (RCRA), include preparedness requirements intended to help prevent incidents involving hazardous waste and to equip facilities for any such incidents that may occur. RCRA's comprehensive regulatory approach establishes these requirements for three different classes of regulated parties: generators of hazardous waste; transporters of hazardous waste; and owners and operators of hazardous waste treatment, storage, and disposal facilities (TSDFs). This chapter focuses solely on generators, whose preparedness, prevention, and emergency procedure requirements are spelled out in 40 C.F.R. subparts I and M.

113. *Id.* § 112.20(f)(1).
114. *Id.* § 112.2.
115. *Id.* § 112.20(h)(8).
116. *Id.* § 112.21(b).
117. *Id.* § 112.21(c).

Who Must Comply?

RCRA's regulations specify slightly different requirements for generators depending on the amount of waste generated. In general terms, a small quantity generator (SQG) is defined as anyone who generates more than 100 kilograms (220 pounds), but less than 1,000 kilograms (2,200 pounds) of hazardous waste per month, while a large quantity generator (LQG) is anyone who generates more than 1,000 kilograms per month.[118]

What Does It Require?

An SQG that operates satellite accumulation areas for hazardous wastes[119] "must maintain and operate its facility to minimize the possibility of a fire, explosion, or any unplanned sudden or non-sudden release of hazardous waste or hazardous waste constituents to air, soil, or surface water which could threaten human health or the environment."[120] Additional requirements from the regulations include:

- An internal communications or alarm system capable of providing immediate emergency instruction (voice or signal) to all personnel;
- A device, such as a telephone (immediately available at the scene of operations) or a handheld, two-way radio, capable of summoning

---

118. 40 C.F.R. § 260.10 (Defines Large Quantity Generator as, in a calendar month, generating (1) greater than or equal to 1,000 kg. [2,200 lbs.] of non-acute hazardous waste, (2) greater than 1 kg. [2.2 lbs.] of certain listed acute hazardous wastes, or (3) greater than 100 kg. [220 lbs.] of any residue or contaminated soil, water, or other debris resulting from the cleanup of a spill, into or on any land or water, of any of the listed acute hazardous wastes. Defines Small Quantity Generator as, in a calendar month, generating (1) greater than 100 kg but less than 1,000 kg. of non-acute hazardous waste, (2) less than or equal to 1 kg of certain listed acute hazardous waste, or (3) less than or equal to 100 kg of any residue or contaminated soil, water, or other debris resulting from the cleanup of a spill, into or on any land or water, of any [of the listed] acute hazardous waste. Note that some states may have a more stringent definition of LQGs; for example, New Hampshire defines a Full Quantity Generator (FQG) as a generator who, among other things, generates more than 100 kg of non-acute hazardous waste in a month or that accumulates greater than 1,000 kg at any time (*See* NH Code of Admin. Rules Env-Hw 103.61 and 503.02, defining FQG).

119. 40 C.F.R. § 262.15(a), (A satellite accumulation area is a location where a generator may accumulate as much as 55 gallons of non-acute hazardous waste and/or either one quart of a listed liquid acute hazardous waste or 1 kg (2.2 lbs) of listed solid acute hazardous waste "in containers at or near any point of generation where wastes initially accumulate which is under the control of the operator of the process generating the waste[.]").

120. 40 C.F.R. §§ 262.15(b)(7), 262.16(b)(8), 262.16(b)(9).

emergency assistance from local police and fire departments, or state or local emergency response teams;

- Portable fire extinguishers, fire-control devices (including special extinguishing equipment using foam, inert gas, or dry chemicals), spill-control materials, and decontamination supplies;
- Water at adequate volume and pressure to supply water hose streams, foam-producing equipment, automatic sprinklers, or water spray systems; and
- Testing and maintenance of all equipment to ensure proper operation.[121]

Other requirements include maintaining sufficient aisle space to allow for unobstructed movement of emergency personnel and equipment, coordination with local emergency response organizations to provide services if needed, having an emergency coordinator on the premises or on call at all times, ensuring that all employees are trained in applicable waste handling and emergency procedures, and ensuring that responses to all emergencies conform to specified action and notification requirements.[122]

LQGs that operate satellite accumulation areas must meet the same requirements as SQGs that operate satellite accumulation areas,[123] and must also meet similar, but heightened, preparedness requirements for all other hazardous waste activities.[124] This includes the requirement to have a written contingency plan that describes the actions facility personnel will take to respond to fires, explosions, or any unplanned sudden or non-sudden release of hazardous waste or hazardous waste constituents to air, soil, or surface water at the facility.[125] If the generator has an SPCC Plan or another emergency or contingency plan, it may develop a single contingency plan that meets all applicable regulatory requirements, in which case EPA recommends that the plan be based on the National Response

121. 40 C.F.R. § 262.16(b)(8)(ii), (iii) and (iv); *see generally* EPA, Managing Your Hazardous Waste: A Guide for Small Businesses (Oct. 2019), https://www.epa.gov/sites/default/files/2019-10/documents/10008_managingyourhazwaste_508pdf_october_16_2019.pdf.

122. 40 C.F.R. §§ 262.16(b)(8)(v), (vi), and (b)(9)(i)–(iv).

123. *Id.* § 262.15(b).

124. *See id.* pt. 262 subpt. M.

125. 40 C.F.R. §§ 262.260, 262.261(a).

Team's Integrated Contingency Plan Guidance.[126] Copies, updates, and amendments of continency plans, as well as a quick reference guide, must be shared with all local emergency responders (including hospitals and state and local emergency response teams).[127]

Among other items the contingency plan must include are:

- A description of arrangements agreed to with the local response organizations;
- An evacuation plan for generator personnel;
- The names and emergency telephone numbers of all persons qualified to act as emergency coordinator;
- A list of all emergency equipment at the facility (including location, physical description, and capabilities); and
- An evacuation plan for personnel, including the signal(s) used to begin evacuation, evacuation routes, and alternative evacuation routes.[128]

Conclusion

While at first blush the often-required details of preparedness (including emergency response or contingency plans) may seem mind numbing or, in some instances, excessive, the process of developing, implementing, and updating an emergency response plan can be extremely educational and valuable for any community or organization. Clear thought and attention to detail come much more easily to most people when they're not faced with the panic or stress of a sudden emergency. Preparedness plans contain descriptions of procedures and many details that can help a person to focus, regain a sense of calm and confidence, and undertake the essential tasks in appropriate ways during the initial and subsequent stages of an incident. Many organizations actively manage their preparedness plans because they know that these plans can prevent accidents from occurring, mitigate against significant damages or losses, save lives,

126. *Id.* § 262.261(b).
127. *Id.* §§ 262.262, 262.263.
128. *Id.* § 262.261.

protect property, and provide a sense of well-being. Legal counsel and technical advisors can play key roles in assisting organizations of all kinds in ensuring that their preparedness efforts and plans meet all applicable legal requirements while also providing the practical information and guidance that will be essential to a successful response to any incident, including those involving releases of hazardous substances or materials.

Chapter 3

Release Reporting[1]

Thomas S. Burack

As soon as a release of hazardous substances, materials, contaminants, or pollutants into the environment is discovered and initially reported, the response process begins. The reporting process itself usually entails a nearly immediate initial reporting obligation (within minutes or hours), as well as follow-up reporting obligations as new information becomes available. Thus, release reporting remains a vital piece of—and in many respects a parallel process to—every other aspect of the overall response process. The response, which always starts with discovery and reporting, can include such measures as emergency response, containment, site investigation, removal actions, remediation, and risk communication before achieving closure. In this book, these parallel and interconnected processes are discussed in serial chapters, this one on reporting obligations, and the next on the response process. The overall response to a release of hazardous substances or materials is most often based on the National Contingency Plan (NCP) (see Chapter 5), which is a component of the National Response Framework for all disaster situations, as discussed in Chapter 1.

1. Portions of the contents of this chapter have been adapted by the author from the chapter he authored, *Environmental Release Reporting Obligations*, Chapter 5 in Environmental Aspects of Real Estate and Commercial Transactions, American Bar Association (5th ed., 2021).

What Constitutes a Release

Regulated Substances and Contaminants

The definitions in most federal, state, and local environmental laws of what constitutes a "release" are intentionally expansive. The basic policy approach underlying many of these laws is to assume the worst and err on the side of requiring parties to report almost anything that has already caused or could in the future cause contamination of water, land, or air, or affect the public health. The overall goal of these regimes is to identify releases as soon as possible so they can be quickly investigated and cleaned up, thereby minimizing the risks to human health and the environment.[2] Hence, while there are some limited exemptions under the various laws, the general expectation is that reporting will trigger any necessary emergency response or removal action, followed by an investigation to determine the nature and extent of the release and whether any longer-term cleanup will be necessary.

Analyzing whether a reportable release has occurred will typically involve three linked determinations: (1) whether the substance in question is physically present and, if so, at what concentration or mass; (2) whether the substance is regulated under a particular statute at the observed, measured, or estimated concentration or mass; and (3) though generally not dispositive, the mechanism or process that may have caused it to arrive there. In most instances, it will not matter whether the act or omission that caused the release or disposal was intentional, accidental, known, unknown, unknowable, or how far in the past it occurred. Thus, if a responsible party makes contemporaneous, eyewitness observations of a release of a hazardous substance, pollutant, or contaminant onto the ground or into the air or water—or if a third party informs a responsible party of such observation—it's highly likely the release will trigger an immediate reporting obligation, unless a specific exemption applies. Absent such eyewitness observations, the presence of oil products,

2. *See, e.g.*, Ctr. for Biological Diversity, Inc. v. BP Am. Prod. Co., 704 F.3d 413, 428 (5th Cir. 2013); United States v. Carr, 880 F.2d 1550, 1552 (2d Cir. 1989) (the reporting requirement of CERCLA section 103(a) ensures the government's ability to "move quickly to check the spread of a hazardous release").

hazardous substances, or hazardous wastes where they don't belong in the environment, and that didn't get there due to a permitted discharge, is also a likely indicator that a reportable release has occurred. Just because there may not have been a witness who observed the leaking, spilling, or dripping does not mean that there was not a release or disposal. In short, how, when, and why these pollutants or contaminants came to be located where they are discovered or observed may be important factors when analyzing which parties have a duty to report or what defenses to liability may be available. However, if pollutants or contaminants are found in the ambient environment at or above reporting thresholds, and their presence isn't covered by a permit or some other exemption, then a release likely occurred and the next issue is determining who has a duty to report the release. Moreover, even if the discovery of an elevated concentration of a substance in groundwater, surface water, or soil does not trigger a release-reporting obligation, it may still trigger a duty to report an exceedance of a state's environmental quality protection standards (e.g., for soil, groundwater, or surface water). A report of such an exceedance usually has the same consequences as the report of a release, namely triggering a process of site investigation and potential remediation as well as a possible emergency response if the contaminant poses significant, short-term toxic risks to human health or the environment.

While the statutory definitions of what constitutes a release are expansive and comprehensive, so too are the definitions of hazardous substances, pollutants, and contaminants—the chemicals whose presence must be reported. Moreover, the federal and state laws often adopt each other's definitions of key terms. For example, the Comprehensive Environmental Response, Compensation and Liability Act (CERCLA), the broad federal environmental cleanup law, defines "hazardous substances" as including various substances that are regulated by the Clean Water Act, the Clean Air Act, or the Solid Waste Disposal Act, but as excluding most petroleum products. At the federal level, definitions and reporting requirements for releases of petroleum products are primarily found in the Clean Water Act and the Oil Pollution Control Act, although other statutes may come into play as well. In some instances, the mere presence of any concentration of a pollutant or contaminant may trigger a reporting obligation. For example, the presence of an oil sheen (whether due to petroleum products or vegetable oil) on waters of the United States may trigger a reporting obligation under the Clean Water Act.[3]

In most instances, one must first determine whether there is an exceedance of a specified reporting threshold—usually denominated as a concentration or a mass—for the particular pollutant or contaminant. For example, CERCLA includes a comprehensive list of hazardous substances, all of which have a Reportable Quantity (RQ) (ranging from 1 to 5,000 pounds); if a release equals or exceeds the RQ in any 24-hour period, then the release is reportable.[4] Arguably, to make such a determination, a party needs volume and concentration data, as well as process knowledge in order to make well-informed assumptions about the extent of the contamination so they can estimate whether the RQ has been equaled or exceeded. While it's likely that a manufacturing, industrial, or government facility would have the data available to be able to make such a calculation quickly, these underlying data may be unavailable to other parties such as a subsequent property owner; a prospective purchaser; the owner or operator of a ship, train, or truck that's in an accident; or a party who simply stumbles upon a messy situation. Under these circumstances, some parties and their counsel conclude that what they don't know, they don't need to know, and they look the other way.[5] Nevertheless, the penalties for failing to report may be substantial, so understanding the applicable analysis and thinking through the relative advantages and disadvantages of reporting a release under CERCLA section 103 or similar provisions is considerably important. Some state laws require reporting the discovery of groundwater or soil contamination (which are indicators that a release has occurred) if the pollutant is present above a certain concentration, thus making sites reportable under state law even if they may not be reportable under federal law.[6] A report under state law may also lead parties to discover additional data or information about a release that could subsequently trigger a reporting duty under federal law.

---

3. 40 C.F.R. § 110.3(b).

4. 42 U.S.C. § 9603(a).

5. *See generally* Valerie Wagner Long, *Note: The Complexity and Lack of Incentives in the Release Reporting Requirements of CERCLA Section 103*, 18 VA. ENV'T L.J. 245 (1999).

6. *See, e.g.*, N.H. ADMIN. CODE § Env-Or 604.02.

In summary, real-time, eyewitness observations of a release of a contaminant into the environment may be all that's necessary to trigger a reporting obligation under federal or state law. In after-the-fact situations, the discovery of substances in soil, groundwater, surface water, or air at concentrations above background levels may be sufficient to trigger the suspicion of a release, which may mandate a report to a government agency.[7] Under either of these scenarios, it may be necessary to perform calculations or consult charts of reporting thresholds to determine whether there is a reporting obligation.

Finally, it is essential to recognize that state laws can be more stringent than federal laws, such as by having lower reporting thresholds or by regulating releases that are not covered by federal laws. Thus, the question of whether the discovery of environmental contaminants has triggered a reporting obligation must be assessed through multiple statutory and regulatory lenses to ensure that all applicable duties have been identified and fulfilled. Reporting to one level of government typically does not also satisfy the requirement to report to another level; federal, state, and local release reporting obligations must all be separately satisfied, and there may even be more than one agency at the federal or state level to which a report must be given. In short, it's vital to understand what substance has been or may have been released, to have an initial understanding of the quantity, extent, and source of the release, and to determine which regulations apply so that the appropriate reporting requirements are identified and followed.

Emerging Contaminants

Complicating things, scientific knowledge is evolving rapidly, and most regulatory regimes are forever playing "catch up" with the latest scientific understandings. Because of this, there is a gap in time (sometimes years or decades) between when the regulators determine that a substance poses a substantial risk and when they promulgate regulations to address that risk. Moreover, different jurisdictions move at different speeds when updating their environmental laws and regulations, so

7. *See* Chapter 5 for additional discussion of the role of background levels, including of naturally occurring and manmade substances, in determining reporting obligations.

reporting requirements for the same substance often differ from state to state or between federal and state laws. For example, there are many "emerging contaminants" or "contaminants of emerging concern," which have included per- and poly-fluoroalkyl substances (collectively known as PFAS), whose release was only recently regulated and reportable under some individual states' laws or regulations and is just now starting to be regulated under federal law. Microplastics, pharmaceuticals, and personal care products may also be regulated at some levels of government or by some jurisdictions but not others.

Notwithstanding the often-slow pace of regulatory responses to new scientific knowledge, even if a contaminant is not regulated at the time of its observed release into, or its subsequent discovery in, the environment, it could still cause harm to other parties or the environment and it could become regulated in the future. Thus, even a release of a nonregulated or emerging contaminant may present significant risks or concerns. These could include nonstatutory (common law) claims or liabilities; complications in purchasing, selling, or financing a project; reputational harm; or simply uncertainties due to the potential for future scientific or regulatory developments with respect to that contaminant. Thus, a party responsible for a release of a nonregulated contaminant may still choose to report such a release to regulatory authorities and to seek some form of voluntary cleanup agreement as a means of trying to obtain regulatory finality with respect to its response obligations.

Case Law Interpreting What Is a Release

The detailed statutory and regulatory provisions discussed herein require parties to report the unpermitted release or disposal of a contaminant. Although that requirement may appear to be straightforward, courts have not provided clear or consistent guidance. For example, under CERCLA or the Resource Conservation and Recovery Act (RCRA), some federal courts have broadly interpreted the terms "release" and "disposal." These courts included within their definitions the mere migration or leaching of contaminants through the soil, even when the landowner has not taken any affirmative action to introduce the contaminant into the environment. Other courts have taken a narrower view, holding that the mere existence of contamination does not necessarily constitute a release.

This divergence of opinion has important consequences in the reporting context as parties weigh whether the discovery of existing contamination constitutes a release that requires reporting. On the other hand, when eyewitnesses observe a release of a contaminant onto the ground or into the air or water in real time (i.e., contemporaneously), there can be no reasonable doubt that the release is reportable, unless it's below the reporting threshold or a specific exemption applies.

The CERCLA case law interpreting the terms "release" and "disposal" has arisen largely, if not exclusively, in connection with government attempts to impose liability for cleanup or cleanup costs on the current and prior owners of contaminated land, or from private party attempts to obtain contribution from other parties for such costs. The gloss given to the statutory language in these kinds of cases involving cleanup costs, effectively puts parties on notice that courts are very likely to adopt a similarly broad interpretation regarding reporting obligations. It's not surprising, then, that almost every year private parties settle rather than litigate claims by the government asserting that they failed to report releases, especially releases of gases such as anhydrous ammonia, as required by CERCLA section 103 and EPCRA section 304.[8]

Courts that have addressed the general issue of what constitutes release or disposal have expressed a range of views on whether the terms require active human conduct. There are differences of opinion within the circuits themselves. The courts that have imposed liability for "passive" release or disposal have focused on both the statutory language and legislative intent. Many have noted that the definitions of "release" and "disposal" include several terms describing how a contaminant can enter the environment. Some require human action (e.g., "discharge," "deposit," and "dumping") and others do not commonly imply an intentional act ("leaking" and "spilling"). These courts have determined that including the term "leaking" in the definition was aimed at imposing liability for passive leakage of hazardous substances.[9] These and other

8. *See, e.g.*, EPA, *EPA Settlement Requires Dyno Nobel to Improve Chemical Safety at St. Helens, Oregon, Facility* (June 25, 2019), https://www.epa.gov/newsreleases/epa-settlement-requires-dyno-nobel-improve-chemical-safety-st-helens-oregon-facility.

9. *See* Nurad, Inc. v. William E. Hooper & Sons Co., 966 F.2d 837, 845 (4th Cir.), *cert. denied*, 506 U.S. 940 (1992); United States v. Waste Indus., 734 F.2d 159, 164–65 (4th Cir. 1984).

courts have noted that to condition liability on affirmative human participation in a contamination would frustrate the statutes' purposes. The statutes emphasize strict liability, providing only certain limited defenses for innocent landowners and others who did not control the property at the time of the release.[10]

By contrast, the courts that have refused to impose liability on "passive" landowners have expressed concern about the inequity of imposing cleanup costs on landowners who simply happened to own the land while contaminants either leaked from sources controlled by previous owners or migrated through the soil after rainfall.[11] For example, the Third Circuit has rejected the argument that passive migration of contamination rendered an otherwise nonculpable landowner liable under CERCLA, and the Second Circuit adopted its reasoning.[12] However, in a case involving release reporting requirements rather than imposition of cleanup liability, this reasoning may not be as persuasive.

Several courts have distinguished between the terms "release" and "disposal" when interpreting the statute. In *United States v. Petersen Sand & Gravel, Inc.*,[13] for example, an Illinois federal court took a hard look at the language of the CERCLA provisions containing the words "release" and "disposal." The court concluded that, although it was "undisputed that a 'release' includes the kind of passive migration at issue," the word "disposal" was not meant to encompass passive events.[14] The court also

10. *See* Lincoln Props., Ltd. v. Higgins, 823 F. Supp. 1528, 1536 (E.D. Cal. 1992) ("Nor is the 'one source' or 'passive owner exception' . . . supported by the overall structure or purpose of CERCLA. The Act is structured to provide for broad coverage"); *Nurad*, 966 F.2d at 846 (opining that the definition of disposal requiring active human conduct is "at odds with CERCLA's strict liability emphasis"); State of N.Y. v. Shore Realty Corp., 759 F.2d 1032 (2d Cir. 1985) (holding defendants who bought land knowing of the existence of waste storage tanks to be liable for the tanks' leakage).

11. *See, e.g.*, Joslyn Mfg. Co. v. T.L. James & Co., 836 F. Supp. 1264, 1269 (W.D. La. 1993); Snediker Developers Ltd. P'ship v. Evans, 773 F. Supp. 984, 989 (E.D. Mich. 1991).

12. United States v. CDMG Realty Co., 96 F.3d 706 (3d Cir. 1996); ABB Indus. Sys., Inc. v. Prime Tech, Inc., 120 F.3d 351, 358 (2d Cir. 1997).

13. United States v. Petersen Sand & Gravel, Inc., 806 F. Supp. 1346, 1351–52 (N.D. Ill. 1992) (finding defendant liable for leakage/disposal from waste storage barrels that were on the land prior to defendant's incorporation).

14. *See also* Carson Harbor, Ltd. v. Unocal Corp. et al., 270 F.3d 863, 878–79 (9th Cir. 2001), *cert. denied*, 535 U.S. 971 (2002) (distinguishing "release" from "disposal" by pointing out that when Congress intended to include passive migration, it used terms such as "leaching," which is included in the definition of "release" but not in "disposal").

noted that the CERCLA reporting requirements create an incentive to clean up that would not be undercut by a limited interpretation of "disposal."

The Ninth Circuit analyzed the "passive migration" issue in *Carson Harbor, Ltd. v. Unocal Corp.*[15] After reviewing the holdings of other circuits, the court concluded that a careful reading of the various circuit decisions reveals not a dichotomy of opinions but "a more nuanced range of views, depending in large part on the factual circumstances of the case."[16] The court held that "disposal" does not include "gradual passive migration of contamination through the soil."[17] However, based upon a review of some of the legislative history of CERCLA, the decision suggested that passive, gradual "leaking," such as from a barrel or a tank, would constitute a "disposal."[18] In a 2003 decision, the Second Circuit adopted the *Carson Harbor* reasoning, as it held that a property owner was not a responsible party under CERCLA where hazardous substances passively migrated from a neighboring polluter's property through the owner's property.[19]

In summary, there's rarely much doubt that there is a reporting obligation when eyewitnesses observe a release in real time. However, when contamination is discovered after-the-fact, and it can't be readily determined when or how the contamination got there, reporting obligations are more likely to turn on laboratory analyses and other factual data to determine whether a reporting threshold has been exceeded. In cases involving the discovery of contamination due to the passive migration of contaminants through soil or groundwater, courts have taken a range of approaches to the issue of liability for investigating and remediating the resulting contamination. Some courts have found that the landowner whose property was contaminated by the migration of contaminants from another property is liable for the cleanup on their property, while the majority view appears to be that the party that was responsible for the initial release that migrated onto the property of a "downgradient"

15. *Id.*; *accord* Servco Pac., Inc. v. Dods, 193 F. Supp. 2d 1183 (D. Haw. 2002).
16. *Carson Harbor*, 270 F.3d at 875.
17. *Id.* at 879.
18. *Id.* at 885–86; *see Servco*, 193 F. Supp. 2d at 1197.
19. Niagara Mohawk Power Corp. v. Jones Chem. Inc., 315 F.3d 171 (2d Cir. 2003).

landowner is liable for the cleanup of that contamination, regardless of where it comes to be located. Notwithstanding that such a downgradient owner may not be liable for the contamination, if they're the first ones to discover it and the data suggests that a reporting threshold has been exceeded, they would have an obligation to report that discovery.

Who Must Report?

As detailed in the following discussion of specific regulatory programs, most statutes impose reporting obligations on the owner or operator of a facility or vessel from or on which the release occurs, which includes the "person in charge" (typically an employee or officer of an entity). The person in charge may also include a tenant, an individual property owner, or even a homeowner. In some situations, parties who become aware of a release, such as attorneys, environmental consultants, or prospective purchasers, could also have reporting duties, especially if their due diligence activities result in a new release. For example, Licensed Site Professionals (LSPs) in Massachusetts are required under the LSP Rules of Professional Responsibility to notify the Massachusetts Department of Environmental Protection of a release under the limited circumstances in which, while providing professional services other than conducting pre-acquisition environmental due diligence, they identify an imminent hazard, notify their client of the client's statutory obligation to report the hazard, and the client fails to do so within 24 hours.[20] In practically all states, sellers of residential properties (or their agents, which could include realtors) have a duty to disclose known or potential environmental issues,[21] and in some states sellers of commercial properties have similar types of disclosure obligations.[22] If a prospective purchaser discovers a reportable release

20. 309 CMR 4.00, Rules of Professional Conduct, Board of Registration of Hazardous Waste Site Cleanup Professionals § 4.03(4). *See also* 310 CMR 40.0000, 40.0300, 40.0303, 40.0311(7), 40.0321, 40.0950, and 309 CMR 2.02.

21. *See, e.g.*, NH RSA 477:4-a, which requires general disclosures relating to the potential presence of radon, arsenic, lead, and PFAS, as well as flood risks.

22. *See, e.g.*, Michigan Compiled Laws § 324.20116, prohibiting transfer by the owner of an interest in real property without providing written notice to the purchaser of the general nature and extent of a known hazardous substance release on the property and any associated land or resource use restrictions.

during their due diligence activities, most state and federal laws would not require that party to report the discovery, but were they to purchase the property, their knowledge and ownership status would most likely trigger an immediate reporting obligation.

Federal Reporting Requirements

Statutory and Regulatory Provisions

The principal federal reporting requirements are imposed under the Comprehensive Environmental Response, Compensation, and Liability Act (CERCLA, or Superfund),[23] the Brownfields Revitalization and Environmental Restoration Act (Brownfields Amendments of 2002),[24] the Emergency Planning and Community Right-to-Know Act (EPCRA),[25] and the Clean Water Act (CWA).[26] Additionally, reporting obligations are imposed under the Toxic Substances Control Act (TSCA),[27] the Resource Conservation and Recovery Act (RCRA),[28] and the Clean Air Act (CAA).[29] The requirements of these statutes overlap to a significant degree. However, except where expressly provided, compliance with the reporting requirements under one statute does not substitute for compliance with the others' reporting obligations.

Comprehensive Environmental Response, Compensation and Liability Act (CERCLA) Section 103(a)

CERCLA section 103(a)[30] requires parties to give notice of any unpermitted release of a reportable quantity of a hazardous substance. The person in charge of a facility where a release has occurred must report it as soon as he or she has knowledge of such a release.[31] The National

23. 42 U.S.C. §§ 9601 *et seq.*
24. Title II of the Small Business Liability Relief and Brownfields Revitalization Act of 2001, Pub. L. No. 107-118, 115 Stat. 2356 [hereinafter Brownfields Amendments of 2002].
25. 42 U.S.C. §§ 11001 *et seq.*
26. Federal Water Pollution Control Act, 33 U.S.C. §§ 1251 *et seq.*
27. 15 U.S.C. §§ 2601 *et seq.*
28. 42 U.S.C. §§ 6901 *et seq.*
29. *Id.* § 7401 *et seq.*
30. *Id.* § 9603(a).
31. *Id.*

Response Center (NRC) receives the notification[32] and in turn notifies all appropriate governmental agencies, including the governor of any affected state. EPCRA also requires that the reporting party notify state and local officials of the incident.

Section 101(14) of CERCLA defines "hazardous substances" as those designated under these federal statutes:[33]

- Section 311(b)(2)(A) of the Clean Water Act;[34]
- Section 102 of CERCLA;[35]
- Section 3001 of RCRA[36] (which includes both listed substances and those having the characteristics described in section 3001);
- Section 307(a) of the Federal Water Pollution Control Act;[37]
- Section 112 of the Clean Air Act;[38] and
- Section 7(f) of TSCA.[39]

A current list of these chemicals is set forth at 40 C.F.R. § 302.4.

Not all releases must be reported—only those involving a release within a 24-hour period of a "reportable quantity" of the substance in question. Reportable quantities for each substance have been promulgated pursuant to CERCLA section 102[40] and are set forth at 40 C.F.R. §§ 302.4 and 302.5. Fortunately, EPA has developed a helpful compendium of all the substances for which release reports are required under CERCLA, EPCRA, and section 112(r) of the Clean Air Act. Known as the "List of Lists," this consolidated list of chemicals is sorted alphabetically and by Chemical Abstract System (CAS) number, making it easy

32. The National Response Center was established pursuant to the federal Clean Water Act, 33 U.S.C. § 1321(b)(5); 33 C.F.R. § 153.203. The center's phone number is (800) 424-8802.

33. Note that the definition of hazardous substances under section 101(14) of CERCLA "does not include petroleum, including crude oil or any fraction thereof which is not otherwise specifically listed or designated as a hazardous substance . . . [or] natural gas, natural gas liquids, liquefied natural gas, or synthetic gas usable for fuel (or mixtures of natural gas and such synthetic gas)." 42 U.S.C. § 9601(14).

34. 33 U.S.C. § 1321(b)(2)(A).

35. *Id.* § 1321(b)(2)(A).

36. 42 U.S.C. § 6921.

37. 33 U.S.C. § 1317(a).

38. 42 U.S.C. § 7412.

39. 15 U.S.C. § 2606(f).

40. 42 U.S.C. § 9602.

to determine if a release is reportable and, if so, the pertinent reportable quantity, threshold planning quantity, threshold quantity, or RCRA code.[41]

The person in charge of the facility at which the release occurred gives the notification as soon as he or she has knowledge of the release by placing a call to the Coast Guard's National Response Center (800-424-8802), which is staffed 24/7.[42] The National Contingency Plan, 40 C.F.R. §§ 300 *et seq.*, provides the reporting requirements for CERCLA section 103(a), which requires "information that will help to characterize the release," including but not limited to: location of the release, type(s) of material(s) released, an estimate of the quantity of material released, possible source(s) of the release, and date and time of the release.[43]

Penalties for failure to report can be severe, including adjustments for inflation; currently, civil penalties of up to $71,545 per day can be assessed, or up to $214,637 per day for a second or subsequent violation of the CERCLA reporting obligations.[44] In 2018, as part of a settlement involving multiple violations associated with operations at its refineries, Chevron USA, Inc. paid penalties to EPA and the state of Mississippi totaling $2.95 million. These included penalties assessed pursuant to CERCLA section 103(a) for failure to timely notify federal authorities of a 2012 hydrogen sulfide release and pursuant to EPCRA section 304

41. *See* List of Lists, Consolidated List of Chemicals Subject to the Emergency Planning and Community Right-To-Know Act (EPRCA), Comprehensive Environmental Response, Compensation and Liability Act (CERCLA), section 112(r) of the Clean Air Act (CAA), and section 311(j)(5) of the Clean Water Act (CWA), EPA 550-B-24-001 (Oct. 2024), https://www.epa.gov/system/files/documents/2024-11/consolidated-list-of-lists_updated-october-2024.pdf. Special rules apply for mixtures of chemicals and "continuous and stable" releases. *See* 42 U.S.C. § 9603(f). There are also certain other exceptions found in the statute or implementing regulations. They include federally permitted releases, such as those under National Pollutant Discharge Elimination System (NPDES) permits (*see* 42 U.S.C. § 9603(a) and 33 U.S.C. § 1342); and releases that expose only persons in the workplace, such as those in totally enclosed buildings (*see* 42 U.S.C. § 9601(22)(A), definition of release). In addition, under CERCLA, releases of solid pieces of certain metals (antimony, arsenic, beryllium, cadmium, chromium, copper, lead, nickel, selenium, silver, thallium, and zinc) that have a diameter greater than 100 micrometers (0.004 inches) do not need to be reported (*see* footnote III after Table 302.4 in 40 C.F.R. § 302.4).

42. *See* 40 C.F.R. § 302.6.

43. *See id.* 300.405(d). Again, special rules apply to continuous releases. *See id.* § 302.8.

44. *See* 42 U.S.C. § 9609(b) and 40 C.F.R. § 19.4, Table 1.

for failure to notify state and local agencies of the same release.[45] Due to the accrual of penalties and because failure to report is deemed a continuing violation, penalties can mount quickly. A criminal conviction under CERCLA section 103(a) can result in imprisonment for up to three years, or up to five years for a subsequent conviction.[46]

CERCLA Section 103(c)

An often-overlooked reporting provision is CERCLA section 103(c),[47] which requires parties to notify the administrator of the EPA facilities that have treated, stored, or disposed of hazardous wastes. The statute requires notification by June 9, 1981, leading many to assume that facilities discovered after that date are not subject to reporting under section 103(c).[48] However, commonly referring to section 103(c) as "the lasting provision," the agency takes the position that this notification requirement is an ongoing obligation that creates a continuous reporting obligation that attaches anytime it is determined that a facility once treated, stored, or disposed of hazardous wastes.[49] While such situations are not likely to arise frequently, given that nearly 45 years have passed since this notification deadline, this is nonetheless a point to be considered in transactions or activities involving facilities whose environmental compliance status has not been evaluated during that time period.

---

45. United States of America and the State of Mississippi v. Chevron U.S.A., Inc., Consent Decree (N.D. Cal.), Oct. 24, 2018; *see* EPA, *Chevron Settlement Information Sheet*, https://www.epa.gov/enforcement/chevron-settlement-information-sheet (last updated Feb. 27, 2025).

46. 42 U.S.C. § 9603(b).

47. *Id.* § 9603(c).

48. The person responsible for notification is "any person who owns or operates, or who at the time of disposal owned or operated, or who accepted hazardous substances for transport and selected a facility at which hazardous substances . . . are or have been stored, treated, or disposed of." *Id.* § 9603(c).

49. *See* EPA, *RCRA, Superfund & EPCRA Hotline Training Module, Statutory Overview of CERCLA* (updated February 1998) 5, https://nepis.epa.gov/Exe/ZyNET.exe/P100K203.TXT?ZyActionD=ZyDocument&Client=EPA&Index=1995+Thru+1999&Docs=&Query=&Time=&EndTime=&SearchMethod=1&TocRestrict=n&Toc=&TocEntry=&QField=&QFieldYear=&QFieldMonth=&QFieldDay=&IntQFieldOp=0&ExtQFieldOp=0&XmlQuery=&File=D%3A%5Czyfiles%5CIndex%20Data%5C95thru99%5CTxt%5C00000035%5CP100K203.txt&User=ANONYMOUS&Password=anonymous&SortMethod=h%7C-&MaximumDocuments=1&FuzzyDegree=0&ImageQuality=r75g8/r75g8/x150y150g16/i425&Display=hpfr&DefSeekPage=x&SearchBack=ZyActionL&Back=ZyActionS&BackDesc=Results%20page&MaximumPages=1&ZyEntry=1&SeekPage=x&ZyPURL.

Notification is made to the National Response Center (NRC) pursuant to the requirements of the National Contingency Plan, including the same information as would be provided for a release reported under CERCLA section 103(a). The penalty for not reporting is a fine of up to $10,000, imprisonment for up to one year, or both.[50]

CERCLA Section 103(f)

A release that is "continuous and stable in quantity and rate" does not have to be reported under CERCLA section 103(a) or (c) provided it has previously been reported as a "continuous" release under CERCLA section 103(f). The regulations define a continuous release as one that "occurs without interruption or abatement or that is routine, anticipated, and intermittent and incidental to normal operations or treatment processes."[51] Examples of a continuous release could include radon released from a stockpile, benzene released during the production of polymers, or a hazardous substance released from a tank vent each time a tank is filled.[52] The rules include, inter alia, detailed requirements for the initial telephone notification to the NRC, a follow-up written notification within 30 days, an annual notification report, and notifications of changes in the release.

CERCLA Section 111(g)

Another little-understood or discussed aspect of CERCLA is the requirement included in section 111(g) for EPA to promulgate regulations specifying the notice to be provided to potential injured parties by an owner and operator of any vessel, or facility from which a hazardous substance has been released."[53] EPA has not yet proposed or promulgated rules on this topic, arguably exempting parties from needing to comply with such requirements, at least until EPA adopts final rules on the issue. However, the final sentence of section 9611(g) reads: "Until the promulgation

50. 42 U.S.C. § 9603(c).

51. 40 C.F.R. § 302.8.

52. EPA, Reporting Requirements for Continuous Releases of Hazardous Substances; A Guide for Facilities on Compliance 3 (1997), https://www.epa.gov/epcra/reporting-requirements-continuous-releases-hazardous-substances-guide-facilities-compliance.

53. 42 U.S.C. § 9611(g).

of such rules and regulations, the owner and operator of any vessel or facility from which a hazardous substance has been released shall provide reasonable notice to potential injured parties by publication in local newspapers serving the affected area." There are no known instances yet in which an owner or operator has explicitly sought to comply with this provision by means of placing written notice of a release in a local newspaper. Based on the extensive reporting under section 103(a) to the NRC, which in turn must notify the affected governments,[54] and the various steps of the National Contingency Plan, which require the government to publish notice in a "major local newspaper,"[55] the potential affected parties receive the intended notice through multiple press releases, newspaper notices, or other public information or outreach efforts by governmental agencies.[56] This issue has not been litigated in any widely available forum.

Brownfields Act Sections 221 and 222(a)

The Brownfields Amendments of 2002 were enacted in January 2002, creating exemptions from liability under CERCLA to attract prospective purchasers to contaminated properties known as "brownfields." The statute amended CERCLA to make important changes to the "innocent landowner" (IL) defense[57] and to provide the now well-known exemptions from liability for bona fide prospective purchasers[58] (BFPPs) and

---

54. The final sentence of 42 U.S.C. § 9603(a) reads: "The National Response Center shall convey the notification expeditiously to all appropriate Government agencies, including the Governor of any affected State."

55. *See* 40 C.F.R. §§ 300.415(n), 300.425(e), 300.430(c), (f), 300.435(c), 300.815(a), 300.820(a).

56. *But see* Notification Requirements; Reportable Quantity Adjustments, 50 Fed. Reg. 13456, 13464 (Apr. 4, 1985) (a final rule amending the NCP, in which the following response to comment appears under the heading, "Newspaper Notification Requirement:" "One commenter asked whether the RQ notification requirements revoke section 111(g). The newspaper notification requirement established by section 111(g) of CERCLA is not affected by any of the notification requirements in today's rule.").

57. *See* Brownfields Amendments of 2002, *supra* note 4, at § 223 (amending CERCLA § 101(35), 42 U.S.C. § 9601(35)). For the convenience of the reader, all statutory citations will be both to the relevant section of the Brownfields Amendments of 2002 and the section of CERCLA amended by the Brownfields Amendments of 2002.

58. Brownfields Amendments of 2002 § 222, CERCLA § 101(40).

contiguous property owners[59] (CPOs). One of the requirements for exemption for both BFPPs and CPOs is that they provide "all legally required notices with respect to the discovery or release of any hazardous substances at the facility."[60]

Although Congress did not define what it meant by "legally required notices," EPA issued interim guidance on this topic in 2003. This was superseded by final guidance issued in 2019,[61] which announced, among other things, that "[t]he ongoing "legally required notices" obligation ensures that EPA and other appropriate entities are made aware of hazardous substance releases in a timely manner."[62] The 2019 guidance takes a very broad approach, stating that "'[l]egally required notices' may include those required under federal, state, and local laws, and under ICs [institutional controls] and settlement agreements." The guidance identifies the following provisions as examples of "legally required notices" under federal law: CERCLA section 103, notification requirements regarding released substances; EPCRA section 304, emergency notification; and RCRA section 9002, notification provisions for underground storage tanks. The guidance also states that "BFPPs and CPOs have the burden of ascertaining what notices are legally required in a given instance and of complying with those notice requirements." The guidance concludes by stating that "providing legally required notices is an ongoing obligation of any landowner desiring to maintain its status as a BFPP or CPO," and includes language authorizing EPA regional offices to require that BFPPs and CPOs self-certify their compliance with these requirements.

---

59. Brownfields Amendments of 2002 § 221, CERCLA § 107(q).

60. Brownfields Amendments of 2002 § 222, CERCLA § 101(40) (discussing the requirements for qualifying as a bona fide purchaser); Brownfields Amendments of 2002 § 221, CERCLA § 107(q)(1) (discussing the requirements for qualifying as a contiguous landowner).

61. *See* EPA, *Memorandum from the Assistant Administrator for the Office of Enforcement and Compliance Assurance to Regional Counsels and Superfund National Program Manager (July 29, 2019), Enforcement Discretion Guidance Regarding Statutory Criteria for Those Who May Qualify as CERCLA Bona Fide Prospective Purchasers, Contiguous Property Owners, or Innocent Landowners ("Common Elements")*, https://www.epa.gov/sites/production/files/2019-08/documents/common-elements-guide-mem-2019.pdf.

62. *Id.* at 21.

Emergency Planning and Community Right to Know Act (EPCRA) Section 304

EPCRA section 304[63] requires the owner or operator to issue notifications regarding releases of reportable quantities of "extremely hazardous substances." Substances covered by these requirements, as well as the reporting thresholds, are listed at 40 C.F.R. § 355, Appendix A. If no reporting threshold has been set for a substance, the reportable quantity is set by statute at one pound.[64] Because of the substantial overlap in reporting obligations between CERCLA and EPCRA, the regulations include a matrix showing the various parties that must be notified in the event of a release of an extremely hazardous substance (EHS).[65] For example, releases of substances not deemed extremely hazardous but otherwise reportable under CERCLA must also be disclosed to local emergency planning committees (LEPCs) and state emergency response commissions (SERCs).[66] The appointment of the LEPCs is governed by EPCRA section 301(c),[67] which directs each state and local emergency planning commission to designate an official to serve as a coordinator for information received by the LEPCs.

If EPCRA requires that notice of a release be given to a party, whether it is the National Response Center, an LEPC (local fire or police chiefs are often the designees), or a SERC (typically a state's director of emergency response or homeland security), the initial notification must be given immediately.[68] To the extent that it is known at the time of the notice, the notification must specify the following:

- the chemical name and identity of the substance;
- whether the substance is on the list of "extremely hazardous chemicals;"

63. 42 U.S.C. § 11004.
64. *Id.* § 11004(a)(3).
65. 40 C.F.R. § 355.60.
66. EPA maintains on its website a list of the points of contact for each SERC and recommends contacting the applicable SERC to obtain the contact information for the LEPC in a given community; *see* EPA, *State Emergency Response Commissions Contacts*, https://www.epa.gov/epcra/state-emergency-response-commissions-contacts (last updated Apr. 18, 2025).
67. 42 U.S.C. § 11001(c).
68. 40 C.F.R. § 355.40(a).

- an estimate of the quantity released into the environment;
- the time and duration of the release;
- the medium or media into which the release occurred;
- known or anticipated health risks associated with the substance as well as medical advice for exposed individuals;
- proper precautions to take regarding the release; and
- the name and telephone number of the person(s) to be contacted for further information.[69]

As soon as practicable after a release, a party must create a written follow-up report indicating the actions taken to respond to and contain the release, the resulting known or anticipated health risks, and advice regarding medical attention for individuals exposed to the release.[70] Failure to report can result in a civil fine of up to $71,545 per day, or $214,637 per day for a subsequent violation, and imprisonment for up to two years, or five years for a subsequent violation.[71]

Such releases must also be reported on a facility's Annual Toxic Chemical Release Form (Form R) under EPCRA section 313, the Toxics Release Inventory (TRI) program.[72] Of likely significant consequence due to their near-ubiquity in the environment, the 2020 National Defense Authorization Act that was signed into law on December 20, 2019, included a provision that immediately added 160 per- and polyfluoroalkyl substances (PFAS) to the list of TRI chemicals, and requires EPA to bring additional PFAS under TRI reporting requirements if they meet certain designated criteria.[73] New PFAS subject to this reporting obligation have been added annually in each of calendar years 2021

69. 42 U.S.C. § 11004(b)(2); 40 C.F.R. § 355.40(a).

70. 42 U.S.C. § 11004(c); 40 C.F.R. § 355.40(b).

71. 42 U.S.C. § 11045(b)(2), (4); 40 C.F.R. § 19.4, Table 1.

72. 42 U.S.C. § 11023; *see also* Pollution Prevention Act of 1990, 42. U.S.C. §§ 13101 *et seq.* The information that must be reported on the annual Form R includes, among other things, the following for toxic chemicals manufactured, processed, or otherwise used in reportable quantities during the previous year: an estimate of the maximum amount of the chemical present at the facility at any time; for each waste stream, the disposal method and estimated treatment efficiency achieved by that method; and the annual quantity of each toxic chemical entering each environmental medium.

73. Pub. L. No. 116-92 § 7321, amending EPCRA § 313; *see also* EPA, *Addition of Certain PFAS to the TRI by the National Defense Authorization Act*, https://www.epa.gov/toxics-release-inventory-tri-program/list-pfas-added-tri-ndaa (last updated Jan. 17, 2025).

through 2024, bringing some 205 PFAS under this statutory requirement for Reporting Year 2025 (reporting forms due by July 1, 2026).[74] Effective November 30, 2023, EPA designated all PFAS listed on the TRI as chemicals of special concern, and thereby lowered the reporting threshold for all PFAS to 100 pounds per year.[75] EPA has not announced any plans to modify this TRI reporting threshold for PFAS

Clean Water Act (CWA) Section 311(b)(5)

Section 311(b)(5)[76] of the CWA requires parties to report unauthorized discharges of oil or hazardous substances in harmful quantities into the navigable waterways, adjoining shorelines, or waters of the contiguous zone, or discharges affecting natural resources belonging to or under the management of the federal government. For oil, the reportable quantity is any amount that violates applicable water quality standards, causes a sheen on the water, or causes a sludge or emulsion on the water surface or shoreline.[77] The reportable quantity of hazardous substances varies by substance and is set forth at 40 C.F.R. § 117.3.

The person in charge of the vessel or facility must make a report as soon as he or she has knowledge of the discharge and determines that it equals or exceeds the reportable quantity.[78] The report is made to the National Response Center, which in turn notifies the relevant state agencies. The information to be reported is the same as that required under CERCLA section 103(a), as specified in the National Contingency Plan.

Penalties for nonreporting can be as much as $23,647 per violation (up to a maximum of $59,114) or $23,647 per day (up to a maximum of $295,564).[79] Moreover, in the case of oil spills, failure to report can make the liability limits that would apply under the Oil Pollution Act of 1990 inapplicable.[80]

---

74. *See* https://www.epa.gov/toxics-release-inventory-tri-program/addition-certain-pfas-tri-national-defense-authorization-act; *see also* 90 Fed. Reg. 573 (Jan. 6, 2025).
75. 88 Fed. Reg. 74360 (Oct. 31, 2023).
76. 33 U.S.C. § 1321(b)(5).
77. *See* 40 C.F.R. § 110.
78. 33 U.S.C. § 1321(b)(5).
79. *Id.* § 1321(b)(6), (7); 40 C.F.R. § 19.4, Table 1.
80. 33 U.S.C. § 2704(c)(2)(A).

Resource Conservation and Recovery Act (RCRA)

RCRA contains a variety of reporting requirements. A leak from a hazardous waste tank system or secondary containment at a hazardous waste treatment, storage, or disposal facility (TSDF) must be reported to the EPA Regional Administrator by the tank owner or operator within 24 hours of discovery.[81] The report should include the following:

- The generator's name and address;
- The facility's EPA identification number, if applicable;
- The date, time, and type of incident;
- The quantity of hazardous waste released;
- The extent of any injuries; and
- The quantity and disposition of any materials recovered from the spill.[82]

Under 40 C.F.R. § 264.56,[83] the emergency coordinator designated by the owner or operator of a TSDF is required to report a release, fire, or explosion that could threaten human health or the environment outside of the facility in question. The report must be made to the National Response Center or the local government official designated as the on-scene coordinator for the affected area. It must also include the following:

- The name and telephone number of the person making the report;
- The name and address of the facility;
- The time and type of incident;
- The name and quantity of material(s), to the extent known;
- The extent of injuries, if any; and
- The possible hazards to human health or the environment outside of the facility.

Failure to file a report required under RCRA is punishable by fines of up to $124,426 per day.[84]

---

81. *See* 40 C.F.R. §§ 264.196(d)(1), 265.196(d)(1) (report a leaking tank system or secondary containment system with 24 hours of detection; provide a follow-up report to the EPA Regional Administrator within 30 days of detection, *see* 40 C.F.R. §§ 264.196(d)(3), 265.196(d)(3)).
82. 40 C.F.R. §§ 264.196(d), 265.196(d); *see also* 40 C.F.R. § 302.6.
83. *See* C.F.R. §§ 264.56(d)(2), 265.56(d)(2).
84. 42 U.S.C. § 6928(a)(3); 40 C.F.R. § 19.4, Table 1.

Underground storage tank (UST) leaks of regulated substances other than hazardous waste—such as petroleum products like gasoline and heating oil—must be reported by owners or operators within 24 hours of discovery or during any other period required by the relevant state agency. The content of the report is not specified under federal regulations but will typically be governed by state provisions. The owner or operator must take immediate action to prevent further releases (including removing the substance from the UST, thoroughly inspecting the tank, and monitoring) and must act promptly to remediate any contamination from the spill. Follow-up reports are also required.[85]

Toxic Substances Control Act (TSCA)

An emergency incident reporting requirement under TSCA was first created in a 1978 EPA enforcement policy statement. It was later suspended in 1991 and then reinstated in 2003 for various reasons, including that "[a]lthough many release incidents are covered under other statutes, there may be instances where chemicals that have not yet been reviewed for release reporting under other EPA programs have the requisite hazard characteristics to require a response/notification if there is a release to the environment."[86] The policy requires parties to report within 30 days "emergency incidents of environmental contamination" that "because of the pattern, extent, and amount of contamination (1) seriously threatens humans with cancer, birth defects, mutation, death, or serious or prolonged incapacitation or (2) seriously threatens non-human organisms with large-scale or ecologically significant population destruction[.]"[87]

This TSCA-based policy does not have the force of regulation, and for the most part has been superseded by more recent and comprehensive reporting requirements under CERCLA, EPCRA, RCRA, and the CWA. Moreover, because no report must be made under TSCA if the EPA has this information from another source,[88] it is of limited applicability today.

85. 40 C.F.R. § 280.62(b).

86. *See* 43 Fed. Reg. 11,110 (1978); 56 Fed. Reg. 28,458 (1991); 68 Fed. Reg. 33,129, 33,135 (2003).

87. 68 Fed. Reg. 33129, 33138 (June 3, 2003).

88. 68 Fed. Reg. 33129, 33139 (2003).

TSCA's reporting requirements for polychlorinated biphenyls (PCBs) are considerably more important. As a general matter, the PCB spill reporting obligation applies to a release of more than one pound of material containing more than 50 parts per million (ppm) of PCBs.[89] Untested mineral oil is presumed to contain more than 50 ppm of PCBs.[90] To be reportable, the release must have directly contaminated surface water, sewers, drinking water supplies, animal grazing lands, or vegetable gardens.[91]

Spills meeting these criteria must be reported by the responsible party (such as the owner, facility manager, or foreperson)[92] as soon as possible and, in any event, within 24 hours of discovery.[93] Notification must be made to the National Response Center and the EPA Regional Office's branch of the Office of Pesticides and Toxic Substances.[94] Although there are very few remaining in service today, if a fire occurs in an electrical transformer containing PCBs, it must be reported immediately by the owner to the National Response Center.[95]

Clean Air Act (CAA)

Pursuant to regulations promulgated by the Chemical Safety and Hazard Investigation Board (CSB) in February 2020, accidental releases of certain air pollutants into the ambient air and the air inside a stationary source must be reported to the CSB.[96] The CSB reporting rules must be understood in the broader context of section 112(r) of the Clean Air Act, which imposes substantial requirements on certain facilities to develop and implement Risk Management Plans (RMPs) for the prevention of

89. 40 C.F.R. § 761.125(a).
90. *Id.* § 761.123 (defining a spill).
91. *Id.* § 761.125(a)(1)(i), (ii).
92. *Id.* § 761.123 (defining responsible party).
93. *Id.* § 761.125(c)(1).
94. *Id.* § 761.125(c)(1)(i).
95. *Id.* § 761.30(a)(1)(xi).
96. *Id.* pt. 1604; 85 Fed. Reg. 10074 (Feb. 20, 2020). The Clean Air Act imposes a "general duty" on the owners and operators of stationary sources that produce, process, handle, or store various substances, in the same manner as required under the Occupational Safety and Health Act, *see* 29 U.S.C. § 654, to prevent and minimize the risks associated with accidental releases of those substances. *See* 42 U.S.C. §§ 7412(r)(1), (r)(6)(C)(iii). The CSB is required to "establish by regulation requirements binding on persons for reporting of accidental releases into the ambient air subject to the Board's investigatory jurisdiction."

accidental releases. RMPs should include detailed regulations and extensive guidance documents that cover practically everything, including providing notice of releases to LEPCs.[97]

The CSB's new reporting obligations apply to an accidental release from any "stationary source" that causes a death or inpatient hospitalization, or property damage (including damage, destruction or loss of use of tangible public or private property) at or outside the stationary source exceeding $1 million.[98] An accidental release is "an unanticipated emission of a regulated substance or other extremely hazardous substance into the ambient air from a stationary source."[99] For purposes of the rule, a stationary source includes "any buildings, structures, equipment, installations, or substance-emitting stationary activities which belong to the same industrial group, which are located on one or more contiguous properties, which are under the control of the same person (or person under common control), and from which an accidental release may occur."[100] Notably, this definition differs from that of a stationary source under the Clean Air Act generally, which includes "any building, structure, facility, or installation which emits or may emit any air pollutant."[101]

The owner or operator must submit a report to the CSB within eight hours of the accidental release, or alternatively may submit the NRC identification number to the CSB within 30 minutes of having reported the matter to the National Response Center within four hours of the release.[102] If there are multiple owners or operators, they may agree among themselves to file a single, consolidated report on behalf of one or more of the parties.[103] The report to the CSB must include:

- The name and contact information for the owner/operator and the person making the report;
- The location information and facility identifier;
- The approximate time and a brief description of the release;

97. *See* 40 C.F.R. pt. 68 (Chemical Accident Prevention Provisions).
98. 40 C.F.R. § 1604.3(a).
99. *Id.* § 1604.2 (defining an "accidental release").
100. *Id.* (defining a "stationary source").
101. 42 U.S.C. § 7411(a)(3).
102. 40 C.F.R. § 1604.3(b), (c).
103. *Id.* § 1604.3(d).

- An indication of whether there has been a fire, explosion, death, serious injury, or property damage;
- The name(s) and Chemical Abstract Number(s) of the material(s) released;
- If known, the amount released, number of fatalities, and number of serious injuries;
- Estimated property damage at or outside the stationary source;
- Whether the release resulted in an evacuation order impacting the general public or others, including the number evacuees, approximate radius of the evacuation zone; and
- The type of persons subject to the order (employees, general public, or both).[104]

The CSB will report potential violations of these reporting obligations to the EPA for appropriate enforcement action, which may include administrative penalties or civil or criminal actions.[105]

Nuclear and Radiological Materials

Releases by licensees of the Nuclear Regulatory Commission at facilities handling byproduct, source, or special nuclear materials must make immediate reports to the Nuclear Regulatory Commission of any releases that meet thresholds specified in 10 C.F.R. § 20.2022, and follow-up written reports within 30 days thereafter pursuant to 10 C.F.R. § 20.2023. Releases of certain radionuclides are also reportable pursuant to CERCLA section 103. Additionally, under regulations promulgated by the Department of Transportation (DOT), a telephone report must be made to the National Response Center (800-424-8802 or 202-267-2675) whenever during the transportation in commerce (including loading, unloading, and temporary storage) of radioactive materials, either (1) fire, breakage, spillage, or suspected radioactive contamination occurs, or (2) if, as a direct result of the radioactive material: a person is killed or hospitalized; the general public is evacuated for one hour or more; a major transportation artery or facility is closed or shut down for one hour or more; or, the operational flight pattern or routine of an aircraft

104. *Id.* § 1604.4.
105. *Id.* § 1604.5.

is altered.[106] This must be done within 12 hours of the incident by each person in physical possession of the radioactive material,[107] and each such person must also submit to DOT a Hazardous Materials Incident Report on DOT Form F 5800.1 (01/2004) within 30 days of discovery of the incident.[108]

Infectious Substances

Under regulations promulgated by the Department of Transportation (DOT), a telephone report must be made to the National Response Center (800-424-8802 or 202-267-2675) whenever during the transportation in commerce (including loading, unloading, and temporary storage) of an infectious substance, either (1) fire, breakage, spillage, or suspected contamination occurs involving an infectious substance other than a regulated medical waste occurs, or (2) if, as a direct result of the infectious substance other than a regulated medical waste: a person is killed or hospitalized; the general public is evacuated for one hour or more; a major transportation artery or facility is closed or shut down for one hour or more; or, the operational flight pattern or routine of an aircraft is altered.[109] The telephone report must be made within 12 hours of the incident by each person in physical possession of the infectious substance,[110] and each such person must also submit to DOT a Hazardous Materials Incident Report on DOT Form F 5800.1 (01/2004) within 30 days of discovery of the incident.[111]

Notifications are also required for releases of certain biological agents and toxins that have the potential to pose a severe threat to human, animal, and plant health, or to animal and plant products. Specifically, the Public Health Security and Bioterrorism Preparedness and Response Act of 2002[112] includes as Title II, Subtitle B, the Agricultural Bioterrorism

106. 49 C.F.R. § 171.15(a), (b)(1).

107. *Id.* § 171.15(a), (b)(2); *see also id.* § 176.48 (relating to radioactive contamination on vessels).

108. *Id.* §§ 171.15(c) and 171.16.

109. *Id.* § 171.15(a), (b)(1), (3).

110. *Id.* § 171.15(a), (b)(3).

111. *Id.* §§ 171.15(c) and 171.16.

112. 6A U.S.C. §§ 201 *et seq.* (PL 107-188).

Protection Act of 2002,[113] which governs facilities registered with the Centers for Disease Control and Prevention (CDC) to possess, use, or transfer a list of select biological agents or toxins.[114] There is also a list of overlap select agents and toxins that are subject to regulation by both the CDC and the Animal and Plant Health Inspection Service (APHIS) of the U.S. Department of Agriculture (USDA).[115] The CDC and APHIS regulations require each registered individual or entity to develop and implement a written incident response plan that includes planning and coordination with local emergency responders, as well as procedures for notifying federal, state, or local law enforcement agencies of specified suspicious activities.[116] Moreover, a registered individual or entity must immediately notify CDC or APHIS upon discovery of the theft or loss of a select agent or toxin, or the release of a select agent or toxin causing occupational exposure or outside of the primary barrier of the biocontainment area, and must also submit a completed APHIS/CEDC form within seven calendar days.[117]

State Law Reporting Requirements

A wide variety of state statutes and regulations govern disclosure obligations for environmental contamination. Typically, these statutes mirror federal requirements for reporting releases of hazardous substances or materials, pollutants or contaminants, as well as discharges from USTs. The principal variations among state requirements are in what quantities are reportable, how and to whom to make the report, what the report should contain, and follow-up requirements. Some states, however, may require reporting releases that are not regulated at the federal level. In most instances, parties will first report a release by calling 911 or some other local or state-level emergency response number to notify the local emergency or first responders (e.g., fire and police). While these central services may subsequently notify state-level personnel, it is prudent for a party to independently make those additional reports.

113. 7 U.S.C. §§ 8401 *et seq.*
114. 42 C.F.R. § 73.3.
115. *Id.* § 73.4.
116. 9 C.F.R. § 121.14(e), (f) and 7 C.F.R. § 331.14(e), (f).
117. 9 C.F.R. § 121.19 and 7 C.F.R. § 331.19.

Because state reporting requirements are neither superseded nor preempted by federal requirements, knowledge of state statutory or regulatory reporting schemes is essential for full compliance in this area. Moreover, there are many potential traps for the unwary. For example, under New Hampshire law, "*any person* who becomes aware of an oil discharge" is obligated to immediately report it to the state regulators.[118] The implementing regulations identify five conditions that, if all are met, would obviate the reporting requirement, which mandates immediate notification (i.e., "as soon as practical but within one hour") to the state's environmental agency.[119] However, those conditions effectively place any person who has knowledge of a discharge of oil into the environment (and not just the party responsible for the oil facility, carrier, or vessel that discharged the oil) in the unenviable position of having to determine if, for example, the discharge was less than 25 gallons and has had no impact or potential impact to groundwater or surface water. Thus, in New Hampshire, attorneys, environmental consultants, and even innocent bystanders must report an oil discharge that has not already been reported if they become aware of such a discharge through discussions with other parties involved in a site or release incident, review of an environmental site assessment or other technical report, or a site visit. While the statute does not impose any legal liability on such a person for failing to report (as it does for the "person responsible" for the facility), it raises serious ethical concerns for any person who finds themself in this situation. This may be an outlier among the laws of the various states, but it highlights the importance of paying close attention to the statutory and regulatory reporting obligations in each state in which a release occurs, as well as those in any neighboring states that may be affected by the release. Fortunately, most state environmental agencies have posted information about their respective reporting obligations on their websites, and 911 services are often able to assist parties in identifying additional parties that should be notified of an incident.

118. New Hampshire R.S.A. 146-A:5, ii ("Any person who becomes aware of an oil discharge in violation of this chapter shall immediately notify the department of environmental services.") (emphasis added).

119. NH Code of Admin. Rules Env-Or 604.06.

Conclusion

In summary, making all the necessary initial and follow-up reports of a release of hazardous substances or materials, or other pollutants, contaminants, radionuclides, or infectious substances, is an essential first step and ongoing component in the overall incident response process. The sooner an incident is reported and appropriate response measures are implemented, the greater the likelihood that the harms can be minimized and more significant risks, dangers, and liabilities averted. Individuals, organizations, and entities that routinely handle hazardous, infectious, or radioactive substances or materials will usually be well prepared for releases, spills, or other disasters and will have incident response plans that they exercise routinely and that include detailed guidance on reporting requirements. However, in the absence of any such training or written plans, a call to 911 is always a prudent first step in providing notification of a newly discovered release.

Chapter 4

FEMA Response and Recovery

Jordan Wimpy

Introduction

The Federal Emergency Management Agency, or FEMA, was created on April 1, 1979, when President Jimmy Carter signed Executive Order 12127.[1] Though the executive order delegated to FEMA some limited duties previously implemented by the Department of Commerce, nearly a decade passed before Congress actually established explicit authority for FEMA's current emergency and disaster response missions with enactment of the Robert T. Stafford Disaster Relief and Emergency Assistance Act (Stafford Act).[2] The purpose of FEMA's new authority was to facilitate and expedite "the rendering of aid, assistance, and emergency services, and the reconstruction and rehabilitation of devastated areas."[3]

Under the Stafford Act, FEMA's charge is to "to provide an orderly and continuing means of assistance by the Federal Government to State and local governments in carrying out their responsibilities to alleviate the suffering and damage which result from disasters."[4] FEMA staff of more than 20,000 employees implements this mission from the agency's

1. Executive Order No. 12,127, 3 C.F.R. 376 (1979), https://irp.fas.org/offdocs/eo/eo-12127.htm.

2. Stafford Act, Pub. L. No. 93-288 *as amended* 42 U.S.C. §§ 1521–5208.

3. 42 U.S.C. § 5121(a).

4. *Id.* § 5121(b).

headquarters in Washington, D.C., ten regional offices located across the county, and local offices established in disaster-impacted areas.[5] This chapter takes a high-level look at FEMA's response and recovery processes and programs and briefly discusses the intertwined hazard mitigation programs.

FEMA response and recovery assistance can be understood as one part federal *coordination* and one part federal *resources.* The combination of the two is dependent on the circumstances of each declared "emergency" or "major disaster." An emergency means "any occasion or instance for which . . . Federal assistance is needed to supplement State and local efforts and capabilities to save lives and to protect property and public health and safety, or to lessen or avert the threat of a catastrophe in any part of the United States."[6] The President issues emergency declarations under section 501 of the Stafford Act. A major disaster is:

> Any natural catastrophe (including any hurricane, tornado, storm, high water, winddriven water, tidal wave, tsunami, earthquake, volcanic eruption, landslide, mudslide, snowstorm, or drought), or, regardless of cause, any fire, flood, or explosion, in any part of the United States, which . . . causes damage of sufficient severity and magnitude to warrant major disaster assistance . . . to supplement the efforts and available resources of States, local governments, and disaster relief organizations in alleviating the damage, loss, hardship, or suffering caused thereby.[7]

The President issues a major disaster declaration under section 401 of the Stafford Act. The statute also authorizes presidential declarations for Fire Management Assistance Grants under section 420.[8] The remainder of this chapter will focus on emergency and major disaster declarations.

5. FEMA, *About Us*, https://www.fema.gov/about (last visited Dec. 2, 2024).

6. *Id.* § 5122(1); *see also* 44 C.F.R. § 206.35.

7. *Id.* § 5122(2); *see also* 44 C.F.R. § 206.36.

8. 42 U.S.C. § 5187 (providing "assistance, including grants, equipment, supplies, and personnel to any State or local government for the mitigation, management, and control of any fire on public or private forest land or grassland that threatens such destruction as would constitute a major disaster").

In addition to its statutory authority and its implementing regulations, FEMA's coordination in both phases is enabled by two key framework documents: the *National Response Framework* (NRF)[9] and the *National Disaster Recovery Framework* (NDRF).[10] Frameworks like the NDRF "establish a common platform and forum for how the whole community builds, sustains, and *coordinates delivery of recovery capabilities*."[11] Though outlined in these different frameworks and discussed as different phases, FEMA describes the response and recovery phases as a spectrum or continuum of coordinated activities. In simple terms, the phases include pre-disaster preparedness, immediate response activities and planning that occurs over the days and weeks just after a disaster, and post-disaster recovery and rebuilding spanning months and years. The continuum demonstrates "how recovery efforts begin alongside response activities, and gradually scale up during response operations."[12] Mitigation and planning toward resilience are a thru line strategy spanning FEMA's continuum.[13]

Federal assistance resources available through FEMA under a Stafford Act declaration typically include some mix of public assistance (PA)[14] for the affected state, local, territorial, or tribal governments and certain private nonprofit organizations; individual assistance (IA)[15] for affected individuals and households; and hazard mitigation (HM)[16] to support mitigation and resiliency programs to protect against future disasters. The range and amount of financial assistance available for disbursement by FEMA depends on the type of declaration and, as rumor and reporting

---

9. U.S. Department of Homeland Security (DHS), *National Response Framework*, 4th ed. (Oct. 28, 2019), https://www.fema.gov/sites/default/files/documents/NRF_FINALApproved_2011028.pdf [hereinafter NRF].

10. DHS, National Disaster Recovery Framework (3d ed., Dec. 10, 2024), https://www.fema.gov/sites/default/files/documents/fema_national-disaster-recovery-framework-third-edition_2024.pdf (hereinafter NDRF).

11. *Id.* at i (emphasis added).

12. *Id.* at 3, Fig. 2.

13. *Id.*

14. 42 U.S.C. §§ 5170a, 5170b, 5173, 5185, 5186, 5192.

15. *Id.* § 5174.

16. *Id.* § 5170c.

on recent disasters demonstrates,[17] the amount of money appropriated to FEMA's Disaster Relief Fund.[18]

Background

Before detailing FEMA's various programs and processes for disaster response and recovery, it is useful to step back and observe, briefly, the general framework for the nation's emergency and major disaster response efforts.

For most of its history, and continuing through to today, emergency response in the United States has been a local effort. Local responders inherently include the survivors, first responders, search and rescue, community leaders, and elected officials in the impacted community.[19] Many, and perhaps even most, incidents can be managed directly and locally.[20] When the capacity of local resources is exhausted or overwhelmed, local leaders by and large look first to relevant state, territorial, or tribal governments to supplement the local resources.[21] Local governments may also look to nongovernmental voluntary organizations or governments in adjacent or nearby jurisdictions through "mutual aid agreements" that provide the "terms under which one party provides resources—personnel, teams, facilities, equipment, and supplies—to another party."[22] FEMA's federal support is the last resort. And, though it brings experience,

---

17. Stephen Fowler, *Fact-Checking Falsehoods About FEMA Funding and Hurricane Helene*, NPR (Oct. 7, 2024, 6:47 p.m.), https://www.npr.org/2024/10/07/nx-s1-5144159/fema-funding-migrants-disaster-relief-fund.

18. The DRF is an appropriate allowing FEMA to direct, coordinate, manage, and fund response and recovery efforts consistent with the Stafford Act. The most recent DRF appropriation was set forth in the Fiscal Year 2025 Continuing Appropriations and Extensions Act, Pub. L. No. 118-83, which extended the FY Department of Homeland Security Appropriations Act (Pub. L. No. 118-47). Pursuant to DRF authorities, FEMA publishes monthly reports with information on the DRF, then-available funds, and future projected funding needs. *See* FEMA, *Disaster Relief Fund: Monthly Reports*, https://www.fema.gov/about/reports-and-data/disaster-relief-fund-monthly-reports (last updated Jan. 14, 2025).

19. NRF, *supra* note 9, at 6.

20. *Id.* at 12.

21. *Id.* at 30–31.

22. FEMA, National Incident Management System Guideline for Mutual Aid 1 (Nov. 2017), https://www.fema.gov/sites/default/files/2020-07/fema_nims_mutual_aid_guideline_20171105.pdf.

coordinating efficiency, and significant federal assistance to bear, FEMA's participation in emergency and major disaster response remains focused on supporting, supplementing, and standing up local response and recovery operations.[23]

Thus, the federal government's leadership on recovery and response is exercised only in the most significant circumstances. Even then, the federal response is nearly always in support of local and state, territorial, and tribal efforts. The Stafford Act does allow that certain emergencies may invoke primary responsibility from the federal government. These would include emergencies that involve "a subject area for which, under the Constitution or laws of the United States, the United States exercises exclusive or preeminent responsibility and authority."[24] But, in general, FEMA is a supporting and supplementing entity.

Presidential Declaration

FEMA engagement in either the response or recovery phase of an "emergency" or "major disaster" first requires a presidential declaration of such event pursuant to the Stafford Act. Congress drafted the Stafford Act with plain language stating the authority for the declarations lies solely with the executive branch. As defined, both types of incident declaration rely on "the determination of the President."[25]

A presidential declaration under the Stafford Act requires first a formal request from an impacted state, territorial, or tribal government where the "incident" will or did occur.[26] The request must come from the state's governor or the chief executive of the affected tribal government. It must inform the President that the "situation is of such severity and

23. 42 U.S.C. § 5122(2) (defining "major disaster" and noting the presidential declaration is made only when determined necessary "to *supplement* the efforts and available resources of States, local governments, and disaster relief organizations") (emphasis added).

24. *Id.* § 5191(b); *see also* NRF, *supra* note 9, at 34 (noting "the Federal Government may play a leading role in response where the Federal government has primary jurisdiction or when incidents occur on federal property (e.g., national parks and miliary bases)").

25. 42 U.S.C. § 5122(1), (2).

26. 44 C.F.R. § 206.32(e) defines an "incident" as "[a]ny condition which meets the definition of major disaster or emergency as set forth in § 206.2 which cause damage or hardship that may result in a Presidential declaration of a major disaster or emergency."

magnitude that effective response is beyond the capabilities of the State or affected local governments" and, therefore, the resources of the federal government are necessary to support and supplement local efforts.[27] As a prerequisite for either declaration, the governor or chief executive must "take appropriate response action under State law and direct the execution of the State's emergency plan."[28] As to form and substance, the request must provide certain general information:

- For an emergency, the governor or chief executive must furnish information "describing the State and local efforts and resources which have been or will be used to alleviate the emergency" and "define the type and extent of Federal aid required."[29]
- For a major disaster, the governor or chief executive must furnish information "on the nature and amount of State and local resources which have been or will be committed to alleviating the results of the disaster" and certify that "State and local government obligations and expenditures (of which State commitments must be a significant portion) will comply with all applicable cost-sharing requirements" of the Stafford Act.[30]

Taken together, the state must demonstrate the incident exceeds its capability to respond. The state must also define the type of assistance (e.g., PA, IA) needed to properly respond to save lives and property.[31] Finally, FEMA's deliberative review process also requires parties to submit specific information—for example, the amount and severity of damages—along with the details and discussion of the affected area and population.[32]

Preliminary Damage Assessments

The detailed information is developed and collected through a Preliminary Damage Assessment (PDA) process, which is required for a

27. 42 U.S.C. § 5170 (major disaster); *id.* § 5191 (emergency).
28. *Id.* §§ 5170(a), 5191(a).
29. *Id.* § 5191(a).
30. *Id.* § 5170(a).
31. 44 C.F.R. §§ 206.35, 206.36, 206.40(a).
32. *Id.* §§ 206.35, 206.36, 206.40(a) (providing list(s) and description(s) of information to supplement a request for Presidential declaration).

presidential declaration under the Stafford Act. The PDA process works "to determine the impact and magnitude of damage and the resulting unmet needs of individuals, businesses, the public sector, and the community as a whole."[33] Notably, the initial PDA process requirements may be waived for "incidents of unusual severity and magnitude" that "do not require field damage assessments to determine the need for supplemental federal assistance."[34] Even in those circumstances, however, the expedited federal assistance is limited in nature and extent, and parties are still obligated to compile and submit PDA information to document what long-term federal resources will be necessary to recover. This process may trigger a reconciliation of the initial damage findings.[35]

FEMA developed a guide detailing the damage assessment information required by legal authorities.[36] Impacted local, state, territorial, or tribal governments may seek a Joint PDA with FEMA when the incident itself overwhelms the government's ability to complete even the assessment. When requesting a Joint PDA, the impacted government first prepares and verifies a pre-assessment slate of information.[37] If the incident requires federal action, the Joint PDA "team" will be formed and will include at least one state, territorial, or tribal official; at least one federal official (most often from the relevant FEMA regional office); and one local official who knows the area impacted by the incident.[38] Other state and federal agencies or relevant local relief organizations may also be invited to join the team.[39] The state representative is responsible for coordinating the schedule and requirements of the state and local participation in the Joint PDA process.[40] FEMA, for its part, "will brief team members on damage criteria, the kind of information to be collected for the particular incident, and reporting requirements."[41]

---

33. *Id.* § 206.33.
34. *Id.* § 206.33(d); *see also id.* § 206.36(d).
35. *Id.* § 206.33.
36. FEMA, FEMA Preliminary Damage Assessment Guide (Aug. 2021), https://www.fema.gov/sites/default/files/documents/fema_2021-pda-guide.pdf.
37. 44 C.F.R. § 206.33(a).
38. *Id.* § 206.33(b).
39. *Id.*
40. *Id.*
41. *Id.*

Once the Joint PDA team completes the PDA, including reconciling any differences from the preliminary assessment,[42] the governor or chief executive may proceed with submitting the declaration request.

Submission and Review

Federal regulations specify the deadlines, time frame, and process for submitting the declaration request. For both incident types, emergency and major disaster, the request is submitted to the President through the appropriate FEMA Regional Administrator "to ensure prompt acknowledgement and processing."[43] The deadline and time frame differ depending on the type of declaration. For an emergency declaration, the request "must be submitted within 5 days after the need for assistance under title V becomes apparent, but no longer than 30 days after the occurrence of the incident, in order to be considered."[44] A major disaster declaration request "must be submitted within 30 days of the occurrence of the incident in order to be considered."[45] The 30-day deadline for submission of a request for major disaster is strictly enforced.[46] Both deadlines may be extended when a request to extend is properly and timely submitted.

Upon submission, FEMA evaluates a series of enumerated regulatory factors to make recommended determinations about the need for the presidential declaration and federal involvement. For public assistance (PA) FEMA evaluates the following:

- Estimated cost of assistance
- Localized impacts
- Insurance coverage in force
- Hazard mitigation
- Recent disaster history
- Programs of other federal agencies[47]

42. *Id.* § 206.33(c).
43. *Id.* § 206.35(a) (emergency); *see also id.* § 206.36(a) (major disaster).
44. *Id.* § 206.35(a).
45. *Id.* § 206.36(a).
46. *See* State of Kan. *ex rel.* v. U.S., 751 F. Supp. 1495 (D. Kan. 1990) (affirming validity of 30-day deadline to submit).
47. 44 C.F.R. § 206.48(a)(1)–(6).

When evaluating the need for supplemental support for individuals and households (IA), FEMA looks to the following factors:

- State fiscal capacity
  - Total taxable resources
  - Gross domestic product
  - Per capital personal income by local area[48]
- State resource capacity
  - State, tribal, and local government; nongovernmental organizations (NGO); and Private Sector Activity
  - Cumulative effect of recent disasters
- Uninsured home and personal property losses
  - The cause of damage
  - The jurisdictions impacted and concentration of damage
  - The number of homes impacted and degree of damage
  - The estimated cost of assistance
  - The homeownership rate of impacted homes
  - The percentage of affected households with sufficient insurance coverage appropriate to the peril
  - Other relevant preliminary damage assessment data[49]
- Disaster impacted population profile
  - The percentage of the population determined to be living in poverty status
  - The percentage of the population already receiving government assistance such as Supplemental Security Income and Supplemental Nutrition Assistance Program benefits
  - The pre-disaster unemployment rate
  - The percentage of the population 65 years old and older
  - The percentage of the population 18 years old and younger
  - The percentage of the population with a disability
  - The percentage of the population who speak a language other than English and speak English less than "very well"

---

48. *Id.* § 206.48(b)(1).
49. *Id.* § 206.48(b)(2).

    - Any unique considerations regarding American Indian and Alaskan Native Tribal populations raised in the state's request for a major disaster declaration that may not be reflected in the other data points required by FEMA rules[50]
- Impact to community infrastructure
    - Life-saving and life sustaining services
    - Essential community services
    - Transformation infrastructure and utilities[51]
- Casualties[52]
- Disaster-related unemployment.[53]

The full list of review factors is included here to illustrate and emphasize the volume of detailed information the Joint PDA team must assemble to meet FEMA's review requirements.

With the necessary information in hand and the relevant factors considered, the FEMA Regional Administrator will "promptly prepare a summary of the PDA findings."[54] "The data is analyzed and submitted with a recommendation to the Assistant Administrator for the Disaster Assistance Directorate" at the conclusion of its review.[55] The recommendation is provided to the President along with the governor or chief executive's request. Consistent with the Stafford Act, the President's review will result in a presidential declaration of an "emergency" or "major disaster," or denial.[56]

50. *Id.* § 206.48(b)(3).
51. *Id.* § 206.48(b)(4).
52. *Id.* § 206.48(b)(5).
53. *Id.* § 206.48(b)(6).
54. *Id.* § 206.37(b).
55. *Id.* § 206.37(c); *see also* Update to FEMA's Public Assistance Regulations, 89 Federal Register 54,966 (proposed July 2, 2024) (proposing updated references to FEMA positions and offices including replacing "Disaster Assistance Directorate with "Recovery Directorate") (to be codified at 40 C.F.R. pt. 206).
56. *Id.* § 206.38; *see also id.* § 206.46(a) (providing for the governor or chief executive's right of appeal directly to the President and spelling out the necessary timeline and requirements).

Declaration Approved: The Coordination of Resources

The process of federal coordination begins immediately after the President issues an emergency or major disaster declaration, commencing with FEMA notifying the governor or chief executive, as well as other federal agencies and/or interested parties of the declaration.[57] FEMA's first substantive step is to "determine and designate the types of assistance to be made available," based in part on the governor or chief executive's request.[58] At the same time, FEMA, through the Assistant Administrator for the Disaster Assistance Directorate, will "designate the affected areas eligible for supplementary Federal assistance under the Stafford Act."[59] An "affected area designated by the Assistant Administrator for the Disaster Assistance Directorate includes all local government jurisdictions within its boundaries."[60] Operationally, the Administrator, or designee, will appoint necessary disaster officials:

- Federal Coordinating Officer (FCO). The FCO shall initiate action immediately to ensure that federal assistance is provided in accordance with the declaration, applicable laws, regulations, and the FEMA-State Agreement.[61]
- Federal Disaster Recovery Coordinator (FDRC). The FDRC are the primary field leaders responsible for facilitating disaster recovery coordination and collaboration between federal, state, territorial, and local governments.[62]
- State Disaster Recovery Coordinator (SDRC) (previously referred to as the State Coordinating Officer, or SCO). The SDRC works closely with state and local officials to communicate local recovery priorities and resources to federal officials.[63]

---

57. *Id.* § 206.39.
58. *Id.* § 206.40(a).
59. *Id.* § 206.40(b).
60. *Id.*
61. *Id.* § 206.41(a); *see also* NDRF, *supra* note 10, at 6.
62. NDRF, *supra* note 10, at 6.
63. 44 C.F.R. app. C-4.

- Governor's Authorized Representative (GAR). The GAR shall administer federal disaster assistance programs on behalf of the state and local governments and other grant or loan recipients. The GAR is responsible for the state compliance with the FEMA-State Agreement.[64]

Once appointed, the FCO takes the helm in "mak[ing] an initial appraisal of the types of assistance most urgently needed."[65] The FCO works with the SDRC in "establishing field offices and Disaster Application Centers . . . to coordinate and monitor assistance programs, disseminate information, accept application, and counsel individuals, families and business concerning available assistance."[66] When the initial appraisal and setup are complete, the FCO implements two key coordination functions: (1) "[c]oordinate the administration of relief" that includes "activities of State and local governments, activities of Federal agencies[,]" and relief organizations such as the American Red Cross and Salvation Army;[67] and (2) take action to "make certain that all of the Federal agencies are carrying out their appropriate disaster assistance roles under their own legislative authorities and operational policies[.]"[68]

The FCO, in carrying out its obligations, "may activate [and deploy] emergency support teams, composed of Federal program and support personnel" into the affected area.[69] The teams "assist the FCO in carrying out his/her responsibilities."[70] At the state level, the SDRC operates as the "principal point of contact regarding coordination of State and local disaster relief activities and implementation of the State emergency plan."[71]

In order to document the assistance and the consideration and obligations of the various parties, the "understandings, commitments, and conditions for assistance under which FEMA disaster assistance [is] provided" are outlined in a FEMA-State Agreement (or FEMA-Tribal

64. *Id.* § 206.41(d).
65. *Id.* § 206.42(a)(1).
66. *Id.* § 206.42(a)(2).
67. *Id.* § 206.42(a)(3).
68. *Id.* § 206.42(a)(4).
69. *Id.* § 206.43.
70. *Id.*
71. *Id.* § 206.42(b).

Agreement).[72] Execution of the FEMA-State Agreement is required after a presidential declaration.[73] In fact, FEMA funding will not be authorized—with the exception of essential emergency services or housing assistance—until the FEMA-State Agreement is in place.[74] The provisions of the agreement are "binding obligations on FEMA, States, their local governments and private nonprofit organizations" and remain, therefore, legally enforceable.[75] For these reasons, the FEMA-State Agreement is the keystone document:

> describ[ing] the incident and the incident period for which assistance will be made available, the type and extent of the Federal assistance to be made available, and contain[ing] the commitment of the State and local government(s) with respect to the amount of funds to be expended in alleviating damage and suffering by the major disaster or emergency.[76]

The NRF further describes the coordination process and explains implementation of the coordination process. The NRF, now in its fourth edition, relies on the federal Emergency Support Function (ESF) "coordinating structure, to help mitigate the impact of catastrophic incidents on community lifelines."[77] A community lifeline "enables the continuous operation of critical government and business functions and is essential to human health and safety or economic security."[78] FEMA's NRF identifies seven community lifelines: safety and security; food, water, shelter; health and medical; energy (power and fuel); communications; transportation; and hazardous material.[79] The NRF makes "[s]tabilizing community lifelines [] the primary effort during response" in order to "lessen threats and hazards to public health and safety, the economy, and security."[80] The ESFs, which now number 15, operate as "groups of organizations that

72. *Id.* § 206.44(a).
73. *Id.*
74. *Id.*
75. *Id.*
76. *Id.* § 206.44(b).
77. NRF, *supra* note 9, at 3.
78. *Id.* at 8.
79. *Id.*
80. *Id.* at Table 1.

work together to deliver core capabilities to stabilize [the] community lifelines in support of an effective response."[81]

The NRF includes the following example of the ESF coordination structure to stand up and stabilize the health and medical lifeline during incident response operations:

ESF	Example of Supporting Actions or Capabilities
ESF #1 Transportation	Coordinate the opening of roads and manage aviation airspace for access to health and medical facilities or services.
ESF #2 Communications	Provide and enable contingency communications required at health and medical facilities.
ESF #3 Public Works and Engineering	Install generators and provide other temporary emergency power sources for health and medical facilities.
ESF #4 Firefighting	Coordinate federal firefighting activities and support resource requests for public health and medical facilities and teams.
ESF #5 Information and Planning	Develop coordinated interagency crisis action plans addressing health and medical issues.
ESF #6 Mass Care, Emergency Assistance, Temporary Housing, and Human Assistance	Integrate voluntary agency and other partner support, including other federal agencies and the private sector, to resource health and medical services and supplies.
ESF #7 Logistics	Provide logistics support for moving meals, water, or other commodities.
ESF #8 Public Health and Medical Services	Provide health and medical support to communities and coordinate across capabilities of partner agencies.
ESF #9 Search and Rescue	Conduct initial health and medical needs assessments.
ESF #10 Oil & Hazardous Materials Response	Monitor air quality near health and medical facilities in close proximity to the incident area.
ESF #11 Agriculture and Natural Resources	Coordinate with health and medical entities to address incidents of zoonotic disease.
ESF #12 Energy	Coordinate power restoration efforts for health and medical facilities or power-dependent medical populations.
ESF # 13 Public Safety and Security	Provide public safety needed security at health and medical facilities or mobile teams delivering services.

81. *Id.* at 21.

ESF	Example of Supporting Actions or Capabilities
ESF #14 Cross-Sector Business and Infrastructure	Be informed of and assess cascading impacts of health or medical infrastructure or service disruptions, and deconflict or prioritize cross-sector requirements.
ESF #15 External Affairs	Conduct public messaging on the status of available health and medical services or public health risks.

Source: FEMA, National Response Framework Table 3.

Within this structure, the "departments and agencies supporting federal ESFs may be selectively activated by FEMA or as requested by a lead federal agency to support response activities."[82] Notably, the current NRF added ESF #14, Cross-Sector Business and Infrastructure, to further "coordinate multi-sector response operations between (or across) the government *and private sector*."[83]

Because it is such a critical part of its mission, FEMA continually reviews, revises, and updates its coordination structure.

Declaration Approved: The FEMA Assistance Programs

A vital component of the presidential declaration and the FCO determination—perhaps the most vital component—is the disbursement of significant federal resources. Those federal resources, as previously noted, typically fall into one of three buckets: public assistance, individual or household assistance, and hazard mitigation.

Public Assistance (PA)

FEMA's PA program resources are most often the first out the door following an emergency or major disaster declaration. PA directly supplements the resources and needs of states, tribes, territories, local governments, and eligible nonprofits (i.e., the public entities) in the area affected by the incident. The PA program includes forms of direct assistance

82. *Id.* at 22.
83. *Id.* at iii (emphasis added).

as well as grants to help implement emergency protective measures,[84] conduct emergency debris removal,[85] and, ultimately, make permanent repair or replacement of damaged public facilities.[86] These categories are further broken down into the type of work, either emergency work or permanent work.

Emergency work is the "work which must be done immediately to save lives and to protect improved property and public health and safety, or to avert or lessen the threat of a major disaster."[87] This work includes the debris removal and emergency protective measures.[88] Permanent work also includes "the restorative work that must be performed through repairs or replacement, to restore an eligible facility on the basis of its predisaster design and current applicable standards"[89] as well as work to reduce future disaster impacts.[90] FEMA's permanent work designation includes five select groups: roads and bridges; water control facilities; buildings and equipment; utilities; and parks, recreational, and other facilities.[91]

The FEMA distinctions carry weight. Emergency work may be authorized for an emergency or major disaster declaration, while permanent work is authorized only for a major disaster declaration. Moreover, performance requirements for each type of work include specifically defined time limits for completion; examples follow.

Completion Deadlines	
Type of Work	**Months**
Debris Clearance	6
Emergency Work	6
Permanent Work	18

Source: 44 C.F.R. § 206.204(c)(1).

84. *See, e.g.*, 42 U.S.C. §§ 5170b (essential assistance), 5185 (emergency communications), 5186 (emergency public transportation).

85. 42 U.S.C. § 5173.

86. *Id.* § 5172.

87. 44 C.F.R. § 206.201(b).

88. FEMA, Public Assistance and Policy Guide 51 (June 2020), https://www.fema.gov/sites/default/files/documents/fema_pappg-v4-updated-links_policy_6-1-2020.pdf.

89. 44 C.F.R. § 206.201(i).

90. 42 U.S.C. § 5172(e)(1)(A)(ii).

91. Public Assistance and Policy Guide, *supra* note 88, at 51.

All PA program resources, regardless of work type, must be properly documented in the FEMA-State Agreement.

Direct Federal Assistance

Direct federal assistance under the PA program is available when the state or local entity "lack[s] the capability to perform or to contract for eligible emergency work and/or debris removal."[92] In that situation, the state or other recipient "may request the work be accomplished by a Federal agency."[93] FEMA, in turn, provides for reimbursement to the other federal agency.[94] Direct federal involvement requires the relevant state to (1) provide "all lands, easements and rights-of-ways necessary to accomplish" the work; (2) hold harmless the United States from damages because of the work and indemnify the federal government against any claims arising from the work; and (3) provide reimbursement for the non-federal share of the cost.[95] The state must also act as local facilitator in local jurisdictional matters,[96] including "securing local building permits and rights of entry, control of traffic and pedestrians, and compliance with local building ordinances."[97]

Direct assistance is implemented through a "mission assignment letter" from the FEMA Regional Administrator to the relevant federal agency "defin[ing] the scope of eligible work, the estimated cost of the eligible work and the billing period frequency."[98] This assistance has a short fuse for initiation and completion. In fact, the regulations require that the relevant federal agency complete the work under the mission assignment within "60 days after the President's declaration."[99] The performing federal agency manages the assistance and the agency "shall ensure that the work is completed in accordance with the Regional Administrator's approved scope of work, costs and time limitations."[100] The performing

92. 44 C.F.R. § 206.208(a).
93. *Id.*
94. *Id.*
95. *Id.* § 206.208(b)(1)(i)–(iii).
96. *Id.* § 206.208(b)(iv).
97. *Id.* § 206.208(e)(2).
98. *Id.* § 206.208(c)(1).
99. *Id.* § 206.208(d).
100. *Id.* § 206.208(e)(1).

federal agency must also keep the Regional Administrator and recipient "advised of work progress and other project developments" and must ensure the work is completed in "compliance with applicable Federal, State and local legal requirements."[101] Each direct assistance project concludes with a final inspection report.[102]

Public Assistance Grants

Most PA programming is delivered and administered through public assistance grants. The grants are implemented as part of the FEMA-State Agreement, whereby the authorized state, tribe, or territory becomes the grant recipient.[103] The recipient then administers the PA grant for counties authorized to receive federal assistance under the declaration.[104] As administrator of the PA grant, the recipient is responsible for:

- Providing technical advice and assistance to eligible subrecipients;[105]
- Providing state support for project identification activities to include small and large project formulation and the validation of small projects;[106]
- Ensuring that all potential applicants are aware of available public assistance;[107] and
- Submitting documents necessary for the award of grants.[108]

PA projects administered by the recipient via subgrants are typically processed using standard grant application reimbursement procedures.[109] Applicants may include "a State agency, local government, or eligible private nonprofit organization . . . submitting an application to the recipient

---

101. *Id.*
102. *Id.*
103. *Id.* § 206.201(m) (defining recipient); *see also id.* § 202.202(b).
104. *Id.* § 206.202(b).
105. *Id.* § 206.202(b)(1).
106. *Id.* § 206.202(b)(2).
107. *Id.* § 206.202(b)(3).
108. *Id.* § 206.202(b)(4).
109. Alternative procedures for "capped costs" type arrangements are available and may be appropriate in certain circumstances. *See generally* 42 U.S.C. § 5189f.

for assistance under the State's grant."[110] For *each* applicant requesting public assistance, the recipient must send the completed FEMA forms to the Regional Administrator "within 30 days after designation of the area where the damage occurred."[111] PA eligibility must then be established for *each* project. Together, the Stafford Act, implementing regulations, and FEMA policy statements establish criteria for project eligibility that include the applicant, facilities, work, and costs. FEMA refers to these criteria as the PA program "eligibility pyramid."[112] "Applicant" is defined earlier in the chapter, and the other criteria are summarized here:

- *Facility* includes facilities belonging to a public entity,[113] private nonprofit facilities owned and operated by an organization meeting the definition of a private nonprofit organization found in section 206.221(f),[114] and facilities serving a rural community or unincorporated town or village if owned by a private nonprofit organization and providing an essential governmental service to the general public.[115]
- *Work* must be required as the result of the emergency or major disaster event, located within the designated area of a major disaster or emergency declaration, and be the legal responsibility of an eligible applicant.[116]
- *Costs* must be "reasonable," meaning that "in its nature and amount, it does not exceed that which would be incurred by a prudent person under the circumstances prevailing at the time the decision was made to incur the cost."[117] Under the Stafford Act, costs are estimated (1) on the basis of the pre-disaster design, (2) in conformity with the latest consensus-based codes and standards (including applicable hazard mitigation and floodplain

110. 44 C.F.R. § 206.201(a).
111. *Id.* § 206.202(c).
112. Public Assistance and Policy Guide, *supra* note 88, at 38.
113. 44 C.F.R. § 206.223(c).
114. *Id.* § 206.223(b).
115. *Id.* § 206.223(d).
116. *Id.* § 206.223(a)(1)–(3).
117. 2 C.F.R. § 200.404.

management criteria), and (3) in a manner allowing the facility to meet the definition of resilient.[118] PA grants may not reimburse costs funded by other means, such as private insurance.[119]

Finally, the award of a PA subgrant brings with it several requirements. Chief among the requirements is the nonfederal cost share where the final or remaining 25 percent of eligible project costs is the responsibility of the recipient, which can be passed further down to the applicant.[120] The nonfederal portion may be covered by means other than matching money, including applying (i.e., quantifying and taking credit for) the value of donated goods, resources, and labor.[121] PA subgrants may also include insurance requirements to protect against future loss.[122] Finally, for permanent work approved by the PA program, FEMA also requires that the recipient have a state hazard mitigation plan in place.[123]

Individual Assistance (IA)

IA is the chief assistance program for providing disaster survivors with financial and other forms of direct assistance. The Stafford Act and implementing regulations provide several forms of individual assistance to those directly impacted by an incident:

- Crisis Counseling Assistance and Training Program (CCP)[124]
- Disaster Case Management (DCM)[125]
- Disaster Legal Services (DLS)[126]
- Disaster Unemployment Assistance (DUA)[127]
- Individuals and Households Program (IHP)[128]

118. 42 U.S.C. § 5172(e)(1)(A)(i)–(iii).
119. 44 C.F.R. § 206.250(c).
120. *See, e.g.*, 42 U.S.C. § 5193(a) (stating that "[t]he Federal share for assistance provided under [the Emergency Assistance Programs] shall be equal to not less than 75 percent of the eligible costs").
121. 2 C.F.R. § 200.306(e)–(j).
122. 44 C.F.R. § 206.250–206.253.
123. *Id.* § 206.226(b).
124. 42 U.S.C. § 5183.
125. *Id.* § 5189d.
126. *Id.* § 5182.
127. *Id.* § 5177.
128. *Id.* § 5174.

As with other federal assistance programs, the type of presidential declaration matters. In this case, all forms of IA are potentially available in the event of a major disaster declaration, while only the IHP and CCP are available when the President issues an emergency declaration.[129]

IA funding comes directly from the DRF, with federal funds covering 100 percent of approved CCP, DCM, DLS, DUA, and IHP (housing) assistance. The IHP is the only IA that provides grants directly to individuals and households to supplement recovery. IHP directly addresses housing and other similar needs. For IHP needs beyond direct housing assistance, FEMA requires 25 percent nonfederal cost share. This is most often picked up by the relevant state, territory, or tribe. Implementation of the IA program is carried out in no small part through FEMA's comprehensive program guidance.[130] What follows is a brief overview of each of the IA programs identified earlier.

Crisis Counseling and Assistance Training Program

The CCP supports and supplements state and local efforts with community-based efforts by "provid[ing] professional counseling services, including financial assistance to State or local agencies or private mental health organizations to provide such services or training of disaster workers, to victims of major disasters" to address "mental health problems caused or aggravated" by the major disaster or its aftermath.[131] Such services can include crisis counseling, psycho-education, coping skills development, and links to other resources.[132] FEMA can provide grant funding to state, territorial, tribal, or local mental health services or contract directly with local private providers. FEMA can also fund training for the individuals providing the services.[133] CCP services range from short term (60 days following the IA approval with a 30-day extension)[134] or longer term (nine months following the IA approval with a 90-day extension).[135]

---

129. *Id.* § 5192(a)(6).

130. FEMA, Individual Assistance Program and Policy Guide, v. 1.1, FP 104-009-03 (May 2021), https://www.fema.gov/sites/default/files/documents/fema_iappg-1.1.pdf [hereinafter IAPPG].

131. 42 U.S.C. § 5183(a).

132. IAPPG, *supra* note 130, at 8.

133. 42 U.S.C. § 5183(b).

134. 44 C.F.R. § 206.171(f).

135. *Id.* § 206.171(g).

Disaster Case Management

DCM programs establish a framework for planning and managing recovery for disaster survivors—individuals and families. This framework pairs up case managers and survivors to prepare for unmet needs and establishes a single point of contact for understanding and accessing the various resources.[136] DCM offers immediate- and longer-term assistance. Immediate DCM programs focus on the first 90 to 180 days, with long-term services relying on a period of performance up to 24 months from the date of declaration. The funding may be directed to the state, territorial, tribal, or local government, or to qualified private organizations.[137] Similar to PA grants, DCM is made available to nonfederal entities after an assessment of need and the submission of an application.[138]

Disaster Legal Services

DLS facilitates legal advice and representation by attorneys to low-income individuals through non-fee generating matters. The emphasis is to counsel individuals accessing the various benefits and assistance authorized by the Stafford Act.[139] The program is supplemented through FEMA agreements with the American Bar Association's Young Lawyers Division and is made available through a toll-free hotline.[140] DLS services are available for as long as is necessary.[141]

Disaster Unemployment Assistance

DUA authorizes the state, territory, or tribal authority's unemployment compensation agency to provide temporary DUA unemployment benefits for up to 26 weeks. The benefits are available to individuals previously employed, or self-employed, and rendered jobless or unable to work as a direct result of the incident.[142]

---

136. IAPPG, *supra* note 130, at 183.
137. *Id.* at 184.
138. *Id.* at 191–92.
139. 44 C.F.R. § 206.164(a).
140. IAPPG, *supra* note 130, at 235.
141. *Id.* at 235.
142. *Id.* at 239.

Individuals and Households Program

The IHP provides two types of housing assistance—direct assistance and financial assistance—in addition to other individual needs assistance resources. The IHP sits at the heart of the IA program, working to meet basic needs and support basic, individual recovery efforts. Notably, IHP assistance is capped and adjusted on an annual basis. In the 2025 fiscal year, the cap was $43,600.[143] IHP benefits require survivors to meet certain eligibility requirements and complete necessary IHP application forms. Each type of assistance may trigger separate eligibility reviews and determinations. IHP programs include those shown in the following table.

Housing Assistance and Other Needs Assistance		
Direct Housing Assistance	**Financial Housing Assistance**	**Other Needs Assistance**
• Lodging Expense Reimbursement • Rental Assistance • Home Repair Assistance • Home Replacement Assistance	• Multifamily Lease & Repair • Transportable Temporary Housing Units • Direct Lease • Permanent Housing Construction	• Serious Needs Assistance • Displacement Assistance • Personal Property Assistance • Transportation Assistance • Group Flood Insurance Policy • Funeral Assistance • Medical and Dental Assistance • Childcare Assistance • Assistance for Miscellaneous Items • Moving and Storage Assistance • Clean and Sanitize Assistance

Source: IAPPG Figure 5 and Figure 28; *see also* Congressional Research Service, *FEMA Individual Assistance Programs: An Overview*, Table 1, CRS R46014 (Apr. 17, 2024).

143. *See* Notice of Maximum Amount of Assistance Under the Individuals and Households Program, 89 Fed. Reg. 84,923 (Oct. 24, 2024).

Hazard Mitigation Grant Program

FEMA defines hazard mitigation as "[a]ny cost effective measure which will reduce the potential for damage to a facility from a disaster event."[144] It further defines activity under the Hazard Mitigation Grant Program (HMGP) to mean "any mitigation measure, project, or action proposed to reduce risk of future damage, hardship, loss or suffering from disasters."[145] Hazard mitigation is about the future, near term, and long term. Its aim is to reduce risk.

HMGP mitigation support is authorized directly under the Stafford Act[146] and is developed and implemented pursuant to implementing regulations.[147] And, like the other assistance programs, it is supported by guidance from FEMA.[148] Because hazard mitigation focuses on predicting, planning, and mitigating future risk, it is perhaps the broadest and most nuanced of any of FEMA's assistance programs. The HMGP guidance includes many example scenarios that may be helpful to community members, leaders, and planners, and to their legal counsel and technical advisors.

The HMGP is triggered by a major disaster declaration from the President, and, like other FEMA assistance programs, it is funded by the DRF. The HMGP works to ensure that recovery, and particularly rebuilding, after a major disaster takes advantage of opportunities to reduce loss of life and property from future disasters. HMGP is awarded to the state, territorial, or tribal government as ***recipient***,[149] with funding passed through to sub-applicants that may include state agencies and local governments, as well as private nonprofit organizations (including qualified conservation organizations).[150] Local and tribal subgrantees must have approved mitigation plans in place to be eligible.[151]

144. 44 C.F.R. § 206.2(14).
145. *Id.* § 206.431.
146. 42 U.S.C. § 5170c.
147. 44 C.F.R. §§ 206.430–206.440.
148. *See* https://www.fema.gov/grants/mitigation/learn/hazard-mitigation [hereinafter HMAPPG].
149. 44 C.F.R. § 206.434(a)(1).
150. *Id.* § 206.434(a)(2)–(3).
151. *Id.* § 206.434(b)(1).

Eligible HMGP activities include both planning and projects. Up to 7 percent of a state's HMGP award may be distributed to assist local and tribal governments with the development of mitigation plans.[152] Mitigation projects "may be of any nature that will result in protection to public or private property."[153] Activities already being implemented are not eligible for HMGP program assistance. FEMA's enumerated examples of eligible projects include the following:

- Structural hazard control or protection projects
- Construction activities that will result in protection from hazards
- Retrofitting of facilities
- Property acquisition or relocation
- Development of state or local mitigation standards
- Development of comprehensive mitigation programs with implementation as an essential component
- Development or improvement of warning systems[154]

FEMA also established minimum project criteria, requiring that HMGP projects and activities:

- Conform to the State Mitigation Plan and Local or Tribal Mitigation Plan approved under 44 C.F.R. part 201; or for Indian Tribal governments acting as recipients, conform to the Tribal Mitigation Plan approved under 44 C.F.R. 201.7;
- Have a beneficial impact on the designated disaster area, whether or not located in the designated area;
- Conform to 44 C.F.R. part 9, Floodplain Management and Protection of Wetlands, and other applicable environmental and historic preservation laws, regulations, executive orders, and agency policy;
- Solve a problem independently or constitute a functional portion of a solution where there is assurance that the project as a whole will be completed; and

152. *Id.* § 206.434(d)(1).
153. *Id.* § 206.434(d)(2).
154. *Id.*

- Be cost-effective and substantially reduce the risk of future damage, hardship, loss, or suffering resulting from a major disaster.[155]

The recipient state retains responsibility for reviewing, identifying, and selecting eligible projects that align with the State Mitigation Plan.[156] Consistent with other FEMA assistance programs, the state, acting as recipient, must establish an administrative program for implementation of the HMGP[157] and maintain primary responsibility management of HMGP projects.[158]

Other FEMA Program Procedures and Considerations

FEMA's emergency and major disaster assistance programs are administrative functions. Authorized by public law, FEMA promulgated implementing regulations for each aspect of each assistance program. FEMA's programs are typical of most federal administrative regimes in that they include procedures appropriate for review and appeal of administrative determinations.[159] FEMA's assistance programs—direct and grant administered—also require that approved work or activity comply with other applicable laws and regulations.[160] These compliance obligations are typically spelled out in the FEMA-State Agreement and subrecipient awards. Finally, because of the amount of federal funds typically involved in the response to a declared emergency or major disaster, the Stafford Act and FEMA regulations give vigorous consideration to progress reports,[161] review and audit requirements,[162] and final inspection reports.[163]

---

155. *Id.* § 206.434(c).

156. *Id.* § 206.435(a).

157. *Id.* § 206.437.

158. *Id.* § 206.438.

159. *Id.* §§ 206.46 (administering the appeal of declaration determinations), 206.115 (administering the appeal of IA eligibility determinations, denials, cancelations, and related decisions, 206.206 (administering the appeal of PA determinations), 206.440 (administering the appeal of HMGP determinations).

160. 2 C.F.R. § 200.300 (requiring all recipients serving as pass through entities for federal funds to ensure the funding is implemented in "full accordance with the U.S. Constitution, applicable Federal statutes and regulations—including provisions protecting free speech, religious liberty, public welfare, and the environment, and those prohibiting discrimination").

161. 44 C.F.R. § 206.204(f).

162. *Id.* §§ 206.16, 206.207(c).

163. *Id.* § 206.208(e)(1).

Conclusion

As noted at the outset of this chapter, local and state governments drive disaster response in the United States. This holds true even when the President issues an emergency or major disaster declaration under the Stafford Act. FEMA participation in the response and recovery effort brings with it federally authorized assistance programs, federal funding, and federal operational experience to lead the planning and coordination effort. But state and local officials, along with approved disaster relief organizations, remain the driving force for implementation of response and recovery activities beyond direct federal assistance. Accordingly, community leaders and planners, and their legal counsel and technical advisors, must be prepared when federal assistance is called upon *and* made available. This requires responsible officials to maintain well-prepared and up-to-date emergency response and mitigation plans. It demands familiarity with the key points of contact at each level of the coordination framework. And it calls for a working knowledge of the factors supporting a request for a presidential declaration, the geographic scope of the declaration, and the programmatic reach of the FEMA State Agreement.

Chapter 5
The National Contingency Plan

Susan Parker Bodine and Mary Ellen Ternes

Overview of the NCP

Promulgated pursuant to CERCLA and the Clean Water Act (CWA),[1] and codified at 40 C.F.R. Part 300, the National Contingency Plan (NCP) establishes the standard process for notifying, responding to, and removing releases of oil, hazardous substances, pollutants, or contaminants. It was initially developed in response to the spill of 37 million gallons of oil from an oil tanker off the coast of England. Observing the lack of coordination in the response to this disaster, U.S. officials developed a coordinated approach to respond to oil spills in the United States. This initial plan provided for a response headquarters, a national reaction team, and regional reaction teams. Congress subsequently required this coordinated approach to be codified and expanded to include hazardous substance releases.

1. The NCP is authorized by the Comprehensive Environmental Response, Compensation and Liability Act (CERCLA) § 104, 42 U.S.C. § 9604, as amended by the Superfund Amendments and Reauthorization Act of 1986 (SARA), Pub. L. No. 99-499, and by the Clean Water Act (CWA) § 311(d), 33 U.S.C. § 1321(d), as amended by the Oil Pollution Act of 1990 (OPA), Pub. L. 101-380. In Executive Order (E.O.) 12777 (56 FR 54757, Oct. 22, 1991), the President delegated to EPA the responsibility for the amendment of the NCP. Amendments to the NCP are coordinated with members of the National Response Team (NRT) prior to publication for notice and comment. This includes coordination with the Federal Emergency Management Agency (FEMA) and the Nuclear Regulatory Commission in order to avoid inconsistent or duplicative requirements in the emergency planning responsibilities of those agencies. The NCP is applicable to response actions taken pursuant to the authorities under CERCLA and section 311 of the CWA.

Response authority comes from the CWA (as amended by the Oil Pollution Act), CERCLA, the Oil Pollution Act, and the Robert T. Stafford Disaster Relief and Emergency Assistance Act (the Stafford Act) (for hazardous materials incidents resulting from a presidentially declared disaster or emergency).[2]

The NCP establishes the National Response Team (NRT)[3] and enumerates its roles and responsibilities in the National Response system. This includes planning and coordinating responses, providing guidance to Regional Response Teams (RRTs), coordinating a national program of preparedness planning and response, and facilitating research to improve response activities. EPA serves as the lead agency within the NRT.

Under the NCP, the roles and responsibilities of the RRTs include coordinating preparedness, planning, and response at the regional level.[4] The RRTs consist of standing teams made up of representatives of each federal agency that is a member of the NRT, as well as state and local government representatives from that region. RRTs also include an incident-specific team made up of members of the standing team that are activated for a specific response. RRTs have several responsibilities, including conducting oversight and consistency review of area plans within a given region.

Through the NRT and RRTs, the NCP establishes the unified command structure for managing responses to discharges through coordinated personnel and resources of the federal government, the state government(s), and the responsible party or parties.[5] The NCP also identifies the responsibilities of federal agencies that may be called upon during response planning and implementation to provide assistance in their respective areas of expertise consistent with the agencies' respective capabilities and authorities.[6] In addition, the NCP defines the objectives, authority, and scope of Federal Contingency Plans, including the NCP, Regional Contingency Plans (RCPs), and Area Contingency Plans (ACPs).[7]

2. 42 U.S.C. §§ 5121, *et seq.*
3. 40 C.F.R. § 300.110.
4. *Id.* § 300.115.
5. *Id.* § 300.135(d).
6. *Id.* §§ 300.170, 300.175.
7. *Id.* § 300.210.

The NCP establishes the general responsibilities for federal on-scene coordinators (OSCs),[8] who the NCP authorizes to direct all federal, state, and private response activities at the site of a discharge.[9] The OSCs submit to the Regional Response Team (RRT) or the National Response Team (NRT) a report on all removal actions taken at a site.[10]

As discussed in Chapter 1, the NCP is part of a larger, government-wide framework for responding to disasters, called the National Response Framework (NRF). The NRF is a guide to how the nation responds to all types of disasters and emergencies. It is built on scalable, flexible, and adaptable concepts identified in the National Incident Management System (NIMS) to align key roles and responsibilities across the nation. The NRF describes specific authorities and best practices for managing incidents that range from the serious but purely local to large-scale terrorist attacks or catastrophic natural disasters. The NRF provides coordinating mechanisms to bring in additional agencies and components as needed.[11]

The NRF's Emergency Support Function Annexes (ESFs) organize capabilities and resources into functions most likely needed during an incident. A large-scale natural disaster or significant terrorist incident can require the activation of all ESFs. A localized flood or tornado might only require activation of a few ESFs.

Each ESF has one or two coordinating federal agencies that orchestrate federal support and manage staff and resources for that functional area, and additional agencies that have supporting roles. EPA and the U.S. Coast Guard are the primary agencies for overseeing Emergency Support Function (ESF) #10, Oil and Hazardous Materials Response Annex. ESF #10 provides a coordinated federal response to actual or potential oil and hazardous materials incidents. Response under ESF #10 occurs when there has been a presidential disaster declaration under the Stafford Act or there is a need to support a response taken under the NCP with additional resources.

8. *Id.* § 300.120.

9. *Id.* § 300.135(a).

10. *Id.* § 300.165.

11. For more information on the National Response Framework, *see* FEMA, *National Response Framework*, https://www.fema.gov/emergency-managers/national-preparedness/frameworks/response (last updated Jan. 10, 2025).

Figure 5.1 displays the hierarchy of federal responses to oil and hazardous substance releases.[12] The federal OSC (FOSC in the figure) evaluates the release report to determine if federal assistance is needed. If a response is needed but state, local, tribal, and territorial governments (SLTT in the figure) will provide oversight, and if the responsible party (RP in the figure) is adequately responding, no federal resources will be required. If the OSC determines a federal response is needed, then the NCP is triggered. This response can be as little as providing oversight over a responsible party response.

Depending on the severity of the release, additional resources beyond those provided by the OSC, the state and local governments, and the responsible party may be needed. If the release is designated as a spill of national significance (SONS in the figure), the senior agency official (SAO in the figure) or the national incident commander (NIC in the figure) assists the OSC with coordinating resources. If multiple agency resources are needed then the appropriate ESFs can be triggered. Finally, if the President declares a major disaster under the Stafford Act then FEMA is the lead federal agency and designates a federal coordinating officer.

Figure 5.1 Federal response coordination constructs

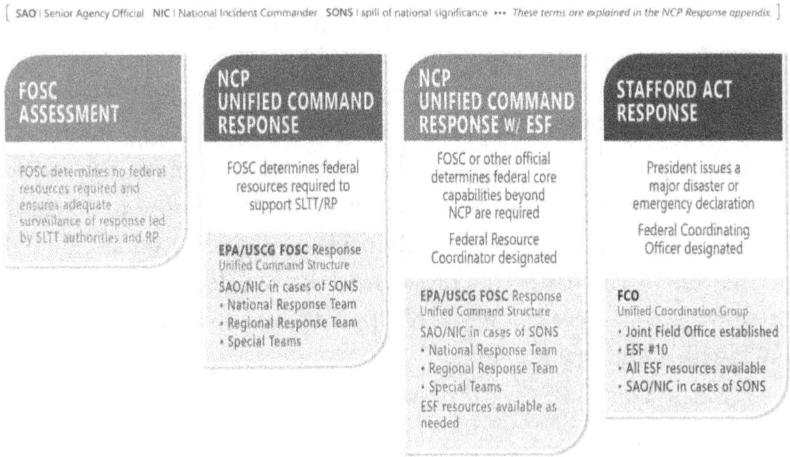

12. *See generally* Oil and Chemical Incident Annex to the Response and Recovery Federal Interagency Operational Plans 21 (Feb. 2023), https://www.fema.gov/sites/default/files/documents/fema_incident-annex-oil-chemical.pdf.

The vast majority of releases require no federal response or NCP-only response actions. Accordingly, the remainder of this chapter focuses on response under the NCP.

Scope of the NCP Authority

Authority under the NCP is triggered by a release of oil, hazardous substances, pollutants, or contaminants into the environment.[13] The NCP adopts the Clean Water Act's definition of "oil" at section 311(a)(1), which includes:

> [O]il of any kind or in any form, including, but not limited to, petroleum, fuel oil, sludge, oil refuse, and oil mixed with wastes other than dredged spoil. Oil, as defined by section 1001 of the OPA means oil of any kind or in any form, including, but not limited to, petroleum, fuel oil, sludge, oil refuse, and oil mixed with wastes other than dredged spoil, but does not include petroleum, including crude oil or any fraction thereof, which is specifically listed or designated as a hazardous substance under subparagraphs (A) through (F) of section 101(14) of the Comprehensive Environmental Response, Compensation, and Liability Act (42 U.S.C. 9601) and which is subject to the provisions of that Act.

EPA interprets this definition of oil to include *any amount* of oil mixed with another substance, like water.[14]

The NCP uses CERCLA's definition of "hazardous substances." This definition includes listed categories of materials regulated under other statutes.[15] EPA also has the authority to add substances to the list,

13. 40 C.F.R. § 300.3(a)(2).

14. *See* EPA, *Mixture with Oil as an Additive (e.g., Oil-Based Paint)*, https://www.epa.gov/oil-spills-prevention-and-preparedness-regulations/mixture-oil-additive-eg-oil-based-paint (last updated May 31, 2024).

15. CERCLA, 42 U.S.C. § 9601(14). The term "hazardous substance" means (A) any substance designated pursuant to section 311(b)(2)(A) of the Federal Water Pollution Control Act [33 U.S.C. 1321(b)(2)(A)], (B) any element, compound, mixture, solution, or substance designated pursuant to section 9602 of this title, (C) any hazardous waste having the characteristics identified under or listed pursuant to section 3001 of the Solid Waste Disposal Act [42 U.S.C. 6921] (but not including

which it utilized for the first time in 2024 to add perfluorooctanoic acid (PFOA) and perfluorooctanesulfonic acid (PFOS) to the CERCLA list of hazardous substances.[16] The resulting list is arguably the most comprehensive such list in any federal statute.[17]

The CERCLA list of hazardous substances includes elements, compounds, mixtures, solutions, and substances. It lists metals, including arsenic, barium, cadmium, chromium, lead, mercury, selenium, and silver, despite their natural presence in soil, or for some, in our vitamin supplements; acetone, despite being a common laboratory contaminant; benzene, despite being found in petroleum, while petroleum is expressly excluded from the definition of hazardous substances; and some listed substances are regulated pursuant to other statutes. For example, pentachlorophenol is a listed hazardous substance but is also a hazardous waste designated with the code D037 at levels above 100 mg/L and the code F027 when in a discarded, unused formulation.

This list of hazardous substances includes almost any material associated with industrial sectors in the United States that could present a substantial threat to public health and the environment should exposure occur, based on toxicity or hazard and prevalence in industry. In historically industrialized areas, it is common to detect low concentrations of hazardous substances with the use of standard EPA analytical methods designed for characterizing impacts to environmental media, for example, soil and water. These methods are intended to detect these substances even where operations have long since been abandoned, and assignment of specific waste code listings under RCRA are no longer possible, because

any waste the regulation of which under the Solid Waste Disposal Act [42 U.S.C. 6901 et seq.] has been suspended by Act of Congress), (D) any toxic pollutant listed under section 307(a) of the Federal Water Pollution Control Act [33 U.S.C. 1317(a)], (E) any hazardous air pollutant listed under section 112 of the Clean Air Act [42 U.S.C. 7412], and (F) any imminently hazardous chemical substance or mixture with respect to which the Administrator has taken action pursuant to section 7 of the Toxic Substances Control Act [15 U.S.C. 2606]. The term does not include petroleum, including crude oil or any fraction thereof which is not otherwise specifically listed or designated as a hazardous substance under subparagraphs (A) through (F) of this paragraph, and the term does not include natural gas, natural gas liquids, liquefied natural gas, or synthetic gas usable for fuel (or mixtures of natural gas and such synthetic gas).

16. 89 Fed. Reg. 39,124 (May 8, 2024) (utilizing the authority of section 102, 42 U.S.C. § 9602).

17. 40 C.F.R. § 302.4, Designation of Hazardous Substances.

either the waste was generated before RCRA was enacted or there is no longer an owner or operator available who could make a hazardous waste determination and assign a waste code. These analytical methods are compiled in EPA's Methods for Evaluating Solid Waste, Physical/Chemical Methods (SW-846).[18] The SW-846 manual contains procedures for field and laboratory quality control, sampling, determining hazardous constituents in wastes, determining the hazardous characteristics of wastes (toxicity, ignitability, reactivity, and corrosivity), and determining physical properties of wastes. It also contains guidance on how to select appropriate methods.[19] Of course, because natural elements like metals are included on the CERCLA list, one is sure to detect "hazardous substances" in virgin forest soil. Thus, a significant question is whether the hazardous substance is present in concentrations above "background," so as to distinguish what hazardous substances were present before a release, and not the result of a release.[20]

Even if a substance is not a "hazardous substance," it could still be a "pollutant or contaminant." The NCP adopts CERCLA's definition, which includes just about anything else, except petroleum and natural gas:

> [A]ny element, substance, compound, or mixture, including disease-causing agents, which after release into the environment and upon exposure, ingestion, inhalation, or assimilation into any organism, either directly from the environment or indirectly by ingestion through food chains, will or may reasonably be anticipated to cause death, disease, behavioral abnormalities, cancer, genetic mutation, physiological malfunctions (including malfunctions in reproduction) or physical deformations, in such organisms or their offspring; except that the term "pollutant or contaminant" shall not include petroleum, including crude oil

---

18. These analytical methods are adopted as guidance unless they are required to be used to identify hazardous waste, in which case they are promulgated as part of EPA's RCRA regulations. These methods are available at https://www.epa.gov/hw-sw846.

19. *See* EPA, *Hazardous Waste Test Methods/SW-846,* https://www.epa.gov/hw-sw846 (last updated Dec. 26, 2024).

20. CERCLA does not give agencies authority to respond to undisturbed, naturally occurring substances. 42 U.S.C. § 9604(a)(3)(A).

> or any fraction thereof which is not otherwise specifically listed or designated as a hazardous substance under subparagraphs (A) through (F) of paragraph (14) and shall not include natural gas, liquefied natural gas, or synthetic gas of pipeline quality (or mixtures of natural gas and such synthetic gas).[21]

The NCP also defines the terms "releases" and "environment" very broadly, relying on CERCLA's definitions of these terms:

> The term "environment" means (A) the navigable waters, the waters of the contiguous zone, and the ocean waters of which the natural resources are under the exclusive management authority of the United States under the Magnuson-Stevens Fishery Conservation and Management Act [16 U.S.C. 1801 et seq.], and (B) any other surface water, ground water, drinking water supply, land surface or subsurface strata, or ambient air within the United States or under the jurisdiction of the United States.[22]

> The term "release" means any spilling, leaking, pumping, pouring, emitting, emptying, discharging, injecting, escaping, leaching, dumping, or disposing into the environment (including the abandonment or discarding of barrels, containers, and other closed receptacles containing any hazardous substance or pollutant or contaminant), but excludes (A) any release which results in exposure to persons solely within a workplace, with respect to a claim which such persons may assert against the employer of such persons, (B) emissions from the engine exhaust of a motor vehicle, rolling stock, aircraft, vessel, or pipeline pumping station engine, (C) release of source, byproduct, or special nuclear material from a nuclear incident, as those terms are defined in the Atomic Energy Act of 1954 [42 U.S.C. 2011 et seq.], if such release is subject to requirements with respect to financial protection established by the Nuclear Regulatory Commission under section 170 of such Act [42 U.S.C. 2210], or, for the purposes of section 9604 of this title or any other response action, any

21. 40 C.F.R. § 300.5 (incorporating the CERCLA definition, 42 U.S.C. § 9601(33)).
22. 42 U.S.C. § 9601(8).

release of source byproduct, or special nuclear material from any processing site designated under section 7912(a)(1) or 7942(a) of this title, and (D) the normal application of fertilizer.[23]

Release Reporting

Pursuant to the Clean Water Act, unpermitted releases of oil are prohibited and required to be reported immediately if they may be harmful to public health or the environment.[24] EPA has determined that harmful releases include spills that violate applicable water quality standards; spills that cause a "sheen" (discolored film) on surface water or shorelines; and spills that cause a sludge or emulsion (heavy mix of oil and water) beneath the surface of the water or along the shoreline.[25]

Pursuant to CERCLA, the Emergency Planning and Community Right to Know Act (EPCRA), and the NCP, releases of hazardous substances above a reportable quantity must be reported to the National Response Center (NRC),[26] the State Emergency Response Commission (SERC), and the Local Emergency Planning Committee (LEPC) by any person in charge of a vessel or facility. This must be done *immediately upon knowledge* of any release of a hazardous substance over the assigned "reportable quantity" for that material within a 24-hour period.[27]

As a practical matter, the reporting requirements in the CWA and CERCLA and implementing regulations provide some leeway to allow the person in charge of the facility to determine whether a harmful quantity (oil) or a reportable quantity (hazardous substances) has been released

---

23. *Id.* § 9601(22).

24. 33 U.S.C. § 1321(b)(3), (b)(5).

25. 40 C.F.R. § 100.3, and *id.* § 300.300. *See* EPA, Oil Discharge Reporting Requirements (Dec. 2006), https://www.epa.gov/sites/production/files/2014-06/documents/spccfactsheetspill reportingdec06-1.pdf (providing useful explanation of the "sheen rule"). The CWA Spill Prevention Containment and Countermeasure (SPCC) regulations also require reporting spills that exceed 1,000 gallons, or if there are more than two, over-42-gallon spills within any 12-month period. 40 C.F.R. pt. 112. *See also* EPA, Spill Prevention, Control, and Countermeasure (SPCC) Regulation: A Facility Owner/Operator's Guide to Oil Pollution Prevention (June 2010), https://www.epa.gov/sites/production/files/documents/spccbluebroch.pdf.

26. NRC release reports are called into 1-800-424-8802.

27. 42 U.S.C. § 9603(a). 40 C.F.R. pt. 302 provides the list of reportable quantities for listed hazardous substances.

because the reporting obligation is based on knowledge.[28] The reportable quantities of each hazardous substance, whether specifically listed or identified by category, are included in the list of hazardous substances.[29] However, once it is known or should be known (i.e., a catastrophic release) that a reportable quantity has been released within a 24-hour period, the reporting requirement is triggered. As a matter of enforcement discretion, EPA's Enforcement Response Policy for calculating proposed penalties for civil administrative actions, and for settlement offers concerning EPCRA sections 304, 311, and 312 and CERCLA section 103(a) states that EPA expects reporting to occur within 15 minutes of actual or constructive knowledge of a reportable release.[30]

Release reports for hazardous substances should include the chemical name; whether it is extremely hazardous; an estimate of the quantity released; the time and duration of the release; whether the release occurred to the air, water, or land; any known or anticipated acute or chronic health risks; proper precautions such as evacuation or sheltering in place; and the name and telephone number of a contact person.[31]

Releases of oil permitted pursuant to the CWA National Pollution Discharge and Elimination System Permits do not need to be reported pursuant to the NCP.[32] Releases of hazardous substances permitted under a federal permit (or a permit issued by a state implementing a federally delegated or authorized program) do not need to be reported, and are

28. 33 U.S.C. § 1321(b)(5)(reporting by the person in charge is required "as soon as he has knowledge" of the spill of oil in harmful quantities); 42 U.S.C. § 9603(a) (reporting by the person in charge is required "as soon as he has knowledge" of a release of a reportable quantity within a 24-hour period).

29. 40 C.F.R. § 302, Table 302.4.

30. EPA, Enforcement Response Policy for Sections 304, 311 and 312 of the Emergency Planning and Community Right-to-Know Act and Section 103 of the Comprehensive Environmental Response, Compensation and Liability Act (Sept. 30, 1999), https://www.epa.gov/sites/default/files/documents/epcra304.pdf. Under this penalty policy, the longer a facility operator waits to issue a report, the higher the penalty may be.

31. *See* EPA, *When Are You Required to Report an Oil Spill and Hazardous Substance Release?*, https://www.epa.gov/emergency-response/when-are-you-required-report-oil-spill-and-hazardous-substance-release (last updated July 10, 2024); *see also* EPA, *EPCRA Emergency Release Notifications*, https://www.epa.gov/epcra/epcra-section-304 (last updated Apr. 1, 2024).

32. 40 C.F.R. § 112.1 (excluding releases of oil permitted pursuant to NPDES permits from the definition of "discharge").

exempt pursuant to the "federally-permitted release exemption."[33] However, CERCLA section 107(j) expressly preserves claims under other laws to recover costs or damages resulting from federally permitted releases.[34]

While the specific analysis depends on the type of permit pursuant to which the release is purported to be authorized, as a general rule, courts have held that to be exempt from CERCLA liability, the discharge or release must have been explicitly authorized either in the permit itself or in the administrative record upon which the permit issuance relied.[35] Moreover, courts have held that the defense was not available where the permit did not authorize the release of contaminants to groundwater, although it was authorized to discharge to surface water.[36]

A release above a reportable quantity under the NCP often also constitutes a release that requires reporting to the SERC and to the LEPC under EPCRA.[37] The requirements for reporting accidental releases of "extremely hazardous substances" defined by EPCRA also are triggered immediately. Like CERCLA reporting obligations, enforcement can result if a responsible party waits longer than 15 minutes to make a report once they have actual or constructive knowledge of a reportable release.[38] These initial release reports must be supplemented with a written follow-up notice to the SERC and LEPC.[39] To assist in evaluating CERCLA versus EPCRA reporting requirements, most helpful is EPA's "List of Lists"

---

33. 42 U.S.C. § 9601(10) (defining to term release to exclude permitted releases).

34. *Id.* § 9607(j) (providing that the defense does not "affect or modify in any way the obligations or liability of any person under any other provision of State or Federal law including common law, for damages, injury, or loss resulting from a release of any hazardous substance or for removal or remedial action or the costs of removal or remedial action of such hazardous substance").

35. *See* State of Idaho v. Bunker Hill Co., 635 F. Supp. 665, 673–74 (D. Idaho 1986) (allowing state to recover under CERCLA for damages caused by releases not expressly allowed by the permit or occurring at a time no permit existed).

36. U.S. v. United Nuclear Corp., 814 F. Supp. 1552, 1565 (D. N.M. 1992). The Supreme Court recently blurred the bright line between discharges to surface water and discharges to groundwater and held that a Clean Water Act permit may be required for a release to groundwater if the release to groundwater reaches surface water and is the "functional equivalent" of a release to surface water. Cnty. of Maui v. Haw. Wildlife Fund, 590 U.S. 165 (2020). Accordingly, under certain fact patterns, a Clean Water Act permit could cover a discharge to groundwater.

37. *See* 40 C.F.R. § 355.60.

38. 42 U.S.C. § 11004; 40 C.F.R. pt. 355, subpt. C, Emergency Notification Release.

39. *See EPCRA Emergency*, *supra* note 31.

that compiles EPCRA, CERCLA, and Clean Air Act 112(r) lists into a single reference.[40]

Initiating a Response

The National Response Center (NRC) is located at the Coast Guard headquarters and serves as the clearinghouse for release reports. Upon receipt of a release report, the NRC notifies the appropriate OSC. Pursuant to Executive Order No. 12580 (Superfund Implementation), the NCP gives EPA the lead for release response in the inland zone and gives the Coast Guard the lead for releases in the coastal zone.[41] Other federal agencies also have the lead for responding to releases on facilities under their jurisdiction and control. Release reports are available at the NRC website.[42]

Release reports are transmitted to the OSCs in the appropriate geographic area. An OSC investigates the release to determine the level of threat.[43] The NCP establishes national priorities for responding to a release.[44] The OSC may be dispatched to the release location to determine if there is a "substantial threat" to the public health or welfare, in which case the OSC directs the response.[45] Identification of a substantial threat is based on the size and character of the discharge, and its proximity to human populations and sensitive environments.[46] Classification of the threat includes classifications for spills of national significance requiring national coordination,[47] as well as worst case discharges requiring

---

40. *See Consolidated List of Chemicals Subject to the Emergency Planning and Community Right-to-Know Act (EPCRA), Comprehensive Environmental Response, Compensation and Liability act (CERCLA) and Section 112(r) of the Clean Air Act (CAA), and Section 311(j)(5) of the Clean Water Act CWA)* EPA 550-B-15-001 (Oct. 2024), https://www.epa.gov/system/files/documents/2024-11/consolidated-list-of-lists_updated-october-2024.pdf. This "List of Lists" also provides RCRA hazardous waste codes.

41. 40 C.F.R. § 300.120.

42. United States Coast Guard, *National Response Center*, https://nrc.uscg.mil (last visited Jan. 15, 2024).

43. 40 C.F.R. § 300.320.

44. *Id.* § 300.317.

45. *Id.* §§ 300.130(c), 300.322.

46. *Id.* § 300.322.

47. *Id.* § 300.323.

notification of the National Strike Force Coordination Center.[48] The level of threat identified by the OSC determines whether the RRT and other federal agencies are mobilized and whether various Emergency Support Functions under the National Response Framework (discussed earlier and in Chapter 1) are triggered. The OSC also informs the Federal Emergency Management Agency if there is a potential major disaster[49] and the Department of Health and Human Services if there is a possible public health emergency.[50]

As a practical matter, most releases do not rise to the level of a substantial threat. As already noted, for a substantial threat, the NCP authorizes the OSC to direct all federal, state, and private response activities at the site of a release to mitigate the substantial threat, and to establish a unified command structure.[51]

The NCP and Oil Spills

For oil spills, the NCP establishes national priorities for responding to a release. It authorizes the OSC to determine whether a release poses a substantial threat to the public health based on the size and character of the discharge and its proximity to human populations and sensitive environments. As noted earlier, this includes classifications for spills of national significance requiring national coordination, as well as worst-case discharges requiring notification of the National Strike Force Coordination Center. In such cases, the OSC is authorized to direct all federal, state, or private response and recovery actions. The OSC may pull in resources from other federal agencies or special teams, as well as require implementation of the worst-case portion of the Clean Water Act mandated tank vessel (cargo vessels operating on navigable waters) and Facility Response Plans and the Area Contingency Plan.[52]

48. *Id.* § 300.324.
49. *Id.* § 300.125.
50. *Id.* § 300.135(h).
51. *Id.* §§ 300.135, 300.322.
52. *Id.* (referencing CWA § 311(j)(4) and (5), 42 U.S.C. § 1321(j)(4) and (5)).

Funding for oil spill response may be available from the Oil Spill Liability Trust Fund, provided certain criteria are met.[53] The responsible party is liable for federal removal costs and damages as detailed in section 1002 of the Oil Pollution Act. Federal agencies assisting in a response action may be reimbursed. Other federal agencies may also provide financial support for removal actions.

The NCP and Hazardous Substance Removal Actions

A removal action is defined as cleanup or removal of hazardous substance releases and taking such actions as are necessary to prevent, minimize, or mitigate damage to the public health or welfare or the environment.[54]

In accordance with CERCLA, the NCP authorizes the lead agency to initiate appropriate removal action in the event of a hazardous substance release and provides the OSC with authority to direct actions to mitigate or remove the hazardous substance release. Decisions for action are based on the following criteria:

- Threats to human or animal populations
- Contamination of drinking water supplies or sensitive ecosystems
- High levels of hazardous substances in soils
- Weather conditions that may cause migration or release of hazardous substances
- Threat of fire or explosion
- Other significant factors affecting public health or the environment[55]

Funding for a hazardous substance response is available through the Superfund Trust Fund. Generally, OSCs are delegated the authority to spend up to $50,000 for a nonemergency removal action and up

53. 40 C.F.R. § 300.335.

54. 42 U.S.C. § 9601(23). The term also includes evacuations and provision of alternative water supplies and any emergency assistance provided under the Stafford Act.

55. 40 C.F.R. § 300.415.

to $250,000 where the site conditions constitute an emergency. Subsequent expenditures are authorized in action memoranda.[56] Except for the enforcement sections, these action memoranda are publicly available and are part of the administrative record. Ostensibly, the NCP caps fund-financed removal actions at $2 million and 12 months.[57] However, the exceptions for continued response actions to address immediate risk or a determination that the removal action will be consistent with an eventual remedial action tend to swallow this rule. Under CERCLA section 107, the responsible party is liable for all costs of response.

The amount of detail, public notice, and public availability of removal decision documentation depends on the classification of the removal action. In general, if the OSC determines that a planning period of at least six months exists before an action is required, the agency performs an engineering/cost analysis (EE/CA) and makes it available for public comment before initiating the removal.[58] This is called a non-time-critical removal action. If action is needed more quickly (a time-critical removal), then the NCP requires the OSC to put documents in the administrative record describing the removal action being taken and, as appropriate, allow for public comment, within 60 days after the activity is initiated.

The OSC provides reports on the initiation and status of all removal actions to the Regional Response Team or the National Response Team.[59] These reports are called "Pollution Reports" and are publicly available but can be difficult to find online.[60]

---

56. *See* EPA, Superfund Removal Guidance for Preparing Action Memoranda (Sept. 2009), https://semspub.epa.gov/work/HQ/190041.pdf.

57. 40 C.F.R. § 300.415(l).

58. *Id.* § 300.820.

59. *Id.* § 300.165.

60. For a description of the information found in pollution reports, *see* EPA, *Superfund Removal Procedures: Removal Response Reporting: POLREPs and OSC Reports* (June 1994), https://semspub.epa.gov/work/06/9337492.pdf.

The NCP and Hazardous Substance Remedial Actions

While a removal action is often the only action needed to mitigate the risk from a release, some releases require a permanent remedy, called a remedial action.[61] For remedial actions, the NCP sets forth very detailed requirements.[62]

EPA is not authorized to spend Superfund Trust Fund dollars on a remedial action unless the site is listed on the National Priorities List (NPL).[63] A site is eligible for listing on the NPL if (1) it scores sufficiently high under the hazard ranking system (HRS), (2) it is designated by a state as its highest priority, or (3) the Agency for Toxic Substances and Disease Registry has issued a health advisory for the release and EPA determines there is both a significant threat to public health and that it is more cost effective to use remedial authority to respond.[64]

The HRS is a numerical scoring system designed to rank sites from 1 to 100 based on risk, with greater weight given to human exposure.[65] In the early days of Superfund, EPA arbitrarily set 28.5 as the cut-off for placing a site on the NPL. The cut-off was established to create an initial NPL list of about 400 sites and was never changed. In practice, a site's HRS score does not determine site priority because as soon as a site scores 28.5 or above, EPA stops evaluating the site for listing purposes. As a result, EPA does not know which sites would be ranked higher and, therefore, might be considered a higher priority. The HRS only determines whether a site can be placed on the NPL.[66]

---

61. 42 U.S.C. § 9601(24).
62. 40 C.F.R. §§ 300.420–.440.
63. *Id.* § 300.425(b)(1).
64. *Id.* § 300.425(c). According to the Association of State and Territorial Solid Waste Management Officials, as of 2017, 44 states and territories have exercised their one-time authority. See Mechanisms for Placing Sites on the National Priorities List (NPL), https://astswmo.org/files/Resources/CERCLA_and_Brownfields/SAFG-NPL-Designation-Paper-8-22-17.pdf. Fourteen sites have been placed on the NPL based on an ATSDR health advisory. See Agency for Toxic Substances and Disease Registry (ATSDR) National Priorities List Sites, https://www.epa.gov/superfund/agency-toxic-substances-and-disease-registry-atsdr-national-priorities-list-npl-sites.
65. 40 C.F.R. pt. 300, app. A.
66. As of October 2024, there were 1,341 sites on the NPL and an additional 428 sites have been deleted. *See* Superfund National Priorities List (NPL), https://www.epa.gov/superfund

As soon as a site is listed on the NPL, a remedial project manager (RPM) takes over management of the site from the OSC (if an OSC had been assigned to the site). The RPM oversees the remedial investigation and feasibility study (RI/FS) that is the basis for a record of decision (ROD) that recommends a remedy.[67] Rather than EPA conducting the RI/FS at each NPL site, EPA policy allows responsible parties to perform the RI/FS under EPA oversight, consistent with an "enforcement first" approach to site cleanup.[68]

Remedy Selection

Both CERCLA and the NCP carefully prescribe the process for selecting remedies. EPA has further explained its process and policies in its official guidance.

Statutory Overview

Under section 121, a long-term cleanup action (a remedial action) must be consistent with the NCP to the extent practicable and must provide for cost-effective response.[69] In addition, at a minimum, all remedies must protect human health and the environment.[70] Cost-effectiveness is determined based on short- and long-term costs, including operation and maintenance.[71] For long-term cleanup actions, the statute establishes a preference for treatment over off-site disposal.[72] In the NCP, EPA interprets this provision to apply to principal threats only.[73] If waste is

---

/superfund-national-priorities-list-npl. On December 24, 2024, EPA added the Upper Columbia River to the NPL, bringing the total number of NPL sites to 1,342. 89 Fed. Reg. 100,751 (Dec. 24, 2024).

67. 40 C.F.R. § 300.430.

68. EPA, Promoting Enforcement First for Remedial Investigation/Feasibility Studies at Superfund Sites, OSWER Directive 9200.2-109 (Mar. 20, 2012), https://www.epa.gov/sites/default/files/2013-10/documents/rifs-first-2012.pdf.

69. 42 U.S.C. § 9621(a).

70. *Id.* § 9621(d)(1).

71. *Id.*

72. *Id.* § 9621(b).

73. 40 C.F.R. § 300.430(a)(1)(iii)(A); *see* EPA, A Guide to Principal Threat and Low-Level Threat Wastes, OSWER Directive No. 9380.3-06FS (Nov. 1991); EPA, Rules of Thumb for Superfund Remedy Selection, OSWER Directive 9355.0-69 (Aug. 1997).

to remain onsite, it must meet standards promulgated under other federal environmental laws as well as state law, but only if EPA determines that each such standard is legally applicable or is relevant and appropriate (ARAR) under the circumstances of the release.[74] The statute also identifies Maximum Contaminant Level Goals (MCLGs) under the Safe Drinking Water Act and Clean Water Act water quality criteria as goals or criteria that must be met where relevant and appropriate.[75] Even if legally applicable, CERCLA exempts cleanup actions from the need to obtain a permit for on-site activities.[76] If hazardous wastes or PCB wastes are transferred off-site, they can only be sent to a facility operating under either a RCRA hazardous waste permit or a TSCA PCB disposal permit.[77]

Overview of Remedy Selection Under the NCP

Remedies are shaped by certain "expectations" identified in the NCP.[78] A remedial action is selected based on nine criteria:

1. Overall protection of human health and the environment
2. Compliance with applicable or relevant and appropriate requirements (ARARs)[79]
3. Long-term effectiveness and permanence
4. Reduction in toxicity, mobility, or volume through treatment
5. Short-term effectiveness
6. Implementability

74. 42 U.S.C. § 9621(d)(2). Standards that are applicable or relevant and appropriate are called ARARs. Potential ARARs are identified in EPA's "Compliance with Other Laws" manuals, https://www.epa.gov/superfund/applicable-or-relevant-and-appropriate-requirements-arars.

75. 42 U.S.C. § 9621(d)(2)(A). In the NCP, EPA does not require compliance with MCLGs have been set at zero. 40 C.F.R. § 300.430(e)(2)(i)(C).

76. 42 U.S.C. § 9621(e).

77. *Id.* § 9621(d)(3).

78. 40 C.F.R. § 300.430(a)(1)(iii) (use of treatment to address principal threats where practicable, use of engineering controls for low long-term threats or where treatment is not practicable, use of both treatment and engineering controls to achieve protection, use of institutional controls to prevent exposure but not as the sole remedy unless active measures are not practicable, use of innovative technology, and return of usable groundwater to beneficial use where practicable).

79. Federal and state ARARs are identified in EPA's Compliance with Other Laws Manuals. Part 1 is available at https://semspub.epa.gov/work/HQ/174076.pdf. Part 2 is available at https://semspub.epa.gov/work/HQ/174077.pdf.

7. Cost
8. State acceptance
9. Community acceptance[80]

Overall protection of human health and the environment is the threshold criterion that all remedies must meet. The next five are the primary balancing criteria, and state and community acceptance are modifying criteria.[81] However, both state and community involvement in remedy selection are required.[82]

The NCP provides that exposure to carcinogens is unacceptable if the exposure represents an excess upper bound lifetime cancer risk to an individual of between 10^{-4} and 10^{-6}.[83] For non-carcinogens, EPA uses a hazard quotient of 1 to identify unacceptable exposure.[84]

In the absence of ARARs or when an ARAR is not protective, EPA has established a hierarchy of human health toxicity values that the Superfund program considers "best available science" and relies on when selecting remedies. Tier 1 of this hierarchy consists of EPA's own Integrated Risk Information System (IRIS) values. If a chemical has an IRIS value, then EPA will not look further for risk information. Tier 2 of the hierarchy is populated by EPA's Provisional Peer Reviewed Toxicity Values (PPRTVs). Tier 3 includes toxicity values from EPA and non-EPA sources, and gives priority to values that are current, transparent, and from peer-reviewed sources.[85] However, notwithstanding risk values, EPA generally will not set cleanup levels at concentrations that are below natural background levels.[86]

---

80. 40 C.F.R. § 300.430(e)(9)(iii).

81. *Id.* § 300.430(f)(1)(i).

82. *Id.* § 300.430(c) (community relations) and § 300.500 (state involvement).

83. *Id.* § 300.430(e)(2)(i)(A).

84. EPA, Role of the Baseline Risk Assessment in Superfund Remedy Selection Decision, OSWER Directive 9355.0-30 (Apr. 22, 1991), https://www.epa.gov/sites/default/files/2015-11/documents/baseline.pdf.

85. EPA, Human Health Toxicity Values in Superfund Risk Assessments, OSWER Directive 9285.7-53 (Dec. 5, 2003), https://www.epa.gov/sites/default/files/2015-11/documents/hhmemo.pdf.

86. EPA, Role of Background in the CERCLA Cleanup Program, OSWER Directive 9285.6-07P (Apr. 26, 2002), https://www.epa.gov/sites/default/files/2015-11/documents/bkgpol_jan01.pdf.

In accordance with the NCP, EPA has preliminary discussions with a state regarding remedy selection.[87] EPA then proposes a remedial action and takes public comment for at least 30 days before signing the ROD.[88] EPA may make a significant change to a ROD (such as a significant change in the scope, performance, or cost) through a ROD amendment or through an explanation of significant differences (ESD).[89] A ROD amendment, which requires the same public notice and comment process as the original ROD, is required if the change would fundamentally alter the remedy. As a practical matter, EPA has a great deal of discretion in deciding what amount of change to a remedy is significant, insignificant, or fundamental in this context. In cases in which substantial uncertainty remains and the final remedy will be identified following remedial design, EPA may issue a "contingent ROD" that includes two or more alternatives, thereby avoiding the need to amend the remedy after remedial design is complete.[90]

A state may decide that it does not concur with a remedy. If a state is seeking enhancements that EPA determines are not necessary, EPA can agree to change the remedy only if a state agrees to fund all the additional costs associated with the enhancement.[91]

Identifying and Applying ARARs

ARARs are often a subject of controversy in remedy selection. State and tribal environmental standards only apply to a remedy if EPA determines that the standard is an ARAR, and EPA has a great deal of discretion

---

87. 40 C.F.R. § 300.430(e).

88. *Id.* § 300.430(f)(3). PRPs are well advised to comment on proposed remedies. In developing comments, it can be useful to point to examples of flexibilities adopted by EPA in other RODs. EPA's remedy decisions documents are posted online at https://www.epa.gov/superfund/search-superfund-decision-documents.

89. *Id.* § 300.435(c)(2).

90. EPA, A Guide to Preparing Superfund Proposed Plans, Records of Decision, and Other Remedy Selection Decision Documents, OSWER 9200.1-2P § 8 (July 1999), https://www.epa.gov/sites/default/files/2015-02/documents/rod_guidance.pdf.

91. 40 C.F.R. § 300.515(f). Remedy enhancements that are not necessary are "betterments." For example, if a soil removal remedy destroys septic systems, a Superfund remedy can only replace the septic systems. It cannot build a wastewater treatment facility for the community. EPA cannot spend Superfund dollars to carry out a betterment. Nor can EPA use its enforcement authorities to compel a private party to fund a betterment.

when making that determination. Even if EPA determines a standard is an ARAR, it still may select a remedy that does not comply if EPA waives compliance for one of six specified reasons.[92] In situations where the cleanup is financed by the Superfund, EPA may waive an ARAR based on a determination that compliance will cost too much. This is referred to the "fund-balancing" waiver. In practice, EPA seldom waives compliance with ARARs. It often is easier for EPA to simply determine that a standard is not applicable or relevant and appropriate.

Under the NCP, ARARs are "frozen" at the time the ROD selecting the remedy is signed. That is, if a state or EPA later promulgates a new standard that may be applicable or relevant and appropriate, the ROD is not reopened.[93] However, a ROD may always be reopened if EPA determines that a remedy is no longer protective.

If a state disagrees with EPA over whether a state standard is an ARAR, the state has no recourse if the cleanup is fund financed. If the cleanup will be carried out by a responsible party, a state may intervene in the settlement before a consent decree is entered by a court and argue that EPA's decision was not supported by substantial evidence.[94]

EPA takes the position that NEPA is not an ARAR and that CERCLA remedy selection is exempt from the NEPA process. Although CERCLA contains no NEPA waiver, as stated in its "Notice and Procedures for Voluntary Preparation of National Environmental Policy" documents, EPA argues that CERCLA exempts EPA from compliance with procedural requirements of environmental laws, including NEPA, and that EPA's procedures and environmental reviews are functionally equivalent to NEPA.[95] In the early years after CERCLA's enactment in 1980, private parties tried, unsuccessfully, to challenge this position.[96]

---

92. 42 U.S.C. § 9621(a).

93. 40 C.F.R. § 300.430(f)(1)(ii)(B)(1).

94. 42 U.S.C. § 9621(f)(2)(B).

95. Notice of Policy and Procedures for Voluntary Preparation of National Environmental Policy Documents, 63 Fed. Reg. 58,045 (1998).

96. Lone Pine Steering Committee v. United States EPA, 600 F. Supp. 1487 (D.N.J. 1985) (holding the plaintiffs lacked standing to bring a NEPA claim), *aff'd*, Lone Pine Steering Comm. v. United States Env't Protection Agency, 777 F.2d 882 (3d Cir. 1985).

State standards apply to a remedy only to the extent provided in section 121 of CERCLA.[97] Thus, for CERCLA remedy decisions, state standards are preempted by the remedy selection provisions of CERCLA.[98]

Groundwater

The NCP establishes an expectation that usable contaminated ground water be returned to its beneficial use, wherever practicable within a time frame that is reasonable.[99] Groundwater remedies are often controversial because "pump and treat" remedies can be costly, energy intensive, and unreliable.

Congress added section 121, "Cleanup Standards," to CERCLA in the 1986 Superfund Amendments and Reauthorization Act, which included a requirement for EPA to consider the designated or potential use of groundwater when identifying relevant and appropriate water quality criteria.[100] EPA's Superfund program used the EPA Office of Water's 1986 "Ground-Water Protection Strategy" to identify groundwater beneficial uses. Under that strategy, groundwater is classified as Class I (high value drinking water sources), Class II (current or potential drinking water sources), or Class III (unsuitable for human consumption unrelated to a specific contamination source such as groundwater with high total dissolved solids).[101] In 1992, EPA issued the "Final Comprehensive State Ground Water Protection Program (CSGWPP) Guidance," which establishes a process for state groundwater classification and EPA approval.[102] In 1997, EPA issued "The Role of CSGWPPs in EPA Remediation Programs," which makes it clear that EPA can use EPA-approved

97. 42 U.S.C. § 9621(d) (requiring CERCLA remedies to comply with legally applicable state standards but then allowing EPA to determine what is legally applicable, exempting compliance with state standards under in certain circumstances, such where they would effectively resulting a statewide prohibition on land disposal, and allowing EPA to exempt compliance under certain conditions).

98. The applicability of state standards after a CERCLA remedy is complete remains unclear despite Supreme Court consideration of this issue in the context of an ongoing cleanup. Atlantic Richfield Co. v. Christian, 590 U.S. 1 (2020).

99. 40 C.F.R. § 300.430(a)(1)(iii)(F).

100. P.L. 99-499, § 121 (1986).

101. 55 Fed. Reg. 8666, 8732–33 (Mar. 8, 1990) (NCP preamble).

102. EPA 100-R-93-001 (Dec. 1992).

groundwater classification systems in remedy determinations.[103] Unfortunately, once EPA stopped providing funding to states to develop CSGWPPs, few states have reexamined their groundwater classifications, so the flexibility offered by EPA in 1997 is rarely used.

EPA can also determine that restoration of groundwater is technically impracticable.[104] These "TI waivers" are also rarely used. Further, even if the presence of dense non-aqueous phase liquids (DNAPLs) or another condition is preventing groundwater restoration, TI waivers are generally not considered until a second technology is tried and fails.[105]

Finally, EPA can determine that restoration is not practicable within a reasonable time frame. In 2012, the National Research Council of the National Academy of Science found that "[s]ignificant limitations with currently available remedial technologies persist that make achievement of [Safe Drinking Water Act standards] throughout the aquifer unlikely at most complex groundwater sites in a time frame of 50–100 years."[106] EPA used to report data on the status of remedies, which made it clear that many groundwater pump and treat remedies did not reach restoration goals. In the "Treatment Technologies for Site Cleanup: Annual Status Report (Twelfth Edition)," EPA reported that of the 73 pump and treat remedies that had been shut down, only 30 were discontinued because they met project goals.[107] The report also noted that 100 pump and treat remedies had been changed to other groundwater remedies.

Due to the limitations of groundwater pump and treat remedies, EPA has increasingly relied on monitored natural attenuation as a component of a groundwater remedy. EPA recognizes that the NCP requirement to treat principal threat sources does not apply to groundwater, as it is not

---

103. OSWER Directive 9283.1-09 (Apr. 1997).

104. "Guidance for Evaluating the Technical Impracticability of Ground-Water Restoration," OSWER Directive 9234.2-25 (Sept. 1993), https://semspub.epa.gov/work/06/9351189.pdf.

105. EPA, Groundwater Road Map: Recommended Process for Restoring Contaminated Groundwater at Superfund Sites, OSWER Directive 9283.1-34 (July 2011), https://semspub.epa.gov/work/HQ/174480.pdf.

106. Nat'l Rsch. Council, Alternatives for Managing the Nation's Complex Contaminated Groundwater Sites 7 (Nov. 2012), https://nap.nationalacademies.org/read/14668/chapter/1.

107. EPA, Treatment Technologies for Site Cleanup: Annual Status Report 4-13, Appx. G (12th ed. Sept. 2007), https://www.epa.gov/sites/default/files/2015-09/documents/asr12_full_document.pdf.

a source.[108] EPA also recognizes that monitored natural attenuation does treat organic and some inorganic (radionuclides) compounds.[109] Finally, EPA recognizes that continuing to operate pump and treat programs that are making little or no progress could have adverse environmental effects, due to greenhouse gas emissions.[110]

To reevaluate remedies that were not working, EPA established a policy of reviewing cleanup decisions, called remedy "optimization." While initially EPA optimized remedies only at fund-lead sites, it has expanded the practice to PRP-lead sites.[111] At groundwater sites, remedy optimization can lead to turning off pump and treat systems and relying instead on monitored natural attenuation.[112]

As discussed in Chapter 7, it is difficult for any person to challenge an EPA remedy before EPA takes an enforcement action. However, EPA needs private parties to carry out cleanups. Accordingly, EPA's policies and precedents with respect to the selection of remedies can be used by private parties that are negotiating agreements to carry out a CERCLA remedy to ensure that the remedy is cost-effective.

In addition, many implementation decisions are made by an RPM after a private party has agreed to carry out a remedial action. These policies and precedents also can be useful when negotiating remedy implementation with RPMs.[113]

---

108. EPA, Use of Monitored Natural Attenuation at Superfund, RCRA Corrective Action, and Underground Storage Tank Sites, OSWER Directive 9200.4-17P (Apr. 1999), https://www.epa.gov/sites/default/files/2014-02/documents/d9200.4-17.pdf.

109. *Id.*

110. EPA, Green Remediation: Incorporating Sustainable Environmental Practices into Remediation of Contaminated Sites (Apr. 2008), https://www.epa.gov/sites/default/files/2015-04/documents/green-remediation-primer.pdf.

111. EPA, National Strategy to Expand Superfund Optimization Practices from Site Assessment to Site Completion, OSWER Directive 9200.3-75 (Sept. 2012), https://semspub.epa.gov/work/HQ/174096.pdf.

112. Responsible parties seeking to reevaluate the efficacy of a groundwater remedy may find good information in the recommendations of the Superfund Remedy Review Board, found at https://www.epa.gov/superfund/national-remedy-review-board-nrrb.

113. RPM's tend to be very risk adverse but pointing out that the flexibility sought is endorsed by EPA Headquarters can help overcome a reluctance to provide flexibility.

Conclusion

The Superfund NCP is the "bible" for responding to releases of oil and hazardous substances. However, it is important to remember that EPA also has developed many policy documents that provide further direction and often flexibility. Any person faced with a significant release should be familiar with both the NCP and those policies.

Chapter 6

Responses to Transportation-Related Hazardous Materials Incidents: Trains, Pipelines, Ships, and Trucks

Greg Dillard and Emily Mott

This chapter examines key legal considerations for responding to transportation incidents, highlighting four common events: railway derailments and railcar releases, pipeline spills, maritime spills, and roadway accidents. The manner in which the responsible party or parties respond to such incidents is crucial to minimizing the negative regulatory and business impacts and improving the ultimate outcome and resolution of the situation. For example, a poorly coordinated or disorganized response exposes a responsible party (or even a government agency) to community backlash, media criticism, and material reputational harm. Conversely, a well-run transportation incident response reduces legal liability, timely communicates relevant information to government agencies and the public, and assists the responsible party in identifying and implementing remedial recommendations and best practices to avoid a re-occurrence. While there are many aspects to an integrated, well-run incident response, this chapter focuses on reporting and notifications, agency authority, incident management, investigations, emergency preparedness, and potential liability issues associated with transportation-related environmental incidents. Many of these topics broadly apply to most, if not all, incidents—whether transportation related or not.

Railways: Train Derailments and Railcar Releases

Incident Reporting and Notifications

One of the first considerations after an incident is making a timely report and notification to the relevant government agencies. Depending on the type of incident, there are usually several government agencies that will need to be notified under law. The reporting obligations differ based on the type and amount of material released, whether the release occurred to land, water, or air, and in which jurisdiction(s) the release occurred. There may also be state and federal reporting obligations.

As detailed in Chapter 3, a crucial early step in every response is to identify the substance(s) released and make an initial determination or approximation as to how much of each substance was released. This is essential because certain reporting requirements are triggered based on the released quantities (e.g., should the amount released be over the "reportable quantity," reporting will likely be required).

The reporting of releases from railroad incidents is governed by Title 49 of Code of Federal Regulations Part 225, administered by the Federal Railroad Administration (FRA). The Hazardous Materials Transportation Act (HMTA)[1] and its implementing regulations, 49 C.F.R. Parts 171 and 172, relate to the reporting of releases from any transportation of hazardous materials in commerce.[2] Generally, each person[3] in physical possession of hazardous material[4] that was involved in certain transportation-related[5] reportable incidents must give notice to the National

1. 49 U.S.C. §§ 5101–5127.

2. Functions not subject to these requirements are listed in 49 C.F.R. § 171.1(d).

3. "Person" means an individual, corporation, company, association, firm, partnership, society, joint stock company, or a government, Indian tribe, or authority of a government or tribe offering a hazardous material for transportation in commerce or transporting a hazardous material to support a commercial enterprise. 49 C.F.R. § 171.8.

4. "Hazardous Material" is a substance or material that the Secretary of Transportation has determined is capable of posing an unreasonable risk to health, safety, and property when transported in commerce and designated as hazardous under Section 5103 of the Federal Hazardous Materials Transportation Act. The term includes hazardous substances, hazardous wastes, marine pollutants, elevated temperature materials, materials designated as hazardous, and materials meeting defining criteria for hazard classes and divisions in 49 C.F.R. Part 173. 49 C.F.R. § 171.8. Hazardous substances are listed in Appendix A to 49 C.F.R. § 172.101.

5. "Transportation" means the movement of property and loading, unloading, or storage incidental to that movement. *Id.* § 171.8.

Response Center (NRC) as soon as practical but no later than 12 hours after the occurrence of the reportable incident.[6]

Depending on the factual scenario, transportation incidents must be reported to the NRC via telephone on its 24-hour hotline, (800) 424-8802.[7] The NRC will then notify federal, state, and local responders. Nevertheless, reporting to the NRC usually does not also satisfy the independent legal obligations of responsible parties under the laws of most states to also make timely reports directly to one or more state or local agencies. Similarly, reports made to state or municipal agencies are commonly not forwarded to the NRC.

The notice to the NRC must provide the following information: (1) the name of the reporter; (2) the name and address of the person represented by the reporter; (3) the phone number where the reporter can be contacted; (4) date, time, and location of the incident; (5) the extent of any injuries; (6) class or division, proper shipping name, and quantity of hazardous materials involved, if available; and (7) the type of incident and nature of hazardous material involvement and whether a continuing danger to life exists at the scene.[8]

In addition to the initial notice provided to the NRC within 12 hours of the incident, each responsible party must also file a written Hazardous Materials Incident Report within 30 days after discovery of the incident.[9]

Because it is often difficult in the initial stages of an incident response to determine with certainty the full list of all the hazardous substances or materials or the precise amounts of each that were released, initial notifications and written reports will typically steer away from including premature conclusions. It is common in the notifications to include "wiggle room" phrases, such as "estimated," "preliminary calculation," or "based upon information known at this time." Agencies usually, but not always, acknowledge that responsible parties may not have their arms around all the relevant facts during the first hours of an incident

6. *Id.* § 171.15(a).

7. 49 C.F.R. § 171.15(a). For a listing of incidents which require reporting to the NRC, *see* 49 C.F.R. §§ 171.15(b), 171.16.

8. 49 C.F.R. § 171.15(a).

9. The Hazardous Materials Incident Report (currently DOT Form F 5800.1, Rev. 1/2004), https://www.phmsa.dot.gov/sites/phmsa.dot.gov/files/docs/IncidentForm010105.pdf. *See also* 49 C.F.R. § 171.16(a).

response. Accordingly, to help avoid providing premature or potentially false information to an agency, it is common for responsible parties to supplement their notifications as additional data and calculations become available. Further, responsible parties are neither asked nor expected to report any data beyond those enumerated in the applicable statutes or rules, or to raise any legal arguments or defenses in their release notifications. The assertion of legal arguments or defenses by a responsible party during the reporting phase may be perceived as a red flag by an agency.

Responsible parties often find that they can improve their follow-up notifications by quickly initiating a fulsome internal investigation—often under the attorney-client privilege and/or attorney work product doctrine—in order to more accurately describe the type of release, how it occurred, and whether it created an actual hazard to the environment, public, and employees. Such in-depth investigations can enable a responsible party to correct initial, conservative (i.e., high-end) reporting, mitigating preliminary factual errors that could otherwise negatively impact agency enforcement and third-party lawsuits.

Agency Actions and Authorities

The earliest phases of a response involving a railroad incident are commonly directed by local emergency first responders in the municipalities or counties in which the incident occurs, because they are the first to be notified if a report is made via a 911 call. Depending on the nature and scale of the release and the extent of actual or potential impacts to human health or the environment, subsequent reports to the state or federal agencies may cause state authorities to exert control under state law or to defer to one or more federal agencies. These agencies may mobilize to the site and take overall responsibility and authority for directing the response.

Upon receipt of the initial notification, even before deciding to deploy personnel to an incident site, an agency may take a range of imminent actions. This includes but is not limited to sending a written notice to preserve all evidence related to the incident (requiring the responsible party to preserve both the incident scene, as well as remote electronic and operational data), requesting documents or videos, and conducting initial interviews by remote means.

Upon the occurrence of a train-related incident, for investigation, compliance, or enforcement purposes, an incident site may be simultaneously visited by multiple federal agencies, including the National Transportation Safety Board (NTSB), the Environmental Protection Agency (EPA), the Department of Transportation (DOT), or the Occupational Safety and Health Administration (OSHA). Both the FRA and the Pipeline and Hazardous Materials Safety Administration (PHMSA) are DOT agencies that have jurisdiction over rail activity involving the transportation of hazardous materials. Governing regulations can be found at 49 C.F.R. Parts 100–199 for the FRA and 49 C.F.R. Parts 200–299 for PHMSA. The FRA and PHMSA share responsibility for regulating the transportation of hazardous materials by rail.

In response to incidents that have large-scale community impacts, teams from the Federal Emergency Management Agency, the U.S. Department of Health and Human Services, or the Centers for Disease Control and Prevention frequently visit with affected residents, generate community update communications, and gather situational awareness about ongoing citizen concerns or unmet needs. For responsible parties, ensuring effective multi-agency communications can be challenging during an incident. When responsible parties effectively coordinate their agency communications, they exponentially increase the probability that affected community stakeholders will be timely notified of significant updates and the public will have access to available resources, such as public health testing and assessments by medical personnel and toxicologists. For example, within hours after the highly publicized train derailment incident in East Palestine, Ohio, multiple federal agencies were already collaborating to address numerous issues, including the associated public health concerns.[10] The responsible parties, when feasible, often see it as being in their best interest to be involved in, or at the least made aware of, those assessments and communications—ensuring they are well-informed and updated regarding the agencies' actions and areas of interest and the affected communities' concerns.

---

10. *See Fact Sheet: Biden-Harris Administration Deploys Additional Federal Resources to East Palestine, Ohio* (Feb. 17, 2023), https://bidenwhitehouse.archives.gov/briefing-room/statements-releases/2023/02/17/fact-sheet-biden-harris-administration-deploys-additional-federal-resources-to-east-palestine-ohio/.

National Transportation Safety Board

The NTSB is an independent federal investigative agency charged by Congress with the primary authority to investigate significant accidents and develop safety recommendations in multiple modes of transportation, including aviation, railroad, highway, marine, and pipelines. The NTSB has the authority to investigate highway accidents and incidents, including incidents at railway grade crossings, in cooperation with a state.[11] While local, state, and federal agencies may support an NTSB investigation, or conduct their own investigations, which may be informed by the NTSB investigation, the NTSB is the lead federal agency responsible for conducting the safety investigation.[12] The NTSB does not investigate potential criminal activity and has no enforcement or penalty authority. However, its findings may be used by other agencies that are probing potential civil or criminal charges for violations of environmental or other laws.

As the typical lead investigative agency for train derailments, the NTSB usually deploys to the incident site within hours of notification to commence its investigation. While the NTSB frequently issues a preliminary report within a matter of weeks, including confirmed facts underlying the incident, the NTSB's fulsome investigation and final report may take upwards of a year to complete (depending on the complexity of the incident). Some federal agencies may wait to complete their investigation until the NTSB has issued its final report, but some agencies (such as OSHA) have shorter limitations periods in which they are required to complete their investigation and independently issue a citation for violations.

In recognition of the fact that it does not always have within its ranks all the necessary expertise or ready access to all the necessary information, the NTSB follows a "party system" investigation process.[13] The list of entities invited to be "parties" is at the sole discretion of the NTSB, and often includes the entities or representatives of entities that are the targets

11. 49 U.S.C. § 1131(1)(c).
12. *Id.* § 1131(2)(a).
13. 49 C.F.R. § 831.11.

of the investigation, including, for example, the railroad company, the manufacturers of the involved railcars, and organizations that represent locomotive engineers. The NTSB's investigative team typically includes hazardous material investigators; equipment specialists; and mechanical, operations, and train track experts. The NTSB accepts information, analysis, and reports from the parties, but the agency is the exclusive author of its final report.

Federal Railroad Administration

The FRA is responsible for enforcing federal rail safety and hazardous materials laws, rules, and regulations as applied to passenger and freight railroads. FRA enforcement actions usually involve civil penalties levied against a railroad, individuals, or companies that offer hazardous materials for rail transportation. The FRA investigates hazardous material releases that result from train accidents, as well as hazardous material releases from non-accident release events. In some incidents, the FRA or PHMSA will play a supporting role in the NTSB's investigation, but will also conduct its own, separate investigation "to determine root causation, and any contributing factors, so that parties can implement corrective actions to prevent similar incidents in the future. Such corrective actions cover a broad range of activities, including, but not limited to ensuring that simple repairs are made; changing operating rules; modifications to equipment and infrastructure inspection procedures; or developing a new federal regulation or safety standard."[14] Thus, FRA investigations target both safety improvements and enforcement violations.

- In 2022, the FRA reported 3,775 recommended violations relating to hazardous materials, 2,525 relating to safety standards, and 1,628 relating to railroad operating practices, obtaining $14,152,533 in civil penalty assessments and settlements.[15]

14. USDOT, *Federal Railroad Administration Accident Investigation Fact Sheet* (Sept. 2016), https://railroads.dot.gov/sites/fra.dot.gov/files/2019-11/FRA%20Accident%20Investigation%20Fact%20Sheet.pdf.

15. USDOT, *Federal Railroad Administration's Fiscal Year 2022 Enforcement Report* (2022), https://railroads.dot.gov/elibrary/fiscal-year-2022-enforcement-report.

- In 2023, the FRA reported 2,325 recommended violations relating to hazardous materials, 3,103 relating to safety standards, and 1,605 relating to railroad operating practices, obtaining $15,630,602 in civil penalty assessments and settlements.[16]

Environmental Protection Agency

As discussed in detail in Chapter 5, The National Contingency Plan, the EPA typically leads large-scale cleanup operations and is the federal government agency in charge of responding to the release of hazardous substances into the environment. Whether the cleanup is performed by industry, local, state, or federal entities, EPA will ensure the cleanup is appropriate, timely, and minimizes human risks and environmental damage. In some situations, EPA may undertake control of the cleanup itself. However, the responsible party may be liable for reimbursing the expenses EPA incurs relating to the work. In addition to identifying potential enforcement violations against the company, EPA will often conduct air and water sampling or monitoring to ascertain the safety of the surrounding area and community. Responsible parties usually endeavor to participate jointly with EPA in such monitoring as part of its incident response so they can effectuate the coordinated interagency and community communications discussed in this chapter.

Pipeline and Hazardous Materials Safety Administration

PHMSA is responsible for developing and enforcing regulations for the safe, reliable, and environmentally sound transportation of energy and other hazardous materials by all modes of transportation, whether on land, sea, or air, including railroads and pipelines.[17] Practically, when PHMSA investigates railroad incidents, it frequently takes a subordinate role to other agencies.

16. USDOT, *Federal Railroad Administration's Fiscal Year 2023 Enforcement Report* (2023), https://railroads.dot.gov/elibrary/fiscal-year-2023-annual-enforcement-report.

17. USDOT, *PHMSA Regulations*, https://www.phmsa.dot.gov/regulations (last updated May 5, 2021).

Occupational Safety and Health Administration

When a railway incident occurs, a responsible party should expect federal OSHA or the applicable state-sponsored safety agency (i.e., state-plan OSHA) to be part of the response and investigation process. OSHA will focus its investigation and enforcement on personnel safety, which frequently in railcar chemical releases and train derailments is covered by a variety of safety regulations. Responsible parties involved in the physical cleanup are legally obligated to ensure that its personnel are complying with OSHA's HAZWOPER (Hazardous Waste Operations and Emergency Response) standard, at 29 C.F.R. § 1910.120.[18] OSHA and the FRA have complementary responsibilities with respect to protecting workplace safety and health.

Incident Management

The elements of successfully managing a railway incident are universal to most transportation incidents. Select aspects that apply more commonly to distinct transportation incidents will be addressed throughout this chapter. The incident response management process can be intensive, lengthy, and demanding, often requiring substantial resources and personnel of the responsible parties to be responsive to all engaged governmental authorities. Responsible parties that are not accustomed to these sudden and substantial burdens may find it especially important to focus on ensuring that they are dedicating enough financial resources and personnel to assist in the emergency response efforts, including for such tasks as evidence preservation, witness interviews, site walkthroughs, responding to document requests, report writing, and other time-sensitive tasks. Due to the fact-intensive nature of incident responses and the related investigations, responsible parties will also often seek to limit staffing turnover to maintain consistency in data collections and productions and to maintain an overall knowledge base about the incident.

18. *See generally* OSHA, *Hazardous Waste Operations and Emergency Response (HAZWOPER)*, https://www.osha.gov/emergency-preparedness/hazardous-waste-operations/standards (last visited Feb. 12, 2025).

While a responsible party and government agencies have some overlapping and some divergent response objectives, the unified initial focus in every railway incident response is on ensuring the safety of personnel, the public, and the environment. One of the very first incident management steps is to establish an incident command post at a safe location from the incident scene. Under the National Incident Management System (NIMS), which is also discussed in Chapter 1, effective incident command is a key building block to successfully achieving short- and long-term objectives. Unless the responsible party's own personnel are able to fully mitigate the hazards, initial emergency response actions such as personnel rescues, release mitigations, and fire suppression will be undertaken by local first responders or mutual aid response teams directed by the incident commander (typically, the local fire chief). Once the incident location has been deemed safe for others to enter, the incident commander will direct that environmental investigation and cleanup activities quickly commence. At some point, typically soon after the initial emergency response actions have been completed, either a state or federal official may assume the role of incident commander, or a unified command structure may be implemented.

Both to protect onlookers from site hazards and to help ensure evidence preservation, the incident location will be cordoned off at the direction of the incident commander. The geographic area surrounding the incident (and any equipment located on it) is usually treated as evidence and will likely be the subject of a preservation notice issued by a state or federal agency. In many instances, the incident commander will also establish a temporary exclusion zone to limit further access, thereby preserving the scene for investigators, minimizing loss of evidence, and mitigating later claims of spoliation. However, in all instances one of the incident commander's foremost responsibilities is ensuring safety, and most states' law is developed so that they may take all actions they deem necessary to achieve this objective without regard to whether an action could result in the loss or spoliation of evidence.

For this and other reasons, responsible parties will often move quickly after an incident's imminent hazards have been mitigated to compile photographic and other records of the incident. This may include engaging a third-party evidence custodian whose services can be engaged under privilege by a responsible party's legal counsel or hired under a nonprivileged structure depending on the specific potential legal liabilities and operational needs of that responsible party. In addition to immediate scene and evidence preservation, responsible parties will also typically check for video footage or recordings from its own property or equipment as well as that of nearby properties or sites controlled by others, assess and preserve any relevant electronic data systems, and issue preservation demands to third parties, where applicable. Site control agreements are often drafted and proffered by responsible parties to agencies and involved third-party entities as a means of securing the cooperation of all involved private and governmental entities to preemptively address physical evidence preservation procedures, limit the exclusion zone to only necessary preservation areas, and establish a procedure for identifying potential evidence by all involved parties.

Streamlined communication pathways are key to keeping the multiple agencies and responders timely and consistently informed, while running an efficient and integrated emergency response. At the beginning, the incident commander will usually put an overall communication strategy in place to facilitate their charge of overseeing all personnel involved in the safety response, in which case the responsible party's teams will usually be integrated into this communications structure. But after the incident command has been removed and control of the site is returned to a combination of the responsible parties and investigating agencies, there remains a need for coordinated interagency communications and public announcements. It is now standard practice for responsible parties to include media relations as a key component of their overall response to an incident. Having staff—whether internal or hired from an external company—whose primary focus is on managing external communications regarding the incident and the ongoing response can help a responsible party timely report out relevant information and keep the community updated. To help protect their own credibility, responsible parties will typically vet their factual updates with their legal counsel before releasing them to the agencies, media, and the public.

Another area of consideration in the aftermath of a train derailment incident is specialized contractor engagement and supervision. Specifically, while government agencies may perform initial and ongoing environmental monitoring, it is common practice in these situations for the responsible party to promptly engage its own experts and specialized contractors, such as a monitoring company for sampling air, soil, surface water, or groundwater impacts or an environmental spill response and control company to implement spill control measures. These immediate monitoring activities can provide key insights into potential environmental and community risks and impacts, and frequently they provide responsible parties with the necessary information to accurately share verifiable, collected environmental impact updates to the governmental agencies, media outlets, and their own personnel.

Investigations by Responsible Parties and Coordination with Governmental Authorities

In the immediate wake of a railway incident, a responsible party frequently finds it either legally necessary or simply prudent to conduct an internal investigation, which may be privileged, nonprivileged, or a combination of the two. Investigations may be performed exclusively internally or may include a third-party consultant. Privileged investigations are typically much broader than nonprivileged causal investigations. While privileged and nonprivileged investigations both involve site evidence analyses, document reviews, and employee interviews, the scope of the privileged investigation typically is broader and intentionally structured to assess potential topics of legal liability, evaluate enforcement exposure, and provide legal advice. Privileged investigations can review and analyze potential areas of concern beyond the direct, indirect, and root causes of the incident, thereby providing the responsible party with a more fulsome assessment of its policies, practices, and programs, as well as the actions that were directly involved in the incident. By contrast, a nonprivileged root cause investigation is typically more limited in scope and focused more acutely on identifying the proximate and root causes of the incident and developing tailored recommendations relating to only those causes. Where legal risk appears more significant from a large-scale incident, a responsible party may find it advantageous to consider the benefits of conducting simultaneous "dual track" privileged and non-privileged internal investigations.

When legal risk appears less significant, a responsible party may choose to conduct a single, nonprivileged root cause investigation. Even in those cases, there is a role for the company's lawyer. This strategy incorporates a cross-discipline approach addressing a company's environmental, safety, operations, and legal needs; a lawyer does not look at issues the same way as an engineer or an operations specialist. The role of the lawyer can be to highlight issues or potential areas of investigation for the investigation team that they may not have thought of themselves. Lawyers tend to think about and focus on two principal issues: (1) how to make sure this kind of incident does not happen again, and (2) what information would be helpful in defending the responsible party against future government enforcement or tort litigation. A typical responsible party's investigation team is not as focused on the second issue, but rather is focused on what happened, how and why it happened, and what were the safety and environmental impacts. Thus, the lawyer, even in a supporting resource role for the investigation team, may have guidance and insight into certain topics that could bolster the investigation team. However, because this particular type of investigation is nonprivileged, it is not being directed by legal counsel. The lawyer is not making demands but instead monitoring the team's work and suggesting topics to explore. When conducted holistically with support from a lawyer, these nonprivileged investigations tend to be collaborative processes that are more likely to robustly assess all relevant incident topics.

It is important for responsible parties to be aware of the internal resource burdens they will need to plan for when concurrently conducting an internal investigation(s) and managing one or more agency investigations. For example, a responsible party must ensure that its investigation team includes personnel with necessary knowledge of the relevant equipment and processes, but those personnel were not involved in the activities that led up to the incident, and that it has sufficient staff to respond to agency requests for information, documents, evidence, and site visits. Responsible parties must ensure that they have sufficient internal and external staffing to be able to respond in a timely, complete, and accurate manner to each request. For example, a responsible party is usually allowed to have one of its lawyers or managers attend and take notes during agency interviews of that party's supervisory employees. Responsible parties generally find it beneficial to have their counsel sit in on these agency interviews; helpful information may be gleaned from these interviews that may assist the party's own internal investigation and help to protect the party from later government enforcement. These staffing and resource needs are best achieved when planning for them occurs prior to an incident, not after.

Emergency Preparedness

Railroads are required to comply with a range of general and specific rules and regulations intended to promote emergency response preparedness. For example, each hazardous material that is offered for transportation by railroad must bear a standard label or placard that specifically identifies the hazardous material so that incident responders can promptly understand the potential hazards and determine the appropriate response mechanisms.[19] Railroads that operate passenger train services, as well as passenger or freight railroads that host the operations of passenger train services, and certain contractors to all such railroads, must also comply with additional regulations that mandate emergency preparedness planning.[20]

An integrated and well-run emergency response starts with planning and preparation. This is accomplished by creating an emergency response plan, conducting training and response exercises, and evaluating practice and real-life incident response performance to identify and implement lessons learned. Most railroads find it helpful to develop and maintain open lines of communication with local emergency management and response groups in advance of incidents in order to promote effective consultations on emergency preparedness. Standard good practices for preparedness may involve a railroad and the local, state, or federal emergency response agencies jointly undertaking simulated, integrated practice responses, such as tabletop drills and field exercises, which include multiple disciplines and hierarchies of communication. These kinds of

19. 49 C.F.R. pt. 172. These regulations also apply to other transportation means, for example, truck, barge, and pipeline.

20. *Id.* pt. 239.

practice exercises can help to identify additional channels of communication and notifications that may be needed in the case of an actual incident, as well as potential environmental spill contractors and necessary equipment for response efforts.

The Association of American Railroads also has online materials relating to rail preparedness and response, including an overview of the various federal laws that may apply to releases of hazardous substances.[21]

Potential Legal Liability

After a railway incident, a responsible party will find it helpful to broadly evaluate its legal exposure. The surrounding community, impacted individuals, or environmental groups may choose to file suit for alleged damages to persons, property, or the environment. Various negligence theories may be employed by different parties, and they frequently overlap and interconnect. For example, civil penalties imposed by government agencies may later form the basis of negligence per se allegations (depending on the jurisdiction). Claims sounding in trespass and public or private nuisance are also routinely alleged. Individuals or businesses impacted by the incident, or the response activities, may also file suit for damages for loss, seeking recovery costs and consequential damages. Depending on the situation, businesses surrounding the railway incident site may seek damages for inability to operate their business. Individuals, such as local residents and rail workers, may seek to hold a company liable for toxic torts, health damages, or wrongful death as a result of the incident.

Also, as mentioned earlier, EPA can enforce against violations of environmental laws subsequent to derailment or railcar release in several ways: civil administrative actions (for example, directing cleanup activities or imposing civil penalties for regulatory violations), civil judicial actions (for example, lawsuits for past and future costs of environmental cleanup or disputed regulatory violations), and criminal actions.

A recent incident highlights the high-value legal risks associated with these types of incidents. The U.S. Department of Justice (DOJ) filed suit, on behalf of the EPA, against Norfolk Southern for the unlawful discharge of pollutants, oil, and hazardous substances, asserting liability against the

21. For example, *see* https://www.aar.org/issue/freight-rail-hazmat-safety/.

company for past and future costs incurred, as a result of a February 2023 derailment of a Norfolk Southern freight train in Palestine, Ohio. The parties eventually reached a settlement in May 2024, valued at over $310 million, including a $15 million civil penalty and injunctive relief relating to improving safety, health monitoring for surrounding communities, long-term environmental monitoring, and other actions to protect nearby waterways and drinking water resources. According to EPA's press release issued on May 23, 2024, "[t]ogether with other response costs and rail safety enhancements, Norfolk Southern estimates that it will spend more than $1 billion to address the contamination and other harms caused by the East Palestine derailment and improve rail safety and operations."[22] These government settlements were in addition to hundreds of residential and impacted business claims pending in state and federal courts in Ohio. This illustrates the material financial damages and legal liability that companies face in the wake of serious railway incidents.

Pipeline Incidents

Pipelines are essential to the transport of numerous energy products produced, refined, and used across the nation, including natural gas, crude oil, and petroleum-based refined products. Pipelines are the most frequent transport method for moving the products that are critical to national security and the U.S. economy, including gasoline, home heating oil and kerosene, diesel fuel, and jet fuel. In addition to these products, pipelines also transport a broad range of industrial and petrochemical fuels: carbon dioxide, ethylene, ethanol, propane, butane, ammonia, and biofuels. Due to the high flammability and explosion risks of pipeline incidents, it is critical that responsible parties understand the regulatory scheme and enforcement mechanisms that may be employed in the event of a pipeline incident and be prepared to address all aspects of its response.

---

22. *See* EPA, *United States Reaches Over $310 Million Settlement with Norfolk Southern to Address Harms Caused by East Palestine Train Derailment* (May 23, 2024), https://www.epa.gov/newsreleases/united-states-reaches-over-310-million-settlement-norfolk-southern-address-harms#:~:text=WASHINGTON%20%E2%80%93%20Today%2C%20May%2023%2C,damage%20caused%20by%20the%20Feb.

Incident Reporting and Notifications

In addition to the general notification best practices described earlier under the discussion of railways, it is important to know that pipeline incidents[23] and accident[24] reporting regulations are located at 49 C.F.R. Parts 191 and 195. Operators of gas,[25] hazardous liquids,[26] or carbon dioxide pipelines must report accidents and incidents at the earliest practicable moment following discovery, but no later than one hour after confirmed discovery, with certain limited exclusions.[27] These notifications must be made to the NRC either by telephone (800-424-8802) or electronically at http://www.nrc.uscg.mil.[28] The following information must be provided: (1) the operator/company name; (2) the location of the accident; (3) the time of the incident; (4) the number of fatalities and/or personal injuries; (5) the phone number of the operator; (6) the

---

23. For gas pipelines, "incident" means any of the following events: (1) An event that involves a release of Gas from a pipeline, Gas from an underground natural gas storage facility, liquefied natural gas, liquified petroleum gas, refrigerant gas, or gas from an LNG facility and results in one or more of the following consequences: (a) A death or personal injury necessitating in-patient hospitalization, (b) Estimated property damage of $122,000 or more, including loss to the operator and other, or both, but excluding the cost of the Gas lost. Check the Pipeline and Hazardous Materials Safety Administration's website for the current property damage reporting threshold, (c) Unintentional estimated gas loss of three million cubic feet or more; (2) An event that results in an emergency shutdown of an LNG Facility or an underground natural gas storage facility (activation of an emergency system for reasons other than an actual emergency does not constitute an incident); or (3) An event that is significant in the judgment of the operator, even if it did not meet other criteria in paragraph (1) or (2) of this definition. *See* 49 C.F.R. § 191.3.

24. For hazardous liquid or carbon dioxide pipelines, an accident report is required for a release resulting in any of the following: (1) Explosion or fire not intentionally set by the operator; (2) Releasing 5 gallons (19 liters) or more of Hazardous Liquid or carbon dioxide, except no report is required for a release of less than 5 barrels (0.8 cubic meters) resulting from a pipeline maintenance activity if the release is (a) not otherwise reportable, (b) not one described in 49 C.F.R. § 195.52(a)(4), (c) confined to company property or pipeline right-of-way, and (d) cleaned up promptly; (3) Death of any person; (4) Personal injury necessitating hospitalization; or (5) Estimated property damage, including cleanup and recovery cost, value of lost product, and damage to property of the operator or others, or both, exceeding $50,000. *See* 49 C.F.R. § 195.2.

25. "Gas" means natural gas, flammable gas, or gas which is toxic or corrosive. *See* 49 C.F.R. § 191.3.

26. "Hazardous Liquid" means petroleum, petroleum products, anhydrous ammonia, and ethanol or other non-petroleum fuel, including biofuel, which is flammable, toxic, or would be harmful to the environment if released in significant quantities. *See* 49 C.F.R. § 195.2.

27. *Id.* §§ 191.1, 195.1.

28. *Id.* §§ 191.5, 195.52.

telephone number of the operator's on-site person; and (7) any other significant facts.[29]

Further, within 48 hours after the confirmed discovery of a pipeline accident or incident, to the extent practicable, an operator must revise or confirm by telephone to the NRC its initial telephonic notice with an estimate of the amount of product released, an estimate of the number of fatalities and injuries, and all other significant facts known by the operator that are relevant to the cause of the incident or accident.[30] Even if there are no changes or revisions to the initial report, it may be beneficial to the operator to confirm in this follow-up telephone notice the estimates in its initial report.[31]

Follow-up written reports may also be required depending on the type of accident or incident involved.[32] This written reporting requirement must be completed within 30 days after discovery of the accident or incident.[33]

Lastly, depending on the release scenario, a Comprehensive Environmental Response, Compensation, and Liability Act (CERCLA) reporting requirement may be triggered, as detailed in Chapter 3.[34] Generally, a person[35] in charge of a pipeline or midstream facility must immediately report a release[36] of a reportable quantity of a CERCLA hazardous substance.[37] As soon as the person in charge has knowledge of the release of a reportable quantity in any 24-hour period, the person must immediately

---

29. *Id.* §§ 191.5, 195.52.

30. *Id.* §§ 191.5(c), 195.52(d).

31. *Id.* §§ 191.5(c), 195.52(d).

32. *Id.* §§ 191.9(a), 191.15(a)–(c), 195.54(a).

33. *Id.* §§ 191.9(a), 191.15(a)–(c), 195.54(a).

34. *See* CERCLA § 103(a) and 40 C.F.R. pt. 302.

35. A "person" includes an individual, firm, corporation, association, partnership, consortium, joint venture, commercial entity, U.S. government, state, municipality, commission, political subdivision of a state, or any interstate body. 42 U.S.C. § 9601(21); 40 C.F.R. § 302.3; 52 Fed. Reg. 13378, 13393.

36. "Release" means any spilling, leaking, pumping, pouring, emitting, emptying, discharging, injecting, escaping, leaching, dumping, or disposing into the environment. 42 U.S.C. § 9601(22); 40 C.F.R. § 302.3.

37. The reportable quantity must have been released within a 24-hour period to trigger the requirement to report. 42 U.S.C. § 9603(a); 40 C.F.R. § 302.6.

report the release to the NRC at its 24-hour hotline (800-424-8802).[38] The NRC must be notified that the release has occurred or is occurring, after which the NRC likely will request additional information.[39]

Under CERCLA, a "facility" includes any "building, structure, installation, equipment, **pipe or pipeline** (including any pipe into a sewer or publicly owned treatment works), well, pit, pond, lagoon, impoundment, ditch, landfill, storage container, motor vehicle, rolling stock, or aircraft."[40] Thus, pipeline releases of certain amounts involving CERCLA hazardous substances[41] must be reported. Notably, concurrent releases of the same substance from different sources at the same facility must be considered together to determine if a reportable quantity has been released within any 24-hour period from a facility.[42] Further, as relevant to some pipeline operators, CERCLA hazardous substances contain an exclusion for "petroleum, including crude oil and any fraction thereof which is not otherwise specifically listed or designated as a hazardous substance . . . and . . . natural gas, natural gas liquids, liquified natural gas, or synthetic gas usable for fuel (or mixtures of natural gas and such synthetic gas)."[43]

Agency Actions and Authority

The United States has more than 2.6 million miles of pipelines (not including water and sewer pipes).[44] The federal pipeline safety laws

38. 42 U.S.C. § 9603(a); 40 C.F.R. § 302.6.

39. 42 U.S.C. § 9603(a); 40 C.F.R. § 302.6.

40. "Facility" also includes any site or area where a hazardous substance has been deposited, stored, disposed of, or placed, or otherwise come to be located; but does not include any consumer product in consumer use or any vessel (emphasis added).

41. A CERCLA hazardous substance is any listed or unlisted hazardous substance. A listed hazardous substance is any substance listed in 40 C.F.R. § 302.4, Table 302.4. *See* 42 U.S.C. § 9601(14); 40 C.F.R. §§ 302.3, 302.4. An unlisted hazardous substance is any solid waste, as defined in 40 C.F.R. § 261.2, not excluded from regulation under 40 C.F.R. § 261.4(b), that exhibits any of the characteristics of hazardous waste identified in 40 C.F.R. §§ 261.20–261.24. These characteristics are (1) ignitability, (2) corrosivity, (3) reactivity, and (4) toxicity. *See* 42 U.S.C. § 9601(14); *see also* 40 C.F.R. §§ 302.3, 302.4.

42. 42 U.S.C. § 9601(9), (17), (18); 40 C.F.R. § 302.3; 50 Fed. Reg. 13456, 13459.

43. 42 U.S.C. § 9601(14); 40 C.F.R. § 302.4.

44. *See* USDOT, *General Pipeline FAQs*, https://www.phmsa.dot.gov/faqs/general-pipeline-faqs (last updated Nov. 6, 2018).

(49 U.S.C. Chapter 601) designate the Department of Transportation's PHMSA as the lead enforcement authority and provide it with the authority to issue and enforce standards to protect the public, property, and the environment from potential risks associated with pipeline transportation. Pursuant to this authority, PHMSA issued pipeline safety regulations (49 C.F.R. Parts 190–199) that are designed to protect the public, property, and the environment. Accordingly, PHMSA's Office of Pipeline Safety is responsible for regulating the safe design, construction, testing, operation, maintenance, and emergency response of U.S. oil and natural gas pipeline facilities. PHMSA regulates and oversees both interstate and most intrastate pipelines.

While PHMSA regulates pipelines, the NTSB typically investigates major pipeline accidents to determine the cause of the accident and make needed safety recommendations. In certain situations, OSHA also has the authority to respond to pipeline accidents and issue safety violations to the company. EPA may also respond to spills of oil, hazardous substances, or hazardous materials from pipelines and provide additional assistance to state and local responders, if needed. There are memoranda of understanding issued between the agencies outlining when EPA or OSHA have regulatory authority.[45]

Incident Management

As part of an initial pipeline incident response, an incident commander is commonly designated. There are several additional actions routinely taken by a responsible party (some of which are similar to those described earlier under railways) if the incident commander is not otherwise doing so. In addition to planning for initial notifications that must be made by the responsible party, it is common for the responsible party to initially secure the area in the vicinity of the incident, establish proper hazard/exclusion zones, establish an incident command post, and begin a site assessment. Part of an initial site assessment entails determining the nature of the incident and release and recording details of the site and

45. *See* USDOL, Memoranda of Understanding, https://www.osha.gov/laws-regs/mou/publicationdate (last visited Feb. 18, 2025).

the potential impact of the incident. Most significantly, if hazardous materials are involved in the release, prudence dictates that only properly equipped responders approach the site at this stage. All involved entities and personnel benefit, and overall risks are reduced by a responsible party who makes it a priority to communicate with emergency responders the known hazards associated with the products being transported in the affected pipeline or process equipment. Until the released substances and their hazards have been identified, it is important to communicate to first responders that the responsible party cannot confirm the hazards, thereby mitigating the risks of a responder rushing in and encountering a hazard for which she is not prepared. Establishing an exclusion hazard zone is a good practice before the hazards of the products being transported are confirmed.

Not every pipeline incident will be the same, as the material involved, location, and circumstance will differ. However, initial post-release site assessments will often include consideration of the following:

- Location/pipeline identification information
- Materials and amounts involved
- Hazards of materials involved (consider compatibility with surrounding areas or other materials)
- Severity of incident (e.g., any injuries)/any dangers to life, health, and the environment
- Status of incident/pipeline
- Distance to nearest populated areas and evacuation points
- Nearby waterway(s) and potential impacts from runoff
- Additional hazards (e.g., potentially impacted utilities, nearby facilities, etc.)

Investigations by Responsible Parties and Governmental Authorities

PHMSA tracks pipeline incidents, such as spills impacting people or the environment. In 2023, PHMSA tracked thousands of incidents resulting in harm to the environment, persons, or property, as shown in Table 6.1.

Table 6.1 U.S. Department of Transportation, Pipeline and Hazardous Materials Safety Administration, Office of Hazardous Material Safety, 2024 Hazmat Summary by Results[46]

Result	Incidents	Hospitalized	Non-Hospitalized	Fatalities	Damages
Environmental Damage	21	0	0	0	$31,690,491
Explosion	5	0	1	0	$1,944,224
Fire	75	0	8	0	$22,594,334
Material Entered Waterway/ Sewer	23	0	0	0	$27,337,068
None	1,548	0	0	0	$328,431
Spillage	25,574	6	81	0	$59,402,030
Vapor (Gas) Dispersion	150	1	7	0	$23,930,699

As part of its response and investigation into pipeline incidents, PHMSA may use enforcement mechanisms to identify and require correction of noncompliance with cited requirements. PHMSA may also require pipeline operators to make certain repairs to ensure the integrity of the pipelines. PHMSA's federal safety standards are in 49 C.F.R. Parts 192 and 193.

Frequently, a pipeline incident can trigger liability for a responsible party under both federal and state pipeline regulations. Therefore, many PHMSA investigations are conducted in coordination with the respective state agency that regulates the relevant intrastate pipeline operations. These dual federal and state investigations can create additional burdens on a responsible party.

Further, a pipeline incident investigation may also be performed by the NTSB. The NTSB's jurisdiction includes pipeline incidents involving a fatality, substantial property damage, or significant injury to the environment.[47] While the NTSB does not have regulatory authority and cannot assess fines against pipeline operators, it can issue findings and

46. Data available at USDOT, *Incident Statistics,* https://www.phmsa.dot.gov/hazmat-program-management-data-and-statistics/data-operations/incident-statistics (last updated Mar. 19, 2024).

47. 49 C.F.R. § 1131.

recommended corrective actions to the pipeline operator. The findings and recommendations of all NTSB investigations are available to the public on the CAROL (Case Analysis and Reporting Online) database.[48]

Emergency Preparedness

PHMSA requires pipeline operators to establish emergency plans and written procedures to minimize hazards associated with a pipeline emergency. As part of an operator's emergency plan, they must implement procedures that allow them to establish and maintain adequate communication with appropriate emergency response officials, take appropriate actions to protect the public, and notify and coordinate with emergency response personnel any planned or actual responses taken during such an emergency.[49]

It is advisable for pipeline operators to regularly review, update, and practice their emergency response program(s). Common preparations and corporate practices to respond to a pipeline release include training company management on response procedures and policies, identifying qualified company employees or contractors to participate in NTSB investigations, having trained emergency response teams and preselected third-party specialists trained in extinguishing and mitigating a chemical release, and cooperating with local responders.

As a helpful guide to assist coordination between pipeline operators and local first responders, the Pipeline Association for Public Awareness published a Pipeline Emergency Response Guideline in 2024; it contains an incident response checklist.[50]

Potential Legal Liability

PHMSA uses a range of enforcement mechanisms under which pipeline operators are required to take corrective actions for safety violations and implement preventative measures to prevent future incidents. For

48. *See* NTSB, *CAROL Database*, https://data.ntsb.gov/carol-main-public/basic-search (last visited Feb. 12, 2025).

49. *See* 49 C.F.R. § 192.615 (applicable to natural and other gas pipelines); *see also* 49 C.F.R. § 194.107 (applicable to onshore oil pipelines).

50. Pipeline Association for Public Awareness, Pipeline Emergency Response Guidelines (2024), https://pipelineawareness.org/perg.

example, in 2023, PHMSA initiated 198 enforcement actions and closed 185 cases.[51] In connection with these matters in 2023, PHMSA proposed $5,632,134 in civil penalties, ultimately assessing $3,863,565 in civil penalties, as part of 36 cases.[52] OSHA and EPA apply their standard enforcement penalties and remedial action options on responsible pipeline parties.

Plaintiffs may attempt to use the findings and recommendations made by the NTSB or PHMSA in subsequent litigation against the pipeline operator, which is usually the principal—if not the sole—responsible party in the event of a pipeline incident. Further, failure to follow NTSB recommendations, whether because they are cost prohibitive or otherwise, typically reflects poorly on the pipeline operator in the court of public opinion and may lead to undue criticism. Therefore, most pipeline operators robustly respond to pipeline incidents and attempt to quickly resolve regulatory findings.

Most enforcement actions are resolved either by the pipeline operator accepting the alleged violations or through negotiation and settlement. However, should the enforcement action not be able to be timely resolved, the DOJ may step in and file a civil or criminal action in federal court on behalf of PHMSA (or EPA or OSHA).

Depending on the incident, pipeline owners or operators may have more legal liability exposure to injured workers, contractors, property owners, or community members than the enforcing agencies. For example, if a pipeline leak caused an explosion and fire that injured a worker and burned down a home, it would not be surprising for multiple parties to bring a personal injury lawsuit against the pipeline owner or operator, usually based in negligence. It is also not uncommon for environmental groups and surrounding community members to band together and assert liability claims for damages to the environment, businesses, property, or public enjoyment.

For example, in 2021, Amplify Energy owned a pipeline that burst and released approximately 25,000 gallons of crude oil into the Pacific

51. USDOT, *Summary of Enforcement Activity: Nationwide*, https://primis.phmsa.dot.gov/enforcement-data/summaries (last visited Feb. 12, 2025).

52. USDOT, *Summary of Cases Involving Civil Penalties*, https://primis.phmsa.dot.gov/enforcement-data/civil-penalties/penalties-resolved (last visited Feb. 12, 2025).

Ocean near Southern California.[53] As part of a settlement agreement following the incident, the company agreed to pay $50 million to property owners, tourism shops, and thousands of fishermen harmed by the spill.[54] This settlement was largely based on the resulting economic effect of the release to nearby business who were negatively impacted due to a sudden lack of tourism and leisure enjoyment in the area.[55]

Marine Incidents: Spills, Allision, Collision, and Grounding

The world's oceans facilitate more than 90 percent of all U.S. international trade, including the transport of millions of barrels of oil per day.[56] Unfortunately, the occasional oil spill occurs, typically as a result of allision (when a moving vessel hits a stationary object, such as the March 26, 2024, disaster when the container ship *Dali* struck and caused the collapse of the Francis Scott Key Bridge in Baltimore),[57] collision, or grounding, frequently subjecting responsible parties to high legal liability and resulting financial damages from the environmental consequences.

Marine transportation activities are subject to various federal and state statutory schemes that can impose significant liability, lengthy claims processes, response costs, and civil and criminal penalties, among other things. The Oil Pollution Act of 1990 (OPA) primarily governs

---

53. City News Service, *$50-million Huntington Beach Oil Spill Settlement Wins Final Approval*, Daily Pilot (Apr. 25, 2023), https://www.latimes.com/socal/daily-pilot/news/story/2023-04-25/50-million-huntington-beach-oil-spill-settlement-wins-final-approval.

54. *Id.*; *see also* Gutierrez v. Amplify Energy Corp., Case No. SA 21-CV-1628-DOC-JDE (C.D. Cal. May 25, 2022).

55. *Id.*

56. Bureau of Transportation Statistics, *Crude Oil and Petroleum Products Transported in the United States by Mode*, https://www.bts.gov/content/crude-oil-and-petroleum-products-transported-united-states-mode (last visited Feb. 12, 2025); National Oceanic and Atmospheric Administration (NOAA), *Ports*, https://coast.noaa.gov/states/fast-facts/ports.html (last visited Feb. 12, 2025).

57. *See, e.g.*, Kirk Moore, *Baltimore Bridge Collapse "the Hallmark of All Disasters,"* WorkBoat (Nov. 12, 2024), https://www.workboat.com/international-workboat-show/baltimore-bridge-collapse-the-hallmark-of-all-disasters#:~:text=Outbound%20from%20Baltimore%20for%20Sri,steel%20debris%20in%20the%20water; *see also* https://www.cbsnews.com/baltimore/news/usdj-announces-100-million-settlement-against-dali-owners-for-francis-scott-key-bridge-collapse/#:~:text=DALI%20owner%2C%20manager%20in%20Key,for%20harbor%20cleanup%20%2D%20CBS%20Baltimore.

liability associated with marine oil spills in U.S. waters.[58] The OPA imposes a comprehensive regulatory scheme on the maritime industry that regulates liabilities associated with cleanup and removal, imposing strict joint and several liability to defined categories of responsible parties. The OPA imposes civil penalties of up to $25,000 a day for violations (adjusted for inflation), in addition to damages.[59] Moreover, other federal laws, including the Clean Water Act (CWA), National Marine Sanctuaries Act, Refuse Act of 1899, Migratory Bird Treaty Act, Endangered Species Act, and Marine Mammal Protection Act, may also apply depending on the incident. Some coastal states, such as Texas and Louisiana, also have specific oil pollution laws.[60] Aside from economic damages, vessel owners and operators involved in a significant spill almost always suffer reputational harm. Accordingly, most vessel owners and operators find that preparing to effectively participate in a quick and well-integrated incident response helps them manage the high-value risks resulting from shipping incidents.

Incident Reporting and Notifications

Any person in charge of a vessel[61] who has knowledge of a reportable discharge[62] of oil or of a CWA Hazardous Substance into the navigable waters of the United States,[63] adjoining shorelines, or waters of

58. 33 U.S.C. §§ 2701 *et seq.*

59. *Id.* § 2716a(a).

60. *See* Texas Oil Spill Prevention and Response Act of 1991, Tex. Nat. Res. Code §§ 40.001 *et seq.*; *see also* Louisiana Oil Spill Prevention and Response Act of 1991, La. Rev. Stat. §§ 30:2451 *et seq.*

61. "Vessel" means every description of watercraft or other artificial contrivance capable of being used for transportation on water other than a public vessel (which is a vessel owned or chartered and operated by the United States, or by a State or political subdivision thereof). 33 U.S.C. § 1321(a)(3), (4); 40 C.F.R. § 116.3.

62. "Discharge" includes, but is not limited to, any spilling, leaking, pumping, pouring, emitting, emptying, or dumping, with some exclusions. 33 U.S.C. § 1321(a)(2); 40 C.F.R. § 116.3.

63. "Navigable waters" means waters of the United States, including the territorial seas. "Waters of the U.S." includes the territorial high seas and traditional navigable waters; perennial and intermittent tributaries; lakes, ponds and impoundments that contribute to traditional navigable waters in a typical year; and wetlands that are adjacent to jurisdictional waters. 40 C.F.R. §§ 110.1, 117.1(i), 120.2.

the contiguous zone[64] shall immediately report the release, with certain exclusions.[65]

A reportable discharge of oil[66] is a discharge of oil in quantities that "may be harmful." A discharge of oil may be harmful if it (1) violates applicable water quality standards, (2) causes a film or sheen[67] upon, or discoloration of the surface of the water or adjoining shorelines,[68] or (3) causes a sludge[69] or emulsion to be deposited beneath the surface of the water or adjoining shorelines.[70] Further, a discharge of a CWA Hazardous Substance that exceeds the reportable quantity in any 24-hour period is reportable.[71]

If a CWA reportable discharge occurs, a telephone notification must be made to the NRC[72] as soon as the person in charge has knowledge of any prohibited discharge (i.e., release of a reportable quantity of oil or a CWA hazardous substances).[73] Notification should be made to the NRC via its 24-hour hotline at 800-424-8802. However, if direct reporting to the NRC is not practicable, reports may be made to the Coast Guard or EPA predesignated On-Scene Coordinator (OSC) for the geographic area where the discharge occurs. All such reports shall be promptly relayed to the NRC. If it is not possible to notify the NRC or the predesignated OSC immediately, reports may be made immediately to the nearest Coast

64. "Waters of the contiguous zone" are waters established as such by the United States under Article 24 of the Convention on the Territorial Sea and the Contiguous Zone. 40 C.F.R. § 117.1(h).

65. 33 U.S.C. § 1321(b)(3), (5); 40 C.F.R. §§ 110.6 (oil), 117.21 (hazardous substances). The exclusions are identified in 33 U.S.C. § 1321(a)(2), 40 C.F.R. § 110.5, and 40 C.F.R. § 117.11.

66. "Oil" means oil of any kind or in any form, including but not limited to, petroleum, fuel oil, sludge, oil refuse, and oil mixed with wastes other than dredged spoil. 33 U.S.C. § 1321(a)(1).

67. Under 40 C.F.R. § 110.1, "sheen" means iridescence on the surface of the water.

68. There is not a de minimis defense under the CWA reporting and civil penalty provisions for discharges of oil in quantities large enough to create a sheen on the surface of the water. Chevron, U.S.A., Inc. v. Yost, 919 F.2d 27, 30 (5th Cir. 1990).

69. Under 40 C.F.R. § 110.1, "sludge" means an aggregate of oil or oil and other matter, of any kind and in any form other than dredged spoil, that has a combined specific gravity equivalent to or greater than water.

70. 33 U.S.C. § 1321(b)(3); 40 C.F.R. § 110.3.

71. 40 C.F.R. § 116.4. The reportable quantity is listed in 40 C.F.R. § 302.4, Table 302.4. If the substance is not listed in Table 302.4, the reportable quantity is listed in 40 C.F.R. § 117.3, Table 117.3. Any substance listed in 40 C.F.R. § 116.4, Table 116.4A is a CWA Hazardous Substance.

72. Given the substantial number and potential severity of water-based incidents, it is perhaps not surprising that the NRC is operated by the U.S. Coast Guard.

73. 33 U.S.C. § 1321(b)(5); 33 C.F.R. § 153.203; 40 C.F.R. §§ 110.6 (oil), 117.21 (hazardous substances).

Guard unit, provided that the person in charge of the vessel or onshore or offshore facility notifies the NRC as soon as possible.[74]

When reporting a discharge incident, responsible parties find it helpful to be thoughtful and careful when providing information that will assist the NRC in characterizing the release, such as the location of the release, type(s) of material(s) released, possible source of the release, and date and time of the release.[75] As with other transportation incidents, when a responsible party obtains more accurate information about the type and amounts of materials released, it can and is effectively required to update its notifications to the relevant regulator(s).

Agency Actions and Authorities

Under 33 U.S.C. §§ 1251–1387, the CWA identifies the federal government and the U.S. Coast Guard as being in charge of ensuring that spills are adequately and timely cleaned up. The Coast Guard actively manages and oversees water-based cleanup and response efforts. In the aftermath of a large marine oil spill, the Coast Guard will establish a Unified Command to coordinate and manage the government's response to the spill. The Coast Guard very consistently and rigorously activates and implements its Unified Command response structure. State agencies and local government officials will generally consult with and provide support to the Coast Guard, but the Coast Guard will maintain the primary response leadership role.

If the federal government perceives that the responsible parties are not adequately responding to the oil spill, the Coast Guard has statutory authority to take over the cleanup operation and hire commercial contractors to undertake the cleanup at the expense of the responsible parties.[76] Even if federal officials determine that responsible parties have met their cleanup obligations, state agencies or local authorities do have authority to require that the cleanup operation be continued to meet state and local requirements.

74. 33 C.F.R. § 153.203.
75. 40 C.F.R. §§ 110.6; 300.405(d).
76. 33 U.S.C. § 1321(c).

Depending on the incident (size, location, fault, etc.), the Coast Guard may provide a criminal referral to the DOJ for further prosecution. However, the Coast Guard's past position has been to encourage cooperation with cleanup and response efforts, rather than pursue criminal referral. If a criminal investigation were to commence, it would likely involve several federal agencies, such as the Coast Guard, EPA, and DOJ. Criminal penalties under the CWA (enhanced by the OPA),[77] are available to prosecutors for "negligent" or "knowing" violations of the act.[78] Under these criminal penalty provisions, DOJ prosecutors may impose fines of up to a million dollars and imprisonment for up to 15 years.[79] The DOJ's strategy may involve the threat of criminal prosecution to gain leverage in settlement negotiations with responsible parties over damages associated with oil pollution events. In the unfortunate event that an owned, operated, or managed vessel is involved in an oil spill, immediate and accurate reporting along with transparent cooperation with government officials are often effective means by which responsible parties seek to limit their exposure to damages and removal costs and to avoid a situation that would encourage or warrant a DOJ criminal investigation.

In addition to civil penalties, cleanup costs, and potential criminal liability, marine spills can have a devastating impact on natural resources, the environment, marine life, and human use. Resource management agencies are designated to serve as resource trustees on the public's behalf and to spend recoveries on "restoration, rehabilitation, replacement, or acquisition of the equivalent resources."[80] When it comes to paying for natural resource damages, the responsible parties may either pay the amount determined by the government or develop and implement their own (government-approved) restoration plan. Responsible parties typically retain experts to develop independent damage estimates and compare them with those developed by the government's experts before deciding on their preferred approach to addressing and resolving a natural resource damage claim.

77. *See id.* § 1319(c).
78. *Id.*
79. *Id.*
80. 33 U.S.C. § 2706(c)(1)(C).

Incident Management

The key to properly executing a marine spill response is for vessel owners and operators to have an effective plan to timely mobilize resources. Resources must be put to work at the most appropriate locations to contain and minimize the oil spill as soon as possible. This requires the utmost cooperation between vessel interests and federal, state, and local officials. From the very first moments of the reported incident, it is crucial that the responsible party gather the pertinent information, confirm its accuracy, and provide a detailed report to government authorities. It is also important for the responsible party to establish a clear line of communication with government authorities and to gain the trust of the individual officials involved in the management of the spill.

Investigations by Responsible Parties and Governmental Authorities

Either the Coast Guard or the NTSB will typically perform an investigation into a marine incident. The Coast Guard has been given the power to "make inquiries, examinations, inspections, searches, seizures, and arrests upon the high seas and waters over which the United States has jurisdiction, for the prevention, detection, and suppression of violations of laws of the United States."[81] In the interests of helping to prevent future incidents and to promote marine safety, the Coast Guard's purpose in conducting an investigation is to determine the cause of the incident and whether any failure of material contributed to the incident.[82]

The NTSB also has the authority to investigate marine incidents to establish the facts, circumstances, and cause or probable cause of an incident occurring on the navigable waters, internal waters, or the territorial sea of the United States. However, the NTSB only becomes involved in instances of major marine incidents.[83] In some instances, both the Coast Guard and the NTSB will perform investigations, working independently or in partnership. The Coast Guard and NTSB do have a Memorandum of Understanding in place agreeing to interagency cooperation

81. 14 U.S.C. § 522.
82. 46 U.S.C. § 4.07-1.
83. 49 U.S.C. § 850.

and mutual assistance in their investigations, including the sharing of information.

Vessel owners and operators, and their counsel, often assist with or participate in these investigations, such as through the organized collection of evidence, production of documents and electronic information, and arrangement of witness interviews and testimony. In some instances, responsible parties may want to perform their own internal investigations to identify causal and contributory factors, recognize incident trends, and implement corrective and preventative actions.

The Coast Guard and NTSB prepare and publish reports of their investigations, almost all of which contain findings and recommendations.[84] These investigation reports often provide useful "lessons learned" that vessel owners or operators may find valuable to incorporate into their own operations in order to prevent an incident and its attendant emergency response activities and otherwise to help mitigate an incident's impacts.

Emergency Preparedness

In the immediate aftermath of a maritime-related incident, the responsible party may find it necessary to quickly issue a distress signal, sound onboard alarms, record relevant data, assess damage, take safety precautions (such as activating onboard fire suppression equipment or deploying life rafts), initiate the shipboard oil pollution emergency plan, and report the incident to the National Response Center. Depending on the type and severity of the incident, it may also be important for a vessel's crew to take soundings (i.e., check the fluid levels) of important tanks onboard, as impact shocks have been known to crack tanks and cause accidental releases. If fuel or oil tanks are damaged, there may be an imminent danger of an oil spill, triggering implementation of the

84. U.S. Coast Guard, *Marine Casualty Reports of Investigation, Reports of Marine Boards, and Other Marine Safety Reports and Studies*, https://www.dco.uscg.mil/Our-Organization/Assistant-Commandant-for-Prevention-Policy-CG-5P/Inspections-Compliance-CG-5PC-/Office-of-Investigations-Casualty-Analysis/Marine-Casualty-Reports/ (last visited Feb. 12, 2025); NTSB, *Investigation Report*, https://www.ntsb.gov/investigations/AccidentReports/Pages/Reports.aspx?mode=Marine (last visited Feb. 12, 2025).

Shipboard Oil Pollution Emergency Plan required under MARPOL (the International Convention for the Prevention of Pollution from Ships).[85]

When pre-identified and pre-planned, these emergency actions can effectuate an efficient and well-integrated response that effectively marshals shipboard and shoreside resources. For example, the first response to an incident may need to include triage and acute traumatic injury medical care. Having a plan in place to quickly mobilize resources is essential to successfully managing and mitigating the impact of an incident.

Potential Legal Liability

In addition to claims/enforcement actions by the government discussed earlier under Agency Authority, third parties may also bring legal claims following a major incident involving a significant discharge of oil or other hazardous chemicals into the water. Third-party claims could include tort claims, property damage claims, contract claims, claims by investors, as well as claims related to injuries or the death of workers or other persons under the Death on the High Seas Act,[86] the Jones Act,[87] the Longshore and Harbor Workers' Compensation Act,[88] general maritime law, and applicable state worker's compensation statutes and common law. These lawsuits could be filed individually or as class actions, encompassing numerous plaintiffs. For example, commercial fishermen, shrimpers, seafood processors, charter boat operators, and nearby hotels and restaurants have been known to file suit in the wake of marine spill incidents.

Roadway Accidents

While usually less severe than other incidents addressed in this chapter, roadway-based vehicular accidents that result in spills of hazardous

85. International Maritime Organization, *Shipboard Marine Pollution Emergency Plans*, https://www.imo.org/en/OurWork/Environment/Pages/Shipboard-Marine-Pollution-Emergency-Plans.aspx#:~:text=Regulation%2037%20of%20MARPOL%20Annex%20I%20requires,approved%20Shipboard%20Oil%20Pollution%20Emergency%20Plan%20(SOPEP).&text=Regulation%2017%20of%20MARPOL%20Annex%20II%20makes,pollution%20emergency%20plan%20for%20noxious%20liquid%20substances (last visited Feb. 12, 2025).

86. 46 U.S.C. §§ 30301 *et seq.*

87. *Id.* § 55102.

88. 33 U.S.C. §§ 901 *et seq.*

materials to the ground, air, and waterways are the most frequent incident that causes harm to the environment.[89]

Incident Reporting and Notifications

Depending on the material released and the quantity of material released as a result of the vehicular accident,[90] a reporting obligation may be triggered under the federal Hazardous Material Transportation Act (HMTA).[91] Generally, under the HMTA, each person[92] in physical possession of hazardous material[93] that was involved in certain transportation-related reportable accidents[94] must give notice as soon as practical but no later than 12 hours after the occurrence of a reportable accident.[95]

Notice may be made by telephone or online to both state and federal authorities. The State Operations Center is available at (512) 424-2208 or (800) 832-8224. With respect to federal authorities, notification is to be made to the National Response Center at its 24-hour hotline, (800) 424-8802, or online at http://www.nrc.uscg.mil.[96] This required notice must include the following information: (1) the name of the reporter; (2) the name and address of the person represented by the reporter; (3) the phone number where the reporter can be contacted; (4) date, time, and location of the incident; (5) the extent of any injuries; (6) class

89. Stephen Stock, *Hazmat Road Accidents in the U.S. Have More Than Doubled in the Past Decade*, CBS News (May 9, 2023), https://www.cbsnews.com/news/hazardous-materials-trucks/ ("[F]or every hazardous materials incident involving a train, there are 33 hazmat incidents involving big rigs on our roadways.").

90. A list of hazardous substances is available in Appendix A to 49 C.F.R. § 172.101.

91. 49 U.S.C. §§ 5101–5127; 49 C.F.R. pts. 171 and 172.

92. "Person" means an individual, corporation, company, association, firm, partnership, society, joint stock company, or a government, Indian tribe, or authority of a government or tribe *offering a hazardous material for transportation in commerce or transporting a hazardous material to support a commercial enterprise*. 49 C.F.R. § 171.8 (emphasis added).

93. "Hazardous Material" is a substance or material that the Secretary of Transportation has determined can pose an unreasonable risk to health, safety, and property when transported in commerce and designated as hazardous under Section 5103 of the Federal Hazardous materials Transportation Act. The term includes hazardous substances, hazardous wastes, marine pollutants, elevated temperature materials, materials designated as hazardous, and materials meeting defining criteria for hazard classes and divisions in 49 C.F.R. Part 173. *See* 49 C.F.R. § 171.8.

94. "Transportation" means the movement of property and loading, unloading, or storage incidental to that movement. 49 C.F.R. § 171.8.

95. *Id.* § 171.15(a).

96. *Id.*

or division, proper shipping name, and quantity of hazardous materials involved, if available; and (7) type of incident and nature of hazardous material involvement and whether a continuing danger to life exists at the scene.[97]

Within 30 days after discovery of the accident, a written report of the accident must be made[98] to state[99] and federal authorities.[100] The written report must be provided via the Hazardous Materials Incident Report Form DOT F 5800.1.[101] The information collected through the report is then used by PHMSA and other agencies to mitigate risk, analyze gaps, and enhance safety. Responsible parties must retain a copy of the report for at least two years.[102] Further, under certain circumstances,[103] the accident report must be updated within one year of the date of the occurrence of the accident.

Additionally, most states have independent, additional reporting obligations that may be triggered, such as the Texas Land and Water Release Reporting Code, which applies to certain discharges and spills from motor vehicles.[104]

Agency Actions and Authorities

The Department of Transportation regulates the transportation of hazardous materials under the HMTA.[105] The Secretary of the DOT has delegated the primary authority for regulating transport of hazardous

---

97. *Id.*

98. *Id.* § 171.16(a).

99. For state authorities, send the written report to Texas Division of Emergency Management 1033 La Posada, Suite 300 Austin, Texas 78752-3824.

100. For federal authorities, send the written report to Information Systems Manager, PHH-63 Pipeline and Hazardous Materials Safety Administration Department of Transportation East Building 1200 New Jersey Ave., SE Washington, D.C. 20590-0001. Alternatively, incidents may be reported online by submitting an electronic Hazardous Material Incident Report to the Information System Manager, PHH-60, Pipeline and Hazardous Materials Safety Administration, Department of Transportation, Washington, DC, 20590-0001 via: http://hazmat.dot.gov/.

101. 49 C.F.R. § 171.16(a); Hazardous Materials Incident Report form, https://www.phmsa.dot.gov/sites/phmsa.dot.gov/files/docs/IncidentForm010105.pdf.

102. 49 C.F.R. § 171.16(b).

103. Listed in *id.* § 171.16(c).

104. Texas Water Code § 26.039 and 30 Texas Admin. Code ch. 327.

105. 49 U.S.C. §§ 5101 *et seq.*

materials on roadways to the Federal Motor Carrier Safety Administration (FMCSA).[106] Although, the NTSB, PHMSA, EPA, OSHA, and a state's environmental agency may also participate in investigating spills from roadway accidents. For example, in Texas, the Texas Commission on Environmental Quality (TCEQ) is frequently the lead agency for hazardous material spill response.[107] When an environmental release occurs on a public or private roadway, the first governmental responder is usually county or municipal police, followed soon thereafter by multiple agencies—including fire and rescue services as well as environmental regulators.

Incident Management

Because vehicle accidents usually occur on public roadways where other vehicles and people are quickly encountered, personnel safety is a paramount focus. It is standard procedure for workers operating a vehicle that has lost containment of a hazardous material to prioritize their own safety and that of the public nearby—whether in vehicles or in adjacent areas to the accident. If people are in danger, the first call is to 9-1-1. Directing people to evacuate the immediate area can also be an effective protective action.

After acting to protect people exposed to the accident, and completing required notifications, isolating the area can limit additional damage. For example, based on training provided to personnel by responsible parties, it may be appropriate to restrict access with traffic cones or direct traffic away from the spill. The immediate goal is to limit damage of the spill until professional cleanup arrives. Depending on the circumstance, it may be appropriate to move a leaking vehicle from the traveled portion of the highway, but only if it is safe to operate the vehicle. Unless the vehicle driver or passengers have the necessary training and expertise,

---

106. Regulations issues by the FMCSA are published in the Federal Register and compiled in the U.S. Code of Federal Regulations, https://www.fmcsa.dot.gov/regulations.

107. Texas Parks and Wildlife, *Oil Spill and Hazardous Substance Response Agencies*, https://tpwd.texas.gov/landwater/water/environconcerns/damage_assessment/response.phtml#:~:text=Texas%20Commission%20on%20Environmental%20Quality,local%20regional%20office%20of%20TCEQ (last visited Feb. 12, 2025).

containment and safe disposal of the leaked materials is a job for trained personnel, who may take time to reach the site. Depending on the material released and the training provided to the driver or passengers, some basic mitigation efforts that do not involve contact with the released material may be permitted. For example, such measures could include digging trenches to divert or collect the material away from streams or sewers.

Because police or other law enforcement are usually the first on the scene, they usually take control of the scene, and company personnel are not immediately responsible for evidence preservation, interviewing witnesses, and investigating the incident. It is good practice, when possible, for responsible parties to obtain the identities of the law enforcement authorities and contact information so police reports and other investigation materials can more readily be collected at a later date.

Once it is confirmed safe to do so by law enforcement, it is standard practice for a responsible party to conduct an internal investigation in the same manner as after other transportation incidents. The responsible party will also have the same evidence preservation obligations once law enforcement releases equipment in the accident back to the responsible party. One often overlooked aspect of incident management activities is to develop an equipment preservation plan for the vehicle(s) involved as soon as possible after an accident. An effective preservation plan will include notifying third parties of their duty to preserve evidence when their vehicles are involved in the accident.

Because roadway hazardous material accidents can result in releases to the ground, water, and air, a responsible party will typically notify its preselected environmental cleanup contractor to arrive at the accident scene as soon as reasonably practicable. Roadway incidents can occur in remote locations and environmental damage mitigation can take time to effectuate. Beginning to execute the environmental mitigations and cleanup are commonly an important part of media messaging to the public and nearby communities. Delays in contacting or engaging a qualified contractor can be viewed as callous or even negligent by damaged third-party landowners and residents.

Investigations by Responsible Parties and Governmental Authorities

On average, the federal government receives 12 reports of hazardous substance releases every day.[108] Depending on the circumstances of the accident and specific hazardous material(s) spilled or released as a result of the accident, investigations may be performed by a variety of government entities, including FMCSA, NTSB, PHMSA, EPA, OSHA, and/or a state's environmental agency. It is also a standard practice for transportation companies and carriers to perform their own internal investigations after each accident involving their equipment. These investigations should determine the likely cause(s) of the accident and identify lessons learned. Corrective actions must then be developed, scheduled, and implemented to improve the fleet's safety and reduce the risk of similar future accidents.

Emergency Preparedness

Training personnel to quickly communicate the type of substance spilled from a regulated vehicle is an important preparedness action. Trained personnel should know which agencies to notify in the event of a spill. Responsible parties may find it helpful to keep this information in written form in the commercial vehicle for use during the stressful period immediately following an incident. Required warning labels and placards are intended to help the responsible party and emergency responders to quickly identify the spilled substance and its potential hazards (i.e., flammable, toxic, corrosive, etc.). Other transportation information, such as bills of lading or safety data sheets, may also contain hazardous material information that should be communicated to emergency responders.

Vehicles transporting hazardous materials in certain amounts pursuant to the Hazardous Materials Regulations must display placards on the sides and ends of the transport vehicle.[109] These placards are intended to

---

108. EPA, *Emergency Response and Recognizing Hazardous Substance Releases,* https://www.epa.gov/emergency-response/emergency-response-and-recognizing-hazardous-substance-releases (last updated Sept. 26, 2024).

109. *See* 49 C.F.R. pt. 172, subpt. F for complete placarding regulations.

visually identify the type of hazardous material being transported. This assists emergency responders in taking appropriate safety precautions depending on the hazardous material at issue. Warning labels may also be required to be affixed to packages, representing the hazards of the material contained in the package.[110]

It is also good practice to train company personnel to immediately prioritize safety of people in the vicinity of the spill by isolating the area, notifying emergency services, and making sure responders are aware of the spilled chemical(s) and their known hazards. This will assist responders to select the appropriate personal protective equipment.

In addition, the U.S. Department of Transportation Federal Highway Administration has published release mitigation practices for responding to hazardous material vehicular spills that may be helpful to responsible parties whose personnel or equipment experience vehicular accidents.[111]

Typically, responsible parties that routinely transport hazardous materials on public or private roadways have an environmental cleanup contractor already selected and under contract to assist in the event one of their vehicles causes or contributes to a spill.

Potential Legal Liability

According to PHMSA data, over the last ten years, the number of tractor-trailer accidents involving hazardous materials has jumped two and a half times, an increase of 155 percent.[112] And the severity of the accidents is also high. For example, in 2020, a tractor trailer crash on a Massachusetts highway caused nearly 10,000 gallons of gasoline mixed with ethyl alcohol to spill onto the highway and into a nearby saltwater marsh. While there were no personal injuries, the cost of the tractor trailer, loss of material, and cleanup of the marsh exceeded $1.1 million dollars.[113]

As with all transportation incidents, vehicular accidents involve legal liability that may stem from personal injury, wrongful death, property

---

110. *See id.* for complete labeling regulations.

111. USDOT, *Traffic Incident Management in Hazardous Materials Spills in Incident Clearance*, https://ops.fhwa.dot.gov/publications/fhwahop08058/60.htm (last visited Feb. 12, 2025); *see also* Texas Commission on Environmental Quality, *What to Do After a Spill*, https://www.tceq.texas.gov/response/spills/actions.html (last visited Feb. 12, 2025).

112. Stock, *supra* note 89.

113. *Id.*

damage, environmental damage, mitigation and cleanup, loss of high-value hazardous material products, and agency enforcement penalties. The frequency of these incidents makes emergency response preparedness, quick incident management actions, and thorough post-accident investigations critical steps in appropriately responding to roadway accidents and limiting a responsible party's legal liability.

Conclusion

There are many aspects to running a well-coordinated, integrated response after a hazardous material transportation incident. A well-run incident response can improve responsible parties' ability to limit legal liability, timely gather and evaluate evidence and information, perform targeted internal investigations, respond to government inquiries and investigations, and position the responsible party to defend against subsequent agency enforcement and private litigation.

Regardless of whether responding to a railway, pipeline, maritime, or roadway incident, reporting and notifications are usually the first priority—timely informing relevant agencies of the incident in order to fulfill regulatory obligations. Simultaneously, responsible parties, along with emergency responders and incident command, are usually deploying to and handling the immediate safety concerns associated with the incident—the goal being to first make the incident location as safe as possible, while preserving evidence for future investigation. Subsequent investigations focus on identifying the causal and contributory factors leading to the incident, including root causes that address underlying contributors, and recommending corrective actions to prevent similar incidents from occurring in the future. These investigations are commonly performed under legal privilege to provide legal advice and counsel to the responsible party in anticipation of litigation relating to the incident. Due to the numerous workstreams created after hazardous material incidents, the number of agencies that may potentially get involved, and the likelihood of litigation following the incident, responsible parties should take care to be as prepared as possible in the event of a transportation-related incident.

Chapter 7

Liability and Defenses for Hazardous Substance Incidents

Susan Parker Bodine and Kevin R. Murray[1]

Potential statutory liability—particularly under the Comprehensive Environmental Response, Compensation, and Liability Act (CERCLA; also known as Superfund)[2]—has for several decades drawn most of the attention of those evaluating the risks associated with releases of hazardous substances. The strict, retroactive, and potential joint and several liability under CERCLA is far reaching and makes CERCLA a powerful statute. However, CERCLA only addresses the costs of responding to releases of hazardous substances and damages to natural resources caused by those releases. It does not overlap with common law claims for personal injury and property damage. Further, it only preempts common law to the extent that a common law claim is for the same response costs.

The first part of this chapter discusses liability for hazardous substances releases under CERCLA and the second part discusses liability

---

1. The authors wish to acknowledge Mary Ellen Ternes, Earth & Water Law, LLC, for her contribution to this chapter through the disaster law compilation initially prepared by Mary Ellen Ternes, Earth & Water Law, LLC; Thomas S. Burack, Sheehan Phinney Bass & Green, PA; and Kevin R. Murray, Holland & Hart, for educational purposes at The Judge Alfred P. Murrah Center for Homeland Security Law & Policy 2019 National Summit, which was held at Oklahoma City University in 2019.

2. Comprehensive Environmental Response, Compensation, and Liability Act, 42 U.S.C. §§ 9601 *et seq.*

under state common law. While this chapter does not directly address liability or defenses under other federal or state laws that may apply to releases of hazardous materials, pollutants, or contaminants that fall outside of CERCLA's jurisdiction, such as liablity for releases of petroleum under the Clean Water Act and the Oil Pollution Act, many of the statutory principles and common law theories discussed in this chapter may be useful in analyzing liability or defenses for this broader set of potential types of releases. While there may be other applicable federal and state environmental statutes, CERCLA has by far the broadest scope and so is most commonly used as the tool for response and liability.

CERCLA Legal Liability and Defenses

As a general matter, any person who incurs costs to respond to a release or threatened release of a hazardous substance may require responsible parties to pay those costs.

The elements of liability are a release or threatened release of a hazardous substance (unless federally permitted), from a facility, resulting in costs or damages or that may present an imminent and substantial endangerment.

A release of oil or hazardous substances warranting response pursuant to the NCP also often violates one environmental statute or another.[3] Thus, along with liability pursuant to CERCLA for response costs, the responsible party may also face liability for statutory or regulatory violations.

Additionally, pollution impacting other properties or resulting in exposure to toxic substances or personal injury may trigger common law claims, such as negligence, trespass, and nuisance by impacted property owners or other persons.

---

3. For example, a release of hazardous substances above an applicable federally permitted release threshold constitutes a violation of that permit, whether it be a Clean Air Act permit, a Clean Water Act permit, or other federal permit.

CERCLA Liability

Responsible Parties

CERCLA assigns liability to the following classes of persons:

1. the owner and operator of a vessel or a facility;
2. any person who at the time of disposal of any hazardous substance owned or operated any facility at which such hazardous substances were disposed of;
3. any person who by contract, agreement, or otherwise arranged for disposal or treatment, or arranged with a transporter for transport for disposal or treatment, of hazardous substances owned or possessed by such person, by any other party or entity, at any facility or incineration vessel owned or operated by another party or entity and containing such hazardous substances; and
4. any person who accepts or accepted any hazardous substances for transport to disposal or treatment facilities, incineration vessels or sites selected by such person, from which there is a release, or a threatened release which causes the incurrence of response costs, of a hazardous substance.[4]

There is extensive case law on what places a person into one or more of these categories of liable parties. Courts have interpreted liability broadly, sweeping in persons who had nothing to do with the disposal,[5] including any current or past owner of impacted property, whether or not they participated in the disposal,[6] and any generators, whether or not they selected the disposal site or contracted with someone else to haul off their waste.[7] In many cases, liability is established by the testimony

---

4. 42 U.S.C. § 9607(a)(1)–(4).

5. United States v. Atlantic Rsch. Corp., 551 U.S. 128, 136 (2007) ("[E]ven parties not responsible for contamination may fall within the broad definitions of PRPs in §§ 107(a)(1)–(4).").

6. *See, e.g.*, Atl. Richfield Co. v. Christian, 590 U.S. 1, 18 (2020) (finding owners of land where contamination came to be located by the actions of others to be responsible parties).

7. *See, e.g.*, United States v. Aceto Agric. Chems. Corp., 872 F.2d 1373, 1379–82 (8th Cir. 1989) (citing arranger liability cases).

of truck drivers, even in the absence of bills of lading or other contract documents demonstrating the origin of the hazardous substances.

The Supreme Court has not been willing to pierce the corporate veil to establish operator liability for parent corporations under CERCLA, absent evidence that the parent "manage[d], direct[ed] or conduct[ed] operations [of the subsidiary's facility] specifically related to pollution, . . . [or] the leakage or disposal of hazardous waste, or decisions about compliance with environmental regulations."[8]

Whether a person other than the current owner or operator of a facility is liable depends on the definition of the term "disposal." CERCLA defines it by reference to the definition in the Solid Waste Disposal Act.[9] The Eighth Circuit has held that disposal includes tearing a building down.[10] The Ninth Circuit has held that disposal does not include aerial deposition.[11] EPA gets around the aerial deposition limit by arguing that once a hazardous substance is on the ground it can be washed off by rainfall or blown off by wind, a second disposal.

According to the Supreme Court, whether a person is liable as an "arranger" requires an intent to dispose.[12] In *Burlington Northern*, Shell Oil sold product that was shipped by rail. Shell was aware that some spilling occurred during off-loading. The Court held that such knowledge was not sufficient to turn the sale of a product into an intentional disposal.[13]

In a 2024 decision, the Fourth Circuit overturned a district court that held that arranger liability requires not only an intent to dispose but also knowledge that a substance is hazardous.[14] While this was a case

8. United States v. Bestfoods, 524 U.S. 51, 67–68 (1998).

9. 42 U.S.C. § 9601(29).

10. United States v. Dico, Inc., 920 F.3d 1174 (8th Cir. 2019) (sale of building known to be contaminated is arranging for disposal of hazardous substances).

11. Pakootas v. Teck Cominco Metals, Ltd., 830 F.3d 975 (9th Cir. 2016) (definition of disposal does not include hazardous substances deposited at a Superfund site via aerial deposition from a remote source).

12. Burlington Northern v. United States, 556 U.S. 599, 611 (2009) (interpreting the word "arrange" to mean taking an action to bring about a specific purpose).

13. *Id.* at 612–13.

14. 68th St. Site Work Grp. v. Alban Tractor Co., 105 F.4th 222 (4th Cir. 2024).

of first impression it is likely that the issue was not litigated previously because, as the court pointed out, the statute clearly does not include a knowledge element.

Scope of Liability

Responsible parties can be held liable for the following costs:

> (A) *all costs of removal or remedial action* incurred by the United States Government or a State or an Indian tribe *not inconsistent with* the national contingency plan;
>
> (B) any *other necessary costs* of response incurred by any other person *consistent with* the national contingency plan;
>
> (C) *damages* for injury to, destruction of, or loss of natural resources, including the reasonable costs of assessing such injury, destruction, or loss resulting from such a release; and
>
> (D) the costs of any health assessment or health effects study carried out under section 9604(i) of this title.[15]

Section 107(a) goes on to specify that "amounts recoverable in an action under this section shall include interest[.]"

In addition, agencies that have the lead for exercising the President's response authority under CERCLA (described earlier) also have been delegated the President's authority to order responsible parties to conduct a cleanup where the agency determines that there may be an imminent and substantial endangerment due to the release or threatened release of a hazardous substance.[16] Section 106 orders are enforceable in federal court, and any person who fails to comply may be liable for daily penalties and three times the costs of response. EPA has been very successful in arguing that "imminent and substantial endangerment" means any level

15. 42 U.S.C. § 9607(a) (emphasis added).

16. *See* 42 U.S.C. § 9606(a) (order authority); Executive Order 12,580 (delegating order authority to EPA and the Coast Guard); Executive Order 13,016 (a 1996 Executive Order amending Executive Order 12,580 to delegate order authority to the Secretaries of the Interior, Agriculture, Commerce, Defense, and Energy for releases on property under their jurisdiction and control).

of harm and any point in time in the future.[17] Faced with the threat of treble damages, very few persons defy a 106 order. A person who complies with such an order but believes he is not liable may make a claim against the Superfund for reimbursement.[18]

Finally, once a court finds a party is liable for CERCLA response costs, the court may issue a declaratory judgment and order the party to carry out any additional needed response actions.[19]

As noted earlier, removal and remedial action are defined broadly, and expressly include the enforcement costs of the United States and EPA's costs of overseeing cleanup work carried out by responsible parties. Courts have also held that recoverable costs include EPA's indirect costs.[20] It is difficult for a defendant to demonstrate that the government's costs are not inconsistent with the NCP. While CERCLA and the NCP require

---

17. *See* B.F. Goodrich Co. v. Murtha, 697 F. Supp. 89, 96 (D. Conn. 1988) (an unquantified risk of harm is sufficient); United States v. Conservation Chemical, 619 F. Supp. 162, 193–94 (W.D. Mo. 1985) (an endangerment may be "imminent" if factors giving rise to it are present, even though the harm may not be realized for years and an endangerment may be "substantial" if there is a reasonable cause for concern that someone or something may be exposed to a risk of harm by a release or a threatened release of a hazardous substance). *See generally* EPA, *OECA Cookbook on Imminent and Substantial Endangerment* (Nov. 12, 1997), https://nepis.epa.gov/Exe/ZyNET.exe/910220FQ.TXT?ZyActionD=ZyDocument&Client=EPA&Index=1995+Thru+1999&Docs=&Query=&Time=&EndTime=&SearchMethod=1&TocRestrict=n&Toc=&TocEntry=&QField=&QFieldYear=&QFieldMonth=&QFieldDay=&IntQFieldOp=0&ExtQFieldOp=0&XmlQuery=&File=D%3A%5Czyfiles%5CIndex%20Data%5C95thru99%5CTxt%5C00000037%5C910220FQ.txt&User=ANONYMOUS&Password=anonymous&SortMethod=h%7C-&MaximumDocuments=1&FuzzyDegree=0&ImageQuality=r75g8/r75g8/x150y150g16/i425&Display=hpfr&DefSeekPage=x&SearchBack=ZyActionL&Back=ZyActionS&BackDesc=Results%20page&MaximumPages=1&ZyEntry=1&SeekPage=x&ZyPURL.

18. 42 U.S.C. § 9606(b).

19. *Id.* § 9613(g)(2). In actions under 107 of CERCLA, declaratory judgment under section 113(g)(2) is mandatory ("the court shall enter a declaratory judgment on liability for response costs or damages that will be binding on any subsequent action or actions to recover further response costs or damages"). In contribution actions under section 113 of CERCLA, courts are divided as to whether declaratory judgment is available under section 113(g)(2) or whether the Declaratory Judgment Act (28 U.S.C. §§ 2201 *et seq.*) controls. *Compare* Boeing Co. v. Cascade Corp., 207 F.3d, 1177, 1191 (9th Cir. 2000) (section 113(g)(2) applies to contribution claims) *and* United States v. Davis, 261 F.3d 1 (1st Cir. 2001) (same), *with* Reichhold Chems., Inc. v. Textron, Inc., 888 F. Supp. 1116, 1123–24 (N.D. Fla. 1995) (section 113(g)(2) applies only to 107 actions).

20. *See, e.g.*, United States v. R.W. Meyer, 889 F.2d 1497, 1502–03 (6th Cir. 1989), *cert. denied*, 494 U.S. 1057 (1990); United States v. Ottati & Goss, 900 F.2d 429, 444 (1st Cir. 1990). Indirect costs are general costs of operating EPA that EPA allocates to a site. Indirect costs can nearly equal direct costs, creating an incentive for responsible parties to carry out a cleanup action themselves to limit EPA's involvement to oversight.

that a response action be "cost-effective," defenses based on cost-effectiveness have not been successful. Courts have held that the government can recover costs unless the government's decision to incur the costs is arbitrary and capricious.[21]

As a general rule, it is difficult for a defendant to show that EPA's actions were arbitrary and capricious. One exception to this general rule is *Emhart Industries v. New England Container Co.*[22] Emhart had been found liable for response costs in an earlier proceeding. The 2017 opinion followed a 13-day evidentiary trial on whether EPA's remedy was arbitrary and capricious and whether Emhart had good cause to refuse to comply with an EPA administrative order directing them to carry out the remedy.[23] The judge allowed Emhart to go outside the administrative record and introduce expert testimony under the exception for supplementing a record where a court finds that the additional testimony by experts will aid to understanding the record, finding that EPA had an obligation to explain the assumptions that underpin its remedy.[24] After considering the expert testimony, the court found that EPA had failed to justify its assumptions that restoration of groundwater would be practicable and effective, making groundwater at the site a potential source of drinking water.[25] The court also found that EPA's assumptions regarding the type and amount of fish consumed when setting cleanup levels to protect human health were arbitrary.[26] According to the court, these errors made EPA's selection of a remedial action "arbitrary, capricious, or otherwise not in accordance with law" and the court stayed the enforcement order until EPA addressed those issues, including by reopening its remedial investigation and feasibility study and amending the remedy.[27]

21. *R.W. Meyer*, 889 F.2d at 1508.

22. Emhart Indus. v. New England Container Co., 274 F. Supp. 3d 30 (D.R.I. 2017).

23. A responsible party cannot challenge an EPA remedy unless and until EPA brings an enforcement action or a party complies with an order and seeks reimbursement from the Superfund under section 106(b) of CERCLA. 42 U.S.C. § 9613(h). In the *Emhart Industry* case, Emhart refused to comply with an order and EPA brought an enforcement action.

24. *Emhart*, 274 F. Supp. 3d at 46, 49.

25. *Id.* at 67.

26. *Id.* at 78.

27. *Id.* at 80–81.

While the *Emhart* case appears to be a primer on how to successfully challenge an EPA remedy, EPA eventually made some accommodations to Emhart on remedy implementation and settled the case, including obtaining an agreement from Emhart to not oppose vacatur of the 2017 opinion. The court entered that settlement and vacated its earlier decision.[28]

As a general rule, liability under section 107 of CERCLA is joint and several. That means EPA can target any responsible party and make that person pay all the response costs. That person can then turn around and sue other responsible parties for contribution.[29] However, in 2009 the Supreme Court held that Superfund liability is *not* joint and several where the defendant can prove that the harm is divisible.[30]

Private Party Actions

CERCLA provides two causes of action for a private party who has incurred response costs: (1) contribution under section 113(f)(3)(B), and (2) cost recovery under section 107(a). Contribution and cost recovery are distinct remedies available to PRPs in different procedural situations. Both are means by which a PRP can recover at least some portion of its costs related to a cleanup effort, but they differ in what costs a party can potentially recover, burdens of proof, and statutes of limitation.

A section 107(a) cost recovery claim generally allows a PRP to impose a greater share of the liability (at least if attorney fees are considered) on another PRP. Case law from federal circuits around the country has been inconsistent on when a party qualifies to bring a contribution action versus a cost recovery action for a given set of cleanup costs.

A section 113(f)(3)(B) contribution claim allows a PRP who has taken actions to clean up hazardous substances to seek monetary contribution from others who are also responsible for the contamination when the PRP has paid more than its fair share. A right to contribution may arise where a PRP has been sued under sections 106 or 107 or has settled

28. Emhart Indus. v. New England Container Co., 2019 U.S. Dist. LEXIS 61119 (D.R.I. 2019), *aff'd sub nom* Emhart Indus. v. U.S. Dep't of the Air Force, 988 F.3d 511 (1st Cir. 2021).

29. 42 U.S.C. § 9613.

30. Burlington Northern, 556 U.S. at 599 (allowing an allocation defense to joint and several liability if the defendant can prove the harm is divisible).

its liability with a state or the United States through an administrative or judicially approved settlement.[31]

The distinction between section 107 and section 113 is important not only because of joint and several liability but because the two sections have different statutes of limitation. A claim under section 113 must be brought within three years but a party has six years to bring a claim under section 107 for remedial costs.[32] In a 2022 case following decades of CERCLA litigation over PCB contamination in the Kalamazoo River, the Sixth Circuit held that a 1998 declaratory judgment against a party began the statute of limitations for a contribution action by one of the parties found liable under the 1998 declaratory judgment. The court held that this was true even if the contribution action was against a person who was not subject to the 1998 declaratory judgment. In this case, it meant that any party found liable under the 1998 declaratory judgment needed to file contribution actions against other parties (whether part of the 1998 declaratory judgment or not) within three years, for costs covered by the declaratory judgment (which in this case were all response costs). That meant a 2010 contribution action filed by a party that was found liable in 1998 was time-barred.[33]

In 2021, a unanimous Supreme Court weighed in on the statute of limitations for CERCLA contribution actions. In *Guam v. United States*, the Court summarily rejected a Department of Defense argument that a Clean Water Act consent decree between Guam and the United States started the clock on the statute of limitations for a CERCLA contribution action by Guam against the Navy for the cost of cleaning up the Ordot Dump, where the Navy had disposed of toxic military waste for decades.[34]

---

31. 42 U.S.C. § 9613(f)(1), (f)(3)(B); *see also* United States v Atlantic Rsch. Corp., 551 U.S. 128, 138 (2008), ("Contribution is . . . the 'tortfeasor's right to collect from others responsible for the same tort after the tortfeasor has paid more than his or her proportionate share, the shares being defined as a percentage of fault'" (quoting Black's Law Dictionary 353 (8th ed. 2004)).

32. *Compare* 42 U.S.C. § 9613(g)(2) *with* 42 U.S.C. § 9613(g)(3).

33. Georgia-Pacific Consumer Products LP v. NCR Corp., 32 F.4th 534 (6th Cir. 2022), *cert. denied*, 144 S. Ct. 69 (2023).

34. Guam v. United States, 593 U.S. 310, 312 (2021) (holding that CERCLA contribution requires resolution of a CERCLA-specific liability).

The Supreme Court has also weighed in on the issue of whether a private party can bring an action under section 107 with joint and several liability or solely an action under section 113 for contribution with several liability. In *Cooper Industries, Inc. v. Aviall Services, Inc.*, the Court held that a party who has not been sued under section 106 or section 107 may not bring a contribution action under section 113.[35] In *United States v. Atlantic Research Corp.*, the Court held that such parties may bring an action under section 107 to recover their costs from responsible parties and that section 113 actions and section 107 actions are mutually exclusive.[36] As explained by the Supreme Court, "costs incurred voluntarily are recoverable only by way of § 107(a)(4)(B), and costs of reimbursement to another person pursuant to a legal judgment or settlement are recoverable only under § 113(f)."[37]

Atlantic Research Corp. did not resolve all the issues surrounding section 113 and section 107. The Ninth Circuit's 2017 opinion in *Asarco LLC v. Atlantic Richfield* clarified some key issues regarding a PRPs eligibility to bring either action, while still leaving some questions open.[38] One thing the *Asarco* opinion made clear is that the two causes of action are mutually exclusive—a PRP cannot be eligible for both, at least with respect to the same cleanup costs.[39]

While cost recovery and contribution actions "offer complementary yet distinct remedies," there is overlap:

> For example, a PRP may undertake its own response actions pursuant to a settlement agreement with the government. That PRP will have incurred its own response costs, meaning it is eligible for cost recovery under 107(a), but it has also settled with the government, giving rise to a contribution action under § 113(f)(3)(B). The question is whether both or only one of these avenues of relief is available.[40]

35. Cooper Industries, Inc. v. Aviall Services, Inc., 543 U.S. 157 (2004).
36. *Atlantic Rsch. Corp.*, 551 U.S. at 128.
37. *Id.* at 139–40 n.6.
38. Asarco LLC v. Atlantic Richfield Co., 866 F.3d 1108, 1117 (9th Cir. 2017).
39. *Id.* at 1117.
40. *Id.* at 1116–17.

Given this potential overlap, the Ninth Circuit applies the following rule: "[A] party who *may* bring a contribution action for certain expenses *must* use the contribution action, even if a cost recovery action would otherwise be available."[41]

To bring a contribution action, the claimant must show: (1) that it is subject to an administrative or judicially approved settlement; (2) that the PRP took response action or incurred response costs subject to that agreement or consent order; and (3) that the agreement or consent order resolved its liability for at least some of the response actions or costs.[42]

In footnote 9 of the *Asarco* opinion, the Court explains that "where a contribution action is unavailable, a PRP may be able to bring a § 107 'cost recovery' action against other PRPs to recoup 'any . . . necessary costs of response incurred' that result from a release of a hazardous substance."[43] In other words, if a PRP has performed work pursuant to a consent order that fails to meet any of the three requirements for a contribution action, the court may essentially ignore the existence of the consent order altogether and permit the PRP to proceed with the usually preferable claim of cost recovery instead.

Allocation of Liability

In most cases liability is not divisible, so joint and several liability will apply. However, if a case is litigated, a court will allocate the liability in phase two of a trial, after liability is established. Section 113(f)(1) provides that "in resolving contribution claims, the court may allocate response costs among liable parties using such equitable factors as the court determines are appropriate."[44] In 1986, Congress added section 122 to CERCLA to authorize EPA to prepare nonbinding preliminary allocations of responsibility (NBARs), when asked to do so by responsible parties, based on factors such as volume, toxicity, mobility, strength of evidence, ability to pay, litigative risks, public interest, precedential value, and inequities and aggravating factors.[45]

41. *Id.* at 1117 (alterations and internal quotation marks omitted).
42. *See id.* at 1118.
43. *Id.* at 1130, n.9.
44. 42 U.S.C. § 9613(f)(1).
45. *Id.* § 9622(e)(3).

As a practical matter, parties do not want to leave their fate to a judge, and parties rarely ask EPA to prepare an NBAR. Instead, parties generally form committees and do their own allocations among themselves, sometimes with the assistance of allocation consultants.[46]

Defenses and Liability Protections

CERCLA liability for releases of hazardous substances is famously fearsome as many courts have held it is strict, joint and several, and retroactive. While there are arguments that may be available given the facts, and the plaintiff always has the burden of proof to show that the elements of CERCLA liability are met, escape is difficult. Given that CERCLA imposes liability based on a person's status, the plaintiff's burden of proof is not difficult to meet.

CERCLA does provide some defenses to liability. When raising a defense, the burden of proof falls on the defendant, so CERCLA defenses are not often successful.

CERCLA provides the following defenses:

> There shall be no liability under subsection (a) of this section for a person otherwise liable who *can establish by a preponderance of the evidence* that the release or threat of release of a hazardous substance and the damages resulting therefrom were caused solely by—
>
> (1) an act of God;
>
> (2) an act of war;
>
> (3) an act or omission of a third party other than an employee or agent of the defendant, or than one whose act or omission occurs in connection with a contractual relationship, existing directly or indirectly, with the defendant (except where the sole contractual arrangement arises from a published tariff and acceptance for carriage by a common carrier by rail), if the defendant establishes

---

46. A PRP allocation process can be very lengthy and expensive, particularly if it relies on extensive data on hazardous substance fate and transport. The allocation of responsibility among PRPs at the Portland Harbor Superfund site has gone on for years.

> by a preponderance of the evidence that (a) he exercised due care with respect to the hazardous substance concerned, taking into consideration the characteristics of such hazardous substance, in light of all relevant facts and circumstances, and (b) he took precautions against foreseeable acts or omissions of any such third party and the consequences that could foreseeably result from such acts or omissions; or
>
> (4) any combination of the foregoing paragraphs.[47]

Act of God Defense

An Act of God is "an unanticipated grave natural disaster or other natural phenomenon of an exceptional, inevitable, and irresistible character, the effects of which could not have been prevented or avoided by the exercise of due care or foresight."[48]

In practice, the Act of God defense is quite narrow.[49] First, the natural disaster must be "grave," which arguably limits the scope of qualifying disasters. Also, the natural disaster must be so exceptional and inevitable that the effects could not have been prevented or avoided.[50] At this time, hurricanes, and their relative strength, are being discussed as foreseeable through the developing area of "Attribution Science."[51] And more is being asked or expected of facilities in the path of these anticipated storms. For example, Arkema, Inc.'s Crosby, Texas, facility was flooded during Hurricane Harvey, resulting in loss of power causing loss of refrigeration, ultimately resulting in degradation of combustible chemicals and a fire that could not be extinguished, triggering civil and criminal litigation.[52] The civil claims asserted by over 140 plaintiffs allege that Arkema failed to adequately prepare for such a major flood

---

47. 42 U.S.C. § 9607(b) (emphasis added).

48. 42 U.S.C. § 9601(1); *see also* 33 U.S.C. § 1321(a)(12).

49. *See, e.g.*, Laurencia Fasayiro, *Invoking the Act of God Defense*, 2 Env. & Energy Law & Pol'y J. 3:2 (2009).

50. *Id.* (*citing* Jacoby v. Town of Gillette, 174 P.2d 505, 509 (Wyo. 1946)).

51. Sophie Marjanac et al., *Acts of God, Human Influence and Litigation*, 10 Nature Geoscience, 616 (2017); Sophie Marjanac, *Extreme Weather Event Attribution Science and Climate Change Litigation: An Essential Step in the Causal Chain?*, 36 J. of Energy & Nat. Res. Law 265 (2018).

52. *See* U.S. Chemical Safety and Hazard Investigation Board, Investigation Report: Organic Peroxide Decomposition, Release and Fire at Arkema Crosby Following

event, "having had the knowledge that such an event was foreseeable," and allege negligence, gross negligence, and negligence per se, among other claims.[53] The criminal claims allege reckless emission of an air contaminant, which requires demonstration of awareness and conscious disregard of a substantial and unjustifiable risk.[54] While not a CERCLA claim, the Arkema facts show how difficult an Act of God defense can be.

Act of War Defense

The Act of War defense requires that the act of war be the sole cause of the release or threat of release of hazardous substances. For that reason, it is not often asserted. However, the defense was successfully utilized by oil companies sued by EPA to recover response costs associated with a hazardous waste site resulting from the World War II aviation gasoline ("av-gas") program. In that case, the court found in favor of the oil companies, stating:

> [T]he war caused the problem and like myriad others the burden must rest on the United States, which is all of us. The United States won the war and all of us paid the costs at the time. This is another such cost merely long delayed.[55]

CERCLA's act of war defense was also upheld in litigation following the post-9/11 emergency response activities, as courts found that the defense did not rely on a congressional declaration of war or martial law.[56]

While not an affirmative defense, responsible parties have been successful in arguing that the War Production Board, not the private owner, was the operator of a facility involved in the production of nylon for parachutes during World War II, and therefore the Commerce Department,

---

Hurricane Harvey Flooding (May 2018), https://www.csb.gov/assets/1/20/final_arkema_draft_report_2018-05-23.pdf.

53. Plaintiffs' Third Amended Complaint at 25, Graves v. Arkema, Inc., Plaintiffs' Third Amended Complaint, U.S. Dist. Ct. (S. Dist. TX, Houston Div.) (4:17-cv-03068).

54. The State of Texas v. Richard P. Rowe, Case No. 160031101010-3, Harris County District Court, Texas, No. 339; The State of Texas v. Leslie Comardelle, Case No. 160031201010-3, Harris County District Court, Texas, No. 339; The State of Texas v. Arkema, Inc., Case No. 201776961, Harris County District Court, Texas, No. 157 (transferred from Court 339 to 157, as "other civil").

55. United States v. Shell Oil Co., 13 F. Supp. 2d 1018, 1030 (C.D. Cal. 1998).

56. Cedar & Washington Associates, LLC v. Port Authority, 751 F.3d 86 (2d Cir. 2014).

as the successor, was responsible for response costs of cleaning up any associated releases.[57]

Third-Party Defense

The third-party defense is commonly asserted, but its scope is strictly limited to true third parties, as well as fulfillment of duties by the alleged responsible party asserting the defense, including the allegedly responsible party's exercise of due care and addressing precautions against foreseeable acts or omissions of the alleged third party, as well as foreseeable consequences of these acts or omissions. It is usually easier to contemplate than to successfully assert and maintain a third-party defense.

Good Samaritan Defense and Actions Undertaken at the Direction of the On-Scene Coordinator

CERCLA also provides defenses for those actions taken to render care, assistance, or advice in accordance with the NCP, known as the Good Samaritan defense, as well as for actions taken at the direction of the OSC:

> Except as provided in paragraph (2), no person shall be liable under this subchapter for costs or damages as a result of actions taken or omitted in the course of rendering care, assistance, or advice in accordance with the National Contingency Plan ("NCP") or at the direction of an on-scene coordinator appointed under such plan, with respect to an incident creating a danger to public health or welfare or the environment as a result of any releases of a hazardous substance or the threat thereof. This paragraph shall not preclude liability for costs or damages as the result of negligence on the part of such person.[58]

---

57. FMC Corp. v. U.S. Dep't of Commerce, 29 F.3d 833, 843 (3d Cir. 1994) (imposing operator liability when the government had "substantial control" over the facility and "active involvement" of the activities there); *compare* PPG Industries, Inc. v. United States of America, 957 F.3d 395 (3d Cir. 2020) (applying the successor liability analysis of *Bestfoods* and declining to find that the United States was liable as an operator as a result of involvement with a chromate ore processing plant during World War I and World War II where the United States was not making day-to-day decisions regarding waste generating operations).

58. 42 U.S.C. § 9607(d).

While these defenses are clearly stated in CERCLA, they are not so clearly applied. For example, CERCLA provides another specific defense for CERCLA remediation contractors.[59] But this exemption applies only to sites that are listed on the National Priorities List. In the litigation following the Gold King Mine disaster, a CERCLA remediation contractor failed to get dismissed from the case filed by the State of New Mexico under both CERCLA and state law. In that matter, EPA was engaging in remediation activities at the Gold King Mine. The CERCLA contractor, Environmental Restoration, LLC, was working specifically at the direction of the EPA's OSC when the release occurred. Nonetheless, the Court held that dismissal was not appropriate at that stage of the case because the plaintiffs alleged sufficient facts to support a determination that the contractor was an operator of the site, arranged for disposal of hazardous substances at the site, and transported hazardous substances to the site, creating liability under CERCLA, and that it was unclear whether EPA provided sufficient direction to the contractors to give rise to a government contractor defense that could provide immunity from state law.[60]

Even before the Gold King Mine event, however, parties were reluctant to engage in recovery operations as Good Samaritans due to the potential to incur liability. Pursuant to EPA's interim guidance for exercising enforcement discretion to forego pursuing Good Samaritans for response costs,[61] EPA does not consider the following parties to be Good Samaritans: a current or past owner of the property; a party that

59. *Id.* § 9619. This section provides that response action contractors shall not be liable under this CERCLA or under any other federal law to any person for injuries, costs, damages, expenses, or other liability (including but not limited to claims for indemnification or contribution and claims by third parties for death, personal injury, illness or loss of or damage to property or economic loss) which results from a release or threatened release of a hazardous substance to which the contractor is responding. This defense is limited where there is negligence and shall not apply: "in the case of a release that is caused by conduct of the response action contractor which is negligent, grossly negligent, or which constitutes intentional misconduct." Further, it applies only at sites listed on the National Priorities List.

60. New Mexico v. U.S. EPA, 310 F. Supp. 3d 1230 (D.N.M. 2018) (denying contractor's motion to dismiss); *see also* U.S. Dep't of the Interior, Technical Evaluation of the Gold King Mine Incident (Oct. 2016), https://www.usbr.gov/docs/goldkingminereport.pdf.

61. *See* EPA, Interim Guiding Principles for Good Samaritan Projects at Orphan Mine Sites and Transmittal of CERCLA Administrative Tools for Good Samaritans (June 6, 2007), https://www.epa.gov/sites/production/files/2015-09/documents/cercla-goodsam-principles-mem-ed2015.pdf.

is potentially liable for the remediation of the existing contamination pursuant to CERCLA section 106 or 107;[62] or a party that is liable under any other federal, state, or local law for the remediation of the existing contamination. Third parties that would otherwise qualify as a Good Samaritan have been reluctant to step forward, fearing that their actions may cause them to incur liability or lose their Good Samaritan status. Moreover, a question of long-term operations and maintenance often comes into play associated with the responsibility to maintain recovery systems or to obtain permits. This is especially true when the incident has not risen to the level requiring appointment of an OSC. For these reasons, Good Samaritans often seek an administrative settlement with EPA to gain liability protection for their cleanup actions, as discussed next.

In December 2024, Congress enacted the Good Samaritan Remediation of Abandoned Hardrock Mines Act of 2024.[63] This law authorizes EPA to issue up to 15 permits for the remediation of historic mine residue at abandoned hardrock mines by persons who are not current or former owners or operators of the abandoned mine, had no role in creation of the mine residue, and are not otherwise liable for cleaning up the mine residue, in other words, "Good Samaritans." The permit would shield the Good Samaritan from liability under both CERCLA and the Clean Water Act. It remains to be seen if this new authority will encourage cleanups of abandoned mines.

Federally Permitted Releases

CERCLA defendants may assert a defense based on the "federally permitted release" exemption.[64] The specific analysis depends on the type

62. 42 U.S.C. §§ 9606, 9607.

63. Pub. L. No. 118-155.

64. 42 U.S.C. § 9601(10) (providing: The term "federally permitted release" means (A) discharges in compliance with a permit under section 402 of the Federal Water Pollution Control Act [33 U.S.C. § 1342], (B) discharges resulting from circumstances identified and reviewed and made part of the public record with respect to a permit issued or modified under section 402 of the Federal Water Pollution Control Act and subject to a condition of such permit, (C) continuous or anticipated intermittent discharges from a point source, identified in a permit or permit application under section 402 of the Federal Water Pollution Control Act, which are caused by events occurring within the scope of relevant operating or treatment systems, (D) discharges in compliance with a legally enforceable permit under section 404 of the Federal Water Pollution Control Act [33 U.S.C. § 1344], (E) releases in compliance with a legally enforceable final permit issued pursuant to section 3005(a) through (d) of the Solid Waste Disposal Act [42 U.S.C. § 6925(a)–(d)] from a hazardous

of permit pursuant to which the release is supposedly authorized. As a general rule, courts have held that the discharge or release must have been explicitly authorized either in the permit itself or in the administrative record upon which the permit issuance relied.[65] The Third Circuit recently held that, due to differences in the statutory language for Clean Air Act (CAA) permitted releases, releases "subject to" a CAA permit do not need to be in compliance with that permit.[66]

Additional Defenses Added in the Small Business Liability Relief and Brownfields Revitalization Act

In January 2002, Congress amended CERCLA in the Small Business Liability Relief and Brownfields Revitalization Act, which added defenses

---

waste treatment, storage, or disposal facility when such permit specifically identifies the hazardous substances and makes such substances subject to a standard of practice, control procedure or bioassay limitation or condition, or other control on the hazardous substances in such releases, (F) any release in compliance with a legally enforceable permit issued under section 1412 of title 33 of 1 section 1413 of title 33, (G) any injection of fluids authorized under Federal underground injection control programs or State programs submitted for Federal approval (and not disapproved by the Administrator of the Environmental Protection Agency) pursuant to part C of the Safe Drinking Water Act [42 U.S.C. §§ 300h, *et seq.*], (H) any emission into the air subject to a permit or control regulation under section 111 [42 U.S.C. § 7411], section 112 [42 U.S.C. § 7412], title I part C [42 U.S.C. §§ 7470, *et seq.*], title I part D [42 U.S.C. §§ 7501 *et seq.*], or State implementation plans submitted in accordance with section 110 of the Clean Air Act [42 U.S.C. § 7410] (and not disapproved by the Administrator of the Environmental Protection Agency), including any schedule or waiver granted, promulgated, or approved under these sections, (I) any injection of fluids or other materials authorized under applicable State law (i) for the purpose of stimulating or treating wells for the production of crude oil, natural gas, or water, (ii) for the purpose of secondary, tertiary, or other enhanced recovery of crude oil or natural gas, or (iii) which are brought to the surface in conjunction with the production of crude oil or natural gas and which are reinjected, (J) the introduction of any pollutant into a publicly owned treatment works when such pollutant is specified in and in compliance with applicable pretreatment standards of section 307(b) or (c) of the Clean Water Act [33 U.S.C. § 1317(b), (c)] and enforceable requirements in a pretreatment program submitted by a State or municipality for Federal approval under section 402 of such Act [33 U.S.C. § 1342], and (K) any release of source, special nuclear, or byproduct material, as those terms are defined in the Atomic Energy Act of 1954 [42 U.S.C. §§ 2011 *et seq.*], in compliance with a legally enforceable license, permit, regulation, or order issued pursuant to the Atomic Energy Act of 1954.). *See also* Guidance on the CERCLA Section 101(10) Federally permitted release Definition for Certain Air Emissions (notice); 74 Fed. Reg. 18,899 (Apr. 17, 2002).

65. *See* State of Idaho v. Bunker Hill Co., 635 F. Supp. 665, 673–74 (D. Idaho 1986) (allowing state to recover under CERCLA for damages caused by releases not expressly allowed by the permit or occurring at a time no permit existed).

66. Clean Air Council v. U.S. Steel Corp., 4 F.4th 204 (3rd Cir. 2021). This is another example of counterintuitive outcomes resulting from inartful legislative drafting.

to CERCLA liability to address certain areas where third-party contribution actions imposed particularly draconian liability and to encourage cleanup and redevelopment of former industrial properties.[67] This act is commonly referred to as the Brownfields bill.

De Micromis Exemption

Under section 107(o) of CERCLA, the *de micromis* exemptions exempt persons from Superfund response cost liability at NPL sites as generators and transporters if the person can demonstrate that the total amount of the material containing hazardous substances they contributed was less than 110 gallons of liquid materials or 200 pounds of solid materials and all or part of disposal, treatment, or transport occurred before April 1, 2001. However, this exemption does not apply if (1) the materials contributed or could contribute significantly, either individually or in the aggregate, to the cost of the response action or natural resource restoration; (2) the person fails to comply with an information request; (3) the person impedes or impeded, through action or inaction, a response action or natural resource restoration at the facility; or (4) the person has been convicted of a criminal violation for conduct to which the exemption would apply.[68]

While, in general, a plaintiff has the burden to establish a prima facie case, in this section of the statute, Congress specifically put the burden of proof on plaintiffs in private party contribution actions to show that the exemption does not apply.[69]

Municipal Solid Waste Defense

EPA generally does not pursue municipal solid waste (MSW) generators. However, private parties did sue MSW generators in contribution claims, arguing that MSW contains hazardous substances and the volume of MSW increased cleanup costs.[70] To deter these third-party claims, Congress added section 107(p) to CERCLA to exempt persons

67. Pub. L. No. 107-118 (2002).

68. 42 U.S.C. § 6907(o).

69. *Id.* § 9607(o)(4). Shifting the burden of proof has the effect of discouraging third party contribution actions.

70. *See, e.g.*, B.F. Goodrich Co. v. Murtha, 815 F. Supp. 539, 540 (D. Conn. 1993) (granting motion of industrial defendants who had entered into a CERCLA consent decree with EPA for the cleanup of two landfills to file third party complaints against eighteen municipalities and over 1,100

from Superfund response cost liability as generators for the disposal of MSW from residential properties, small businesses, and nonprofits, if the person is:

- an owner, operator, or lessee of residential property from which the MSW was generated;
- a business from which the MSW was generated that employed on average not more than 100 individuals in the three years prior to notification of potential liability and is a "small business concern" as defined by the Small Business Act, or
- a nonprofit organization that employed not more than 100 individuals during the preceding year at the location from which the MSW was generated.[71]

However, the MSW exemption does not apply if the President (or the delegated agency, usually EPA) determines that:

- the MSW contributes or could contribute significantly, either individually or in the aggregate, to the cost of the response action or natural resource restoration,
- person fails to comply with an information request, or
- the person impedes or impeded, through action or inaction, a response action or natural resource restoration at the facility.[72]

This section defines MSW as waste material generated by a household and waste material generated by a commercial, industrial, or institutional entity. The commercial waste must be essentially the same as waste normally generated by a household, be collected and disposed of with other MSW as part of normal MSW collection, and contain a relative quantity of hazardous substances no greater than the relative quantity of hazardous substances contained in waste generated by a typical single-family household. Examples of municipal solid waste listed in the statute are food and yard waste, paper, appliances, consumer product packaging, elementary

---

small businesses based on an allegation that the municipalities and businesses arranged for the disposal of municipal solid waste containing hazardous substances at the landfills).

71. 42 U.S.C. § 9607(p).
72. *Id.* § 9607(p)(2).

and secondary school science lab waste, and household hazardous waste. Combustion ash from resource recovery facilities or municipal incinerators and waste material from manufacturing and processing operations are excluded from the definition.[73]

In this section Congress put the burden of proof to show that the exemption does not apply on all (including governmental) plaintiffs for MSW disposal before April 1, 2001, and on plaintiffs in private party contribution actions for MSW disposal on or after April 1, 2001.[74] Non-governmental plaintiffs that bring an action and fail to demonstrate that the exemption does not apply also must pay the prevailing party's costs.[75] Finally, Congress banned all contributions claims by private parties against residential MSW generators.[76] As a practical matter, Congress has achieved its goal of preventing contribution claims for MSW disposal.

Contiguous Property Owner Defense

Congress was aware of the limitations of the third-party defense. To address some of those limitations, Congress added section 107(q) to CERCLA to exempt from owner or operator liability persons that own land contaminated *solely* by a release from contiguous, or similarly situated, property owned by someone else if the person can demonstrate that he or she:

- did not cause or contribute to the release or threatened release;
- is not potentially liable or affiliated with any other person potentially liable;
- exercises appropriate care in respect to the release;
- provides full cooperation, assistance, and access to persons authorized to undertake the response action and natural resource restoration;
- complies with all land use controls and does not impede the performance of any institutional controls;
- complies with all information requests;

73. *Id.* § 9607(p)(4).
74. *Id.* § 9607(p)(5).
75. *Id.* § 9607(p)(7).
76. *Id.* § 9607(p)(6).

- provides all the legally required notices regarding releases of hazardous substances; and
- conducted all appropriate inquiry at time of purchase and did not know or have reason to know of contamination.[77]

Bona Fide Prospective Purchaser Defense

Congress is very supportive of brownfields redevelopment, enacting liability protection for brownfields redevelopers called the bona fide prospective purchaser defense as well as authorizing grants to help fund site assessment, cleanups, and state voluntary cleanup programs.[78] The bona fide prospective purchaser defense is intended to remove legal barriers to redevelopment of brownfields properties by new owners (and their tenants) by exempting such persons from owner or operator liability so long as the person does not impede the performance of a response action or natural resource restoration.

A bona fide prospective purchaser is defined as a person who can demonstrate by a preponderance of the evidence that:

- all disposal took place before the date of purchase;
- person made *all appropriate inquiry* (a defined term);
- person exercises *appropriate care* with respect to any release (defined only in enforcement discretion guidance and the subject of much litigation);
- provides full cooperation, assistance, and access to persons authorized to undertake response actions or natural resource restoration;
- complies with land use restrictions and does not impede performance of institutional controls;
- complies with all information requests;
- provides all legally required notices regarding releases of hazardous substances;
- person is not potentially liable or affiliated with any other person potentially liable.[79]

---

77. *Id.* § 9607(q).

78. The Small Business Liability Relief and Brownfields Revitalization Act, Pub. L. No. 107-118 (2002).

79. 40 U.S.C. § 9601(40) (emphasis added).

Exclusions from Owner or Operator Liability

The CERCLA section 101(20) defines owner or operator in a circular fashion as any person owning or operating a facility. However, the definition also includes a number of exemptions so certain classes of owners and operators cannot be held liable as an owner or operator under section 107. For example, this definition excludes persons who hold indicia of ownership merely to protect a security interest, that is, lenders.[80] It also excludes units of state or local government that acquire ownership through seizure or in connection with law enforcement activity, bankruptcy, tax delinquency, abandonment, or other circumstances where the government acquires property by virtue of its function as sovereign. The exclusion only applies if the state or local government did not cause or contribute to the release or threatened release of a hazardous substance.[81] Finally, it excludes Alaska Native Villages and Native Corporations for liability as owners or operators of often contaminated land that was conveyed to them by the federal government under the Alaska Native Claims Settlement Act.[82]

EPA Interpretation of Certain CERCLA Defenses

EPA cannot create exclusions from CERCLA liability—only Congress has that authority.[83] EPA can exercise enforcement discretion and can develop guidance informing the regulated community on how and when EPA intends to exercise its enforcement discretion.[84] This guidance is not controlling, but courts are likely to consider it.

80. *Id.* § 9601(20)(A), (F), (G), and (H).

81. *Id.* § 9601(20)(D).

82. *Id.* § 9601(20)(E).

83. Kelley v. EPA, 15 F.3d 1100, 1107–08 (D.C. Cir. 1994) (holding that Congress has "designated the courts and not EPA as the adjudicator of the scope of CERCLA liability" and vacating EPA's Lender Liability rule, which purported to exclude lenders from the definition of owner or operator). Congress responded in 1996 by adding a lender exclusion from the definition of owner or operator in CERCLA.

84. *See, e.g.*, the EPA enforcement policies related to *de minimis* parties, *de micromis* parties, inability to pay parties, MSW generators, municipalities, owners of property above contaminated aquifers, and residential homeowners, found here: https://www.epa.gov/enforcement/unique-parties-and-superfund-liability#demin.

In 2019, EPA issued an update to its "Common Elements" guidance.[85] This enforcement discretion guidance addresses the common elements of establishing a defense for certain landowners: bona fide prospective purchasers (BFPPs),[86] contiguous property owners (CPOs),[87] and innocent landowners (ILOs).[88] To be excluded from CERCLA liability, these categories of landowners must perform "all appropriate inquiries"[89] into prior uses of the property before acquisition (all three categories), demonstrate "no affiliation"[90] with a liable party (BFPPs and CPOs), and perform "continuing obligations."[91] The continuing obligations are:

- demonstrating that no disposal of hazardous substances occurred at the facility after acquisition by the landowner (for BFPPs and ILOs);
- complying with land use restrictions and not impeding the effectiveness or integrity of institutional controls (all three categories);
- taking "reasonable steps" with respect to hazardous substance releases affecting a landowner's property (all three categories);
- providing cooperation, assistance, and access to persons authorized to conduct response actions or natural resource restoration;
- complying with information requests and administrative subpoenas (for BFPPs and CPOs); and
- providing legally required notices (for BFPPs and CPOs).[92]

Each of these conditions has been the subject of litigation, which EPA discusses in the "Common Elements" guidance.[93]

---

85. EPA, Enforcement Discretion Guidance Regarding Statutory Criteria for Those Who May Qualify as CERCLA Bona Fide Prospective Purchasers, Contiguous Property Owners, or Innocent Landowners ("Common Elements") (July 29, 2019) https://www.epa.gov/sites/default/files/2019-08/documents/common-elements-guide-mem-2019.pdf [hereinafter Common Elements].

86. 42 U.S.C. §§ 9601(40), 6907(r)(1)) (bona fide prospective purchasers).

87. *Id.* § 9607(q) (contiguous property owners).

88. *Id.* §§ 6901(35), 6907(b)(3) (innocent landowners).

89. *Id.* § 9601(35)(B).

90. *Id.* § 9601(40)(B)(viii).

91. *See* CERCLA §§ 101(40)(B)(i)–(viii) and 107(r) for BFPPs, 107(q)(1)(A) for CPOs, and 101(35)(A)–(B) and 107(b)(3) for ILOs.

92. *See* Common Elements, *supra* note 85, at 8-22.

93. *Id.*

Significantly, EPA makes it clear that while a "disposal" can disqualify a CERCLA liability defense, and case law on what constitutes a disposal is inconsistent,[94] EPA will not pursue enforcement against a property owner for what EPA calls a "secondary disposal," if the owner acted reasonably. That is, recognizing Congress's intent to encourage brownfields redevelopment, EPA reconciles the requirement to take "reasonable steps" to manage existing or ongoing releases with the requirement that a BFPP and ILO not dispose of hazardous substances after acquisition. EPA does this by taking the position that no disqualifying disposal takes place while a party is taking reasonable steps to manage a preexisting release of hazardous substances or if an owner is undertaking site development and construction activities in a reasonable manner.[95] EPA also provides its view of what constitutes "reasonable steps" and embraces the legislative history of the Brownfields bill, which states that an otherwise exempt owner should not have to undertake response actions to maintain its exemption from liability for the costs of response actions.[96]

In 2020, EPA updated its enforcement discretion guidance on CERCLA liability and local government acquisitions, to reflect the statutory changes enacted in the Brownfields Utilization, Investment, and Local Development (BUILD) Act of 2018.[97] The BUILD Act amended CERCLA's section 101(20)(D) liability protection for state and local government acquisitions of contaminated property. It removed the requirement that state and local governments must acquire title to property "involuntarily" while retaining the language that a qualifying government acquisi-

94. *See, e.g.*, Tanglewood E. Homeowners v. Charles-Thomas, Inc., 849 F.2d 1568, 1573 (5th Cir. 1988) ("[T]here may be other disposals when hazardous materials are moved, dispersed, or released during landfill excavations and fillings."); Kaiser Alum. & Chem. Corp. v. Catellus Dev. Corp., 976 F.2d 1338, 1342 (9th Cir. 1992) ("disposal" can occur when a development contractor excavated the site for residential development and spread contaminated soil to previously uncontaminated areas of the property); Bob's Beverage, Inc. v. Acme, Inc., 264 F.3d 692, 697 (6th Cir. 2001) (disposal occurs where active human conduct "cause[s] the spread of contamination into or on previously uncontaminated soil or water.").

95. Common Elements, *supra* note 85, at 10-11.

96. *Id.* at 18-19, Attachment B.

97. Consolidated Appropriations Act, Pub. L. No. 115-141 Division D, 132 Stat. 1052 (Mar. 23, 2018). *See* EPA, Superfund Liability Protections for Local Government Acquisitions after the Brownfields Utilization, Investment, and Local Development Act of 2018 (2018), https://www.epa.gov/sites/default/files/2020-06/documents/local-gov-acquisition-guide-final-2020-esign.pdf [hereinafter Local Acquisition Guide].

tion includes "other circumstances in which the government acquires title by virtue of its function as sovereign."[98] Congress also added "through seizure or otherwise in connection with law enforcement activity," to the nonexclusive list of exempt acquisitions.[99] Unlike the other property owner defenses, the state and local government acquisition exclusion from liability is subject only to the condition that the state or local government does not cause or contribute to the release or threatened release of a hazardous substance from the facility, so continuing obligations do not apply.

Congress did not eliminate all the ambiguities in CERCLA as it relates to state and local government liability. As a sovereign entity, a state or local government could argue that all actions it takes are "by virtue of its function as sovereign."[100] However, EPA applies the principle of statutory interpretation of *ejusdem generis*. That means EPA takes the position that not all government acquisitions are protected from liability under CERCLA because where general words or phrases (like "other circumstances in which the government acquires title by virtue of its function as sovereign") follow a number of specific words or phrases (like "seizure," "in connection with law enforcement activity," "bankruptcy," "tax delinquency," and "abandonment"), the general words are construed as limited. They will apply only to persons or things of the same kind or class as those expressly mentioned.

Applying that principle of statutory interpretation, EPA asserts that acquisitions through purchase, inheritance, bequest, gift, or donation are not uniquely governmental and are not covered acquisitions; a state or local government must therefore take steps to be a BFPP to attain liability protection for such an acquisition.[101] Applying that same principle, EPA takes the position that acquiring property through escheat is covered by section 101(20), even though escheat is included in the innocent landowner defense in CERCLA section 101(35)(A)(ii).[102] Finally, even though eminent domain is also covered by the innocent landowner

98. Pub. L. No. 115-141, § 2.
99. *Id.*
100. 42 U.S.C. § 9601(20)(D).
101. Local Acquisition Guide, *supra* note 97, at 8.
102. *Id.* at 9.

defense, EPA states that eminent domain can be a qualifying state or local government acquisition in under CERCLA section 101(20) if it is for public use of property (uniquely governmental), not private economic development (not uniquely governmental).[103]

Additional Protections from Liability

In addition to the CERCLA defenses to liability discussed earlier, EPA's own CERCLA model documents for resolving claims or ordering respondents to perform obligations with respect to CERCLA projects provide some relief in the force majeure clause. The force majeure clause addresses performance delays relating to any event arising out of the control of a respondent. However, the provision is somewhat limiting and exempts as a force majeure any event that results from a foreseen incident for which a respondent both fails to notify the agency and fails to take actions to prevent or minimize the delay. For example, the 2024 model RI/FS AOC provides,

> Respondents shall send a further notice to EPA that includes: (i) a description of the event and its effect on Respondents' completion oof the requirements of the Settlement; (ii) a description of all actions taken or to be taken to prevent or minimize the adverse effects or delay; (iii) the proposed extension of time for Respondents to complete the requirements of the Settlement; (iv) a statement as to whether, in the opinion of the Respondents, such event may cause or contribute to an endangerment to the public health or welfare, or the environment; and (v) all available proof supporting their claim of force majeure. Failure to comply with the notice requirements herein regarding an event precludes Respondents from asserting any claim of force majeure regarding that event[.][104]

EPA has historically asserted that this language is intended to require a respondent to take all measures necessary to prevent impacts from a

103. *Id.* at 9–10, n.16.
104. EPA, Model RI/FS ASAOC, ¶ 47 (Dec. 2024), https://cfpub.epa.gov/compliance/models/view.cfm?model_ID=792.

foreseen event such as a predictable disaster (a disaster for which a party should have been reasonably aware). As a practical matter, EPA will generally recognize a force majeure that causes a delay and a missed deadline but will not excuse compliance entirely. If compliance is not possible, a PRP must generally seek to reopen and renegotiate the settlement.

Also, the various environmental statutes provide exemptions from the application of environmental authority during an emergency response to assist in response efforts. For example, the Clean Water Act provides an exemption from permitting for exigent discharges at the direction of the OSC.[105] EPA may issue temporary emergency permits to treat, store, or dispose of hazardous waste.[106] An OSC may exempt off-site waste transfers in emergency removal actions.[107]

Settlement and Order Authority

As noted, enforcement authority under CERCLA is broad and can address virtually any release of hazardous substances. For example, section 106 of CERCLA authorizes EPA to use administrative orders, or to seek a court order, whenever there may be an imminent and substantial endangerment to public health, welfare, or the environment not only from hazardous substances but also from pollutants and contaminants.[108] EPA uses these orders and judicial consent decrees as a mechanism for resolving claims, recovering response costs, and defining the scope of any removal or remedial work. If the settlement is voluntary, these settlements will take the form of an Administrative Settlement Agreement and Order on Consent (ASAOC) or a Consent Decree (CD). If it is involuntary, EPA will issue a Unilateral Administrative Order (UAO).

Section 122 of CERCLA gives EPA and DOJ express authority to enter into settlements with any person under which the person performs a response action. Section 122 also gives EPA and DOJ authority to enter into settlements under which the United States accepts funds from a settling party, deposits the funds into "special accounts" within

---

105. Clean Water Act, 33 U.S.C. § 1321(c); 40 C.F.R. § 122.3(d).
106. 40 C.F.R. § 300.40.
107. *Id.* § 270.61(a).
108. 42 U.S.C. § 9606.

the Superfund trust fund, and uses those funds (without the need for an appropriation) for response actions at the site.[109]

If a person settles with EPA, the settling party will generally be given a covenant not to sue for the hazardous substance release that is addressed by the remedial action, to take effect when EPA agrees that the remedial action is complete. The covenant is typically subject to a reopener for conditions that were unknown at the time of the settlement.[110]

The value of the ASAOC and CD is that they define the nature of the settlement, including a description of the work and any payments to be made to the United States. In return, the United States grants the party a covenant not to sue. A settlement with EPA also protects from contribution claims by other parties "regarding matters addressed in the settlement."[111] EPA has developed model documents that serve as the agency's template for all ASAOCs and CDs.[112] For example, the covenant not to sue in the 2024 revision to the Model Remedial Design/Remedial Action (RD/RA) Consent Decree currently provides: "Subject to ¶¶ 71 and 72, the United States covenants not to sue or to take administrative action against Settling Defendants under sections 106 and 107(a) of CERCLA regarding [the Site] [the Work, Past Response Costs, and Future Response Costs]."[113] Paragraphs 71 and 72 contain reservations of rights and outline conditions under which the agreement is "reopened" and EPA has the right to take action.[114] In essence, the covenant not to sue provides that the United States will not sue as long as the PRP completes the defined work, makes the required payments, complies with the

---

109. *Id.* § 9622(a), (b). Special accounts are generally used for cashing out de minimis parties or parties with a limited ability to pay. EPA is unlikely to agree to cash out a PRP with deep pockets and significant responsibility for the site.

110. *Id.* § 9622(f).

111. *Id.* § 9622(h)(4).

112. All of EPA's model Superfund settlement documents are found at: https://cfpub.epa.gov/compliance/models/.

113. EPA, Model Remedial Design/Remedial Action (RD/RA) Consent Decree (July 2024), https://cfpub.epa.gov/compliance/models/view.cfm?model_ID=81&groupID=1.

114. The general reservations in paragraph 72 of the current RD/RA consent decree includes reservations for, among other things, liability for additional response actions that EPA determines are necessary to achieve and maintain Performance Standards or to carry out and maintain the effectiveness of the Remedial Action, but that are not covered by EPA's authority to modify the remedial action as specified in paragraph 21 of the model.

provisions in the agreement related to the site, and none of the reservations are triggered.[115]

As a condition of settlement, EPA's model documents also provide that the settling party waive its rights to challenge the remedy or its liability. For this reason, some parties are willing to forego a covenant not to sue and contribution protection. They instead take a unilateral order to preserve the right to later make a claim against the Superfund for reimbursement of arbitrary and capricious costs or to argue that they were not liable.[116] Implementing a recommendation of the 2019 Superfund Task Force, EPA is also willing to settle with parties who want to redevelop contaminated properties—even if they are BFPPs—and with Good Samaritans who want to clean up a site for which they have no liability.[117] In the context of what constitutes a "disposal," a party who redevelops property or voluntarily cleans it up could technically become an "operator" responsible for disposal activities.

Finality

When a responsible party settles its liability for a hazardous substance release, whether with a state or a local government, the party wants finality. That is, it does not want a regulator to come back for another bite of the apple. A settling party wants to quantify its liability and get it off the party's books.

As discussed earlier, EPA settlements are not final due to reopeners for unknown circumstances and changing estimates of the degree of cleanup needed to protect public health. With respect to settlements with states, Congress acted in the Brownfields bill to support the finality of state settlement agreements by adding section 128(b) of CERCLA.[118]

---

115. The covenant not to sue and the reservation of rights sections of the model documents are part of what many refer to as the "dirty dozen provisions," which EPA generally will not negotiate. While minor modifications are possible, a party generally must agree to these to enter into an order.

116. 42 U.S.C. § 9606(b)(2).

117. EPA, Superfund Task Force Recommendations 16–18 (July 25, 2017), https://www.epa.gov/sites/default/files/2017-07/documents/superfund_task_force_report.pdf.

118. 42 U.S.C. § 9628(b)(1)(A).

Section 128(b) states that at brownfields sites[119] EPA may not take enforcement action for a release that has been addressed under a state cleanup program. However, this section does not bar federal actions if the state asks EPA to intervene, if the contamination crosses state lines, if EPA determines that there may be an imminent and substantial endangerment, or if there is new information and further action is needed to protect public health.[120]

EPA values finality, however. Notwithstanding all the reopeners in EPA settlement agreements, EPA understands that it needs to offer finality to persuade private parties to carry out or fund cleanups. But even if a party resolves its liability to the United States and obtains a covenant not to sue and contribution protection, the question of liability under state law may remain.

The Supreme Court recently addressed some aspects of the interplay between CERCLA liability and state common law claims. In *Atlantic Richfield Co. v. Christian, et al.*, the Court addressed both state jurisdiction and the ability to change a remedy relying on state law.[121] That case arose out of remediation of historic hazardous substances releases from the former Anaconda smelter site in Butte, Montana. The releases impacted surface soils at nearby residences, and EPA selected a response action that called for Anaconda's corporate successor Atlantic Richfield Co. (ARCO) to work at the impacted residences. The selected remedy required excavation and removal of surface soils above risk-based concentration levels but allowed deeper soils to remain in place and capped, with institutional controls to prevent soil disturbance. Impacted property owners argued that EPA's remedy reduced their ability to use their property.

As already noted, CERCLA does not authorize damages for personal injury and property damage and such claims are expressly preserved.[122] Ninety-eight homeowners filed suit against ARCO in the Montana state courts, asserting trespass, nuisance, and strict liability claims under state

119. *See* definitions of "brownfield site" and "eligible response site," 42 U.S.C. § 9101(39), (41). In general, these definitions exclude NPL sites, RCRA corrective action sites, and sites where EPA or an authorized state has taken enforcement action under a federal environmental law.

120. *Id.* § 9628(b)(1)(B).

121. Atl. Richfield Co. v. Christian, 590 U.S. 1 (2020).

122. 42 U.S.C. § 9614(a).

common law and sought restoration damages.[123] Under Montana state law, restoration damages can exceed the reduction in property value, but the damages must be used for restoration.[124] In their state law case, the plaintiffs sought to compel ARCO to fund a restoration plan that included removing soil contaminated with arsenic above 15 ppm, not the 250-ppm action level adopted by EPA; excavation of two feet of soil, not one; and collecting groundwater located 15 feet below ground. After the Montana Supreme Court ordered ARCO to fund those actions, ARCO appealed that case to the U.S. Supreme Court.

On the question of jurisdiction, the U.S. Supreme Court rejected ARCO's argument that the state law claims were barred by section 113(h), because section 113(h) only bars challenges to remedies in federal court.[125] The Court also disagreed with ARCO that the state law claims were barred under section 113(b), because that section only bars state court jurisdiction over claims arising under CERCLA, not state law claims.[126] The Court did agree with ARCO that the homeowners could not conduct additional cleanup without EPA approval under section 122(e)(6).[127]

This holding may be unique to Montana, where restoration damages require restoration work, not just payment of monetary damages, giving rise to a potential conflict between the restoration damages and the CERCLA remedy. However, it does raise the possibility of EPA approving additional work sought by property owners, upending CERCLA's carefully crafted remedy selection process.

In the absence of a law like Montana's, *Atlantic Richfield v. Christian* stands for the proposition that monetary damages under common law are *not* precluded by CERCLA. Any entity that has such a spill must be aware of its legal vulnerability to and consequences of both CERCLA and common law claims.

123. *See* Atl. Richfield Co. v. Mont. Second Judicial Dist. Court, 39 408 P.2d 515 (2017).

124. Lampi v. Speed, 261 P.3d 1000 (Mont. 2011).

125. *Christian*, 590 U.S. at 15. Except as specified, federal courts are prohibited from entertaining challenges to EPA's remedy decisions under by CERCLA § 113(h), 42 U.S.C. § 9613(h).

126. *Id.* at 12–13. State courts have no jurisdiction to hear controversies arising under CERCLA under CERCLA § 113(b), 42 U.S.C. § 9613(b).

127. *Id.* at 17. Potentially responsible parties need express EPA approval to conduct additional remediation at an EPA-overseen site pursuant to CERCLA section § 122(e)(6), 42 U.S.C. § 9622 (e)(6).

Common Law Causes of Action for Environmental Claims[128]

CERCLA is a powerful tool for recovery of investigation and cleanup costs, but it is not a vehicle for recovery of damages for personal injury or property damages. They must be sought under the common law instead.[129]

Potential common law liability poses unique challenges to those attempting to avoid or quantify potential environmental liability associated with a hazardous substance release. First, not all of it can be avoided, and sometimes it is broader than a mere hazardous substance release. Second, common law liability exposure is typically more difficult to quantify than statutory liability. Toxic tort plaintiffs—that is, those who have suffered property damage, physical injury, or increased risk of disease—have always relied on common law theories to advance their cases. That is partly because of the broad relief potentially available under such theories, including the possibility of recovering punitive damages and attorney's fees, and partly because such claims can be asserted in state court, which is generally a more favorable forum for plaintiffs.

A host of situations illustrates the continued viability—and the need to consider—common law theories. Common law claims are often invoked where statutory causes of action are unavailable or inadequate, such as in the following situations:[130]

1. Claims that might otherwise be time-barred can sometimes be asserted under the common law "continuing" tort doctrine.[131]

---

128. This section has been adapted from Margo R. Casselman & Christopher D. Thomas, *Common Law Causes of Action for Environmental Claims*, *in* Environmental Aspects of Real Estate and Commercial Transaction (Kevin R. Murray, ed., 5th ed. 2021).

129. Kittok v. Lagasse, No. CIV.A. 01-2441, 2002 WL 1484388, at *3 (E.D. La. July 10, 2002) ("CERCLA does not cover 'compensation to private parties for bodily and economic injury traditionally within the reach of state tort law.'") (citation omitted).

130. Kenneth A. Manaster & Daniel P. Selmi, *Importance of Common Law Doctrines in an Age of Statutes*, 1 State Env't Law § 2:2 (2019) ("[D]espite the comprehensiveness of modern environmental statutes, situations continue to arise in which plaintiffs find those statutes inadequate for the environmental problem at hand and, therefore, they turn to the common law.") (internal footnotes omitted).

131. *See, e.g.*, Mangini v. Aerojet-Gen. Corp., 281 Cal. Rptr. 827, 838 (Ct. App. 1991) ("Where a continuing nuisance is alleged, every continuation of the nuisance gives rise to a separate claim for damages caused by the nuisance.").

Continuing nuisance or trespass is a common theory in cases of continued migration of groundwater contamination.

2. Emerging contaminants that are largely not yet regulated by federal statutes nonetheless might be actionable under common law theories. As the harmful effects of new substances are discovered, plaintiffs will likely continue to rely on creative common law theories until statutory regimes catch up.[132]
3. State common law claims serve an important role in the context of agricultural land, where federal law generally does not preempt state tort law.[133]
4. Although many environmental statutes include provisions allowing individual citizens to sue for violations, those statutes frequently do not provide damages as a remedy. On the other hand, damages are generally available in a tort action.[134]
5. Where the defendant has complied with regulatory requirements and the plaintiff has no statutory or administrative recourse, the plaintiff may still obtain relief under common law theories, provided the common law duty of care is broader than the statutory or permit obligations.[135]

---

132. *See, e.g.*, Oliver Twaddell et al., *Unregulated, Uncertain and Ubiquitous: Environmental Pitfalls of PFAS and 1,4-Dioxane*, 60 No. 6 For the Defense 68 (June 2018) ("While the United States Environmental Protection Agency (EPA) has historically exercised its regulatory authority over many environmental contaminants, there are also many 'emerging contaminants' that are not yet regulated."); Thomas P. Redick, *Tracking Trends in Environmental Torts: Common Law Nuisance, Down on the Farm*, ABA Env't Litig. & Toxic Torts Comm. News 20, 22 (Dec. 2007) ("Evolution applies to environmental law—what is lawful today might be unlawful, and very costly to clean up many years down the road.") (discussing cases where plaintiffs have relied on nuisance theories to sue owners of farms or other agricultural property, including for the commingling of biotech crops with other crops).

133. *See* Bates v. Dow Agrosciences LLC, 544 U.S. 431 (2005); Redick, *supra* note 132, at 20.

134. Manaster & Selmi, *supra* note 130, at § 2.2 ("While environmental statutes may contain so-called 'citizen suit' provisions allowing private individuals to sue to enforce regulatory obligations, those statutes seldom authorize damage claims for environmental harms.") (internal footnotes omitted).

135. *Id.* (citing FPL Farming Ltd. v. Env't Processing Sys., L.C., 351 S.W.3d 306, 310 (Tex. 2011) ("As a general rule, a permit granted by an agency does not act to immunize the permit holder from civil tort liability from private parties for actions arising out of the use of the permit.")).

Typical Causes of Action

Aside from the occasional common law fraud claim between buyer and seller, plaintiffs typically assert one or more of the following claims when they turn to the common law: nuisance (private or public), trespass, strict liability, and negligence. Depending on the jurisdiction, these theories may remain a function of case law or may have been embodied in statute or ordinance, but departures from tradition are generally modest. As with most cases, in the context of hazardous substance releases, plaintiffs generally plead multiple causes of action.

Turner v. Murphy Oil USA, Inc.[136] involved an oil release from a refinery after Hurricane Katrina. It ended in settlement, but the case involved common law claims. The certified claims asserted in the Administrative Master Complaint—negligence, liability of a landowner for activity that deprives his neighbor of enjoyment or causes damages, strict liability, nuisance and trespass, and groundwater contamination—all relate to property damage that the plaintiff class members allegedly suffered when oil spilled onto their properties. As revealed by numerous tests conducted at class members' properties and uncontroverted visual evidence, there is no doubt that oil belonging to Murphy's Tank 250-2 spilled onto many of these properties. Proving that the crude oil damaged the plaintiff class members' properties would not be difficult, so the plaintiffs possessed strong claims for nuisance, trespass, groundwater contamination, and liability of a landowner for activity depriving a neighbor of enjoyment or causing damages. There was also strong evidence that Murphy did not follow its own hurricane protection procedures, which allowed the tank to float and subsequently rupture, suggesting that a jury could have found in the plaintiff class members' favor on the issue of negligence as well.[137] The total value of the settlement was estimated at $330,126,000.

In another case arising out of a natural disaster, in *Henry v. St. Croix Alumina, LLC*,[138] plaintiffs alleged damages for releases related to Hurricane Georges. On September 21, 1998, Hurricane Georges struck the

136. Turner v. Murphy Oil USA, Inc., 472 F. Supp. 2d 830 (E.D. La. 2007).

137. *Id.* at 838.

138. Henry v. St. Croix Alumina, LLC, No. 1999/0036, 2007 U.S. Dist. LEXIS 98205, at *4–6 (D.V.I. Aug. 10, 2007).

island of St. Croix and blew portions of red mud piles into the surrounding neighborhoods. At the time Hurricane Georges hit St. Croix, St. Croix Alumina was the owner and operator of the refinery. In 1999, the plaintiffs alleged that they and their property had been harmed by the defendants' failure to properly contain the red bauxite dust and red mud and filed suit against St. Croix Alumina, Alcoa, and Glencore. Specifically, with respect to Glencore, the plaintiffs alleged that Glencore owned the alumina refinery, shipped bauxite to VIALCO, and oversaw its production into alumina.[139] Plaintiffs further alleged that Glencore "failed to correctly control the storage and containment of the bauxite and its manufacturing process by-products, such that persons adjacent to the Refinery and downwind from the Refinery were exposed to contaminants"[140] and that Glencore "failed to properly store, contain and/or remove the 'red dust' but instead left it in piles on its property."[141]

Plaintiffs asserted the following counts against Glencore: (1) maintaining an abnormally dangerous condition; (2) nuisance per se; (3) public nuisance; (4) private nuisance; (5) intentional infliction of emotional distress; (6) negligent infliction of emotional distress; (7) negligence; and (8) punitive damages. In this case, proving the alleged harms proved to be difficult for plaintiffs. The litigation lasted 15 years and resulted in dismissal of the claims against defendants for failure to prove the release caused the alleged personal injuries and failure to show an ongoing nuisance to be abated.[142] Even though the property damage claim was not dismissed, plaintiffs abandoned their litigation after the Third Circuit Court of Appeals affirmed the district court's denial of the plaintiff's request to bring in new experts.[143]

The following sections contain a general description of the basic causes of action.

---

139. *Id.* Third Am. Compl. at 13–14.

140. *Id.* at 15.

141. *Id.* Compl. at 18.

142. Memorandum, Henry v. St. Croix Alumina, LLC, No. 1999/0036 (Dist. V.I. Aug. 28, 2009) (granting defendant's summary judgment on all compensatory and punitive damages claims), *aff'd* Opinion, Henry v. St. Croix Alumina, LLC, No. 12-1844 (3rd Cir. July 10, 2014).

143. Opinion, Henry v. St. Croix Alumina, LLC, No. 12-1844 (3rd Cir. July 10, 2014).

Nuisance

State-law nuisance doctrine has been instrumental to plaintiffs seeking redress for pollution, release of toxic substances, and other environmental concerns since before the enactment of modern statutory environmental law.[144] Under common law, nuisance actions are characterized as either private or public. Most nuisance actions that arise in environmental litigation between private parties are brought under a private nuisance theory.

Private Nuisance: Elements

Under section 822 of the Restatement (Second) of Torts:[145]

One is subject to liability for private nuisance if, but only if, his or her conduct is a legal cause of an invasion of another's interest in the

144. *See* Taylor v. Culloden Pub. Serv. Dist., 591 S.E.2d 197, 206 (2003) ("[T]his case aptly demonstrates the need for common law remedies in addition to the [West Virginia Water Pollution Control Act], especially where it is arguable that the government agency charged with protecting the public's interests may not be acting with sufficient alacrity to eradicate the alleged nuisance which may be presenting serious public health concerns or posing a potential environmental hazard."); Sharon Steel Corp. v. City of Fairmont, 334 S.E.2d 616, 621 (1985) ("Nuisance law has been particularly effective in addressing environmental problems." . . . "Nuisance actions have challenged virtually every major industrial and municipal activity which is today the subject of comprehensive environmental regulation—the operation of land fills, incinerators, sewage treatment facilities, activities at chemical plants, aluminum, lead and copper smelters, oil refineries, pulp mills, rendering plants, quarries and mines, textile mills and a host of other manufacturing activities.") (quoting William H. Rodgers, Handbook on Environmental Law § 2.1 at 100 (1977)).

145. The Restatement (Third) of Torts is currently in progress and is being released in sections. *See* Restatement (Third) of Torts, Apportionment Liab. Foreword (Am. L. Inst. 2000). Thus far, the reporters have released final sections regarding products liability, the elements of negligence and related principles such as apportionment of liability, strict liability, and liability for economic harm. Given that the Restatement (Third) sections are still relatively new, courts have not yet widely or uniformly adopted them, although there are notable exceptions—including state supreme court decisions adopting certain sections. *See, e.g.*, Thompson v. Kaczinski, 774 N.W.2d 829, 837 (Iowa 2009) (discussing and ultimately adopting the Restatement (Third) sections regarding factual and proximate cause, §§ 26, 29, which were drafted "in an attempt to eliminate unnecessary confusion caused by the traditional vernacular" rather than to effect drastic substantive change); *but see* Alcombrack v. Ciccarelli, 363 P.3d 698, 703 (Ariz. Ct. App. 2015) (declining to adopt Restatement (Third) § 7 because "adoption of the Third Restatement would do more than just modify existing Arizona negligence law; it would substantially change Arizona's longstanding conceptual approach to negligence law by effectively eliminating duty as one of the required elements of a negligence action") (citation omitted). Therefore, this chapter generally refers to the Restatement (Second) but notes differences in the Restatement Third where relevant.

private use and enjoyment of land, and the invasion is either: (1) intentional[146] and unreasonable;[147] or (2) unintentional and otherwise actionable under the rules controlling liability for negligent or reckless conduct, or for abnormally dangerous conditions or activities.[148]

To recover under a private nuisance theory, a plaintiff must prove that the defendant engaged in certain activities or maintained certain conditions that caused an "unreasonable" and "substantial" interference with the plaintiff's use and enjoyment of its land.[149] In other words, the "defendant's activity must cause harm that exceeds 'the customary interferences a land user suffers in an organized society,' and be an appreciable and tangible interference with a property interest."[150]

---

146. Restatement (Second) of Torts § 825 (Am. L. Inst. 1965) (quoted in Crest Chevrolet-Oldsmobile-Cadillac, Inc. v. Willemsen, 384 N.W.2d 692, 695 n.3 (Wis. 1986)); Hughes v. Emerald Mines Corp., 450 A.2d 1, 4–5 (Pa. Super. Ct. 1982). At section 825, the Restatement (Second) defines an intentional invasion as follows: "An invasion of another's interest in the use and enjoyment of land or an interference with the public right is intentional if the actor (a) acts for the purpose of causing it, or (b) knows that it is resulting or substantially certain to result from his conduct."

147. Restatement (Second), *supra* note 146 at § 826 (*quoted in Crest Chevrolet*, 384 N.W.2d at 695); *Hughes*, 450 A.2d at 5; *see also* Frank v. Env't Sanitation Mgmt., 687 S.W.2d 876, 880 (Mo. 1985) ("The easiest way to show a nuisance is to prove defendant's conduct is unreasonable as a matter of law. This category may be called nuisance *per se*."). The unreasonableness of an intentional invasion is set forth in the Restatement (Second) at section 826, which provides:

> An intentional invasion of another's interest in the use and enjoyment of land is unreasonable if
>
> (a) the gravity of harm outweighs the utility of the actor's conduct, or
>
> (b) the harm caused by the conduct is serious and the financial burden of compensating for this and similar harm to others would not make the continuation of conduct not feasible.

148. Restatement (Second), *supra* note 146 at § 822 (quoted in *Crest Chevrolet*, 384 N.W.2d at 695; *Hughes*, 450 A.2d at 4).

149. Hendricks v. Stalnaker, 380 S.E.2d 198, 200 (W. Va. 1989). The plaintiff need not have a fee interest in the property to maintain a private nuisance suit. *See, e.g.*, Mercier v. Pachaug Marina & Campground, No. CV 950128463, 1998 WL 470596, at *1 (Conn. Super. July 30, 1998) (holding that a propriety leasehold is a sufficient interest in the property and the common areas of a campground owned and maintained by defendant); Sallisky v. Treetops Camping Club, No. 328646, 1998 WL 161376, at *3 (Conn. Super. Mar. 30, 1998) (holding that tenancy at a campsite is sufficient property interest for a nuisance suit); Graves v. Diehl, 958 S.W.2d 468, 470 (Tex. App. 1997) (holding that a contract for deed is a sufficient property interest to maintain a private nuisance suit).

150. Dunlop v. Daigle, 444 A.2d 519 (N.H. 1982); *see also* Page Cnty. Appliance Ctr., Inc. v. Honeywell, Inc., 347 N.W.2d 171, 175 (Iowa 1984) ("When the alleged nuisance is claimed to be offensive to the person, courts apply the standard of 'normal persons in a particular locality' to measure the existence of the nuisance. This normalcy standard is also applied where the use of property is claimed to be affected.").

Private nuisance claims are commonly invoked where a property owner's activities have released contaminants into groundwater or soil or exposed plaintiffs to them.[151]

These cases provide just a few examples of the types of activities that may form the basis of a nuisance action. As the Michigan Supreme Court has noted:

> There are countless ways to interfere with the use and enjoyment of land, including interference with the physical condition of the land itself, disturbance in the comfort or conveniences of the occupant including his peace of mind, and threat of future injury that is a present menace and interference with enjoyment.[152]

Some courts, however, are uncomfortable with such a broad concept of nuisance. In Golen v. Union Corp.,[153] a Pennsylvania court complained that Michigan's interpretation of nuisance includes "virtually all harms"[154] and stated that courts need to establish "sensible limits to liability under this potentially sweeping concept."[155] In Golen, the court considered the plaintiff's claim that the environmental contamination present on the defendant's land hindered the plaintiff's ability to sell his property.[156] The court held that a nuisance suit could not provide a remedy because the use of the plaintiff's land was not harmed, only his interest in selling the property.[157] In so holding, the court limited suc-

151. *E.g.*, Cook v. Rockwell Int'l Corp., 790 F.3d 1088 (10th Cir. 2015) (class action for state-law nuisance brought by owners of property near nuclear weapons manufacturing plant that had mishandled radioactive waste, releasing waste into the ground and nearby bodies of water, and the air and soil throughout the area; jury awarded $177 million in compensatory damages and $200 million in punitive damages, plus $549 million in prejudgment interest); Barnett v. Connecticut Light & Power Co., 900 F. Supp. 2d 224 (D. Conn. 2012), *holding modified on reconsideration in part*, 967 F. Supp. 2d 593 (D. Conn. 2013), *aff'd*, 580 F. App'x 30 (2d Cir. 2014) (Plaintiff, a homeowner, stated a claim for private nuisance against Defendant utility company where Defendant "improperly used the [electric utility] easement on the Plaintiff's property in such a way as to cause dangerous levels of EMF radiation to invade her home, resulting in various harms and injuries to the Plaintiff and her family, and interfering with the use and value of her property.").

152. Adkins v. Thomas Solvent Co., N.W.2d 715, 720 (Mich. 1992).

153. 718 A.2d 298 (Pa. Super. 1998).

154. *Id.* at 299.

155. *Id.*

156. *Id.* at 298.

157. *Id.*

cessful nuisance claims to those where there is a "physical presence on the property in order to be perceived."[158] Similarly, other courts have held that "diminution of market value alone, buttressed by no accompanying personal or property damage, does not constitute an unreasonable interference with the 'use and enjoyment' of the land."[159]

The Balancing Test

The law of nuisance attempts to weigh the defendant's right to use and enjoy their property against the neighbors' right to be free from interference with the use and enjoyment of their land. To determine whether the defendant's interference was unreasonable, courts balance the competing interests of those parties.[160]

As one court put it, "[a]lthough balancing tests are always unsatisfactory because they are unpredictable, it nonetheless appears that balancing was at the heart of actions for nuisance from its inception."[161] One commentator stated, "Because the facts of each case are unique and the outcome of each dispute depends on balancing of equitable factors, the law of nuisance has been called a 'quintessential judgment-entitlement' rule in contrast to the more 'mechanical' rule of trespass."[162]

The Restatement (Second) of Torts lists some of the factors to be considered when comparing the gravity of the harm to the plaintiff[163] to the social utility of the defendant's activities alleged to cause the harm. Restatement section 827 lists the following "gravity of harm" factors:

- The extent of the harm;
- The character of the harm involved;

---

158. *Id.*

159. Nat'l Tel. Coop. Ass'n v. Exxon Corp., 38 F. Supp. 2d 1, 14 (D.D.C. 1998); *see also* Smith v. Kan. Gas Serv. Co., 169 P.3d 1052 (Kan. 2007) (discussing the concept of stigma in context of a nuisance suit).

160. *Frank*, 687 S.W.2d at 880 ("The unreasonable use element of nuisance balances the rights of adjoining property owners.").

161. *Hendricks*, 380 S.E.2d at 201.

162. Frona N. Powell, *Trespass, Nuisance, and the Evolution of Common Law in Modern Pollution Cases*, 21 Real Estate L.J. 182–215 (1992).

163. *Crest Chevrolet*, 384 N.W.2d 692 at 696 ("The factors listed in Sec. 827 [of the *Restatement*] are not exhaustive. The fact finder may consider other relevant factors in addition to those listed.").

- The social value that the law attaches to the type of use or enjoyment invaded;
- The suitability of the particular use or enjoyment invaded to the character of the locality; and
- The burden on the person harmed of avoiding the harm.[164]

Restatement section 828 lists the following "utility of conduct" factors:

- The social value that the law attaches to the primary purpose of the conduct;
- The suitability of the conduct to the character of the locality; and
- The impracticability of preventing or avoiding the invasion.[165]

The factors listed in sections 827 and 828 are not exhaustive.[166]

Public Nuisance

While a private nuisance is defined as an invasion of another's interest in the private use and enjoyment of land, a public nuisance is "an unreasonable interference with a right common to the general public."[167] In *Copart Industries, Inc. v. Consolidated Edison Co. of New York, Inc.*,[168] the New York Court of Appeals described public nuisance as follows:

> A public, or as sometimes termed a common, nuisance is an offense against the State and is subject to abatement or prosecution on application of the proper governmental agency. It consists of conduct or omissions which offend, interfere with or

164. Restatement (Second), *supra* note 146, at § 827 (quoted in *Crest Chevrolet*, 384 N.W.2d 692 at 696 (applying the section 827 factors)).

165. Restatement (Second), *supra* note 146, at § 828 (quoted in *Hendricks*, 380 S.E.2d 198 at 200–01 (applying the balancing test to determine that defendant's interference did not constitute a private nuisance)).

166. *See Crest Chevrolet*, 384 N.W.2d at 696.

167. Restatement (Second), *supra* note 146, at § 821B; Wayne Cnty. v. Tenn. Solid Waste Disposal Control Bd., 756 S.W.2d 274 (Tenn. Ct. App. 1988) ("A public nuisance is an act or omission that unreasonably interferes with or obstructs rights common to the public."); *Nat'l Tel. Coop. Ass'n*, 38 F. Supp. 2d at 13; W. Page Keeton, et al., Prosser and Keeton on the Law of Torts § 90 (5th ed. 1984) [hereinafter Prosser on Torts].

168. 362 N.E.2d 968 (N.Y. 1977).

cause damage to the public in the exercise of rights common to all, in a manner such as to offend public morals, interfere with use by the public of a public place or endanger or injure the property, health, safety or comfort of a considerable number of persons.[169]

Two types of parties may bring a public nuisance claim. A public (governmental) plaintiff may bring a nuisance action for interference with public rights such as health and welfare. A private citizen may also bring a public nuisance action, functioning as a quasi-private attorney general to vindicate an injury shared by the community.[170] However, to have standing to sue, the private party must show that it suffered "special or peculiar injuries different in kind, not merely in degree, from the injury to the public at large." Even if the court finds the existence of a public nuisance, a private party's claim will be dismissed if it fails to show this requisite type of injury.[171]

Private citizens' public nuisance claims are frequently dismissed based on the plaintiff's lack of special injury. In *Alaska Natives Class v. Exxon Corp.*,[172] the court dismissed a public nuisance action brought by Alaskan natives seeking recovery for injury to their subsistence fishing practices allegedly caused by the Exxon-Valdez oil spill. In *Taunus Corp. v. City of*

169. *Id.* at 970–71 (citations omitted) (citing Melker v. City of New York, 83 N.E. 565, 567 (N.Y. 1908); Restatement (Second), *supra* note 146, at notes preceding § 822, at 217); *see also* Westwood Pharms., Inc. v. Nat'l Fuel Gas Distribution Corp., 737 F. Supp. 1272, 1281 (W.D.N.Y. 1990), *aff'd*, 964 F.2d 85 (2d Cir. 1992) ("With regard to what constitutes a public nuisance under state law, the Second Circuit has held that 'the release or threat of release of hazardous waste into the environment unreasonably infringes upon a public right and thus is a public nuisance as a matter of New York law'"); Chicago v. Commonwealth Edison Co., 321 N.E.2d 412, 417 (Ill. App. Ct. 1974) ("Earlier cases recognized that the public had a right to clean, unpolluted air and that any deprivation of that right was actionable as a private injury and indictable as a public wrong.").

170. *Wayne Cnty.*, 756 S.W.2d at 283; *see also* Elliot v. City of Waterbury, 715 A.2d 27 (Conn. 1998) (holding that the law of nuisance does not contemplate holding a defendant liable for activities occurring on the adjoining property owner's land).

171. B&D Molded Products, Inc. v. Vitek Rsch. Corp., No. CV 97006030362S, 1998 WL 551943, at *4 (Conn. Super. Aug. 17, 1998) (dismissing plaintiff's public nuisance suit because it lacks standing and suggesting that "an appropriate private party can bring suit or the state could rely on the more wide-ranging, flexible pollution statutes to vindicate the public interest").

172. 104 F.3d 1196 (9th Cir. 1997).

New York,[173] the court dismissed a public nuisance claim brought by owners and occupants of properties in the vicinity of the World Trade Center because the plaintiffs failed to show a particularized injury beyond that suffered by the public after the terrorist attacks of September 11, 2001.

Although private plaintiffs must demonstrate a special injury to recover under a public nuisance theory, this requirement is not insurmountable. In *Blair v. Anderson*, in which the plaintiffs claimed injuries related to the defendants' adjoining landfill, the Indiana Court of Appeals held that the operation or maintenance of an open dump is a "nuisance inimical to human health" under Indiana statutory law.[174] And the resulting blockage of water flow to the creek on the plaintiffs' property was sufficient special injury to provide standing to bring a private action to abate and enjoin the public nuisance.

Similarly, in *Mangini*,[175] the plaintiffs alleged public nuisance under a California statute against tenants of the prior owners arising out of the tenants' disposal of contaminants on the property. Noting that the plaintiffs had been required by a governmental agency to undertake testing of the property subsequent to their purchase, the court held that the plaintiffs had alleged special injury sufficient to support a public nuisance claim.[176]

In *Philadelphia Electric* (PECO), however, the Third Circuit held that special pecuniary injury, when not tied to the impacted common right, does not confer standing under a public nuisance theory.[177] PECO sought reimbursement for a cleanup mandated by the Pennsylvania Department of Environmental Resources (DER), arguing that the expense it incurred constituted the requisite harm for standing. The Third Circuit disagreed:

---

173. 279 F. Supp. 2d 305 (S.D.N.Y. 2003). In Newhall Land & Farming Co. v. Superior Court, 19 Cal. App. 4th 334, 342 (Cal. Dist. Ct. App. 1912), the court noted that though the plaintiff lacked the specialized injury element necessary to a public nuisance claim, he can still support a private nuisance claim, because the civil wrong at issue, an undisclosed contaminant plume from the property's previous owners, interferes with his private property and a private right incidental to his property.

174. 570 N.E.2d 1337, 1340 (Ind. Ct. App. 1991).

175. 281 Cal. Rptr. 827.

176. *Id.* at 1138.

177. *Phila. Elec.*, 762 F.2d at 303.

> Though pecuniary harm certainly may be harm of a different kind from that suffered by the general public, we find in this case no allegation or evidence that PECO suffered this harm "exercising the right common to the general public that was the subject of interference." The public right that was interfered with was the right to "pure water." PECO does not allege that it used the waters of the Delaware River itself, or that it was directly harmed in any way by the pollution of those waters. . . . If [plaintiff]—as a riparian landowner—had suffered damage to its land or its operations as a result of the pollution of the Delaware, it would possibly have a claim for public nuisance. But the condition of the Chester site was not the result of the pollution, it was the cause of it. DER required PECO, as the owner of the Chester site, to remove the sources of the pollution. PECO has been harmed only in the exercise of its private property rights over the Chester site. PECO has suffered no "particular damage" in the exercise of a right common to the general public, and it lacks standing to sue for public nuisance.[178]

If a plaintiff succeeds in making the required showing—of an injury distinct from the general public's injury but still related to the common right—there are significant advantages to a public nuisance action, including that the affirmative defenses of laches and the running of the statute of limitations are unavailable.[179]

Defenses

Defenses to nuisance actions include "coming to the nuisance," consent, preemption, primary jurisdiction, and statute of limitations.

---

178. *Id.* at 315 (citations omitted); *see also Amland Props.*, 711 F. Supp. at 784; *PPG Indus.*, 655 F. Supp. at 1257.

179. Prosser on Torts, *supra* note 167, at § 90, p. 648. According to Prosser, [S]ince the plaintiff does not lose his rights as a landowner merely because others suffer damage of the same kind or even of the same degree, there is general agreement that he may proceed upon either theory, or upon both. Where this is the case, the action founded on the public nuisance may sometimes be preferable, because it is well settled that prescriptive rights, laches, and the statute of limitations do not run against it. (citations omitted); *see also* Drayton v. City of Lincoln City, 260 P.3d 642, 645 (2011).

"Coming to the Nuisance"

The defense of "coming to the nuisance" may apply when the plaintiffs acquired the property knowing that it was in proximity to an operation managing hazardous substances. This defense typically precludes damages, but not injunctive relief.[180]

Consent

Where a possessor of property causes a nuisance, but the affected neighboring property owners have given express or implied consent for the nuisance, those neighboring owners cannot maintain a nuisance action.[181] Express consent may be established when the plaintiff consented to the defendant's conduct with a clear understanding of the conduct and the risks involved. Implied consent exists when the plaintiff failed to object to a nuisance in a timely manner.

Preemption

Federal preemption is the invalidation of a state law that conflicts with federal law. In general, federal cases evaluating the relationship between federal and state environmental regulations and common law claims conclude, with limited exceptions, that federal environmental regulatory schemes like the Clean Air Act and Clean Water Act do not automatically preempt state common law claims.[182] Most major federal environmental

---

180. On the "coming to the nuisance" defense, the *Mangini* court stated: "We are aware that, in his Summary of California Law, Witkin remarks that consent is not a defense to an action for nuisance. However, the text accompanying the remark is as follows: 'The so-called doctrine of 'coming to a nuisance' has generally been repudiated; i.e., the plaintiff may obtain injunctive relief even though the nuisance was already in operation, with his knowledge, when he acquired his own property.'" *Mangini*, 281 Cal. Rptr. at 835–36 (citing B.E. Witkin, Summary of California Law § 150, p. 830 (9th ed. 1990) (citation omitted)).

181. *See* Restatement (Second), *supra* note 146, at § 839 ("A possessor of land is subject to liability for a nuisance caused while he is in possession by an abatable artificial condition on the land, if . . . he knows or should know that it exists *without the consent of those affected by it*[.]") (emphasis added).

182. *See, e.g.*, Int'l Paper Co. v. Ouelette, 479 U.S. 481 (1987) (holding, in the context of state common law nuisance claims brought against a pulp and paper mill, that the savings provisions of the Clean Water Act are intended to preserve state statutory and common law claims so long as they do not conflict with the provisions of the CWA); Bell v. Cheswick Generating Station, 734 F.3d 188 (3d Cir. 2013), *cert. denied* GenOn Power Midwest, L.P. v. Bell 134 S. Ct. 2696 (2014) (extending the Supreme Court's holding in *Ouelette* to the Clean Air Act and holding that the CAA

statutes include a savings clause declaring an intention not to preempt common law nuisance actions.[183] Even in the absence of such savings clauses, courts have been reluctant to preempt private nuisance actions, generally holding that common law actions are consistent with regulatory schemes for controlling pollution.[184]

Primary Jurisdiction

Primary jurisdiction "applies where a claim is originally cognizable in the courts, and comes into play whenever enforcement of the claim requires the resolution of issues which, under a regulatory scheme, have been placed within the special competence of an administrative body."[185] If resolution of an issue has been committed to the special competence of an administrative agency, then a court should not disregard that commitment and resolve the issue itself if doing so would infringe on the agency's function. Furthermore, when an agency designs and enforces a regulatory scheme, the agency may be better equipped than is a court to resolve an issue governed by the regulatory scheme.[186]

This defense may be asserted when an administrative body has both the authority and the expertise to decide a nuisance action. The defendant would argue that the plaintiff must seek relief from the appropriate regulatory agency before litigating the nuisance action. While the primary-jurisdiction doctrine is potentially applicable to environmental

---

did not preempt state common law claims against local electrical utility for nuisance, negligence and trespass caused by "malodorous substances and particulates" generated by the facility); Her Majesty the Queen in Right of the Province of Ontario v. City of Detroit, 874 F.2d 332 (6th Cir. 1989) (the Clean Air Act did not preclude state law which was as strict or stricter than emission limitations established under federal law).

183. *See, e.g.*, 42 U.S.C. § 6972(f) (savings clause in RCRA); 42 U.S.C. § 9652 (savings clause in CERCLA).

184. *See, e.g.*, King v. W. Club, Inc., 587 So. 2d 122, 123–24 (La. Ct. App. 1991); Biddix v. Henredon Furniture Indus., Inc., 331 S.E.2d 717, 724 (N.C. Ct. App. 1985). *But see* Twp. of Elizabeth v. Power Maint. Corp., 417 A.2d 1285 (Pa. Commw. Ct. 1980).

185. United States v. Western Pac. R. Co., 352 U.S. 59 (1956).

186. *Id.* at 64–65; *see also* Baykeeper v. NL Industries, Inc., 660 F.3d 686 (3d. Cir. 2011) (discussing application of primary jurisdiction in the context of citizen suit brought against manufacturer of titanium dioxide pigments for violations of Clean Water Act and Resource Conservation and Recovery Act).

nuisance cases, courts have been reluctant to refer nuisance claims to administrative agencies under this doctrine.[187]

Statute of Limitations

States have adopted statutes of limitations for private nuisance actions, generally ranging from two to five years. The application of the statute of limitations turns on whether the alleged nuisance is "permanent" or "temporary."[188] A temporary nuisance is one that is reasonably abatable; a permanent nuisance usually is the result of "a permanent construction which is injurious as installed, rather than injurious through its use and where abatement would be impracticable or impossible."[189] If the nuisance is permanent, the statute of limitations begins to run when the nuisance is created or first occurs.[190] If the nuisance is temporary (also called "continuing"), every repetition of the continuing nuisance gives rise to a separate claim for damages and, therefore, a new limitations period commences each day the nuisance persists.[191]

Damages

Damages awarded in nuisance cases include diminution in property value;[192] discomfort, inconvenience, annoyance, and personal injury;[193]

---

187. *See, e.g.*, People v. Kerr-McGee Chem. Corp., 492 N.E.2d 1003 (Ill. App. Ct. 1986) (upholding trial court's refusal to stay the action where the defendant argued that the primary jurisdiction over the action lies with the federal Nuclear Regulatory Commission).

188. *See* Sherwin-Williams Co. v. ARTRA Grp., Inc., 125 F. Supp. 2d 739, 758 (D. Md. 2001). In *Frank v. Env't Sanitation Mgmt.*, the court noted:

> Damages for . . . permanent nuisances are measured by the difference in the land's market value immediately before and after injury; damages for temporary nuisances include the decrease in rental or useable value of property during the injury. The character of the source of injury often distinguishes temporary and permanent nuisances. A nuisance is temporary if it may be abated, and it is permanent if abatement is impracticable or impossible.

687 S.W.2d at 883 (citations omitted).

189. *Vermillion*, 918 S.W.2d at 831.

190. *See Mangini*, 281 Cal. Rptr. at 837–38.

191. *Id. See also Nat'l Tel. Coop. Ass'n*, 38 F. Supp. 2d at 5.

192. *See, e.g.*, *Md. Heights*, 706 S.W.2d at 221.

193. *See, e.g.*, Atlanta v. Murphy, 391 S.E.2d 474, 476 (Ga. Ct. App. 1990).

loss of profits directly resulting from the nuisance;[194] punitive damages when there is a showing that the nuisance was knowingly and willfully maintained;[195] consequential damages;[196] and remediation costs.[197] Injunctive relief may also be available.[198]

Trespass

Common law trespass is an unauthorized intrusion or invasion in property that interferes with the right of exclusive possession.[199] Traditionally, no showing of intent or fault was required to impose liability for trespass, and actual damage was not a prerequisite to recovery. Under modern trespass theory, however, a plaintiff must prove that the invasion upon its property was intentional, reckless, or negligent.[200] Some courts further require proof that the defendant was substantially certain that the intentional actions would result in a trespass.[201]

The difference between a trespass and nuisance is not always clear. The primary distinction is that a trespass takes place "upon a tangible

194. *See, e.g.*, *Md. Heights*, 706 S.W.2d at 222.

195. *Id.*

196. *See, e.g.*, Lunda v. Matthews, 613 P.2d 63, 67 (Or. Ct. App. 1980).

197. *Phila. Elec.*, 762 F.2d at 303.

198. *See, e.g.*, Dingwell v. Litchfield, 621 A.2d 213 (Conn. App. Ct. 1985); Bassilakis v. Saland Corp., No. CV 920509867S, 1998 WL 197627 (Conn. Super. Apr. 10, 1998) (denying plaintiff's request for an injunction because the awarded monetary damages were sufficient); Rudd v. Electrolux Corp., 982 F. Supp. 355, 370 (M.D.N.C. 1997); Uland v. S.E. Johnson Co., Inc., No. 95-CI-000095, 1997 Ohio App. LEXIS 6112, at *13–14 (Ohio Ct. App. Mar. 3, 1997), *aff'd*, No. WM-97-005, 1998 Ohio App. LEXIS 942 (Ohio Ct. App. Mar. 13, 1998).

199. *Rudd*, 982 F. Supp. 355 at 370; *Uland*, No. 95-CI-000095, 1997 Ohio App. LEXIS 6112, at *13–14.

200. Socony Mobil, Inc. v. Sw. Bell Tel. Co., 518 S.W.2d 257 (Tex. 1974) (holding that in the absence of proof that omissions by an oil company in maintaining a gas station were willful or intentional, an action for trespass would not be maintained).

201. *See* Martin v. Amoco Oil Co., 679 N.E.2d 139 (Ind. 1997) (delineating this standard). The *Martin* court followed the Washington State Supreme Court's reliance on the *Restatement (Second) of Torts*. *See* Bradley v. Am. Smelting & Ref. Co., 709 P.2d 782, 785 (Wash. 1985) (quoting RESTATEMENT (SECOND), *supra* note 146, at § 158 cmt. b) ("Intent is not, however, limited to consequences which are desired. If the actor knows that the consequences are certain, or substantially certain, to result from his act, and still goes ahead, he is treated by the law as if he had in fact desired to produce the result."). *See also Rudd*, 982 F. Supp. at 370 ("[T]here must be some intent involved. This is not an intent to do injury, but merely an intent to go upon the land of another. Thus, the unintentional and nonnegligent entry onto the land of another does not constitute a trespass unless the actor is engaged in an ultrahazardous activity.").

invasion of plaintiff's property, however slight, whereas a nuisance requires proof that the interference with use and enjoyment is 'substantial and unreasonable.'"[202] There are fact patterns where the elements of both trespass and nuisance are met. When both actions are applicable, courts have found that the plaintiff may choose either action or may proceed under both.[203]

Elements

Possession

The plaintiff must demonstrate either actual possession of a property or legal title from which constructive possession can be presumed.[204] According to the Restatement (Second) of Torts, a possessor is one who:

> (a) is in occupancy of land with intent to control it, or
>
> (b) has been but no longer is in occupancy of land with intent to control it, if, after he has ceased his occupancy without abandoning the land, no other person has obtained possession as stated in Clause (a), or
>
> (c) has the right against all persons to immediate occupancy of land, if no other person is in possession as stated in Clauses (a) and (b).[205]

Possessors of land include owners, lessees,[206] tenants-in-common of condominium common areas, and successors to a possessor at the time of a continuing trespass.

202. *Bradley*, 709 P.2d 782 at 787; *see also* Roger Meiners & Bruce Yandle, *Common Law and the Conceit of Modern Environmental Policy*, 7 GEO. MASON L. REV. 923, 936 (1999).

203. *Am. Smelting*, 709 P.2d at 789. *See also* RESTATEMENT (SECOND), *supra* note 146, at § 821D cmt. e, p. 102.

204. James L. Huitt, Jr. & Roger A. Warin, *Liability and Environmental Problems Under Common Law*, *in* ENVIRONMENTAL DISPUTE HANDBOOK: LIABILITY AND CLAIMS 152 (David A. Carpenter et al. eds., 1991).

205. RESTATEMENT (SECOND), *supra* note 146, at § 157.

206. A landlord may maintain a cause of action for trespass against a tenant for damage to a common area. *See* Colonial Props., Inc. v. Vogue Cleaners, Inc., 86 F.3d 210 (11th Cir. 1996) (reasoning that because the law assigns liability to landlords for injuries that occur in common areas, a landlord may bring a trespass claim against a tenant that causes the common area to become hazardous).

A party that is not a possessor of property has no standing to bring a trespass claim. In *Hennigan v. Atlantic Refining Co.*,[207] several employees of a contractor who were working in Philadelphia's sewer system were injured by an explosion apparently caused by the accumulation of oil in the sewer. Assuming that the leakage of oil from the defendant's facility into the city's sewer system constituted a trespass, the U.S. District Court for the Eastern District of Pennsylvania held that the workers had not suffered an invasion of their property rights. In cases like this, recovery may be available to a nonpossessory party under negligence or strict liability theories.[208]

Some courts have held that a former possessor of the plaintiff's property is not liable in trespass for environmental contamination that occurred during the term of its possession. Because trespass requires "an unprivileged, intentional intrusion on land in the possession of another," in *Wellesley Hills Realty Trust v. Mobil Oil Corp.*,[209] a federal district court held that oil contamination of a former gas station site alleged to have occurred during the period of the defendant Mobil's ownership could not form the basis of a trespass action:

> Mobil owned and was in possession of the property when it allegedly released the oil causing the contamination. Thus, Mobil's releases of oil were not unprivileged, and Mobil clearly was not intruding on land in the possession of another. Mobil's releases of oil on its own land, therefore, cannot constitute a trespass.[210]

Busch Oil Co., Inc. v. Amoco Oil Co.[211] also considered the liability of a former owner of a contaminated property. In 1972, there was a gasoline spill on Amoco's property.[212] The property was subsequently sold to the plaintiff, Busch. When Busch attempted to install USTs on the property years later,[213] it discovered the contamination. Under Michi-

---

207. 282 F. Supp. 667 (E.D. Pa. 1967), *aff'd*, 400 F.2d 857 (3d Cir. 1968), *cert. denied*, 395 U.S. 904 (1969).

208. Carroll v. Litton Sys., Inc., No. 92-2219, 1995 U.S. App. LEXIS 2015 (4th Cir. Feb. 1, 1995).

209. 747 F. Supp. 93, 99 (D. Mass. 1990).

210. *Id.*

211. No. 5:94-CV-175, 1996 U.S. Dist. LEXIS 4705 (W.D. Mich. Feb. 20, 1996).

212. *Id.* at *3.

213. *Id.* at *4.

gan law, a trespass is an "unauthorized entry upon the private property of another."[214] The court stated that because the "spill occurred while Amoco owned the Site . . . Amoco did not trespass because it did not enter onto the private property of another."[215] The court also rejected the plaintiff's argument that the spill was actionable as a "continuing trespass," because Amoco neither "consented" to the spill nor continued to maintain the spill after its possession terminated.[216] Various jurisdictions have similarly held that there can be no trespass when the "thing that intrudes" entered the land during the accused trespasser's lawful possession of the property.[217]

In addition, a party may be liable for damages in trespass even though another party is legally responsible for the trespassing agent.[218] In *Jordan v. Foust Oil Co., Inc.*,[219] the North Carolina Court of Appeals denied the summary judgment motion of a gasoline supplier where evidence indicated that deliveries were made into USTs that the supplier knew, or should have known, were leaking. The court rejected the supplier's argument that, because the tanks were owned by a third party, the supplier was not legally responsible for the gasoline when it escaped from the tanks and therefore could not be liable in trespass. Evidence that the supplier continued to deliver gasoline into the tanks, even though its own records indicated that the tanks were leaking, tended to show that the supplier was at least partially responsible for the continued leakage, and was sufficient to support a trespass claim.[220]

Entry

Unlike nuisance, which requires only that the defendant maintain some activity that constitutes a continuing interference with the plaintiff's use and enjoyment of its property, trespass requires proof of an actual

---

214. *Id.* at *28 (citation omitted).

215. *Id.*

216. *Id.* at *29.

217. *See, e.g.*, 325–343 E. 56th St. Corp. v. Mobil Oil Corp., 906 F. Supp. 669 (D.D.C. 1995); Rosenblatt v. Exxon Co., U.S.A., 642 A.2d 189, 190 (Md. 1994).

218. *See, e.g.*, Dartron Corp. v. Uniroyal Chem. Co., 917 F. Supp. 1173 (N.D. Ohio 1996) (holding that the defendant, who previously owned a piece of property, cannot be found liable for trespass after selling the property to the plaintiffs).

219. 447 S.E.2d 491 (N.C. App. 1994).

220. *Id.* at 498.

entry onto the plaintiff's land, either by the defendant or by some physical or observable object resulting from the defendant's actions. While courts traditionally have required evidence of readily discernible physical intrusion, such as flowing water or errant livestock, modern courts have extended the trespass theory to agents that may be invisible to the human eye but are scientifically discernible, such as airborne particulates and soil and groundwater contaminants.[221]

In *Martin v. Reynolds Metal Co.*,[222] the operator of an aluminum reduction plant was liable under trespass for its emission of fluoride compounds that settled on the plaintiffs' cattle farm, poisoning livestock and contaminating water.[223] The Oregon Supreme Court rejected the defendant's argument that, since the fluoride compounds could not be seen with the naked eye, the plaintiffs' cause of action was grounded in nuisance. The court stated that the important characteristic of a trespassing agent is "the object's energy or force rather than its size."[224]

However, there still must be *some* "physical intrusion." Multiple states have held that "an intangible intrusion may give rise to claim for trespass, but only if an aggrieved party is able to prove physical damage to the property caused by such intangible intrusion."[225] For example, based on this rule, the Colorado Supreme Court rejected a trespass claim premised on "noise, radiation, and electromagnetic fields" because these intrusions were neither tangible nor did they result in some tangible, physical damage to the property.

Some modern courts also have rejected the traditional distinction between "direct" and "indirect" invasions. In a modern trespass action,

> [T]he defendant may be liable for trespass even though a substance was not placed directly on plaintiff's land so long as the force causing the deposit, such as natural flow to the land, was

---

221. *Carroll*, 1995 U.S. App. LEXIS 2015, at *2015.

222. 342 P.2d 790 (Or. 1959).

223. *Id.* at 791. By proceeding under a trespass theory instead of a nuisance theory, the plaintiffs were able to avail themselves of a six-year statute of limitations, instead of the two-year statute of limitations applicable to nontrespassory injuries to land. The six-year statute of limitations allowed the plaintiffs to recover additional damages.

224. *Id.* at 794.

225. Pub. Serv. Co. of Colorado v. Van Wyk, 27 P.3d 377, 390 (Colo. 2001).

> direct. . . . The defendant is liable even though the entry of the "thing" was indirect, rather than direct, so long as the defendant acted with knowledge that an invasion was "substantially certain" to follow as a result of the defendant's actions.[226]

Moreover, the fact that the plaintiff is unable to prove conclusively which one of several sources of contamination polluted the plaintiff's property will not bar recovery from one of the sources.[227]

Intent

Historically, intent has been a necessary element of a trespass action. The exact nature of the required intent, however, is not always clear, as shown in *National Telephone Cooperative Association v. Exxon Corp.*[228] In that case, the plaintiff alleged that petroleum contamination from an Exxon tank migrated to the plaintiff's neighboring property. The plaintiff argued that it was not necessary to prove unlawful intent, and it did not matter that Exxon did not intend for its gasoline to reach the plaintiff's property. Rather, all that mattered was that gasoline was present on the property. The court agreed with the first proposition, but not the second, holding:

> While liability for trespass does not depend on a defendant's specific intent to invade unlawfully the property of another, "what is required, however, is volition, i.e., a conscious intent to do the act that constitutes the entry upon someone else's real personal property. An involuntary entry onto another's property is not a trespass."[229]

Stated another way, the "touchstone of trespassory intent is a volitional action to be present on the property. It does not suffice merely to establish that the defendant acted in a manner that somehow resulted in

---

226. *Id.* at 788, 791.

227. Wilson v. McLeod, 398 S.E.2d 586 (N.C. 1990) (holding that where there is more than one possible source of gasoline contamination, plaintiffs need not prove that some of the contamination came from one of the sources individually).

228. *Nat'l Tel. Coop. Ass'n*, 38 F. Supp. 2d at 11–14.

229. *Id.* at 12 (quoting Balt. Gas & Elec. Co. v. Flippo, 684 A.2d 456, 461 (Md. Ct. Spec. App. 1996)).

an invasion of the plaintiff's property."[230] Because the plaintiff had only shown that Exxon intended to place USTs on its property, not that Exxon intended that its gasoline would migrate to the plaintiff's property, the court awarded Exxon summary judgment on the trespass claim.[231]

Actual Damages

Historically, and under the Restatement (Second) of Torts, a plaintiff need not prove actual damages to prevail on a trespass claim.[232] However, some modern courts have required plaintiffs to prove some degree of harm—especially when the entry is less tangible than a traditional trespass.[233] For example, in *Bradley v. American Smelting Corp.*,[234] the Washington Supreme Court required the plaintiff landowners to show actual and substantial damages to property to recover under a continuing trespass theory for the intrusion of airborne toxic particles onto their land from a neighboring smelter. The court imposed this requirement to restrict the number of plaintiffs who otherwise might have been able to recover under a trespass theory.[235]

Likewise, in *Borland v. Sanders Lead Co.*,[236] the Alabama Supreme Court required the plaintiffs to prove substantial damages to sustain a trespass action for an intentional, indirect invasion of their property by the settling of microscopic lead particulates and sulfoxide deposits from the defendant's neighboring lead smelter.[237]

In *Chance v. BP Chemicals*,[238] the plaintiffs challenged the need to prove actual damages as part of their trespass claim. The plaintiffs claimed that the "injectate," placed below the surface of the defendant's

---

230. *Id.* at 13.

231. *Id.* at 14.

232. Restatement (Second), *supra* note 146, at § 158 ("One is subject to liability to another for trespass, irrespective of whether he thereby causes harm to any legally protected interest of the other[.]").

233. *See, e.g.*, Chance v. BP Chems., Inc., 670 N.E.2d 985 (Ohio 1996) (declining to recognize plaintiff's trespass claim against defendant's practice of disposing of hazardous waste byproducts via "deep well" injection, absent any physical damage or actual interference with the reasonable and foreseeable use of the property).

234. 709 P.2d 782 (Wash. 1985).

235. *Id.* at 791. *But see* Stevenson v. E.I. du Pont de Nemours & Co., 327 F.3d 400, 405 (2003).

236. 369 So. 2d 523 (Ala. 1979).

237. *Id.* at 530.

238. 670 N.E.2d 985 (Ohio 1996).

property, migrated underground to the plaintiffs' property.[239] The court rejected the plaintiffs' argument that any trespass results in damages[240] and held that absent "some type of physical damage or interference with use," plaintiffs may not recover damages for their trespass claim.[241]

Nature of the Trespass

Courts have characterized trespasses as permanent, temporary, continuing, or renewing. These distinctions may be important when determining the measure of damages. Some courts have held that damages from permanent trespass are measured by the difference in a property's value before and after the trespass, while damages from temporary trespass are measured by the property's rental value or the reasonable value of its use during the period of trespass.[242]

A determination of whether the trespass is continuing or renewing may also affect the statute of limitations and, therefore, the plaintiff's ability to recover. In *Wilson v. McLeod*,[243] the distinction between a continuing trespass (one that occurs at a particular moment in time and causes a continuing injury) and a recurring trespass (a series of repeating trespasses, each one of which causes separate damage) was critical. The plaintiff sued after gasoline seeped into the water supply on the plaintiff's property. The seepage had been ongoing for almost seven years before the plaintiff brought suit, and North Carolina law set a three-year statute of limitations on continuing trespass claims. Nonetheless, because the seepage of gasoline into the plaintiff's water supply was a recurring trespass, the plaintiff could maintain the action, although she could only recover damages for the three years immediately preceding her filing of the lawsuit.[244] This is an important issue for buyers and sellers to consider; no matter how long ago the contamination began, there is still potential for liability based on recurring trespass.

239. *Id.*
240. *Id.* at 993.
241. *Id.*
242. *See* Huitt & Warin, *supra* note 204, at 154.
243. *Wilson*, 398 S.E.2d at 586.
244. *See also 325–343 E. 56th Corp.*, 906 F. Supp. 669 (discussing "continuing-tort" doctrine).

Damages

Plaintiffs may recover damages under a variety of theories, including property value diminution and personal injury.[245] Plaintiffs could traditionally receive nominal damages and injunctive relief for trespasses that resulted in no actual harm. However, as discussed earlier, that rule has been abrogated by some modern courts, which increasingly require proof of actual damages, especially in environmental cases involving intangible contaminants. However, nominal damages and injunctive relief are still available for traditional physical invasions in some states.[246]

Defenses

Defenses to trespass include consent, assumption of the risk,[247] and statute of limitations (see the earlier discussion of those defenses in the context of nuisance claims). In addition, under federal statutory schemes, a plaintiff's action for common law trespass may be preempted. For example, in *Feikema v. Texaco, Inc.*,[248] the plaintiff homeowners sued the owner of a gasoline tank farm for injunctive relief and damages, alleging nuisance and trespass based on soil and groundwater contamination. At the time of the plaintiffs' suit, the defendants were subject to a consent order that required them to implement a remediation program approved by the U.S. Environmental Protection Agency (EPA). The U.S. District Court held that the relief sought "would conflict with and frustrate . . . the purpose of Congress in its EPA remediation efforts under [the Resource Conservation and Recovery Act]."[249] The Fourth Circuit agreed that the injunctive relief sought would conflict with the EPA-required remediation and, therefore, was preempted by the consent order. Because the consent order did not provide for payment of damages, however, the

245. *See* Wardrop v. Manhattan Beach, 326 P.2d 15 (Cal. App. 1958) (holding defendant who pumped contaminated water onto the plaintiff's property liable under a trespass theory for the plaintiff's development of polio).

246. Holcomb v. Rodriguez, 387 P.3d 286, 291 ("Indeed, nominal damages are available in actions for trespass.").

247. However, the Maryland Court of Appeals has held that assumption of risk is not a defense in trespass actions. JBG/Twinbrook Metro Ltd. v. Wheeler, 697 A.2d 898, 908–09 (Md. 1997).

248. 16 F.3d 1408 (4th Cir. 1994).

249. *Id.* at 1411.

court held that the state law claims for damages under nuisance and trespass were not preempted.[250]

Conclusion

CERCLA has a vast scope and is generally the tool used to address response and liability, with common law likely second. While CERCLA will be the first tier, as the cases discussed in this chapter illustrate, the common law of torts has adapted to the environmental realities of the modern age. Where environmental statutes have left gaps, creative plaintiffs have filled those gaps using tort claims. Accordingly, in a disaster scenario, parties—in addition to considering compliance with environmental statutes and regulations and potential liability under those laws—should investigate and consider potential common law exposure and the related host of claims and parties.

---

250. In a concurring opinion, the circuit court was urged to view preemption of the plaintiffs' damages claims "to the extent that those damages arise from conduct regulated by the EPA's Consent Order," thereby preventing the plaintiffs from gaining "indirectly, through the threat of monetary damages, what we have expressly prevented them from gaining directly through an injunction—mandatory cleanup measures that are incompatible with those already approved by the EPA." *Id.* at 1419 (Murnaghan, J., concurring).

Chapter 8

The Multifaceted Role of Insurance in Environmental Disasters and Climate Change

Rhonda D. Orin, Marshall Gilinsky, Pamela D. Hans, Regan Samson, and Seán McCabe[1]

Introduction

Insurance steps onto center stage whenever a business encounters a weather-related or environmental disaster. Many types of insurance policies come into play.

The main attraction is the property policy, which provides coverage for losses far beyond structural repairs. Property policies also protect against (1) loss of income when a business is closed or impaired; (2) extra expenses, such as relocation and operating temporarily out of an alternate location; (3) costs incurred while preparing for the event; and more.

Many other insurance policies play supporting roles. General liability and pollution-specific policies protect against environmental or weather-related events that release substances into surrounding locations.

1. The authors are partners and associates at Anderson Kill P.C., which has specialized for more than 50 years in recovering insurance proceeds for policyholders following weather-related events and environmental disasters. The firm has its headquarters in New York, with additional offices in Connecticut, New Jersey, Pennsylvania, and Washington D.C.

Directors' & Officers' policies protect directors and officers accused of negligently failing to protect their businesses from catastrophes. Cyber policies come into play when environmental or weather-related events interfere with computer operations or cause leaks of confidential data from businesses' files.

This chapter reviews coverage from each type of policy, as well as issues that apply to all insurance policies, no matter the type. One example is causation, as every policyholder seeking coverage must prove that its losses were caused by covered events. Another is the process for seeking coverage, such as how to give notice, when to do so, whether a lawsuit is allowed, and when a suit can commence. Finally, this chapter reviews the X factor of climate change, which is already impacting and could alter the entire insurance industry.

Potentially Applicable Insurance Policies

Property Insurance Policies

Property insurance policies are available to businesses as part of comprehensive or package policies and to individuals as homeowners' and renters' policies. They provide first-party coverage for damage to a policyholder's own property caused by "fortuitous and extraneous events."[2] They generally fall into two types: "all-risk" and "named perils."

All-risk policies, which are far more common, cover loss from all perils unless specifically excluded. The typical insuring agreement states that the policy "insures against all risks of physical loss or damage from any cause whatsoever . . . except as hereinafter excluded."[3] Once a policyholder proves a loss, the insurance company must prove the loss is not covered. The policyholder need establish only a prima facie case, showing

2. Andrew C. Hecker & M. Jane Goode, *Wear and Tear, Inherent Vice, Deterioration, etc.: The Multi-Faceted All-Risk Exclusions*, 21 Tort & Ins. L.J. 634, 634 (1986); *see also* Meridian Leasing, Inc. v. Associated Aviation Underwriters, Inc., 409 F.3d 342, 350 (6th Cir. 2005); Int'l Multifoods Corp. v. Com. Union Ins. Co., 309 F.3d 76, 83 (2d Cir. 2002); Avis v. Hartford Fire Ins. Co., 195 S.E.2d 545, 547 (N.C. 1973); John S. Clark Co., Inc. v. United Nat'l Ins. Co., 304 F. Supp. 2d 758 (M.D.N.C. 2004).

3. Port Auth. of N.Y. & N.J. v. Affiliated FM Ins. Co., 311 F.3d 226, 234 (3d Cir. 2002).

(1) the existence of an all-risk policy; (2) an insurable interest in the subject of the insurance contract; and (3) the fortuitous loss of the covered property. Once a policyholder meets its *prima facie* burden, the insurance company must prove that an exclusion applies. The insurance company's burden of proving an exclusion is a heavy one.

Named perils policies are the opposite; they delineate what is covered instead of what is excluded. These policies cover damage or loss caused only by specified perils. A typical insuring agreement provides that the "insurer will pay for direct physical loss of or damage to Covered Property at the premises described in the Declarations caused by or resulting from any Covered Cause of Loss." A "Covered Cause of Loss" typically encompasses "fire, lightning, windstorm, hail, explosion, riot, riot attending a strike, civil commotion, aircraft, vehicles, smoke, leakage from fire protection systems, vandalism and malicious mischief, except as excluded elsewhere in the policy."[4]

Coverage Agreement

The key term in the coverage agreement of a property insurance policy is the term "direct physical loss or damage." Policyholders and insurance companies have engaged in intense disputes about the significance of even small variations of this term, such as: "physical loss *of* or damage *to*" (emphasis supplied). Under any variation, it is relatively easy to prove coverage when there is physical alteration of property, such as a roof blown off by a hurricane. But when nonstructural damage renders property unfit for its intended use, the burden can be met as well. In cases involving nonstructural harm—like the presence of asbestos fibers, odors from a methamphetamine laboratory, and even cat urine in a rental property[5]—courts have found coverage under property policies.

---

4. *See, e.g.*, Yale Univ. v. Cigna Ins. Co., 224 F. Supp. 2d 402, 411 (D. Conn. 2002); *see also* Assurance Co. of Am. v. Wall & Assocs. LLC of Olympia, 379 F.3d 557, 559 (9th Cir. 2004).

5. *See, e.g.*, Sentinel Mgmt. Co. v. N.H. Ins. Co., 563 N.W.2d 296, 300 (Minn. Ct. App. 1997); Farmers Ins. Co. of Oregon v. Trutanich, 858 P.2d 1332, 1334–35 (Or. 1993); Gen. Mills, Inc. v. Gold Medal Ins. Co., 622 N.W.2d 147, 151–52 (Minn. Ct. App. 2001); Mellin v. Northern Security Ins. Co., 115 A.3d 799, 805 (N.H. 2015).

Such precedent extends through the 1950s,[6] the 1960s,[7] the 1970s,[8] the 1980s,[9] the 1990s,[10] and so on.

6. Am. All. Ins. Co. v. Keleket X-Ray Corp., 248 F.2d 920, 925 (6th Cir. 1957) (finding that the policyholder, which manufactured instruments used in measuring radioactivity, had suffered property damage from a release of radon dust and gas which made the building unsafe, and made it impossible to calibrate the instruments prior to sale because of background radiation).

7. Hughes v. Potomac Ins. Co., 18 Cal. Rptr. 650, 655 (Cal. Ct. App. 1962) (finding that the policyholder's home—which became perched on the edge of a cliff after a landslide deprived it of lateral support and stability—was damaged because it became unsafe to live in and was thus, useless); *see also* W. Fire Ins. Co. v. First Presbyterian Church, 437 P.2d 52, 54–55 (Colo. 1968) (en banc) (finding a "direct physical loss" where a church complied with the fire department's order to close because gasoline vapors made "use of the building dangerous").

8. Cyclops Corp. v. Home Ins. Co., 352 F. Supp. 931, 937 (W.D. Pa. 1973) (finding the policyholder entitled to coverage for loss of business income where vibration of motor, without apparent damage, caused the business to be shut down).

9. Hampton Foods, Inc. v. Aetna Cas. & Sur. Co., 787 F.2d 349, 352 (8th Cir. 1986) (finding the policyholder could claim business income coverage where risk of collapse necessitated abandoning a grocery store).

10. In chronological order: Hetrick v. Valley Mut. Ins Co., 15 Pa. D. & C. 4th 271 (Pa. Com. Pl. 1992) (finding there would be coverage for loss of use of a house if an outside oil spill made the house uninhabitable); Largent v. State Farm Fire & Cas. Co., 842 P.2d 445, 446 (Or. Ct. App. 1992) (noting that insurance company conceded methamphetamine fumes could cause "accidental direct physical loss"); Farmers Ins. Co. of Or. v. Trutanich, 858 P.2d 1332, 1335 (Or. Ct. App. 1993) (finding costs of methamphetamine odor covered as direct physical loss or damage); Azalea, Ltd. v. Am. States Ins. Co., 656 So. 2d 600, 602 (Fla. Dist. Ct. App. 1995) (finding damage to sewage treatment plant from chemicals that destroyed a bacteria colony necessary for the plant to operate amounted to "direct damage to the structure"); Arbeiter v. Cambridge Mut. Fire Ins. Co., 1996 WL 1250616, at *2 (Mass. Super. Ct. Mar. 15, 1996) (finding oil fumes present in house after discovery of oil leak constituted physical damage); Sentinel Mgmt. Co. v. N.H. Ins. Co., 563 N.W.2d 296, 300 (Minn. Ct. App. 1997) (finding the presence of asbestos could constitute physical loss or damage); Murray v. State Farm Fire & Cas. Co., 203 W.Va. 477, 493, 509 S.E.2d 1, 17 (1998) (finding a home rendered unlivable by falling rocks had suffered a "direct physical loss to the property"); Shade Foods, Inc. v. Innovative Prod. Sales & Mktg., Inc., 78 Cal. App. 4th 847, 865 (2000) (holding that the intermingling of a quarter pound of wood shavings in 80,000 pounds of almonds caused physical loss or damage to the almonds even though the almonds were structurally unchanged); Matzner v. Seaco Ins. Co., No.CIV.A. 96-0498-B, 1998 WL 566658, at *4 (Mass. Super. Ct. Aug. 12, 1998) (concluding that "direct physical loss or damage" was ambiguous and could mean either "only tangible damage to the structure of insured property" or "more than tangible damage to the structure of insured property," and that "carbon monoxide contamination constitutes 'direct physical loss of or damage to' property"); Columbiaknit, Inc. v. Affiliated FM Ins. Co., No. 98-434-HU, 1999 WL 619100, at *7–8 (D. Or. Aug. 4, 1999) (finding that policyholder could bear its burden to demonstrate that clothes containing mold or mildew suffered "direct physical loss or damage" if it established "at trial a class of garments which has increased microbial counts and that will, as a result, develop either an odor or mold or mildew"); Board of Educ. v. Int'l Ins. Co., 720 N.E.2d 622, 625–26 (Ill. Ct. App. 1999) (citing liability insurance coverage cases finding that incorporation of asbestos into buildings caused "property damage," defined under liability policies to be "physical injury to or destruction of tangible property").

Many courts denied property claims during the COVID-19 pandemic of 2020 to 2023 on various grounds, including that COVID-related losses arose from mandatory governmental shutdowns rather than from property damage. Most of these decisions are distinguishable because of the pandemic's unique features.[11] Other courts followed well-established precedent, holding that the presence of the coronavirus on tangible property—although not visible to the naked eye—can cause physical loss or damage.[12] Thus, although insurance companies may disagree, this precedent remains valid and binding for claims that involve nonstructural property damage.

Exclusions

Separate from the insuring agreement, there is a long list of exclusions in property policies—particularly all-risk policies, where the exclusions define the coverage. As a matter of law, exclusions are construed narrowly against insurance companies and in favor of coverage.[13]

"Water" Exclusion, Including Flood

The most significant exclusion for weather-related and environmental events is the exclusion for losses caused by water-related damage. This exclusion typically bars coverage for water damage in a variety of forms, stating: "We will not pay for loss or damage caused directly or indirectly by . . . Water. (1) Flood, surface water, waves, tides, tidal waves, overflow of any body of water, or their spray, all whether driven by wind or not."[14] The various terms in subsection (1) typically are not defined. Because

11. Some courts found that the virus did not cause property damage because it can easily be wiped from surfaces with cleaning fluids, distinguishing it from contaminants like asbestos that are physically integrated into the building's structure. *See, e.g.*, Carilion Clinic v. Am. Guarantee & Liab. Ins. Co., 583 F. Supp. 3d 715 (W.D. Va. 2022). Others found that the business interruption losses did not arise from property damage, but rather from governmental orders motivated by precautionary health concerns. *See, e.g.*, Cordish Cos. v. Affiliated FM Ins., 573 F. Supp. 3d 877 (D. Md. 2021). Other decisions rested on procedural defects in the policyholders' pleadings. *See, e.g.*, Berkseth-Rojas v. Aspen Am. Ins. Co., 513 F. Supp. 3d 724, 732 (N.D. Tex. 2021).

12. *See, e.g.*, North State Deli, LLC v. Cincinnati Ins. Co., 908 S.E.2d 802 (N.C. 2024); Huntington Ingalls Indus., Inc. v. Ace Am. Ins. Co., 287 A.3d 515 (Vt. 2022).

13. *See, e.g.*, Jordan v. Allstate Ins. Co., 116 Cal. App. 4th 1206, 1214 (Cal. Ct. App. 2004) ("Policy exclusions are strictly construed.").

14. ISO Form CP 00 10 06 95; ISO Form CP 10 20 06 95.

water can cause damage in different ways, a burst of litigation about this exclusion often follows weather-related and environmental events.

The "flood" component of this exclusion, for example, was challenged extensively after Hurricane Katrina in August 2005. A typical definition of "flood" is "an overflowing of water in an area normally dry; inundation; deluge."[15] During Hurricane Katrina, water damage was caused not only by the hurricane itself, but also by water that escaped into the streets of New Orleans when the levees around the city failed. Thus, litigation focused on whether damage attributable to the levee failures was excluded as "flood" or whether it was covered because it arose from other causes, such as construction defects. In one of the largest cases, the federal district court held the exclusion did not apply, but the appellate court held the opposite.[16] That case involved coverage for damage that took place when water overtopped the walls of the 17th Street, Industrial, and London Avenue Canals. Plaintiffs alleged the damage was caused by the failure of the Orleans Levee District to maintain the levees properly, not by "flood." The district court deemed the exclusion ambiguous because the term "flood" is susceptible to two reasonable interpretations—one which limits itself only to a flood that is solely attributable to natural causes, and one which also encompasses a flood that is attributable to negligence or intentional acts.[17] The Fifth Circuit reversed, holding that "what occurred here fits squarely within the generally prevailing meaning" of the term, noting that "[w]hen a body of water overflows its normal boundaries and inundates an area of land that is normally dry, the event is a flood."[18]

The history of the "surface water" portion of this definition is basically the same. The term "surface water" usually is not defined in insurance policies, which forces courts interpreting the term to resort to dictionary definitions of the term. A typical dictionary definition is water that "(1) derives from natural precipitation such as rain or melting snow;

15. *Flood*, Merriam-Webster New World Dictionary (2d ed. 1974).

16. *In re* Katrina Canal Breaches Consol. Litig., 466 F. Supp. 2d 729 (E.D. La.), *aff'd in part, vacated in part sub nom.*, 495 F.3d 191 (5th Cir. 2007).

17. *Id.* at 746–47, 756–57.

18. *See In Re* Katrina Canal Breaches Litig., 495 F.3d 191, 214 (5th Cir. 2007).

(2) flows over or accumulates on the surface of the ground; and (3) does not form a definite body of water or follow a defined watercourse."[19] As with "flood," there are many inconsistencies in the case law. A Georgia court, for example, found the exclusion inapplicable where rainwater flowed into a 13-foot-deep pit that a city had dug under a road adjacent to an insured building. From the pit, the water entered an uncapped pipe and flowed into the basement. The court found this water was not "surface water" because it "is no longer diffused, is no longer on the surface of the ground, has gathered into a body, and has followed a defined course through the pipe and into the building."[20] But a North Dakota court held the opposite when water from a heavy rainstorm entered a tunnel from a sports stadium and damaged property at the tunnel's far end. The court found that the water was "surface water" even though it had been "altered . . . by paved surfaces, buildings, or other structures" and by "being artificially channeled underground."[21]

Policyholders should know that when insurance companies are obligated to pay for losses from weather-related and environmental events, they often respond by tightening the exclusions or adding new ones. The effect is to "hollow out" the coverage—with the risk that, eventually, the policies will serve no purpose at all. This phenomenon is documented exhaustively by the Consumer Federation of America in an eye-popping article by J. Robert Hunter, former Insurance Commissioner of Texas:

> [I]ndustry data demonstrates that insurers have significantly and methodologically decreased their financial responsibility for [catastrophic] events in recent years and shifted much of this risk to consumers and taxpayers. . . . [M]ost of these savings have been achieved by hollowing out the coverage in [ ] insurance policies and raising rates.[22]

---

19. Smith v. Union Auto Indem. Co., 752 N.E.2d 1261, 1267 (2001).

20. Selective Way Ins. Co. v. Litig. Techn., Inc., 606 S.E.2d 68 (2005); *see also* Heller v. Fire Ins. Exch., 800 P.2d 1006, 1009 (Colo. 1990).

21. State Fire and Tornado Fund v. N.D. State Univ., 694 N.W.2d 225 (N.D. 2005).

22. *See* J. Robert Hunter, *The Insurance Industry's Incredible Disappearing Weather Catastrophe Risk: How Insurers Have Shifted Risk and Costs Associated with Weather Catastrophes to Consumers and Taxpayers*, Consumer Fed'n of Am. 1 (Feb. 17, 2012).

Other Exclusions

Faulty workmanship exclusions provide that damage resulting from the faulty, inadequate, defective, or negligent construction of part or all of insured property, whether on or off the premises, is excluded.[23] They typically read: "We will not pay for loss or damage caused by or resulting from . . . [f]aulty, inadequate, defective or negligent: . . . [d]esign, testing, specifications, workmanship, repair, construction, renovation, remodeling, grading or earth compaction; . . . of part or all of any property on or off the described premises." Courts have applied at least two reasonable interpretations of the term "faulty workmanship" – "flawed process," and a "flawed product" – rendering the exclusion ambiguous.[24] Similarly, negligence occurring after a product has been properly completed – such as when its electronic controls are being tested – has been found not to trigger the faulty workmanship exclusion.[25]

Wear and tear exclusions have long been a part of all-risk insurance policies.[26] Courts frequently interpret them in accordance with the popular meaning of the expression. They employ adjectives such as "ordinary" and "natural" to limit the breadth of the exclusion.[27]

Inherent vice/latent defect exclusions bar coverage for loss "caused directly or indirectly by . . . inherent vice [or] latent defect." If not defined in the policy, the meaning of these words is up for debate. A Washington court in *Port of Seattle v. Lexington Ins. Co.* described "inherent vice" as "any existing defects, diseases, decay or the inherent nature of the commodity which will cause it to deteriorate with a lapse of time."[28] It explained that there is no coverage for an "inherent vice" that arises

---

23. *See, e.g.*, El. Rincon Supportive Servs. Org., Inc. v. First Nonprofit Mut. Ins. Co., 803 N.E.2d 532 (Ill. App. 1st. Dist. 2004).

24. Allstate Ins. Co. v. Smith, 929 F.2d 447, 450 (9th Cir. 1991).

25. *See* Otis Elevator Co. v. Factory Mutual Ins. Co., 353 F. Supp. 2d 274, 280–81 (D. Conn. 2005); *see also* City of Burlington v. Hartford Steam Boiler Inspection and Ins. Co., 190 F. Supp. 2d 663, 672 (D. Vt. 2002); Dow Chem. Co. v. Royal Indem. Co., 635 F.2d 379, 387 (5th Cir. 1981).

26. *See, e.g.*, Mellon v. Fed. Ins. Co., 14 F.2d 997, 1002 (S.D.N.Y. 1926).

27. *See, e.g.*, Meridian Leasing, Inc. v. Associated Aviation Underwriters, Inc., 409 F.3d 342, 350 (6th Cir. 2005); *see also* Cyclops Corp. v. Home Ins. Co., 352 F. Supp. 931, 936 (W.D. Pa. 1973).

28. Port of Seattle v. Lexington Ins. Co., 111 Wash. App. 901, 908–10 (Wash. Ct. App. 2002) (quoting Missouri Pacific R.R. Co. v. Elmore & Stahl, 377 U.S. 134, 136 (1964)); *see also* Employers Cas. Co. v. Holm, 393 S.W.2d 363, 367 (Tex. App. 1965).

"entirely from internal decomposition or some quality which brings about its own injury or destruction." The exclusion, however, does not apply when the property is "threatened by an outside natural force."[29] In one of the few Year 2000 cases, the Third Circuit held that the inherent vice exclusion barred coverage for a policyholder's Y2K claim.[30] It reasoned that the cause of loss was the internal data entry by the policyholder in the date field, not an external force.

Latent defect exclusions are substantially similar to inherent vice exclusions and bring many of the same challenges. While "latent defect" is usually undefined, it has been interpreted as meaning "a defect that is hidden, or which could not have been discovered by any known or customary test or examination."[31] The Second Circuit deemed that this exclusion, along with an inherent vice exclusion, barred coverage for damage to a boiler unit in an electric generating facility. It held that the loss was caused by leaking welds and that the leaks arose from the welds themselves rather than from an external cause.[32]

Dampness exclusions are virtually tautological; they bar coverage for "loss caused by or resulting from . . . dampness."[33] One New York court ruled that this exclusion barred coverage in the context of mold contamination. The court deferred to a dictionary to find that the plain and ordinary meaning of "dampness" is "wetness" and "moistness,"[34] and then determined that wetness and moistness was the proximate cause of the mold contamination.[35] The precedential value of this ruling is unclear, however, because the ruling begs the ultimate question of how the wetness and moistness arose. Another court could easily look further back

---

29. Am. Home Assurance Co. v. J.F. Shea Co., Inc., 445 F. Supp. 365, 368 (D.D.C. 1978); *see also* GTE Corp. v. Allendale Mut. Ins. Co., 372 F.3d 598 (3d Cir. 2004) (GTE); Hartford Steam Boiler Inspection and Ins. Co., 190 F. Supp. 2d 663 at 688–89 (D. Vt. 2002).

30. *See GTE Corp.*, 372 F.3d 598 (3d Cir. 2004).

31. *Id.*; *see also* Essex House v. St. Paul Fire & Marine Ins. Co., 404 F. Supp. 978, 992 (S.D. Ohio 1975). Gen. Am. Transp. Corp. v. Sun Ins. Office, Ltd., 369 F.2d 906 (6th Cir. 1966).

32. City of Burlington v. Indem. Ins. Co. of N. Am., 346 F.3d 70, 74 (2d Cir. 2003).

33. *See* ISO Form CG 00 01 04 13.

34. 40 Gardenville, LLC v. Travelers Property Cas. of America, 387 F. Supp. 2d 205, 211 (W.D.N.Y. 2005) (quoting The American Heritage Dictionary of the English Language (4th ed. 2000)).

35. *Id.* at 211.

along the chain of causation and select a different—and covered—proximate cause. For example, if a building recently had a fire, and water from fire-fighting equipment created a damp environment that resulted in mold, a court may find that the proximate cause was the covered fire.[36]

Additional Coverages

Nearly all commercial property insurance policies include additional extensions of coverage that insure against losses that transcend the physical loss or damage to property itself. The scope and breadth of these extensions can vary from one policy to the next, depending on the wording used, but the objective in providing these additional coverages and the nature of the losses to which they respond are generally the same across wordings. Several of the most common and important extensions of coverage are discussed next.

Business Interruption

It is common for businesses to suffer economic losses while they are repairing or replacing property that has suffered physical damage or loss. Accordingly, nearly all modern property polices include an extension of coverage for economic losses sustained due to the interruption of business during that time. This is referred to as "business interruption," "business income," or "time element" coverage.

The basic purpose of business interruption coverage is to do for the policyholder what its business would have done for itself had no loss occurred. [37] Although wordings can vary, the following iteration, drafted by the Insurance Services Office, is a good example:

---

36. *See, e.g.*, Tatalovich v. Pa. Nat. Mut. Cas. Ins. Co., No. 10724, 2003 WL 22844173, at *2 (Pa. C.P. Oct. 10, 2003) (mold exclusion did not apply when the mold was caused by water entering the building from a leak in a roof—a peril that was covered).

37. *See, e.g.*, Fireman's Fund Ins. Co. v. Holland Am. Line-Westours, Inc., No. 00-35059, 2002 WL 21924, at *1 (9th Cir. Jan. 4, 2002) ("the purpose of business interruption coverage . . . is limited to protecting the earnings the insured would have enjoyed had there been no interruption); Prudential LMI Comm'l Ins. Co. v. Colleton Enters., Inc., No. 91-1757, 1992 WL 252507, at *2 (4th Cir. Oct. 5, 1992) (Generally, business interruption insurance "is designed to do for the insured in the event of business interruption caused by [an insured peril], just what the business itself would have done if no interruption had occurred—no more."); Quality Molding Co. v. Am. Nat'l Fire Ins. Co., 272 F.2d 779, 780 (7th Cir. 1960) ("Business interruption insurance is insurance under which the insured is protected in the earnings which the insured would have enjoyed had there been no interruption of business. The purpose of business interruption insurance is to protect the prospective

> We will pay for the actual loss of Business Income you sustain due to the necessary suspension of your "operations" during the "period of restoration." The suspension must be caused by direct physical loss of or damage to property, including personal property in the open (or in a vehicle) within 100 feet, at the premises which are described in the Declarations and for which a Business Income Limit of Insurance is shown in the Declarations. The loss or damage must be caused by or result from a Covered Cause of Loss.[38]

Under this form, "Business Income" is defined as:

> a. Net Income (Net Profit or Loss before income taxes) that would have been earned or incurred; and
>
> b. Continuing normal operating expenses, including payroll, incurred.[39]

---

earnings of the insured business.") (citations omitted); Supermarkets Operating Co. v. Arkwright Mut. Ins. Co., 257 F. Supp. 273, 277 (E.D. Pa. 1966) ("The policy now before the Court belongs to that category of insurance protection that is commonly called 'business interruption' or 'use and occupancy' insurance. It is designed to protect the earnings of profits that a business would have earned, had the event insured against no[t] intervened."); Wood Goods Galore, Inc. v. Reinsurance Ass'n of Minn., 478 N.W.2d 205, 209–10 (Minn. App. 1992) ("The purpose of coverage for business interruption loss is to do for the business what it would have done for itself had no loss occurred."); Fireman's Fund Ins. Co. v. Mitchell-Peterson, Inc., 578 N.E.2d 851, 855 (Ohio App. Ct. 1989) ("The purpose of a business interruption policy is to do for the insured in event of a business interruption . . . just what the business itself would have done if not interruption had occurred") (quoting Am. All. Ins. Co. v. Keleket X-Ray Corp., 248 F.2d 920, 928 (6th Cir. 1957)); Berkeley Inn, Inc. v. Centennial Ins. Co., 422 A.2d 1078, 1080 (Pa. Super. 1980) (Generally, business interruption insurance is intended to return to the insured the amount of profit it would have earned had the event insured against not intervened.) Keetch v. Mut. of Enumclaw Ins. Co., 831 P.2d 784, 786 (Wash. App. 1992) (The essential nature and purpose of a business interruption policy is to protect the earnings which an insured would have enjoyed had there been no interruption of business"); Nat'l Union Fire Ins. Co. v. TransCanada Energy USA, Inc., 153 A.D.3d 1153 (N.Y. App. Div. 2017), *appeal denied*, TC Ravenswood v. Nat'l Union Fire Ins. Co., 34 N.Y.3d 908 (N.Y. 2020).

38. James J. Markham, Property Loss Adjusting 178 (2d ed. 1995).

39. John D. Dempsey & Lee M. Epstein, *Re-examining Business Interruption Insurance*, 49 Risk Mgmt. 40 (2002) ("The framers devised an elegant solution still used as standard language in manuscript policies today: By giving 'due consideration to the experience of the business before the date of damage and the probable experience thereafter had no loss occurred,' the insured and insurer could reach reasonable accommodation regarding the actual loss sustained. Based on past experience and the future probable experience, the insured loss could be determined in a commercially reasonable manner.").

The coverage provided for business interruption extends over a "period of recovery," "period of restoration," or "period of indemnity," which usually starts on the date of the loss (or after the expiration of a certain waiting period, usually 24, 48, or 72 hours) and ends at such time that, with "due diligence and dispatch" or "reasonable speed" (or similar objective language), the property can reasonably be restored to its pre-loss condition. For example, the standard Insurance Services Office form includes a definition of "Period of Restoration" stating that the period:

> a. begins:
>
> > (1) 72 hours after the time of direct physical loss or damage for Business Income coverage; or
> >
> > (2) Immediately after the time of direct physical loss or damage for Extra Expense coverage; caused by or resulting from any Covered Cause of Loss at the described premises; and
>
> b. ends on the earlier of:
>
> > (1) The date when the property at the described premises should be repaired, rebuilt or replaced with reasonable speed and similar quality; or
> >
> > (2) The date when business is resumed at a new permanent location.[40]

Most provisions governing the period of recovery are—like the one preceding—based on the *hypothetical* time to restore the property using reasonable efforts, not the time it actually takes.[41] Typically, the period of

---

40. *See* Markham, *supra* note 38, at 187. Unlike previous forms, this one contains a deductible expressed as a specific period of time. Linda G. Robinson & Jack P. Gibson, *Commercial Property Insurance,* IRMI § II.E.6 (2002) ("Sometimes there is no separate deductible for the business income coverage of a commercial property policy. When a deductible does apply, it may be stated in terms of a specified waiting period rather than as a dollar amount. For example, the ISO business income coverage form imposes a 72-hour waiting period deductible. A 72-hour waiting period deductible eliminates coverage for time element loss suffered during the first 72 hours after the direct damage loss.").

41. *See, e.g.*, Bard's Apparel Mfg., Inc. v. Bituminous Fire & Marine Ins. Co., 849 F.2d 245, 252 (6th Cir. 1988) (finding that the Period of Restoration is hypothetical, "amenable to computation in advance and . . . not subject to vagaries like owner indecision, strikes, or failure of lease negotiations which might affect the actual rebuilding time," and thus that it was error for jury to consider

recovery is not cut off by the end date of the policy.[42] Many policies also include "extended business interruption" coverage, which covers losses that occur during the "ramp up" period after the physical repairs can be completed and until such time that the policyholder's business returns to pre-loss performance levels (often capped at an additional 365 days).[43]

Some polices provide guidance on how to quantify the loss, but the overarching objective is to determine lost profits minus saved expenses following the loss.[44] Performing that calculation typically involves a comparison of expected performance prior to the loss with actual performance in the wake of the loss.[45] Such "forecast versus actual" estimates obviously do not (and cannot) measure the business interruption loss with absolute precision. All that is generally required is that the calculation measure the loss with "reasonable certainty."[46]

---

perilous financial condition of policyholder in computing the Period of Restoration); Duane Reade, Inc. v. St. Paul Fire & Marine Ins. Co., 279 F. Supp. 2d 235, 239 (S.D.N.Y. 2003), *aff'd as modified*, 411 F.3d 384 (2d Cir. 2005) ("On their face, the Restoration Period clauses envision a hypothetical or constructive (as opposed to actual) time frame for rebuilding, as evidenced, for example, by their use of the subjunctive 'would.'").

42. *See, e.g.*, Beautytuft, Inc. v. Factory Ins. Ass'n, 431 F.2d 1122, 1124 (6th Cir. 1970) ("Recovery in the event of loss hereunder shall be the ACTUAL LOSS SUSTAINED by the Insured directly resulting from such interruption of business, but not exceeding the reduction in gross earnings less charges and expenses which do not necessarily continue during the interruption of business, for only such length of time as would be required with the exercise of due diligence and dispatch to rebuild, repair or replace such described property as has been damaged or destroyed, commencing with the date of such damage or destruction and not limited by the date of expiration of this Policy."); Steel Prods. Co. v. Millers Nat'l Ins. Co., 209 N.W.2d 32, 34 (Iowa 1973) ("In the event of such damage or destruction this Company shall be liable for the ACTUAL LOSS SUSTAINED by the Insured resulting directly from such interruption of business, but not exceeding the reduction in Gross Earnings less charges and expenses which do not necessarily continue during the interruption of business, for only such length of time as would be required with the exercise of due diligence and dispatch to rebuild, repair or replace such part of the property herein described as has been damaged or destroyed commencing with the date of such damage or destruction and not limited by the date of expiration of this policy.").

43. *See* Ochsner Clinic Found. v. Lexington Ins. Co., 226 F. Supp. 3d 658, 681 (E.D. La. 2017).

44. *See, e.g.*, Finger Furniture Co., Inc, v. Commonwealth Ins. Co., 404 F.3d 312 (5th Cir. 2005).

45. *See, e.g.*, Citadel Broadcasting Corp. v. Axis Ins. Co., 162 So. 3d 470, 475 (La. App. 4th Cir. 2015).

46. *See, e.g.*, Amerisure Ins. Co. v. Roll Serv., Inc., No. 01 C 5292, 2003 WL 21518310, at *2 (N.D. Ill. June 30, 2003) ("[T]he amount of an award of lost profits need not be proven with absolute certainty, [but] the plaintiff bears the burden of proving such damages with reasonable certainty"); Shade Foods, Inc. v. Innovative Prods. Sales Mktg., Inc., 93 Cal. Rptr. 2d 364, 393–94 (Cal. App. 2000) ("In reviewing the amount of the award of damages, we are governed by the

Of course, the performance of almost every business varies from month to month, and year to year, and the most recent performance is not always the best predictor of future results. Accordingly, it is standard practice to account for current trends[47] and factors like seasonality[48] in making and adjusting the business interruption loss calculations. Similarly, it can be challenging to calculate with reasonable certainty the losses suffered by new businesses or those with limited track records.[49]

Overall, business interruption coverage is an integral and valuable component of property insurance policies. Although large business interruption claims often give rise to disputes between policyholders and insurance companies—on a plethora of issues too numerous to cover in this overview—experienced professionals working for the respective sides

---

principle that '[l]ost profits to an established business may be recovered if their extent and occurrence can be ascertained with reasonable certainty."); Dictiomatic, Inc. v. U.S. Fid. & Guar. Co., 127 F. Supp. 2d 1239, 1243–44 (S.D. Fla. 1999) ("It must also be noted that Florida law is clear that a claim for lost profits must be shown with a reasonable degree of certainty."); Maher v. Cont'l Cas. Co., 76 F.3d 535, 541 (4th Cir. 1996) ("West Virginia law allows for the recovery of lost profits in an action for breach of contract, insofar as such profits are proved with 'reasonable certainty"); Rubbermaid, Inc. v. Hartford Steam Boilers Inspection Co., 645 N.E.2d 116 (Ohio App. 1994) ("It is well established that proof of lost profits must be established with reasonable certainty"); Polytech, Inc. v. Affiliated FM Ins. Co., 21 F.3d 271, 276 (8th Cir. 1994) ("to obtain a damage award for lost profits at trial, [the policyholder] must produce evidence that provides an adequate basis for estimating lost profits with reasonable certainty"); Holt Atherton Indus., Inc. v. Heine, 835 S.W.2d 80, 84 (Tex. 1992) ("Recovery for lost profits does not require that the loss be susceptible of exact calculation;" "The amount of the loss must be shown by competent evidence with reasonable certainty.").

47. *See, e.g.*, Blis Day Spa, LLC v. Hartford Ins. Grp., 427 F. Supp. 2d 621, 629 (W.D.N.C. 2006) (noting policyholder sought to prove Business Income and Extra Expense losses based in part on trends in the business, and permitting proof through "expert testimony, economic and financial data, market surveys and analysis, and business records of similar enterprises"); W.S. Shamban &Co. v. Commerce & Indus. Ins. Co., 475 F.2d 34, 36 (9th Cir. 1973) (reviewing competing experts' adjustments to business interruption loss calculation based on trends affecting performance over the prior two years); Keetch v. Mut. of Enumclaw Ins. Co., 831 P.2d 784, 785 (Wash. Ct. App. 1992) (noting that lower court had set amount of loss by "hearing testimony on the motel's income trends").

48. Patrick A. Gaughan, Measuring Business Interruption Losses 166–68 (2004).

49. *See* Blis Day Spa, 427 F. Supp. 2d at 629 ("The general rule requiring "reasonable certainty" has been applied specifically to lost profit damages for a new businesses without a history of profitability."); Rubbermaid, Inc. v. Hartford Steam Boilers Inspection Co., 645 N.E.2d 116, 118 (Ohio App. 1994) (accepting the policyholder's proof of its business interruption losses, even though "the product upon which [the policyholder] based its claim was newly developed and had been on the market for approximately a year and a half prior to the July breakdown"); Gaughan, *supra* note 46, at 171–78.

usually work out the details and arrive at mutually acceptable resolutions of these claims.

Contingent Business Interruption

It is increasingly common for physical loss or damage *away* from a policyholder's premises to cause significant business interruption losses for the policyholder. Supply chain disruptions following catastrophic weather events in Asia are a well-known example. Many commercial property insurance policies include coverage for such losses, called contingent business interruption (CBI) or "dependent property" coverage.

The gist of the coverage and the measurement of losses is more or less the same as business interruption coverage, but instead of being triggered by damage to the *policyholder's* property, it is triggered by physical loss or damage to property of a *supplier or customer* (and often to a second tier of suppliers and customers) or to a business that attracts customers to the policyholder's business.

The Insurance Services Office's "Business Income from Dependent Properties—Broad Form" provides:

> We will pay for the actual loss of Business Income you sustain due to the necessary suspension of your "operations" during the "period of restoration." The suspension must be caused by direct physical loss of or damage to "dependent property" at a premises described in the Schedule caused by or resulting from any Covered Cause of Loss.[50]

In turn, "Dependent Properties" is defined as follows:

> 1. "Dependent Property," means property operated by others whom you depend on to:
>
> > a. Deliver materials or services to you, or to others for your account (Contributing Locations). With respect to Contributing Locations, services does not mean water, communications or power supply services;
> >
> > b. Accept your products or services (Recipient Locations);

50. ISO Form CP 15 08 10 00.

c. Manufacture products for delivery to your customers under contract of sale (Manufacturing Locations); or

d. Attract customers to your business (Leader Locations).[51]

There are relatively few cases dissecting CBI claims,[52] in contrast to the many cases that address straight business interruption losses. This fact reflects that CBI claims are far less common. Regardless, since extreme weather events in recent years have led to an increased number of supply chain disruptions worldwide, CBI claims are likely to increase proportionately. Every business is advised to be aware of this valuable resource within its property insurance policies.

Extra Expense

Extra expense coverage is a natural counterpart to business interruption coverage. Whereas the latter insures against the losses that follow property damage, the former reimburses the policyholder for additional costs it incurs to minimize such losses or prevent them from occurring altogether. For example, if the policyholder's facility is damaged in a fire, but limited operations can continue during the period of repair by moving undamaged equipment and operations to another location, those relocation costs are covered. Such provisions benefit both policyholder and insurance company, as they protect the policyholder's operations and relationships while reducing the business interruption losses that need to be paid.

A wide variety of policy wordings are used to provide extra expense coverage. The most common are limited to expenses that reduce the business interruption losses to be owed.[53] Broader provisions, called "pure" extra expense, include extraordinary costs that follow catastrophes, such as the costs of security guards to prevent looting at a damaged

51. *See id.*

52. *See* Archer-Daniels-Midland Co. v. Phx. Assurance Co., 936 F. Supp. 534 (S.D. Ill. 1996); S. Hosp., Inc. v. Zurich Am. Ins. Co., 393 F.3d 1137, 1141 (10th Cir. 2004); Pentair, Inc. v. Am. Guar. & Liab. Ins. Co., No. Civ. 02-3696, 2003 WL 21804874, at *2 (D. Minn. July 31, 2003), *aff'd*, 400 F.3d 613 (8th Cir. 2005); Tower Auto., Inc. v. Am. Prot. Ins. Co., 266 F. Supp. 2d 664, 670 n.4 (W.D. Mich. 2003); Phila. Parking Auth. v. Fed. Ins. Co., No. 03 Civ. 6748, 2005 WL 78783 (S.D.N.Y. Jan 14, 2005).

53. Richard Lewis & Nicholas Insua, Business Income Insurance Disputes § 4.01 (2d ed. 2013).

facility, unemployment benefits, or charges imposed by state governments when businesses are forced temporarily to cease operations and lay off employees.[54]

One extra expense provision, based on the Insurance Services Office form, provides:

> We will pay necessary Extra Expense you incur during the "period of restoration" that you would not have incurred if there had been no direct physical loss or damage to property at the described premises, including personal property in the open (or in a vehicle) within 100 feet, caused by or resulting from any Covered Cause of Loss. Extra Expense means expense incurred:
>
> (1) To avoid or minimize the suspension of business and to continue "operations;"
>
> (a) At the described premises; or
>
> (b) At replacement premises or at temporary locations, including:
>
> (i) Relocation expenses; and
>
> (ii) Costs to equip and operate the replacement of temporary locations.
>
> (2) To minimize the suspension of business if you cannot continue "operations;"
>
> (3) To repair or replace any property; or
>
> (4) To research, replace or restore the lost information on damaged valuable papers and records;
>
> to the extent it reduces the amount of loss that otherwise would have been payable under this Additional Coverage or Additional Coverage f., Business Income.[55]

---

54. *Id.*

55. Am. States Ins. Co. v. Creative Walking, Inc., 16 F. Supp. 2d 1062, 1063–64 (E.D. Mo. 1998); *see also* F.P. Woll & Co. v. Valiant Ins. Co., No. 99-0465, 2004 WL 503413, at *2 (E.D. Pa. Mar. 11, 2004); Albertini Rests., Inc. v. Nationwide Mut. Ins., No. 93-CV-0442, 1993 WL 117541,

Sue and Labor

Preparing for an upcoming extreme weather event—or any event that can wreak havoc on businesses—can be expensive. Not preparing for such an event, however, can be even worse. Thus, it is common knowledge among businesses that advance planning, including the expense of taking precautionary actions, is required for every unfortunate event that can be anticipated.

The good news is that these expenses are covered under an oddly named clause in most property policies: the "sue and labor" provision.

The typical sue and labor provision requires policyholders to take steps to avert or minimize losses or damage to property covered under the insurance policy. It also requires insurance companies to reimburse a significant portion of these precautionary costs. The provision reflects that precautionary measures serve the interests of both parties. While there are many variations, a typical sue and labor provision provides:

> In case of actual or imminent loss or damage by a peril insured against, it shall, without prejudice to this insurance, be lawful and necessary for the Insured . . . to sue, labor, and travel for, in, and about the defense, the safeguard, and the recovery of the property or any part of the property insured hereunder;
>
> . . . [The Insurance] Company shall contribute to the expenses so incurred according to the rate and quantity of the sum herein insured.[56]

Today, precautionary measures go far beyond putting out the sandbags before the hurricane arrives. Covered costs may include the installation of security systems, fire suppression, temperature control, electric hurricane shutters, and other protective techniques.

One current controversy is whether protective measures such as physically moving servers off site and securing duplicates of data in other locations are covered under computer equipment. This controversy is part of a larger issue of how computers—both hardware and software—fit

---

at *1–2 (E.D. Pa. Apr. 15, 1993); Nassau Gallery, Inc. v. Nationwide Mut. Fire Ins. Co., No. 00C-05-034, 2003 WL 21223843, at *3 (Del. Super. Apr. 17, 2003).

56. GTE Corp., 372 F.3d at 606

into property policies. Some insurance companies take the position that only the hardware is "physical" and subject to coverage, with no coverage available for "intangible" data. Other insurance companies see the issue differently. Some policies resolve the issue with policy language, specifying that covered or insured property includes "electronic data processing equipment," "records on media," "data," and the like.

Insurance companies often are quick to argue that computer-related remediation costs are not covered because they do not protect "physical loss of or damage to" insured property. The success of such arguments depends on the nature of the property that was protected, the legal precedent about whether such property is covered under property policies and the jurisdiction—or even the particular court or judge—before which the argument is being made.

Sometimes the answer lies in the language of the policies themselves. For example, some insurance policies address head-on whether computer code and data constitute physical property subject to coverage under property policies by adding the following policy provision:

> Physical loss or damage shall include any destruction, distortion, or corruption of any computer data, coding, program or software except as hereinafter excluded.[57]

Policyholders who undertake remediation efforts are not only acting prudently but also are fulfilling the intent of the sue and labor provision. As one federal court noted, the purpose of this clause "is to encourage and bind the [policyholder] to take steps to prevent a threatened loss for which the [insurance company] would be liable if it occurred, and when a loss does occur to take steps to diminish the amount of the loss."[58]

The sue and labor provision also works to the advantage of the insurance company. While remediation costs are substantial, the price tag for failing to take precautionary measures in preparation for predictable weather and environmental events could be catastrophic. It is often recognized that the purpose of the sue and labor clause is to reimburse

57. *Id.* at 605.

58. White Star S.S. Co. v. North British & Mercantile Ins. Co., 48 F. Supp. 808, 813 (E.D. Mich. 1943).

the policyholder for those expenditures that are made primarily for the benefit of the insurance company to reduce or eliminate a covered loss. Moreover, property insurance policies often mandate that the policyholder incur sue and labor expenses to protect insured property. In one case, a federal court of appeals ruled that compliance with the sue and labor clause is not optional.

General Liability Insurance Policies

General liability insurance policies protect businesses when their activities or products harm someone else's property or person. It is sometimes referred to as "litigation insurance" because a general liability policy provides, in most cases, an unlimited defense, outside of the policy limits.[59] This type of protection can be essential because often, litigation costs can end up more extensive than the costs of settlements or judgments themselves.

Coverage Agreement

Typically, insuring agreements in general liability insurance policies require the insurance company to pay sums that the policyholder is legally obligated to pay as damages because of bodily injury or property damage. The following provision of a standard form drafted by the Insurance Services Office is representative:

> We will pay those sums that the insured becomes legally obligated to pay as damages because of "bodily injury" or "property damage" to which this insurance applies. We will have the right and duty to defend the insured against any "suit" seeking those damages.[60]

This form further provides that its coverage "applies to 'bodily injury' and 'property damage' only if: (1) the 'bodily injury' or 'property damage'

59. *See* ISO Form CG 00 01 04 13, at Section I, Coverage, Coverage A—Bodily Injury and Property Damage Liability, 1. Insuring Agreement (2021) ("Our right and duty to defend ends when we have used up the applicable limit of insurance in the payment of judgments or settlements under Coverages A or B or medical expenses under Coverage C.").

60. *See* ISO Form CG 00 01 04 13.

is caused by an 'occurrence' that takes place in the 'coverage territory'; and (2) the 'bodily injury' or 'property damage' occurs during the policy period," among other conditions.[61]

Whether an insurance company has a duty to defend its policyholder is typically triggered by the allegations[62] in the underlying complaint, Potentially Responsible Person (PRP) letter, or other administrative demand—all of which are subject to coverage.[63] The majority of jurisdictions confine their assessment to the four corners of the pleadings, while others look beyond the pleadings to determine if the duty to defend is triggered. Where the claims potentially fall within coverage, there is a duty to defend.[64] The insurance company's duty to defend its policyholder is broader than its duty to pay a settlement or judgment.[65] Courts have held that insurance companies owe a broad duty to defend claims that could be indemnified under the insurance policy, even where the evidence suggests—but does not conclusively establish—that the loss may not be covered.[66]

61. *See id.* § I(1)(b)(1), (2).

62. *See* Am. & Foreign Ins. Co. v. Jerry's Sport Ctr., Inc., 2 A.3d 526 (Penn. 2010) ("[T]he duty to defend is triggered when a claim against the insured is potentially covered by the insurance policy." (citing Casper v. Am. Guar. & Liab. Ins. Co., 184 A.2d 247, 249 (Penn. 1962) (holding that where the acts complained of in the complaint cannot be construed as alleging damages covered by the insurance policy, the claims were not potentially within the scope of the policy and the insurer was under no duty to defend)); Erie Ins. Exch. v. Transamerica Ins. Co., 533 A.2d 1363 (Penn. 1987) ("If the complaint filed against the insured avers facts which would support a recovery that is covered by the policy, it is the duty of the insurer to defend until such time as the claim is confined to a recovery that the policy does not cover."); *compare* Monroe Guar. Ins. Co. v. BITCO Gen. Ins. Corp., 640 S.W.3d 195 (Tex. 2022), *with* Equine Assisted Grown and Learning Ass'n v. Carolina Cas. Ins. Co., 266 P.3d 733 (Utah 2011) (permitting consideration of extrinsic evidence to determine duty to defend)).

63. *See, e.g.*, Aire Frio, S.A. v. U.S. Fidelity & Guar. Co., 309 F. Supp. 1388 (D. Canal Zone 1970) (proceedings before industry board of contract appeal); Madawick Contracting Co. v. Travelers Ins. Co., 120 N.E.2d 520 (N.Y. 1954) (arbitration proceedings); Cmty. Unit Sch. Dist. No. 5, Cnty. of Whiteside and Lee v. Country Mut. Ins. Co., 95 Ill. App. 3d 272 (Ill. App. Ct. 1981) (actions before administrative agencies); Avondale Indus., Inc. v. Travelers Indem. Co., 887 F.2d 1200 (2d Cir. 1989) ("potentially responsible person" letter").

64. A duty to defend an insured arises if any part of the claim is *arguably* within the scope of the policy's coverage, and the burden is on the insurer to prove that a claim clearly falls outside the coverage. *See* Prahm v. Rupp Constr. Co., 277 N.W.2d 389, 390 (Minn.1979).

65. Hartford Cas. Ins. Co. v. Swift Distrib., Inc., 59 Cal. 4th 277 (Cal. 2014).

66. *See id.* at 287 (citing Gray v. Zurich Ins. Co., 65 Cal. 2d 263, 277–78 (Cal. 1966); *see also* Montrose Chem. Corp. v. Superior Court, 6 Cal. 4th 287, 299 (Cal. 1993).

Exclusions

CGL policies often contain an array of exclusions that limit the coverage provided by the insuring agreements. While it is difficult to predict which of the almost two dozen exclusions in a form commercial general liability insurance policy are likely to be the subject of coverage litigation involving climate change claims, two exclusions already have been the subject of much litigation in this area: the exclusions for "expected or intended injury" and "pollution."[67]

The standard form commercial general liability insurance policy excludes coverage for bodily injury or property damage "expected or intended from the standpoint of the insured."[68] Some courts interpret this provision to mean that it is immaterial whether the policyholder's act itself was "expected or intended" and instead focus on the question of whether the policyholder expected or intended the injury or damage.[69] Other courts adopt a different approach and require that an insurance company establish that (1) the policyholder's acts were intentional and (2) the injury was expected.[70] If an insurance company raises this exclusion in response to a demand for coverage for climate change liabilities, courts should expect to hear a robust debate about whether the policyholder's acts were intentional, whether the alleged harm resulted from those intentional acts, and whether the policyholder expected or intended for that harm to occur as a result of those acts.

The pollution exclusion found in many post-1980s commercial general liability insurance policies and its applicability to climate change also has been the focus of litigation thus far, which will continue. That exclusion states, in relevant part, that the policy does not apply to:

---

67. *See* ISO Form CG 00 01 04 13, at Section 1—Coverages, Exclusions ¶¶ 2(a), (f).

68. *Id.* at Exclusions ¶ 2(a).

69. *See, e.g.*, City of Johnstown, N.J. v. Bankers Standard Ins. Co., 877 F.2d 1146 (2d Cir. 1998) (exclusion turns on whether the policyholder intended to cause the harm); *see also* James Graham Brown Found., Inc. v. St. Paul Fire & Mine Ins. Co., 814 S.W.2d 273 (Ky. 1991) (coverage for injury that is not expected or intended from the standpoint of the policyholder even if the act was intentional and the injury was foreseeable).

70. *See, e.g.*, Physicians Ins. Co. v. Swanson, 569 N.E.2d 906 (Ohio 1991); *see also* Certain Underwriters at Lloyd's, London v. NL Indus., Inc., No. 2021-00241, 2022 WL 867910 (N.Y. App. Div. Mar. 24, 2022) (exclusions for expected or intended injury required finding that policyholder actually expected or intended resulting harm).

> (1) "Bodily injury" or "property damage" arising out of the actual, alleged or threatened discharge, dispersal, seepage, migration, release or escape of "pollutants": (a) At or from any premises, site or location which is or was at any time owned or occupied by, or rented or loaned to, any insured[.]

Thus far, much of the litigation concerning the pollution exclusion has focused on whether there has been a "discharge" etc. and whether the substance at issue falls within the definition of "pollutants."[71] In the case of climate change litigation, as with most litigation concerning the pollution exclusion, the disputes may involve questions about whether, for example, the gases alleged to have caused or contributed to climate change, are "pollutants" as defined by the insurance policy.[72] While the U.S. Supreme Court has found in the affirmative on this issue outside of the coverage context,[73] litigation in the context of insurance coverage and the pollution exclusion is starting to follow.

Additionally, insurance companies may assert that the alleged effects of climate change on business operations were foreseeable, and therefore do not meet the definition of "occurrence"—that is, "an accident, including continuous or repeated exposure to conditions, which results in bodily injury or property damage neither expected nor intended from the standpoint of the insured"—so as to trigger coverage under the terms of general liability policies. Courts have held, however, that the policyholder must have "subjectively intended" to cause the injury allegedly resulting from its acts or omissions for such events to be precluded from the definition of "occurrence" under the policies.[74]

If the disputes concerning coverage for environmental claims are any indication, disputes between policyholders and insurance companies about whether commercial general liability insurance policies cover

---

71. *See, e.g.*, Barney Greengrass, Inc. v. Lumbermens Mut. Cas. Co., 445 F. App'x 411, 413 (2d Cir. 2011); Mellin v. N. Sec. Ins. Co., Inc., A.3d 799 (N.H. 2015).

72. EPA, *Overview of Greenhouse Gases*, https://www.epa.gov/ghgemissions/overview-greenhouse-gases (last visited Oct. 25, 2023); *see also* Donaldson v. Urb. Land Ints., Inc., 211 Wis. 2d 224 (Wis. 1997)

73. *See* Massachusetts v. EPA, 49 U.S. 497 (2007); *see* detailed discussion *infra* note 151.

74. *See, e.g.*, Est. of Schuch v. State Farm Fire & Cas. Co., 552 F. Supp. 3d 1154, 1164 (D. Or. 2021).

claims alleging that a policyholder's activities contributed to climate change may become more prevalent. While there have been relatively few such cases at present, there have been an increasing number of creative complaints that attempt to hold American corporations responsible for climate change. A corresponding increase in the number of coverage cases on this topic is inevitable, as policyholders will continue to submit these lawsuits to their commercial liability insurance companies for defense and indemnification. This is an area to watch carefully in the years and decades to come.

Policy Layers: Primary, Umbrella, and Excess

A typical general liability insurance program will have multiple layers of coverage: primary, umbrella, and excess. The first layer is the "primary" layer. The role of the insurance company in the primary layer is to defend claims, pay settlements, and pay judgments up to the limits of the policy. When a judgment exceeds the limits of the first layer of insurance, then the succeeding layers step in to pay the amount that exceeds the limits of the primary layer.

An umbrella policy is different than a follow-form excess policy because, as the term "umbrella" implies, it provides broader coverage than the policies over which it sits. Umbrella insurance policies may contain provisions that obligate the umbrella insurance company to drop down and pay when underlying insurance policies do not. Typical umbrella language provides:

> The Company Shall:
>
> (a) defend any suit against the Insured alleging liability insured under the provisions of this policy and seeking recovery for damages on account thereof even if such suit is groundless, false or fraudulent, but the Company shall have the right to make such investigation and negotiation and settlement of any claim or suit as may be deemed expedient by the Company.[75]

75. Home Ins. Co. v. Nat'l Union Fire Ins. of Pittsburgh, 658 N.W.2d 522, 529 (Minn. 2003), *as modified on denial of reh'g* (Apr. 3, 2003).

One court concluded that such language "obligated the umbrella insurer to pay for defense costs for defending claims arising solely under the umbrella insurer's broader (thus primary) coverage."[76] Thus, policyholders and their counsel should be aware that even if lower layers of insurance deny a claim, there may be coverage under the umbrella policy. An excess insurance policy may have the same policy terms as the primary or umbrella policy, usually achieved by simply "following the form" of that policy, or may have different conditions and exclusions, either through inclusion of an entirely independent policy form or by modifying the underlying form through specific endorsements. In either case, the excess policy usually does not have an active duty to defense until the policyholder incurs expenses in an amount equal to the underlying limits.

Specialized Insurance Policies for Environmental Risks

Because it has been standard since the 1970s for general liability insurance policies to contain exclusions for pollution,[77] many policyholders

---

76. *Id.*

77. *See* State Farm Fire & Cas. Co. v. Dantzler, 852 N.W.2d 918, 930 nn.23, 24 (Neb. 2014) (citing Nautilus Ins. Co. v. Jabar, 188 F.3d 27 (1st Cir. 1999) (applying Maine law); Devcon Intern. Corp. v. Reliance Ins. Co., 609 F.3d 214 (3d Cir. 2010) (applying Virgin Island law)); Keggi v. Northbrook Property and Cas. Ins., 199 Ariz. 43, 13 P.3d 785 (Ariz. App. Ct. 2000); MacKinnon v. Truck Ins. Exch., 31 Cal. 4th 635 (Cal. 2003); Am. States Ins. Co. v. Koloms, 177 Ill. 2d 473 (Ill. 1997); Motorists Mut. Ins. Co. v. RSJ, Inc., 926 S.W.2d 679 (Ky. App. Ct. 1996); Doerr v. Mobil Oil Corp., 774 So. 2d 119 (La. 2000), *corrected on other grounds on rehearing*, 782 So. 2d 573 (La. 2001); Clendenin Bros. v. U.S. Fire, 889 A.2d 387 (Md. 2006); W. Alliance Ins. Co. v. Gill, 426 Mass. 115 (Mass. 1997); Century Sur. Co. v. Casino W., Inc., 130 Nev. 395 (Nev. 2014); Nav–Its, Inc. v. Selective Ins. Co., 869 A.2d 929 (N.J. 2005); Andersen v. Highland House Co., 93 Ohio St. 3d 547 (Ohio 2001); Gainsco Ins. Co. v. Amoco Production Co., 53 P.3d 1051 (Wyo. 2002); Auto–Owners Ins. Co. v. Potter, 105 Fed. Appx. 484 (4th Cir. 2004) (applying North Carolina law); Barney Greengrass, Inc. v. Lumbermans Mut. Cas. Co., No. 09 Civ. 7697 (NRB), 2010 WL 3069560 (S.D.N.Y. July 27, 2010) (memorandum opinion); Nat'l Elect. Mfrs. v. Gulf Underwriters Ins., 162 F.3d 821 (4th Cir.1998) (applying District of Columbia law); Certain Underwriters at Lloyd's v. C.A. Turner Constr., 112 F.3d 184 (5th Cir. 1997) (applying Texas law); Am. States Ins. Co. v. Nethery, 79 F.3d 473 (5th Cir.1996) (applying Mississippi law); Gerdes v. Am. Fam. Mut. Ins. Co., 713 F. Supp. 2d 1290 (D. Kan. 2010); Mountain States Mut. Cas. Co. v. Roinestad, 296 P.3d 1020 (Colo. 2013); Heyman Assoc. v. Ins. Co. of State of Pa., 653 A.2d 122 (Conn. 1995); Deni Assoc. v. State Farm Ins., 711 So. 2d 1135 (Fla. 1998); Reed v. Auto–Owners Ins. Co., 284 Ga. 286, 667 S.E.2d 90 (2008); Bituminous Cas. v. Sand Livestock Systems, 728 N.W.2d 216 (Iowa 2007); McKusick v. Travelers Indem., 246 Mich. App. 329 (Mich. 2001); Midwest Fam. Mut. Ins. Co. v. Wolters, 831 N.W.2d 628 (Minn. 2013); Heringer v. Am. Fam. Mut. Ins. Co., 140 S.W.3d 100 (Mo. App. Ct. 2004); Bituminous Cas. Corp. v. Cowen Constr., Inc., 55 P.3d 1030 (Okla. 2002); Madison Constr. v. Harleysville Mut. Ins., 735 A.2d 100 (Pa. 1999); PBM Nutritionals, LLC v. Lexington Ins. Co.,

choose to purchase either endorsements or stand-alone insurance policies that specifically cover environmental liabilities.

Pollution Legal Liability Insurance Policies

One example of a stand-alone policy is a pollution legal liability (PLL) policy. A PLL policy is an insurance policy that covers risks associated with the environmental harm that may be associated with owning or operating a site. Examples include disposal sites and sites on which contracting or other operations are taking place. In general, a pollution legal liability insurance policy covers both first-party and third-party losses. For example, a PLL policy will generally cover first-party liability for clean-up. That policy may also cover defense and indemnity costs associated with third-party claims.[78]

PLL policies can provide coverage for past, current, and future environmental exposures, which would otherwise be excluded from general liability policies. Additionally, PLL policies can provide business interruption coverage where the loss results from a pollution condition. For example, one of the insurance policies at issue in *TerraMatrix, Inc. v. U.S. Fire Insurance Co.*[79] contained the following provision for contractor's pollution legal liability:

> To INDEMNIFY the INSURED for all sums in excess of the Retention amount . . . which the INSURED shall become legally obligated to pay as DAMAGES as a result of CLAIMS FIRST MADE AGAINST THE INSURED AND REPORTED IN WRITING TO THE COMPANY, IN WRITING, DURING THE POLICY PERIOD . . . for POLLUTION CONDITIONS arising out of the performance of PROFESSIONAL SERVICES rendered by the INSURED[.][80]

---

283 Va. 624 (Va. 2012); Quadrant Corp. v. Am. States Ins. Co., 154 Wash.2d 165 (Wash. 2005); Clipper Mill Fed., LLC v. Cincinnati Ins. Co., No. JFM–10–1647, 2010 WL 4117273 (D. Md. Oct. 20, 2010) (memorandum opinion); CBL & Assoc. Mgmt., Inc. v. Lumbermens Mut. Cas. Co., No. 1:05–CV–210, 2006 WL 2087625 (E.D. Tenn. July 25, 2006) (memorandum opinion).

78. *See* Baxter Dunaway, *Environmental Liability Coverage—The Pollution Legal Liability ("PLL")*, 5 L. Distressed Real Est. § 51:30 (2023).

79. TerraMatrix, Inc. v. U.S. Fire Ins. Co., 939 P.2d 483 (Colo. App. Ct. 1997).

80. *See id.* at 490.

The policy defined "Professional Services" as site assessment, remedial investigations, feasibility studies, environmental impact assessment, hydrogeological and geotechnical investigations, mine and mineral engineering, construction management, asbestos identification/inspection.[81]

Parametric Insurance Policies

Parametric insurance policies are contracts that insure a policyholder "against the occurrence of a specific event by payment of a set amount based on the magnitude of the *event* as opposed to the magnitude of the loss."[82] "The amount of payment, the parameter, and a third party responsible for verifying that the parameter was triggered must all be specified in the contract."[83]

In contrast to traditional insurance policies, with a parametric policy there is no requirement that property damage or loss occur.[84] Thus, the insurance company's obligation to pay is triggered by the parameter being satisfied.[85] With increasingly extreme or unpredictable weather impacting construction and other projects, parametric insurance may be a way to mitigate delay damages when a project is not completed because of extreme weather.[86] A parametric policy that includes a particular weather condition as a parameter may help to transfer the risk and financial impact of those delay damages.[87]

Examples of a parametric policies include: payment of $1 million if rainfall of four inches or more in 24 hours, as measured by the National Weather Service, falls at a particular location; payment of $1 million if an earthquake with magnitude of 4.0 or greater, as measured by the U.S. Geological Survey; and payment of $1 million if windspeeds of 40 mph or more are sustained for four hours, as measured by the National Weather Service, and are sustained at a particular location.

---

81. *Id.*

82. *See* NAIC, *Parametric Disaster Insurance* (June 1, 2023), https://content.naic.org/cipr-topics/parametric-disaster-insurance.

83. *See id.*

84. ZURICH, *Zurich Construction Weather Parametric Insurance* (2022), https://www.zurichna.com.

85. ZURICH, *Weather Parametric Insurance: What Is Parametric Insurance?*, https://www.zurichna.com (last visited Oct. 20, 2023).

86. *See id.*

87. *See id.*

A parametric policy's straightforward approach of "if parameter met, then payment of [pre-set amount] within x days" can be a predicable way for a policyholder to transfer risk of loss under certain specified conditions (i.e., parameters) and avoid the uncertainty, delay, and cost associated with loss adjustment. Insurance companies describe parametric policies as a way to avoid claims adjustment, speed up payment of proceeds, and afford certainty of outcome for both the policyholder and the insurance company.[88]

With the frequency of severe weather events increasing, businesses that are penalized for missing completion deadlines may look to parametric insurance policies that insure specific weather-related risks, even when there is no physical loss or damage caused by the weather event. As described by the National Association of Insurance Commissioners, "the term parametric insurance describes a type of insurance contract that insures a policyholder against the occurrence of a specific event by paying a set amount based on the magnitude of the event, as opposed to the magnitude of the losses in a traditional indemnity policy."[89] Parametric insurance policies are different from the traditional property, builders risk, and other inland marine policies because while those policies tie coverage to physical loss or damage, parametric insurance insures the policyholder against the occurrence of a weather event itself, irrespective of whether there is property damage caused by that event.[90] The event is the parameter that triggers insurance.[91]

Flood Policies Through the National Flood Insurance Program

In response to public concern about the coverage available under property policies for damage from flood, the federal government created the National Flood Insurance Program (NFIP) in 1968. The NFIP had two

---

88. Swiss Re Corporate Solutions, *What Is parametric insurance?* (July 7, 2023), https://corporatesolutions.swissre.com/insights/knowledge/what_is_parametric_insurance.html ("With its transparent and fast claims payment and ability to offer a payout without actual physical damage to an asset, parametric or index-based solutions are often brought to the table of discussion when covering hard to insure risks.").

89. NAIC, *Parametric Disaster Insurance* (June 1, 2023), https://content.naic.org/cipr-topics/parametric-disaster-insurance.

90. *See, e.g.*, ZURICH, *supra* note 81; *see also* ZURICH, *supra* note 82.

91. *See* Andre Martin, *What Is Parametric Insurance?*, Swiss Re Corp. Sols. (Aug. 1, 2018), https://corporatesolutions.swissre.com/insights/knowledge/what_is_parametric_insurance.html.

purposes: to share the risk of flood losses through flood insurance and to reduce flood damages by restricting floodplain development.[92] Managed by the Federal Emergency Management Agency (FEMA), the flood policies are delivered to the public by a network of private insurance companies. FEMA retains responsibility for underwriting all of them. While the coverage is notoriously limited, many policyholders find it preferable to the alternative of not having any flood coverage at all. Still, the program has been extended only until September 30, 2025. Although many proposals have been made to extend it, and there have been continuous [] extensions, the long-term survival of the program is uncertain.

Evolving Insurance Requirements—and Market Limitations

Following the Exxon Valdez oil spill, which at the time was the largest in U.S. history, the U.S. Congress passed the Oil Pollution Act of 1990 (OPA).[93] The OPA established the Oil Spill Compensation Fund, which made the party responsible for the discharge liable for the removal costs and economic and natural resource damage, and required the responsible party for certain sized vessels and offshore facilities to establish financial responsibility sufficient to meet the maximum amount of liability to which such persons could be subjected under the act.[94] As summarized by the Congressional Research Service in 2010, the purpose of the act was "to strengthen the safety and environmental practices in the offshore energy exploration and production business, to create a system of so-called 'financial responsibility laws' and compulsory liability insurance combined with strict liability standards, and to place limitations on liability."[95]

Twenty years later, in 2010, the Deepwater Horizon spill eclipsed the Exxon Valdez spill to become the largest offshore oil spill in U.S. history.[96] Prior to Deepwater Horizon, a responsible party for an offshore

---

92. *See, e.g.*, FEMA, *Earthquake Insurance* (Dec. 8, 2022), https://www.fema.gov/emergency-managers/risk-management/earthquake/insurance.

93. OPA 1012 (33 U.S.C. § 2712).

94. *See* H.R. 1465, 101st Cong. (1990).

95. Rawle O. King, *Deepwater Horizon Oil Spill Disaster: Risk, Recovery, and Insurance Implications*, Congressional Research Service (July 12, 2010), https://sgp.fas.org/crs/misc/R41320.pdf.

96. Damage Assessment, Remediation, and Restoration Program, *Deep Horizon* (Oct. 5, 2022), https://darrp.noaa.gov/oil-spills/deepwater-horizon.

facility would be liable for all removal costs plus up to $137.69 million for damages for each incident.[97] According to an estimate from BP itself, the estimated total cost of the Deepwater Horizon spill was more than $65 billion.

Following that spill and perhaps prompted by the disparity between the limitation on liability and the actual clean-up costs,[98] the U.S. Congress reviewed "clean-up and damage compensation mechanisms, as well as of ways to facilitate future oil spill prevention, response and recovery."[99] Current law does not limit a facility's liability for clean-up costs, but it does limit an offshore facility's liability for economic and natural resources damages to $75 million per incident. In addition, facilities may be required to demonstrate their ability to pay in the event of a loss. Businesses may demonstrate financial ability in many ways, and one way in is by establishing that they have insurance.

In recent years, certain insurance companies have decided not to sell insurance to industries that they consider to be "emission intensive" or particular contributors to climate change. Thus far, as least four insurance companies have announced that they will reduce their exposure to what they refer to as "emission-intensive" sectors.[100] Others have announced "new underwriting criteria for oil and gas extraction projects that will require clients to reduce methane emissions, a byproduct of oil and gas production that are among the most severe greenhouse gases."[101] Policyholders with particular exposure to such risks should be alert to future efforts by insurance companies to impose further restrictions, and may choose to take actions when appropriate to oppose them.

97. U.S. Coast Guard, *Oil Pollution Act Liability Limits in 2020* (Feb. 22, 2021), https://www.uscg.mil/Portals/0/NPFC/docs/PDFs/Reports/2021-02-22_Oil_Pollution_Act_Liability_Limits_in_2020.pdf?ver=ssccbIFAQ6kGAbrDkIv4Zg%3D%3D&timestamp=1614104947084#:~:text=For%20incidents%20involving%20discharges%20from,both%20removal%20costs%20and%20damages.

98. The explosion that occurred on the Deepwater Horizon killed 11 men and injured others.

99. *See* King, *supra* note 91.

100. *See* Kyle Bakx, *How a Lack of Insurance Is a Growing Threat to the Oilsands*, CBC News (May 21, 2021), https://www.cbc.ca/news/business/bakx-oilsands-tmx-insurance-1.6030960.

101. *See* News Releases, *Chubb Announces New Climate and Conservation-Focused Underwriting Standards for Oil and Gas Extraction*, Chubb (Mar. 22, 2023), https://news.chubb.com/2023-03-22-Chubb-Announces-New-Climate-and-Conservation-Focused-Underwriting-Standards-for-Oil-and-Gas-Extraction.

Directors and Officers Insurance Policies

Directors and Officers (D&O) insurance policies provide companies and their executives protection from possible legal liability arising out of climate-related risks. In recent years, as climate change and intensifying natural disasters have generated increased climate-related liability claims, the number of cases implicating D&O coverage have also increased.

Cases Triggering D&O Coverage Related to Climate Change Risks

Cases triggering D&O coverage arise under litigation theories related to directors' duties, including (1) failure to company with environmental regulatory obligations, (2) failure to disclosure climate-related risks, (3) failure to adapt investment strategies, (4) failure to adapt to physical impacts of climate change, and (5) failure to mitigate greenhouse gas emissions. Vehicles for such litigation include shareholder class actions and derivative lawsuits. Shareholder class actions typically allege that a company's share price suffered due to climate change during a time when the executives engaged in misleading or deceptive conduct with respect to the impact of such change. On the other hand, derivative actions arise out of the principle that the shareholders of a company require a remedy to force a company to bring proceedings against directors who, by virtue of the control they exercise over company management, could not otherwise be held accountable. In a derivative action, damages that become payable are awarded to the company rather than the shareholders bringing the claim.

For example, D&O policies increasingly come into play regarding allegations of a director's failure to comply with regulatory obligations. In 2002, Congress passed the Sarbanes-Oxley Act requiring directors and officers of a company to report its environmental liability to the U.S. Securities and Exchange Commission (SEC). More recently, the SEC proposed mandatory reporting of companies' climate risks, including the level of greenhouse gas emissions companies produce, both directly and indirectly, how climate risk affects their business, and their plans to meet climate-related goals.

Various lawsuits—including suits filed by local municipalities and states seeking damages because of climate change, and shareholder suits alleging harm to investors stemming from misrepresentations of climate change risks or of actions allegedly taken to mitigate those risks—have already been brought against companies. For example, in *ClientEarth v. Shell Plc & Ors*, activist shareholders sued the directors of Shell Oil about aspects of climate change.[102] ClientEarth, an environmental law organization, alleged that the directors were personally liable for their failure to prepare for net zero emissions pursuant to the Paris Accords.[103] Specifically, the lawsuit alleges that 11 members of Shell Oil's board are mismanaging climate risk, breaching company law by failing to implement an energy transition strategy that aligns with the landmark 2015 Paris Agreement.[104]

Similarly, the attorneys general of New York, Massachusetts, and the U.S. Virgin Islands instituted investigations to determine whether Exxon Mobil Corporation misrepresented to investors how climate change might impact its business. These investigations resulted in enforcement actions brought by states that in turn resulted in private civil litigation against directors and officers. For example, the New York attorney general alleged that Exxon disclosed a higher "proxy cost" of carbon to the investing public, but for internal purposes used a lower greenhouse gas price in connection with making investment and business decisions.[105] Relatedly, the Massachusetts attorney general alleged that Exxon misled consumers regarding its knowledge of climate change, and deceived investors and consumers regarding systematic financial risks of climate change to the economy.[106] The State of California contended that General Motors Corporation and other auto manufacturers were responsible for "approximately nine percent of the world's carbon dioxide emissions and over thirty percent of emissions from sources within the State of California," making them "substantial contributors . . . to global warming,

102. *See* ClientEarth v. Shell Plc & Ors, et al., [2023] EWHC 1137 (Ch), Decision on Prima Facie Case (Eng. and Wales High Ct. May 12, 2023).

103. *See id.* ¶ 27.

104. *Id.* ¶¶ 27–28.

105. *See, e.g.*, People v. Exxon Mobil Corp., No. 452044/2018, 2019 WL 6795771 (Sup. Ct. N.Y. Cnty. Dec. 10, 2019) (ultimately, after trial, the New York court rejected the New York attorney general's claims).

106. *See* Commonwealth v. Exxon Mobil Corp., 187 N.E.3d 393 (Mass. 2022).

and to the adverse impacts upon California."[107] These cases demonstrate that the potential for directors and officers to face liability related to climate change increases with the development of the legal landscape.

Increasing societal concern regarding climate change is also a major factor in recent corporate emphasis on environmental, social, and governance (ESG) issues. One aspect of ESG is sustainability, including making companies more socially conscious and responsive to climate change. Companies are instituting more aggressive programs to reduce their emissions and carbon footprint, particular favorites of activist investors. A company's failure to meet its goals can result in shareholder suits against the company's officers and directors.[108]

In at least some cases, the wording of the complaints give rise—at the very least—to traditional duties to defend. The complaint in *People v. General Motors*, for example, alleged property damage, such as through erosion of the coastline and shrinkage of the snow pack; bodily injury, such as through respiratory problems, heatstroke, and heart attacks; and actual damages, such as through expenditures needed to reduce and respond to these environmental changes.[109] While the Northern District of California refused to impose liability on grounds that these allegations raised non-justiciable political questions,[110] that does not preclude courts from imposing liability in such cases in the future. It is common for insurance companies to deny coverage when new issues arise—such as asbestos and pollution claims in from the 1970s forward—only to find that such coverage is well established over time.

---

107. *See* Amended Compl. at ¶ 3, People v. Gen. Motors Corp., No. C06-05755 EMC, 2007 WL 2726871 (N.D. Cal. Sept. 17, 2007) (Dkt. No. 6), 2006 WL 3069165.

108. *See, e.g.*, Meyer v. Jinkosolar Holdings Co., Ltd., 761 F.3d 245 (2d Cir. 2014) (Second Circuit held that shareholders could proceed with their "greenwashing" lawsuit—alleging misrepresentations of the success in meeting its environment goals—against the company and its officers, directors, and underwriters).

109. *See* Amended Compl., *supra* note 101 ¶¶ 1, 4, 21, 43–56; *see also* State of California Dep't of Just., *Attorney General Lockyer Files Suit Against "Big Six" Automakers for Global Warming Damages in California* (Sept. 20, 2006), https://oag.ca.gov/news/press-releases/attorney-general-lockyer-files-lawsuit-against-big-six-automakers-global-warming.

110. *See* People v. Gen. Motors Corp., No. C06-05755 MJJ, 2007 WL 2726871, at *10 (N.D. Cal. Sept. 17, 2007) ("The Court finds that injecting itself into the global warming thicket at this juncture would require an initial policy determination of the type reserved for the political branches of government."). This holding, however, raises an interesting question about the potential role of political risk insurance policies.

D&O Coverage Issues

While D&O insurance policies are in place to respond to these types of claims, climate change suits against directors and officers may present difficult coverage issues. Such lawsuits may allege, for example, that a company failed to inform prospective investors of "trends or uncertainties likely to have a material effect on the . . . company's business."[111]

Here again, basic coverage principles will come into play, starting with analysis of the plain language of the D&O policies as well as the complaints. Insurance companies, for example, may attempt to deny coverage by relying on the exclusions that often are found in D&O policies regarding pollution or cleanup costs. They may deny coverage even for defense costs when complaints against the companies rest expressly upon allegations of "pollution" and "contamination." They will presumably look for support in the emerging body of law regarding climate change. In *Massachusetts v. E.P.A.*, for example, the Supreme Court found that the greenhouse gas carbon dioxide constitutes an "air pollutant" as described under the U.S. Clear Air Act,[112] whereas courts often limit a pollution exclusion's application to "traditional environmental pollution."

Proximate cause may become an issue in these cases as well. In *Sealed Air Corp. v. Royal Indemnity Co.*, shareholders alleged that the company and its directors and officers misrepresented the company's environmental exposure.[113] The insurance company denied coverage under the D&O policy citing the policy's pollution exclusion. The New Jersey Appellate Division disagreed with the insurance company's position, however, and found for coverage. The court held that the proximate cause of the loss was not the pollution but the misrepresentations and, therefore, the D&O policy's pollution exclusion did not apply to preclude coverage.

111. *See* Regulation S-K Item 303, 17 C.F.R. § 229.303 (2021).

112. Massachusetts v. E.P.A., 549 U.S. 497 (2007). *See e.g.*, Weaver v. Royal Ins. Co. of America, 674 A.2d 975, 977-8 (1996) (injury caused by ingestion of lead paint dust particles not encompassed by pollution exclusion because exclusion applies only to environmental pollution); Nautilus Ins. Co. v. Jabar, 188 F.3d 27, 30 (1st Cir. 1999) (pollution exclusion applied only to environmental pollution, and not to injury from fumes discharged by roofing products used by policyholder in repairing roof); Beahm v. Pautsch, 180 Wis. 2d 574 (Ct. App. 1993) (exclusion does not "exclude more than coverage for liability for environmental damage"); Karoll v. Atomergic Chemetal Corp., 194 A.D.2d 715, 600 (2d Dep't 1993) (pollution exclusion can "be reasonably interpreted to apply only to instances of environmental pollution.)

113. Sealed Air Corp. v. Royal Indemnity Co., 404 N.J. Super. 363 (App. Div. 2008).

Another exclusion in D&O policies that may present coverage disputes for climate change-related suits is the so-called conduct exclusion. The conduct exclusion purports to exclude coverage for intentional, willful, or deliberate misconduct or criminal acts. This exclusion may limit or eliminate coverage, for example, in lawsuits alleging that the company's directors and officers intentionally implemented a program of regulatory noncompliance, or in lawsuits alleging the deliberate withholding of information relating to the company's climate-change-related vulnerabilities. Importantly, however, this exclusion is often subject to a "final adjudication" requirement, so that it is not triggered until there is a final court decision finding such misconduct. Until that point, the insurance company must fund defense costs as they are incurred. If a final adjudication does eventually find such misconduct, the insurance company may be able to recover the defense costs it advanced.

Cyber Insurance

Cyber insurance is the newest frontier. It dates back only to the 1990s, as a response to the widely feared "Y2K problem."[114] Steve Haase of AIG drafted the first stand-alone cyber policy in 1997.[115] Since then, cyber insurance has grown exponentially.

Cyber insurance is relevant to environmental disasters and climate change in a myriad of ways. Every environmental event, for example, can lead to loss of data, loss of security over data, increased hacking, relocation expenses, and third-party claims arising from such losses.

Issues Specific to Cyber Coverage

When computers and their data are damaged or lost due to environmental events, policyholders submit claims for coverage under their traditional property policies. They reason that computers are physical property, and that data stored in their computers is physical as well. This

114. As policyholders contemplated the risk of widespread computer failures, they realized that their standard-form property and casualty insurance policies—drafted in the 1960s and 1970s—may be out of date. *See, e.g.*, Josephine Wolff, Cyberinsurance Policy: Rethinking Risk in an Age of Ransomware, Computer Fraud, Data Breaches, and Cyberattacks (2022).

115. *See* Andrea Wells, *What Agent Who First Wrote First Cyber Policy Thinks About Cyber Insurance Now*, Ins. J. (Mar. 1, 2018), https://www.insurancejournal.com/news/national/2018/03/01/481886.htm.

approach follows logically from the fact that many assets of a company that were formerly maintained in physical form now are maintained in electronic form. Since the assets were covered when they were maintained physically, they should continue to be covered in their electronic forms.

Unsurprisingly, insurance companies often disagree. They commonly submit that computer data is intangible, so the loss of such data is not the type of physical damage or loss that could ever be covered by property insurance. One such example is *American Guarantee & Liability Insurance Company v. Ingram, Micro Inc.*[116] There, the policyholder sought coverage under its property policy for losses incurred after a power outage damaged the computer system and a matrix switch. The insurance company denied coverage on grounds that the computer itself was not "physically damaged." Fortunately for policyholders, the court disagreed. It found that the computer was physically damaged for the one and a half hours that it took to manually reload the programming information that was lost due to the power outage.[117] It also found that the computer impulse was physically damaged for the eight hours it took to manually bypass the damaged matrix switch.[118] These findings correctly reflected the reality that until this work was completed, the system was inoperable.

Similarly, in *National Ink & Stitch, LLC v. State Auto Property & Casualty Insurance Co.*,[119] the policyholder sought coverage under its property policy for a data loss arising from a ransomware attack. The insurance company denied coverage on grounds that the damage was not physical, but the court ruled for the policyholder. The court relied heavily on that fact that the term "data" was qualified by the words "stored on such media." The court found that these words made clear that the policy provided coverage for the data itself.[120] In *Ashland Hospital Corp. v. Affiliated FM Insurance Co.*,[121] the policyholder sought coverage under

116. Am. Guar. & Liab. Ins. Co. v. Ingram, Micro Inc., No. 99-187 TUC ACM, 2000 WL 726789 (D. Ariz. Apr. 18, 2000).

117. *Id.* at *3.

118. *Id.*

119. Nat'l Ink & Stitch, LLC v. State Auto Prop. & Cas. Ins. Co., 435 F. Supp. 3d 679 (D. Md. 2020).

120. *Id.* at *682.

121. Ashland Hosp. Corp v. Affiliated FM Ins. Co., No. 11-16-DLB-EBA, 2013 WL 4400516 (E.D. Ky. Aug. 14, 2013).

its property policy when a loss of air conditioning caused its network to overheat, which prevented data access for several hours. The policyholder wanted replacement costs for computer hardware that was damaged when the network overheated. The insurance company denied that there was physical damage, as the computer system was not rendered completely inoperable. The court found for the policyholder yet again, holding that once the property was adversely affected by overheating, the resulting loss of reliability was a covered event. Under both an immediacy test and a proximate cause test, the court found the damage to the system to be "direct."[122]

Policies that Cover Cyber Losses

Property policies, or "businessowner's policies," are the first ones pulled off the shelf when policyholders suffer a cyber-related loss, as shown by the aforementioned cases. A major consequence of an environmental loss or a natural disaster can be business interruption, as when a natural disaster knocks out Internet service to a region and prevents policyholders from conducting business online. Increasingly, property policies and endorsements are tailored to such events, like Cyber Business Interruption and Extra Expense policies and System Failure Endorsements. The determination of coverage under such policies or endorsements typically turns on whether the loss can be considered an "actual impairment." That term was interpreted broadly by the U.S. District Court of Connecticut in 2022, and deemed to cover a loss of data, in *New England Systems, Inc. v. Citizens Insurance Company of America.*[123] The same outcome was reached that same year by the U.S. District Court of Minnesota, finding an "actual impairment" to arise from a bad actor's interference with a company's email system in *Fishbowl Solutions, Inc. v. Hanover Insurance Co.*[124]

---

122. *Id.* at *5.

123. New Eng. Sys., Inc. v. Citizens Ins. Co. of Am., No. 3:20-CV-01743 (SVN), 2022 WL 17585966 (D. Conn. Dec. 12, 2022).

124. Fishbowl Sols., Inc. v. Hanover Ins. Co. No. 21-cv-00794 (SRN/DJF), 2022 WL 16699749 (D. Minn. Nov. 3, 2022).

Commercial Crime Policies

Property and businessowners' policies are not the only ones to cover cyber losses. Commercial crime insurance policies may be triggered by cyber losses that arise from third-party interference with or invasion of computer systems. While coverage is available under traditional definitions of theft and fraud, these policies have increasingly added endorsements specifying that coverage for computer-related crime is included. With and without such endorsements, these policies have been found to cover such events as theft of money, theft of payment card and checking account data, fraudulent wire transfers, fraudulent card charges, regulatory counsel fees, and data restoration expenses.[125]

One endorsement commonly added in recent years is for losses arising from "social engineering." Social engineering is a ubiquitous term, typically used to describe the use of deception in email or social media to manipulate individuals into divulging confidential information or taking wrongful actions, such as transferring funds to thieves. Business owners should be cautious of such endorsements, however, as they are often like the proverbial wolf in sheep's clothing. While they are usually presented as expansions of coverage, they are commonly designed to *reduce* coverage—for example by providing very low limits of coverage for this particular type of fraud instead of the full policy limits that would otherwise apply.

The existence of coverage under the full policy limits for "social engineering fraud" is established clearly in *Medidata Solutions, Inc. v. Federal Insurance Co.*[126] There,[127] cybercriminals impersonated a senior executive of the policyholder, using fraudulent emails to direct employees to transfer money to the criminals' bank accounts. The fraudulent scheme worked, in that the money was transferred and then lost. The policyholder sought coverage under its commercial crime policy, and the Southern District of New York awarded more than $5 million to the policyholder for the fraud. The insurance company promptly appealed

125. *See, e.g.*, Valero Title Inc. v. RLI Ins. Co., No. 4:19-CV-443, 2021 WL 5154790, at *1 (S.D. Tex. Mar. 29, 2021), *aff'd sub nom.* Valero Title Inc. v. RLI Ins. Co., No. 22-20155, 2023 WL 1434270 (5th Cir. Feb. 1, 2023).

126. Medidata Sols., Inc. v. Fed. Ins. Co., 729 Fed. Appx. 117 (Mem) (2d. Cir. 2018).

127. *Id.*

to the Second Circuit, arguing there was no coverage because there was no third-party hacking or invasion of the computer system. The principal argument was that third-party crime or theft coverage did not apply because the transfer of funds was initiated by the employees themselves.

Fortunately for the policyholder, and for policyholders everywhere, the appeal was unsuccessful. The Second Circuit found that although the employees physically transferred the funds, they did so only because of an intrusion into the policyholder's email system through deceitful and dishonest means. Moreover, the attack made a change to a data element, as the email system's appearance was altered by the introduction of a code that misidentified the sender.[128] On this basis, the court affirmed the coverage awarded to the policyholder.

Third-Party Liability Policies

Liability policies can provide coverage when cyber incidents lead to third-party claims or litigation. Many cyber policies typically include a liability provision that covers privacy regulation proceedings and investigation expenses. Regulatory liability is a substantial risk, and the fines are becoming increasingly expensive. Although policyholders may rely primarily on their cyber policy to cover these expenses, cyber insurance may be insufficient, and there could be instances where covered claims are denied. When this occurs, other liability policies that may provide the policyholder with another level of protection against cyber claims include D&O insurance, E&O insurance, CGL coverage, and Employment Practices Liability Insurance.

Directors and Officers Liability Policies

Directors and officers insurance is another avenue for coverage after a cyber-related loss. One illustrative example is *Spec's Family Partners, Ltd. v. Hanover Insurance Co.*[129] There, the policyholder suffered two separate hacks of its computer system, exposing credit card numbers and customers' personal information to cybercriminals. The policyholder used a merchant bank to process the credit card transactions. After the cyber incident, the card companies presented the merchant bank with

128. *See id.* at 118.

129. *See* Spec's Fam. Partners, Ltd. v. Hanover Ins. Co., 739 Fed. Appx. 233 (5th Cir. 2018).

a $10 million "liability and assessment charge." Upon receipt, the merchant bank sent a demand letter to the policyholder asserting over $7 million in damages for noncompliance with the PCI Data Security Standards. The policyholder then sought coverage under their D&O policy. After the district court found in favor of the insurance company, the policyholder appealed to the Fifth Circuit, which reversed and found that the demand letters triggered the duty to defend because the claims implicated theories of general negligence and contract law.[130] On remand, the district court ruled that the insurance company was required to defend the policyholder against the claims made via the demand letter and fund the affirmative lawsuit commenced by the policyholder against the merchant bank.

Professional Services Policies

Coverage was found for the policyholder in 2020 in one of the best-known cases involving professional services policies: *FedEx Office & Print Services, Inc. v. Continental Casuality Co.*[131] There, the policyholder (FedEx) suffered a data breach at credit card machines connected to its kiosks around the country. As a result, FedEx faced a series of class action lawsuits that alleged violations of the Fair and Accurate Credit Transactions Act. FedEx sought coverage under its professional services policy, which defined a "Professional Services Claim" as "any Claim arising out of a Wrongful Act in the Performance of Professional Services."[132] The insurance company denied coverage, arguing that the event of "printing a receipt" is not part of "the performance of Professional Services." Applying California law, the court rejected this argument, ruling that printing a receipt "is one part of an integrated process unique to FedEx's business model in the performance of providing professional services through a self-service, multi-function kiosk . . . the user's credit card data is inextricably intertwined with the service itself." On this ground, the court found coverage by granting summary judgment in favor of FedEx.

130. *Id.* at 239.

131. *See* FedEx Off. & Print Servs., Inc. v. Cont'l Cas. Co., No. CV 20-4799-MWF (AGRx), 2020 WL 6804455 (C.D. Cal. Oct 20, 2020).

132. *See id.* at *3.

The court also denied the insurance company's motion for judgment on FedEx's claim for breach of the implied covenant of good faith and fair dealing.[133]

Cyber-Specific Policies

One important decision involving a cyber-specific insurance policy is *P.F. Chang's China Bistro, Inc. v. Federal Insurance Co.*, decided by the District Court of Arizona in 2016.[134] The insurance company aggressively marketed the cyber policy as "a flexible insurance solution designed by cyber risk experts to address the full breadth of risks associated with doing business in today's technology-dependent world" that "[c]overs direct loss, legal liability, and consequential loss resulting from cyber security breaches."[135] In that case, the policyholder suffered a data breach when hackers obtained the credit card numbers of several thousand customers and posted that information on a website. The policyholder incurred millions of dollars in response to the loss, including the imposition by the policyholder's processor of credit card information of a Fraud Recovery Assessment, an Operational Reimbursement Assessment, and a Case Management Fee. Litigation arose over the policyholder's claim for coverage of those assessments and the fee.

Although the court found that the Operational Reimbursement Assessment and the Case Management Fee fell within the scope of the policy's insuring agreements, it ultimately rejected coverage as barred by exclusions. The court barred coverage based on exclusions analogous to contractual liability exclusions in general liability policies, for which there is a well-developed body of case law. It found that the policyholder's contract with the credit card company was a third-party contract from which the assessment and fee arose. The court then found that the policyholder's obligation to pay sums to this third-party was a contractual liability that fell outside the coverage of the cyber-specific insurance policy.[136]

---

133. *See id.* at *5.

134. *See* P.F. Chang's China Bistro, Inc. v. Fed. Ins. Co., No. CV-15-01322-PHX-SMM, 2016 WL 3055111 (D. Ariz. May 26, 2016) [hereinafter P.F. Chang's].

135. *See id.* at *1.

136. *See id.*

Issues Applicable to All Types of Insurance Policies

Causation

Every policyholder seeking coverage for a loss will need to establish causation, that is, that the loss arises from a covered cause. Sometimes, causation is not a challenging issue. A policyholder seeking coverage under a D&O policy, for example, should have no difficulty showing that the claim arises from underlying allegations of wrongdoing against the directors or officers. At other times, however, causation can present a serious obstacle. For example, causation is heavily disputed under property policies where weather-related and environmental events encompass various perils or causes of loss—some covered and some not. Hurricane Katrina is a perfect example. The hurricane involved multiple perils, including wind, wind-driven water, flooding, levee breaches, sewage overflows, power failures, court-ordered evacuations, fire, looting, pollution, and mold. The wind-related losses were covered under most property policies, but the flood losses may have been either excluded or made subject to specific sub-limits. Thus, the issue of causation was intensively litigated for many Katrina claims.

A particularly complex issue is the common situation where a covered peril and an excluded peril combine to cause a loss. Courts have developed tests for determining coverage in these circumstances. Most prominent is the doctrine of "efficient proximate cause." Under this doctrine, the cause to which the loss is attributed is the "dominant, the efficient one, that sets the other causes in operation, and causes which are incidental are not proximate, though they may be nearer in time and place to the loss."[137] Policy exclusions are not supposed to bar coverage unless they pertain to that dominant cause.

Insurance companies responded to the doctrine of "efficient proximate cause" by hollowing out the coverage—the process decried by J. Robert Hunter.[138] They drafted a policy provision that can be found in

137. *See, e.g.*, Mark D. Wuerfel & Mark Koop, *"Efficient Proximate Causation" in the Context of Property Insurance Claims*, 65 Def. Couns. J. 400 (1998).

138. *See* Hunter, *supra* note 22, at n. 21.

most property insurance policies—usually as the lead-in to a portion of the Exclusions section. The provision establishes that coverage is precluded for an entire loss if *any* exclusion bars coverage for *any* part of a loss, no matter how incidental. This provision is called the "anti-concurrent causation" (ACC) clause because it was drafted to counteract the doctrine of efficient proximate cause. Typical language states:

> We will not pay for loss or damage caused directly or indirectly by any of the following. Such loss or damage is excluded regardless of any other cause or event that contributes concurrently or in any sequence to the loss.

Anti-concurrent causation clauses have been the subject of numerous challenges by policyholders, who argue that it would be unfair or unlawful to allow such provisions to eviscerate their coverage. One version has been upheld under the laws of many states, including Alaska,[139] Arizona,[140] Colorado,[141] Indiana,[142] Massachusetts,[143] Missouri,[144] New York,[145] Ohio,[146] Nevada,[147] Utah,[148] and Wyoming[149]—but invalidated under the laws of other states, including California,[150] Mississippi,[151] and Washington.[152] Still, many other states have no precedent on this issue.

For the reasons just shown, causation is one of the most important issues to be addressed by a policyholder seeking coverage under a property

139. *See* State Farm Fire & Cas. Co. v. Bongen, 925 P.2d 1042 (Alaska 1996).

140. *See* Millar v. State Farm Fire & Cas. Co., 804 P.2d 822 (Ariz. Ct. App. 1990).

141. *See* Kane v. Royal Ins. Co., 768 P.2d 678, 684 (Colo. 1989).

142. *See* Ramirez v. Am. Fam. Mut. Ins. Co., 652 N.E.2d 511 (Ind. Ct. App. 1995).

143. *See* Alton v. Mfrs. & Merchs. Mut. Ins. Co., 624 N.E.2d 545 (Mass. 1993).

144. *See* Pakmark Corp. v. Liberty Mut. Ins. Co., 943 S.W. 2d 256 (Mo. Ct. App. 1997).

145. *See* Alamia v. Nationwide Mut. Fire Ins. Co., 495 F. Supp. 2d 362 (S.D.N.Y. 2007) (applying New York law).

146. *See* Front Row Theatre, Inc. v. Am. Mfrs. Mut. Ins. Cos., 18 F.3d 1343 (6th Cir. 1994) (applying Ohio law).

147. *See* Schroeder v. State Farm Fire and Cas. Co., 770 F. Supp. 558 (D. Nev. 1991) (applying Nevada law).

148. *See* Alf v. State Farm Fire & Cas. Co., 850 P.2d 1272, 1277 (Utah 1993).

149. *See* State Farm Fire & Cas. Co. v. Paulson, 756 P.2d 764, 769 n.2 (Wyo. 1988).

150. *See* Garvey v. State Farm Fire & Cas. Co., 770 P.2d 704 (Cal. 1989); *see also* Sabella v. Wisler, 377 P.2d 889 (Cal. 1963); Cal. Ins. Code § 530 (West 2009).

151. *See* Tuepker v. State Farm Fire & Cas. Co., 507 F.3d 346, 354–56 (5th Cir. 2007) (applying Mississippi law).

152. *See* Safeco Ins. Co. of Am. v. Hirschmann, 773 P.2d 413 (Wash. 1989).

policy. In addition to assessing if the loss falls under the insuring agreement and if any exclusion possibly could apply, policyholders also should examine if the policy contains an ACC clause and—if so—whether this clause is enforceable under the applicable state law.

The Process of Seeking Coverage

Despite the differences among insurance policies, the process of pursuing and obtaining coverage is remarkably the same. It starts with timely notice—which seems simple but can be surprisingly complex. After the notice, the insurance company and the policyholder exchange materials, starting with a letter from the insurance company acknowledging coverage and often reserving all rights. The threshold question is whether the policyholder has asserted a covered claim, meaning, one that meets all elements in the policy's insuring agreement. The policyholder also will be required to show that it has met all conditions of coverage, such as timely payment of premiums. The next question is whether the insurance company can show that coverage is precluded by a policy exclusion. Finally, the policyholder will be required to show that its claim is "ripe" and ready for payment, which can involve submission of a formal "Proof of Loss" or other documentation. The following sections explore these steps.

Notice and Other Time-Sensitive Provisions

Insurance policies always contain clauses pertaining to notice of losses or claims. These provisions typically require claimants to provide notice within a certain time. Property insurance policies, for example, may call for notice of a claim and a sworn proof of loss within 30, 60, or 90 days of the loss. There are other time-sensitive provisions as well. Most insurance policies limit the time within which policyholders may sue insurance companies for failure to pay claims. Property policies typically require policyholders to replace damaged property within two years of a loss, or else notify the insurance companies of their intent to replace property within a specified period. If this requirement is not met, the recovery may be limited to the actual cash value of the depreciated property, rather than the much higher cost of replacing it. While the enforceability of such provisions is questionable when a widespread disaster makes replacement difficult, the better route is for policyholders to secure agreements with their insurance companies to adjourn such deadlines if they are difficult to meet. Then, by agreement of the parties, the timing issues can be avoided.

Policyholders should treat these notice and suit limitation provisions seriously. They should provide notice of a claim or potential claim as soon as they realize that one may exist, even if they do not yet know the scope of their losses or exactly what coverage they will seek. There is no harm to providing notice prematurely or incompletely—but serious potential harm if notice is provided late. Insurance companies often contend that their policyholders forfeited coverage by being late in providing notice or filing suit. Some courts agree that late notice forfeits coverage even if it had no effect on the insurance company.

The Claims Adjustment Period

Every policyholder that files an insurance claim learns quickly that a protracted adjustment process tends to be the norm, rather than the exception. A slow pace suits the insurance companies' interests, as it enables them to hold onto—and earn interest on—insurance proceeds for as long as possible. As insurance companies unilaterally control the pace of their investigation and the length of time to resolution of a claim, they have adapted their claims handling practices accordingly.

Policyholders, however, can take steps to expedite the process and receive the largest possible recovery. These steps include the following:

- *Be proactive in providing information to the insurance company.* Immediately after filing claims, policyholders can ask insurance company adjusters what information they will need to resolve the claims. Doing so will enable the policyholders to get a head start on gathering and compiling the information to be requested—a task that can be formidable and expensive. Policyholders should collect and submit loss data as it is developed, without waiting until the supporting documentation for the entire claim is complete. The period of restoration for a business interruption loss might be several months or longer. A lot can be done during that period to expedite the path to resolution.

- *Decide upon a reasonable deadline for resolving the claim—and tell the insurance company that an agreement must be reached by that date.* Some policyholders are reluctant to take a hard line with the insurance adjuster for fear of biting the hand that feeds them, but that attitude often only result in a claim being assigned a low priority. Assertiveness when pursuing claims is a good thing. The deadline should give the insurance company sufficient time to evaluate the claim after all relevant information has been submitted. In some states, by submitting proofs of loss, the policyholder can trigger 30- or 60-day periods in which the insurance company must provide a coverage determination.

  Policyholders can establish such deadlines in their responses to insurance companies' reservations of rights letters. They should include demands for detailed coverage determinations, reminding their insurance companies that a failure to provide a timely and specific coverage determination may constitute bad faith. Similarly, policyholders can, and may be advised to, demand segregated payments, if not accountings, for each element of their claims. For example, a dispute over the period of restoration for business interruption coverage under a property policy should not delay payment for the repair and replacement costs for the property that is damaged physically. If insurance companies will not agree to make partial payments, then policyholders may submit partial proofs of loss, which will trigger deadlines for payment under most states' unfair claims handling statutes.
- *Make a written record to the insurance company of everything that transpires with respect to the claim.* It is remarkably easy for policyholders to fire off emails in real time, memorializing every conversation they have with their insurance companies about their claims. In these emails, policyholders should verify all instructions they have received, all actions they have taken in response to those instructions, all assurances they have received regarding the time to resolution, and any other information that seems relevant. This process will ensure that policyholders have written records of all key events regarding their claims, to use (if necessary) in disputes about whether they cooperated in the claims process, what

information they provided or offered to their insurance companies, and whether their insurance companies acted in bad faith.

In sharp contrast, it can be virtually impossible to recreate written records after the fact. Thus, there is every reason to be diligent about sending out these emails—and no good reason not to do so.

- *Do not be shy about demanding relief for dilatory claims handling or outright bad faith.* In some states, policyholders obtain legal advantages when insurance companies fail to process claims promptly. For example, in Louisiana, the period of restoration for a business interruption loss may be extended by an insurance company's untimely payment of the property loss. Also, the insurance company may be liable for the consequential damages that flow from their failure to make timely payments.
- *Require the insurance company to pay undisputed amounts before negotiating contested amounts.* Particularly with property policies, it is common for insurance companies to make good faith partial payments of claims and then pay little or nothing more until a final negotiation over all open issues. This approach allows insurance companies to earn interest on funds for as long as possible, while using the unpaid yet badly needed funds to increase their leverage over settlement negotiations. Policyholders can counter this strategy by pressuring their insurance companies to commit to positions regarding coverage and immediately to pay at least those amounts due under its own analysis of the claim.
- *Assemble a claim team with the skills needed to maximize the recovery.* Although most policyholders only communicate with an adjuster, the insurance company has a team of attorneys, accountants, and in-house claims personnel who often are working hard to minimize the payment of your claim, through coverage defenses and the calculation of the loss. The policyholder's knowledge of its own business goes a long way to leveling the playing field, but there are many arcane coverage issues and claims adjustment practices that require special expertise.
- *Before sitting down with the insurance company to try to resolve the difficult issues, have a clear idea of what the claim will be worth if it*

ends up in litigation. This analysis must include the likelihood of success on the disputed coverage and quantification issues, as well as anticipated legal fees and the time and aggravation associated with a lawsuit. Unless businesses are willing to sacrifice dollars for the sake of principle, they should be prepared to settle based on a realistic value of the claim. On the other hand, a professional evaluation of your claim may reveal that it is more valuable than you think, which will raise your settlement goal.

- *Be mindful of all deadlines imposed.* The key to getting insurance claims satisfactorily resolved within a reasonable time is for policyholders to take control of the process and to demonstrate a resolve to secure the coverage they paid for. This requires hard work, but it will pay handsome dividends.
- *If the claim cannot be resolved through negotiation, you may have a choice of proceeding either to appraisal or litigation.* Appraisal is a form of arbitration provided for under many property insurance policies that either party can demand to resolve disputes over the amount of the loss. It can be a quick and inexpensive way to quantify the claim. However, appraisal is not required, and may not be appropriate when there are coverage issues to be resolved. For example, if the parties disagree over the amount of a business interruption loss because of a dispute over whether market conditions after the hurricane should be considered when calculating damages, the policyholder would be entitled to have that coverage issue decided in court. Appraisers, who are typically in the building trades, are generally not qualified to address such issues. Also, bad faith claims fall outside the scope of an appraisal clause and will have much greater value if placed before a jury. So, the policyholder must carefully consider its options and not necessarily feel compelled to agree to an appraisal simply because the quantification of damages is in dispute.

Climate Change and Insurance Policies

Plaintiffs have been trying for years to hold corporate America liable for climate change. Thus far, the question has been whether such claims can be brought at all. Examples of climate change lawsuits that have been attempted include the following:

- *People v. General Motors*.[153] A class action by the State of California against General Motors on grounds that auto sales caused excess releases of carbon dioxide, leading to certain changes in weather patterns that some people identify as "climate change." The lawsuit notably sought actual damages, rather than just regulatory changes, and for alleging actual examples of bodily injury and property damage, such as coastal erosion, heatstroke, and other injuries. It was brought under the tort theory of public nuisance, which could have given rise to interesting questions of coverage. But the case did not reach those questions because the action was promptly dismissed. The court found that it arose from "political questions" that were reserved under the U.S. Constitution for the legislative and executive branches of government, not the judiciary.[154]
- *Massachusetts v. EPA*.[155] The attorneys general of 12 states and several cities sued the U.S. Environmental Protection Agency (EPA) for failing to take action against the release of carbon dioxide and other greenhouse gases. The EPA took the position that federal law does not authorize the agency to regulate greenhouse gas emissions. The U.S. Supreme Court ruled that these substances "fit well within the [Clean Air Act's] capacious definition of air pollutant."[156] The Court remanded the action back to the EPA, requiring the agency to articulate a reasonable basis to avoid regulating greenhouse gases. On remand, the EPA found that greenhouse gases endanger public health and were likely responsible for the recent occurrence of global warming.[157]

---

153. *See* People v. Gen. Motors Corp., No. C06-05755 EMC, 2007 WL 2726871 (N.D. Cal. Sept. 17, 2007).

154. *See id.* at *6–7.

155. *See Massachusetts, supra* note 69.

156. *See id.* at 500.

157. *See* Massachusetts. v. E.P.A., 249 F. Appx. 829 (D.C. Cir. 2007).

- *American Electric Power Co. v. Connecticut.*[158] Decided seven years after Massachusetts v. EPA, the U.S. Supreme Court held that corporations cannot be sued for greenhouse gas emissions under federal common law, primarily because the regulation of these emissions is reserved to the EPA. Here, eight states and other entities sued five private power companies that owned and operated fossil-fuel-fired power plants in 20 states. They sought to cap the permitted emissions as a public nuisance, alleging that they contributed to global warming. The Court held that the federal common law of public nuisance did not apply because it was displaced by the Clean Air Act.
- *Native Village of Kivalina v. ExxonMobil Corp.*[159] This lawsuit was filed by an Alaskan village against 24 oil, energy, and utility companies for reducing the Arctic ice pack through greenhouse gas emissions. Due to reduction in the Arctic ice pack, the village was sinking and destined for total destruction. Following the reasoning of American Electric Power Co. v. Connecticut, the court dismissed the lawsuit. It found that there was no private cause of action under the federal common law for public nuisance, which is how the case was pled.[160]

Perhaps even more rare than lawsuits arising directly from "climate change" are decisions addressing whether lawsuits for climate change can be covered. There are only a handful of such decisions so far:

- *Aloha Petroleum Ltd. v. National Union Fire.*[161] Here, an energy company sued its insurance companies for failing to defend and indemnify it against climate change cases brought by Honolulu and Maui. In September 2023, the federal district court certified two questions of Hawaii law to the Hawaii Supreme Court: (1) can "accident" include recklessness and (2) are greenhouse gases "pollutants" under the pollution exclusion or are they different from "traditional environmental pollution." The following

158. *See* Am. Elec. Power Co. v. Connecticut, 564 U.S. 410 (2011).
159. *See* Native Vill. of Kivalina v. ExxonMobil Corp., 696 F.3d 849 (9th Cir. 2012).
160. *See id.* at 855.
161. *See* Aloha Petroleum v. National Union Fire Ins. Co. 690 F. Supp. 3d 1168 (D. Haw. 2023).

year, the Hawaii Supreme Court ruled for the energy company on the first question, but for the insurance companies on the second question. The effect was to relieve the insurance companies from any duty to defend.[162]

- *Everest Premier Ins. Co. v. Gulf Oil LP.*[163] Two insurance companies sought a declaration in the Massachusetts Superior Court that they were not obligated to defend or indemnify Gulf Oil LP against allegations by the Conservation Law Foundation that it failed to prepare a bulk petroleum terminal for the various impacts of climate change. The insurance companies claimed there was no coverage because there were no allegations of "bodily injury" or "property damage." They also cited to the pollution exclusion. Within months, the insurance companies filed a voluntary dismissal without prejudice.
- *Illinois Farmers Insurance Co. v. Metropolitan Water Reclamation District of Greater Chicago.*[164] Here, several insurance companies filed a putative class action in Illinois state court against municipal entities in Illinois for failing to implement adequate stormwater management plans to prevent flooding that impaired policyholder property. The policyholders promptly filed notices of removal to federal court. The insurance companies responded by filing notices of removal, stating: "[W]e believe our lawsuit brought important issues to the attention of the respective cities and counties, and that our policyholders' interests will be protected by the local governments going forward."[165]
- *Steadfast Insurance Co. v. AES Corp.*[166] This case is the coverage counterpart of *Native Village of Kivalina v. ExxonMobil Corp.*, cited earlier. There, ExxonMobil's insurance company won a declaration in Virginia state court that it had no duty to defend

162. *See* Aloha Petroleum v. National Union Fire Ins. Co. 557 P.3d 837 (Haw. 2024).

163. *See* Compl., Everest Premier Ins. Co. v. Gulf Oil LP, No. 22-1291, 2022WL 2168415 (Mass. Super. Ct. June 9, 2022).

164. *See* Compl., Illinois Farmers Ins. Co. v. Metro. Water Reclamation District of Greater Chicago, No. 2014CH06608 (Ill. Cir. Ct. Apr. 16, 2014).

165. *See, e.g.*, Notice of Dismissal, Illinois Farmers Ins. Co. v. Metro. Water Reclamation District of Greater Chicago, No. 14-CV-03251 (N.D. Cal. June 4, 2014).

166. *See* AES Corp. v. Steadfast Ins. Co., 283 Va. 609 (Va. 2012).

> or indemnity ExxonMobil against the village's allegations. The decision went up to the Virginia Supreme Court, where it was affirmed. The court's reasoning was that the release of greenhouse gases was intentional, not accidental, and therefore was not subject to coverage under a liability insurance policy.[167]

The impacts commonly associated with climate change, such as sea level rise, severe heat waves, drought, wildfires and excessive storms, are often drivers of insurance claims. Insurance companies get constant reminders about the potential gravity of such events—like Hurricane Harvey, which caused $125 billion in damage in 2017 in Texas and Louisiana, and the Australian bushfires that killed more than a billion animals in 2019–20 and caused more than $4.4 billion in damage.[168] Thus, the insurance industry has been studying "climate change" for years.

The 2020 prediction of consulting firm McKinsey & Company that "[t]he projected escalation of climate risk, such as the occurrence of more floods and wildfires, may lead to underinsurance—or to no insurance at all"[169] may be coming true. In May 2023, two major insurers stopped offering new homeowner's policies in California, allegedly because of risks like wildfires.[170] Others have taken similar action in Florida since early 2022.[171] Such actions have prompted a national conversation about whether entire states may become uninsurable due to an increase in such events or, alternatively, due to events that commonly are associated with the ubiquitous term of "climate change."[172]

To put the discussion in context, though, insurance is big business. The global insurance sector topped $5 trillion in 2021, which is in the

---

167. *See id.* at 618–22.

168. *See* Antonio Grimaldi et al., *Climate Change and P&C Insurance: The Threat and Opportunity*, McKinsey & Company, 1 (Nov. 19, 2020), https://www.mckinsey.com/industries/financial-services/our-insights/climate-change-and-p-and-c-insurance-the-threat-and-opportunity.

169. *See id.* at 4–5.

170. *See* Andrew Freedman & Nathan Bomey, *Uninsurable America: Climate Change Hits the Insurance Industry*, AXIOS (June 6, 2023), https://www.axios.com/2023/06/06/climate-change-homeowners-insurance-state-farm-california-florida.

171. *See* Mel Duvall, *The Florida Insurance Crisis: Why Are Insurance Companies Leaving Florida?*, insurance.com (Sept. 28, 2023), https://www.insurance.com/home-and-renters-insurance/home-insurers-leaving-florida.

172. *See id.*

ballpark of the entire U.S. federal budget.[173] The property and casualty segment alone earned $1.6 trillion in premiums. In many cases, these premiums are pure profit—payments by policyholders who make no claims. The cost to the industry of climate-related losses needs to be compared against this lush backdrop.

As the insurance market tightens, some policyholders are looking to alternatives to traditional insurance as protection against major calamities. One example is purchasing catastrophe bonds from insurance companies—high-yield bonds that pay out only in the event of a specified disaster.[174] Governments are looking to solutions as well. Separate from the federal government's creation of the National Flood Insurance Program as a backstop to uninsurable flood losses, state governments are working on programs for buying up properties at risk of coastal flooding and renting them out until they become uninhabitable.[175]

The best advice for policyholders is to put aside the flood maps and the buzz words in assessing what protection to purchase for their properties. The maps have not kept up with the pace of climate change and the buzz words mostly create confusion. Instead, policyholders should focus simply on seeking out and purchasing the broadest possible coverage that they can find against all risks, whether weather related or not. The protection may make the difference between bankruptcy or ongoing operations if calamity strikes—which is the point of insurance in the first place.

173. *See* Umair Irfan, *The $5 Trillion Insurance Industry Faces a Reckoning. Blame Climate Change.*, Vox (Oct. 15, 2021), https://www.vox.com/22686124/climate-change-insurance-flood-wildfire-hurricane-risk.

174. *See id.*

175. *See id.*

Chapter 9

Handling Civil and Criminal Investigations

Robert Ayers and Gregory Goldberg

Preparing for a Government Agency Investigation

Following a significant workplace or environmental incident, it is common for government agencies to conduct investigations. Potential investigating government agencies include the Occupational Safety and Health Administration (OSHA), the Chemical Safety and Hazard Investigation Board (CSB), the Environmental Protection Agency (EPA), the Mine Safety and Health Administration (MSHA), and the Pipeline and Hazardous Materials Safety Administration (PHMSA), as well as various state and local safety and environmental agencies. It is imperative that responsible parties are prepared to receive and manage such inspections. This chapter provides an overview of standard or recommended procedures for responding to civil and criminal investigations. Chapter 6 provides additional insights regarding investigations involving transportation-related incidents.

Responsible parties should train their employees, especially those in environmental, health, and safety roles and those who manage access to a workplace, on what to expect and how to respond when agency employees arrive at a workplace. Issues to address in this training include identifying the agencies most likely to have an interest in the facility; whether to grant access; who to contact in the organization to confirm that access should be granted and any safety, security, or confidentiality conditions that must be applied; how the agency personnel will be escorted though the workplace; and how to respond to requests for information. Several of these issues are discussed in more detail in this chapter, and an attorney can assist in providing or otherwise arranging for this training.

It is also important, prior to the commencement of an investigation, to assign an employee as the point of contact (or representative) for a potential agency investigation. This is generally a supervisory level employee who is located at or near the workplace, commonly in an EHS-related role. A backup point of contact should also be designated in the event the primary point of contact is not available or if it proves helpful to have two facility representatives participate in meetings about the matter. These points of contact should be well organized, possess strong communication skills, and be trained on all aspects of handling a government investigation. Assigning such points of contact prior to the investigation allows "front desk" personnel to quickly put the agency personnel in contact with the appropriate representatives of the facility, which helps to avoid confusion, prevent inadvertent misrepresentations, and build a cooperative relationship from the outset.

Scene Security and Evidence Preservation

The first step in responding to an incident relating to environmental, health, or safety matters is to make the workplace or incident location safe, so as to prevent further damage or injury to personnel or the environment. This may include stopping a release, putting out a fire, closing a valve, ensuring all personnel and visitors are outside of a certain zone, or shutting down a process, system, or operation. Depending on the nature and severity of the event, the workplace or other emergency action plan may need to be implemented. Concurrently with taking these emergency measures, it may also be necessary to notify local emergency responders (typically by dialing 911) or to make release, injury, or fatality reports to federal, state, or local agencies having jurisdiction (see Regulatory Reporting Requirements section).

Once the workplace or other incident location is safe, the employer should secure the scene and preserve potential evidence. It is vitally important to coordinate these steps with the government official who is the incident commander if one has been established (see Chapter 1). Securing the scene may include tape or physical barriers around the area at issue, locking down buildings, and/or shutting down an entire workplace to only essential personnel, such as first responders and incident investigators. If the responsible party does not have security personnel, it is often valuable to hire a third-party security contractor to monitor and control access to the area at issue or workplace as a whole.

Next, potentially relevant evidence should be preserved. Evidence for these purposes can be generally divided into physical evidence and electronic evidence. Physical evidence can include personal protective equipment (PPE), process equipment, damage debris, and physical documentation such as permits and job safety analyses (JSAs). After discussing with responding agencies, the site owner or operator should take steps to preserve all affected and potentially relevant physical evidence.[1] Priority should be given to evidence that may be destroyed, lost, or otherwise damaged by time or the elements. This includes paperwork that is located outside and equipment that is exposed to potentially damaging elements, such as rain or floodwater.

Before any evidence is moved or removed from the scene, it should be photographed in place and a chain of custody should be created. The chain of custody should document (1) a description of the item, (2) where the item was located when it was collected for preservation, (3) who initially collected the item, and (4) when the item was collected. Because it is impossible to know with certainty what may become relevant during a subsequent investigation or litigation, it is better to be overly inclusive during the evidence preservation stage. Depending on the nature of the incident, the amount of physical evidence may be extremely large. In

1. Unless necessary to make the worksite safe, physical evidence should not be disturbed before discussing with the responding agencies.

certain instances, it is necessary to obtain storage space to adequately preserve evidence. This can be accomplished by utilizing publicly available storage units (with appropriate security) or obtaining storage units to store the evidence on-site.

Electronically stored information (ESI) should also be preserved as soon as possible. It is important to remember that ESI is not limited to emails but may also include data systems and video systems. The systems may have collected vital information, such as pressures and volumes, and such information may only be saved for a certain period before being overwritten, so it is crucial to preserve those data as soon as possible. A responsible party's information technology (IT) department should be consulted to determine whether any system settings need to be modified to ensure relevant ESI is not inadvertently deleted. "Legal hold" notices should also be distributed to all relevant employees (and contractors, as necessary) to ensure individuals preserve all potential physical and electronic information.

Regulatory Reporting Requirements

As an integral part of its response to an environmental or safety incident, a responsible party should immediately review federal, state, and local regulatory reporting requirements. Chapters 3, 5, and 6 include in-depth discussions of requirements for reporting environmental releases. The Reporting and Response Timeline provided at the front of this book is also intended to provide some initial guidance on key steps to take early in responding to an incident, including some of the most common reporting requirements. Due to the technical and legal complexities that may be involved in assessing reporting obligations under environmental and some other statutes, facilities may find it helpful to obtain input from legal counsel who have experience with such matters before making a report.

Reporting requirements often have short deadlines. For example, EPA requires a "person in charge" to "immediately" notify the National Response Center (NRC) whenever a hazardous substance is released "in a quantity equal to or exceeding the reportable quantity" thresholds, unless the release is federally permitted.[2] EPA also requires "immediate notification" to the Local Emergency Planning Committee (LEPC) and State Emergency Response Commission (SERC) for certain releases of hazardous substances under EPCRA.[3]

OSHA requires employers to report a work-related fatality to the agency within eight hours.[4] Employers are also required to report a work-related in-patient hospitalization, amputation, or loss of an eye within 24 hours.[5] CSB requires an "owner or operator" to report "any accidental release resulting in a fatality, serious injury, or substantial property damage" within eight hours.[6] However, if the owner or operator has already submitted a report to the NRC pursuant to EPCRA requirements,[7] "the CSB reporting requirement may be satisfied by submitting the NRC identification number to the CSB within 30 minutes of submitting a report to the NRC."[8]

There are several additional reporting requirements that may apply depending on the nature of the incident. It is advisable for facilities that handle hazardous materials of any kind, as well as for all businesses and organizations generally, to develop familiarity with the various federal, state, and local reporting requirements that may be triggered by their operations. Failure to timely report incidents can result in substantial regulatory liability and can also increase the risk of other liability claims due to the delay in ensuring an appropriate and adequate response. It is also important to note that reporting to a state agency may not satisfy the reporting obligations to the corresponding federal agency, and vice versa. Thus, it's vital to comply with all applicable state and federal reporting requirements and deadlines, as they may differ from each other, even to the extent that one may require notification while the other may not.

2. 40 C.F.R. § 302.6; 42 U.S.C. § 9603.
3. 40 C.F.R. pt. 355, subpt. C; 42 U.S.C. § 11004.
4. 29 C.F.R. § 1904.39(a)(1).
5. *Id.* § 1904.39(a)(2).
6. 40 C.F.R. § 1604.3.
7. *Id.* § 302.6.
8. *Id.*

On-Site Inspection

Following a serious environmental or safety incident, it is common for regulators to perform an on-site inspection of the workplace. These inspections are typically initiated following a mandatory report, as discussed in the Regulatory Reporting Requirements section. In addition to having a designated point of contact, as addressed earlier, employers should consider having legal counsel present on-site to assist with key elements of the response to the investigation. Experienced counsel can help the site understand the government investigation process, minimize miscommunication with the agency, protect legal rights, and help ensure the investigation(s) run as smoothly as possible. To this end, it is advisable to establish a cooperative relationship with the investigating agency or agencies at the outset.[9] This should primarily come from the designated point of contact and counsel.

At facilities that are subject to special access restrictions due to national security requirements, the employer should have in place standard protocols for ensuring that the government inspector (and all other persons accompanying the inspector) possess all necessary identification, including all required security clearances, and the employer may also bar the use of a mobile phone or camera in certain areas.

On-site inspections typically include an opening conference and a walk-around. They may also include requests for information and employee interviews, but because requests for information and interviews commonly occur after the initial on-site inspection, those aspects will be addressed in the following sections.

An opening conference, or opening conversation, will address the purpose and expected scope of the agency's inspection. The facility's point of contact (or representative) should take notes at this meeting, documenting all key comments and questions from the agency and the facility's responses. The agency investigators will likely ask questions during the opening conference. In response, the point of contact should avoid speculating and answering questions about topic areas beyond his or her

9. This chapter will not address government agencies' jurisdiction to conduct inspections. Legal counsel should be consulted with respect to agency jurisdiction and the authority of permitting agencies to come on-site to inspect.

area of expertise. If the point of contact is uncertain of the answer, they should make a note of the question, and let the investigator know they will look into it.

The investigator should be escorted by the point of contact at all times during the walk-around. The point of contact should be equipped with a pen and paper (or electronic equivalent) to take notes and a camera to take photographs. If a hot work[10] or similar permit is required to use a camera at the worksite, the point of contact should ensure the permit is completed prior to the walk-around.

All safety rules must be followed by the investigators, and the point of contact should explain all necessary safety information about the workplace at the outset of the walk-around. There is no exception to a safety rule because someone is a government investigator. This means that if a safety orientation is required before individuals are permitted into the workplace, the investigator must complete the safety orientation. Similarly, if employees are not permitted in a certain area without fall protection, neither is the investigator. If a permit is required to use a phone or camera in a work area, the permit must be completed before the investigator can use their phone or camera in the area.

It is common during walk-arounds for investigators to ask questions of employees in the workplace. Investigators generally have the authority to do so, but it is important to keep a few ground rules in mind. First, the employees should understand who the investigator is and why they are at the workplace. The employees should also understand they are not required to speak to the investigator. This issue is addressed further later in the chapter under Employee Interviews. Finally, if an employee is engaged in a work task, and it would create an unsafe condition for the employee to speak with the investigator at that time, the representative (either counsel or the point of contact) should inform the investigator that it is unsafe to distract the employee at this time. If the employee is willing to speak to the investigator, a separate time can be scheduled for an interview at the investigator's request.

---

10. As a general matter, "hot work" means work involving electric or gas welding, cutting, brazing, or similar flame or spark-producing operations. *See* 40 C.F.R. § 68.3.

Before the investigator leaves the workplace, the counsel or the point of contract should confirm any requests that were made during the on-site inspection, such as requests for documentation, and should confirm the deadline to produce any requested documentation or information. If the investigator made verbal requests, counsel or the point of contact should confirm whether the investigator will follow up with requests in writing. If the investigator does not plan to follow up in writing, it is often helpful for counsel or the point of contact to write down the requests and send them to the investigator after the on-site inspection. This helps ensure the investigator and responsible party are on the same page and avoids miscommunication that can lead to improper allegations later in the investigation. For example, several years ago, OSHA issued an employer a citation for failure to have a respiratory protection program. The employer did, in fact, have a respiratory protection program, but the inspector assumed they did not because he recalled asking for the program verbally during an on-site inspection, and the employer never produced it. The employer did not recall the inspector's verbal request, and they did not follow up in writing to confirm the requests, which led to the miscommunication and citation. These errors can be avoided by confirming all verbal requests in writing throughout the investigation.

It should also be noted that during the course of any on-site inspection, whether linked to a previously reported incident or not, government inspectors have the authority to request immediate access to various records that a facility is required to prepare and maintain. Thus, facilities will find it important to ensure that they keep up with all environmental, health, and safety recordkeeping requirements and to be able to produce them quickly if requested during an inspection. Citations and penalties can be assessed against a facility that fails to timely provide such records during an on-site inspections.

Government inspectors often seek to be helpful and may identify specific items of noncompliance during the course of a walk-around or inspection. Facilities often find it advantageous, when time and safety considerations permit, to promptly address the noncompliant items while the government inspector is still at the facility, to let them know that the matter has been addressed, and to offer to return to that location in the facility to confirm that the item has been corrected appropriately. For example, it may only take a few minutes to replace a lightbulb in an exit sign, post a warning sign, open a wider aisle between pallets of drums, add an accumulation start date to a drum label, close a lid on a waste storage drum, or ensure that exits or electric panels are not blocked. Government inspectors may note prompt self-correction measures and may be less likely to issue citations when a facility demonstrates cooperation and good faith efforts to ensure compliance in a timely manner.

Requests for Information

One of the most common methods through which agencies gather information during an investigation is requests for information (RFIs), also referred to as record requests or requests for documentation. RFIs can vary from a simple request for a date to a voluminous request for records. Responding to RFIs appropriately is vital in avoiding miscommunication and limiting unnecessary enforcement. This section addresses key considerations and recommendations in handling RFIs.

Each RFI issued should include a deadline. However, it is not uncommon for an investigator to omit a deadline when issuing an RFI. In such cases, counsel or the point of contact should contact the agency immediately to secure a deadline. Assuming that the omission of deadline means the agency does not need the responses by a certain date is ill-advised. When contacting the agency to secure a deadline, it is common practice for counsel or the point of contact to suggest a reasonable deadline based on the nature and scope of the requests and the estimated number of work hours necessary to assemble and produce the requested materials. For reasons discussed later, it is also common to incorporate into such proposals any additional time needed for legal review of such materials prior to production. Facilities usually find it advantageous to negotiate a sufficiently long timeline so they don't need to seek extensions.

RFIs can be vague or overbroad, leaving a responsible party to guess at the meaning or scope of the request. For example, an RFI may seek "all training records for employees." This request may implicate hundreds of thousands of documents across multiple facilities, most of which are entirely irrelevant to the investigation. Instead of spending significant time gathering such irrelevant information, a responsible party may choose to first contact the agency to request clarity and limitations on the request. Alternatively, a responsible party may reasonably interpret the request based on the nature of the investigation and respond in accordance with its interpretation. Using the preceding example, this could be producing all training records for employees at the location at issue for the last three years. If the responsible party chooses this approach, it should be very clear in its responses to the RFI exactly what it is producing. It should also offer to collect additional information, if requested.

Government inspectors may not be aware that some of the documents they request are confidential in some manner, such as because they contain trade secrets, information subject to national security restrictions, or are classified and can only be viewed by persons holding security clearances issued by the federal government. Under such circumstances, counsel to the facility will typically inform the agency in writing of the restrictions and will negotiate appropriate restrictions or seek a protective order before any documents are produced. There are also standard procedures under various state and federal laws that facilities can invoke to protect confidential business information (CBI). For example, placing a written CBI claim in the header or footer of every page containing CBI may be sufficient to prevent any party other than the government agency's employees from reviewing a document and thereby protect it from being available to the public through a right-to-know or freedom of information request.

Once responsive information and documentation has been collected, the employer should ensure they are produced in a timely and organized manner. Document productions should be Bates labeled, if possible, and a document production log should be maintained. This log typically will also identify any potentially responsive documents that are not being produced because they are subject to a privilege claim. The production log enables the responsible party to track what documents were produced and when, which is particularly helpful in subsequent stages, such as administrative litigation, when thousands of pages of documentation were produced. It is also advisable to include a transmittal letter, or cover letter, when providing information or documentation. This letter should clearly identify what documentation is being produced in response to which requests. It should also include any necessary clarification or disclaimers.

Before producing documents to a government agency, the responding party, in consultation with their counsel, should review all such documents for privileged information, including information covered by the attorney-client communication privilege or the attorney work product privilege, confidential business information, and personal information that would invade an individual's personal privacy. Documentation containing privileged information should be redacted or withheld, as appropriate; documentation containing confidential information should be clearly marked accordingly (on each page); and documentation containing personal information may need to be redacted or marked, as appropriate. Any withholding, redaction, or confidential markings should be identified in the transmittal letter.

Employee Interviews

A key aspect of fact-gathering in government investigations is employee interviews. Agencies conduct interviews to gather information on workplace conditions, potential hazards, safety practices, and employer and employee knowledge, among other topics. Statements by a company manager during an interview may be used to bind that company to a specific position. Accordingly, a representative, including employer's counsel, may be permitted to participate in an interview of a management-level employee. Agencies will generally demand that interviews with non-management employees be private (i.e., that a representative of the employer or employer's counsel not be present). Employers may, however, offer to provide separate legal counsel to such employees at no cost to the employee on the condition that the employer's counsel and the employee's counsel will enter into a joint defense or common interest agreement so that the employer's counsel and the employee's counsel can share information about the matter in confidence, including what may have been discussed at the agency's interview of the employee.

Regardless of position (management or non-management), it is advisable for the employer's counsel to meet with employees before a government interview to ensure they understand the context for the interview and know their rights. Employee rights include the right to a private interview, the right to refuse to be interviewed, and the right to refuse to sign a statement or to acknowledge an inspector's written notes of an interview. Employees also have the right to decline to allow a government inspector to make an audio or video recording of their interview. In addition, employees are entitled to decline to provide their personal information (i.e., home address, personal phone number, and email address) to a government inspector and to instead choose to provide contact details for their employer. Employees who are members of labor unions or otherwise covered by a collective bargaining agreement may enjoy some additional protections. For example, it is common for collective bargaining agreements to include provisions requiring that the union's representative at the facility be informed in advance of any scheduled inspections, walk-arounds, or employee interviews, especially in connection with government investigations of prior incidents. And, at the employee's option, a union representative is often entitled to participate in such inspection or walk-around, attend the employee's preparatory meeting with the facility's legal counsel, and attend the interview conducted by the government inspector.

As an employer's counsel meets with employees before a government interview or to otherwise gather information about an incident, the attorney must provide an *Upjohn* warning to the employee, including among other advisements that the attorney represents the employer and not the individual.[11] An employee should be made aware of whether a subpoena has been issued compelling participation in the interview. Employees should also be made aware that the most important aspect of an interview is to tell the truth. Additional helpful information in preparation for an interview includes listening to each question carefully to the end before starting to formulate an answer, not guessing or speculating in

11. Upjohn Co. v. United States, 449 U.S. 383 (1981).

response to questions, and answering questions directly. The employer's counsel will usually explore with each employee and the relevant government agency the possibility of attending government interviews of that employee.

Special Criminal Considerations

In anticipating or preparing for an agency investigation following a significant workplace incident, the entity that is the target of the investigation and its counsel should remain mindful of issues potentially implicating criminal law, including for the entity as well as for its employees. Although myriad such issues can arise, we highlight several here.

First, it is important for counsel to determine if a government investigation is criminal in nature or whether it is premised on allegations of criminal conduct. Often, the criminal nature of the investigation is obvious from the circumstances, such as involvement by criminal agents or the receipt of a federal grand jury subpoena. Other times, however, the nature of the investigation can be unclear, in which case it is more difficult to ascertain. In those instances, consideration should be given to asking the government whether the investigation is criminal, recognizing that even posing the question could plant seeds in the mind of a government agent or attorney as to whether the matter should be criminal.

Next, in any matter involving a criminal investigation (and in most that involve government civil investigations), a responsible party should consider whether to conduct an internal investigation under the attorney-client privilege and work product doctrine.[12] Such an investigation is imperative in gathering information that could prove critical to counsel's ability to provide informed, strategic legal counsel, including whether a voluntary disclosure by a responsible party is either required or strategically advantageous; whether to cooperate with the government's

---

12. American College of Trial Lawyers, Recommended Practices for Companies and Their Counsel in Conducting Internal Investigations (2020 Update), https://www.actl.com/wp-content/uploads/legacy/default-document-library/position-statements-and-white-papers/2020---recommended-practices-for-conducting-internal-investigations.pdf?sfvrsn=2473e169_2.

investigation; appropriate employment decisions regarding responsible individuals; initiating or responding to press inquiries; and anticipating and developing defense strategies for potential criminal and civil litigation. Several factors are germane to the decision of when and under what circumstances to initiate an internal investigation, including the following:

- The seriousness of the incident, including significant personal injury or death, environmental damage, or risk to public safety
- Whether an investigation is mandated by law or corporate policy
- Whether the incident raises a serious concern of potential liability or requires disclosure to shareholders or regulators
- The cost and time of an internal investigation
- Whether informed decisions can be made absent an investigation
- Assessment of whether an internal investigation would assist the responsible party in defending subsequent criminal charges, civil litigation, or a government enforcement action (Internal investigations are discussed further in the next section.)

Finally, if the responsible party determines that the investigation is or likely is criminal in nature, the responsible party should decide whether, and if so when, to cooperate with the government's investigation. Cooperation during a government investigation often presents little risk and can substantially limit exposure. The U.S. Department of Justice (DOJ) has issued guidance describing mitigating factors assessed by the government in exercising its charging discretion, several of which focus on cooperation.[13] Without proactively conducting an internal investigation, a responsible party might not be in a position to avail itself of these options. Of course, there may be times when the results of the internal investigation and legal analysis indicate that cooperation may not be in the best interest of the responsible party.

13. DOJ, *Principles of Federal Prosecution of Business Organizations*, U.S. Attorneys' Manual § 9-28.700.

Internal Investigations

It is often beneficial for a responsible party to conduct an internal investigation following a disaster or other serious incident. These investigations are separate from the government agency investigations previously discussed in this chapter.

One of the first determinations in conducting an internal investigation is whether, and to what extent, legal privilege will apply in the investigation. There are two main privileges at issue: the attorney-client communication privilege, which protects confidential communications between an attorney and their client for the purpose of seeking legal advice, and the attorney work product privilege, which protects material prepared in anticipation of litigation by the party's attorney or the attorney's representative, including experts engaged by the attorney.

A responsible party should consult with their attorney at the outset to determine the potential applicability of legal privilege. In making this determination, it is important to consider whether the investigation is voluntary or required. Certain regulations require incident investigations and investigation reports that are subject to disclosure upon request. For example, OSHA's process safety management (PSM) standard requires an employer to investigate and create a report for "each incident which resulted in or could reasonably have resulted in a catastrophic release of highly hazardous chemical in the workplace."[14] If a responsible party is going to conduct an internal investigation under legal privilege, it is advisable to document the privileged nature and intent of the investigation at the outset.

Another initial step in conducting an internal investigation is to form the investigation team. Typically, this team should be comprised of personnel from different functions of the organization (i.e., operations, engineer, health and safety, etc.). Individuals who have a direct relationship or connection with the incident should not be part of the investigation team, if possible. These individuals will be vital to the investigation and should likely be interviewed by the investigation team, but inclusion on

14. 29 C.F.R. § 1910.119(m).

the team may create conflicts of interest when, for example, the team is determining the cause(s) of the incident. Another consideration is whether an expert outside of the organization should be a part of the investigation team. In certain cases, the nature of the incident is such that the organization does not have the internal expertise to fully investigate and determine the causes of the incident. This is common in complicated or catastrophic events, such as explosions. In such cases, a third-party expert can be a vital resource to include on the investigation team.

When conducting the investigation, it is important for the investigation team to determine what happened before it determines why it happened. Avoiding premature speculation regarding the cause(s) of the incident is a challenging, but important, step in ensuring the efficacy of the investigation. To this end, the investigation team should also limit its communications with individuals outside of the investigation team to the maximum extent possible while the investigation is ongoing. Frequent "report outs" to management, for example, can lead to the inadvertent spreading of speculation and inaccuracies. It is preferrable to keep all discussion of the potential cause(s) of the incident within the investigation team until the investigation has concluded.

Counsel should be involved throughout the investigation, even when it is not being conducted pursuant to a legal privilege. The role of counsel during an investigation includes ensuring applicable legal requirements are being met, encouraging adherence with investigation best practices, such as document discipline, and helping the team avoid "scope creep." Scope creep can occur, for example, when an investigation team starts to analyze issues and events that are not related to the incident.

Before finalizing the investigation report, each team member should review and approve the content. Disagreements amongst members should be addressed and resolved before the report is finalized. A member of the investigation team should also ensure the report complies with any internal (e.g., company policy) or external (e.g., government regulations) requirements before the document is finalized. Finally, if the report is covered under an applicable legal privilege, the responsible party should ensure it is treated accordingly. Producing a "privileged" investigation report to a third party, such as a government agency, may result in waiver of the privilege.

Index